The Boundaries of Welfare

The Boundaries of Welfare

European Integration
and the New Spatial Politics
of Social Protection

Maurizio Ferrera
Professor of Comparative Public Policy
University of Milan, Italy

OXFORD
UNIVERSITY PRESS

OXFORD

UNIVERSITY PRESS

Great Clarendon Street, Oxford OX2 6DP

Oxford University Press is a department of the University of Oxford.
It furthers the University's objective of excellence in research, scholarship,
and education by publishing worldwide in

Oxford New York

Auckland Cape Town Dar es Salaam Hong Kong Karachi
Kuala Lumpur Madrid Melbourne Mexico City Nairobi
New Delhi Shanghai Taipei Toronto

With offices in

Argentina Austria Brazil Chile Czech Republic France Greece
Guatemala Hungary Italy Japan Poland Portugal Singapore
South Korea Switzerland Thailand Turkey Ukraine Vietnam

Oxford is a registered trade mark of Oxford University Press
in the UK and in certain other countries

Published in the United States
by Oxford University Press Inc., New York

British Library Cataloguing in Publication Data
Data available

Library of Congress Cataloging in Publication Data
Data available

Typeset by SPI Publisher Services, Pondicherry, India

Printed in Great Britain on acid-free paper by
Biddles Ltd., King's Lynn, Norfolk

ISBN 0-19-928466-0   978-0-19-9284665
ISBN 0-19-928467-9 (pbk.)   978-0-19-928467-2 (pbk.)

1 3 5 7 9 10 8 6 4 2

For Ada and Giulia
Who mean the most to me

Preface and Acknowledgements

It is not easy to trace the precise origins of a book project that has been unfolding for several years, in parallel—as always happens—with various other academic initiatives and commitments. In the case of this book, however, I do have a vivid recollection of how it all started. It is a very pleasant recollection: a whole day spent in the Tuscan countryside, in the house of my *maestro* and friend Peter Flora, together with another old friend, Stefano Bartolini. Sitting on Peter's terrace, which revealed a panoramic view, we spoke about our common interests in European integration and the transformation of the nation state and in how to develop a novel research agenda on this topic, anchored in the classical 'state-building' tradition. That stimulating discussion gave me the initial spur to recast my interest in welfare state developments from a wider and richer perspective. To my good friends Peter and Stefano I thus owe much more than the pleasure of their company in beautiful Maremma. Their broad comparative-historical approach and their deep knowledge of, and admiration for, Stein Rokkan's work have greatly contributed to orienting my research towards the themes covered by this book: the changing boundaries of the welfare state and the political implications of these changes; the growing strains between national schemes of social sharing and supranational economic integration; and the search for institutional strategies capable of reconciling 'solidarity' with 'Europe'.

The new interest in such themes evolved into a fully fledged book project thanks to another old friend, Beppe Di Palma. Beppe invited me to join a research group that he had convened at the University of California at Berkeley together with Chris Ansell on 'The Restructuring of Territoriality', aimed at comparing US and European trends in centre-periphery relations. The group met a few times between 1999 and 2002 at Berkeley and at the European University Institute in Florence, with a view to producing a collective volume. Under the spur of Beppe and Chris's initiative, I wrote first an article, 'European Integration and National Social Citizenship: New Boundaries, New Structuring?' (*Comparative Political Studies*, 36/6, 2003) and then a chapter for the collective volume edited by Ansell and Di Palma (*Restructuring Territoriality*, Cambridge University Press, 2004), in which I outlined the basic argument and presented the first findings of my project. I am really grateful to the two conveners and to all the participants in that initiative—in particular, Sergio Fabbrini, Gary

Marks, Alec Stone Sweet, and Sydney Tarrow—for the many insights I gained from them. I am especially grateful to Jim Caporaso for his invaluable comments on the initial article and for his kind encouragement to develop further my theoretical perspective.

The actual writing of the book began during a semester spent at the Institute for Governmental Studies (IGS) at the University of California at Berkeley, in autumn 2002. I am very grateful to its Director, Bruce Cain, and to the staff for the warm and effective hospitality they offered to me. The book has subsequently advanced during more or less prolonged spells of academic retreat at various times and places, including the newly established Research Unit on European Governance (URGE) at the Fondazione Collegio Carlo Alberto of Moncalieri, near Turin.

Several friends and colleagues have taken the trouble to go through the final draft of the book, providing me with innumerable and very valuable comments and suggestions. My gratitude goes in particular to Stefano Bartolini, Mary Daly, Stefano Giubboni, Franca Maino, Philip Manow, Stefano Sacchi, Dorte Sindbjerg Martinsen, Noel Whiteside, Armando Tursi, and Jonathan Zeitlin. I am thankful to two anonymous referees who wrote detailed reports with punctual remarks and very useful suggestions. I deeply regret that my colleague and friend Mario Stoppino could not read the draft. Mario is no longer with us but his theoretical work on power and politics has significantly influenced my thinking over the years.

Various parts of the book have been presented at seminars and conferences on both sides of the Atlantic. I have benefited in particular from discussions held at Maison de Sciences de l'Homme, Nantes; St Antony's College, Oxford; Center for EU Studies, University of Wisconsin at Madison; Max Planck Institute, Cologne; Wissenschaftszentrum Berlin; University of Bremen, Germany; and, last but not the least, my own university in Milan. My sincere thanks to all those who invited me and who offered their thoughts about my research at these various events, and in particular to Jens Alber, Denis Bouget, Jane Lewis, Bruno Palier, Wolfgang Streeck, and Fritz Scharpf.

The project received support from several institutions, which I would like to gratefully acknowledge: the Italian Ministry of Education (PRIN grants), the Department of Political and Social Studies of the University of Pavia, the Center for Comparative Political Research, 'Poleis', at Bocconi University, and the Department of Labour and Welfare Studies of the University of Milan. The project could not have been completed, however, without the generous support of the Fondazione Collegio Carlo Alberto of Moncalieri and URGE in particular. The final text of this book is, indeed, the outcome of my work within URGE since 2003.

My research assistant Ilaria Madama has made an invaluable contribution to data collection, bibliographic research, and text presentation. Matteo Jessoula and Patrik Vesan have assisted me in collecting data on pensions and labour market policies. Lorenzo Giasanti has helped me with legal and case law search and references. Marika Podelli from Poleis has managed with great efficiency the complex process of gathering my scattered typescripts into a coherent set of files for the publisher, while Michael James has made my English more readable. A warm 'thank you' to the staff of Oxford University Press and in particular to Dominic Byatt, who responded in a very encouraging and effective way to my initial proposal and who has shown genuine interest and keen support for my project from beginning to end.

This book is dedicated to my wife Ada and to my daughter 'Guilia' (to use the funny Berkeley spelling of her name), who keenly welcomed the launch of my project, which coincided with a semester that we all spent together 'on Spruce' in 2002 and that will be remembered as one of the happiest periods of our lives. Ada and Giulia's enthusiasm for the project declined, however, when in subsequent years my research and writing commitments started to eat up an inordinate amount of my free time. I apologize to them for the all-too-frequent forfeited opportunities to spend time and do things together. Yes, now *il libro è finito*—the book is really finished, thanks to their understanding, support, and love.

Contents

List of Figures

List of Tables

List of Abbreviations

AGIRC	Association Générale de Retraite de Cadres
ARRCO	Association des Régimes de Retraite Complémentaires
ATP	Allman Tillagpension
CEMR	Council of European Municipalities and Regions
COR	Commitee of the Regions
EC	European Commission
ECJ	European Court of Justice
ECSC	European Coal and Steel Community
EEC	European Economic Community
EES	European Employment Strategy
EMS	European Monetary System
EMU	Economic and Monetary Union
EP	European Parliament
ESF	European Social Fund
EU	European Union
EURES	European Employment Services
EWCs	European Works Councils
FFSA	Fédération Française de Sociétés d'Assurance
ILO	International Labour Organisation
IORPs	Institutions for Occupational Retirement Provisions
LAPs	Local Action Plans
LEA	Livelli essenziali di assistenza
NAPs	National Action Plans
NDC	Notional Defined Contribution
NHS	National Health Service
OMC	Open Method of Coordination
PAYGO	Pay-As-You-Go
RAPs	Regional Action Plans
SEA	Single European Act
TEPS	Territorial Employment Pacts
TEU	European Union Treaty

Introduction

According to a recent Eurobarometer survey, 95 per cent of European Union (EU) citizens think that 'helping others' is extremely important. Moreover, significant majorities of respondents consider 'equality', 'the spirit of cooperation and solidarity', and 'social security and welfare' as precious legacies of the twentieth century. There are, of course, some noticeable cross-country variations. But the readiness to engage in social sharing and the support for those public programmes that organize sharing practices within society stand out as a deep-seated trait of the civic and political culture of Europeans—a trait which sets them apart from their cousins in North America (European Commission 2001*a*).

But who are the 'others' that ordinary citizens are so willing to help? And, when thinking of equality, solidarity, and welfare, what community do they typically have in mind? Such delicate questions were not explicitly posed by the Eurobarometer. But it is highly probable that respondents have in the mind primarily their fellow nationals, and that their home country is the implicit frame of reference for judgements regarding solidarity and redistribution. From other surveys we know that the readiness to share declines rather sharply when people are asked about foreigners and especially about immigrants—even foreigners and immigrants who belong to other member states of the EU (Ferrera 1993*a*). National identity still largely prevails over European identity in opinion polls. On average (EU-15) 43 per cent of respondents feel exclusively nationals of their member states; another 43 per cent feel 'national and European'—but strictly in that order. In virtually all member states, citizens tend to be very jealous of the decision-making prerogatives of their own government in the core areas of sharing: with few variations over time, about two-thirds of Eurobarometer respondents declare, for example, that responsibility for 'health and social security' should remain firmly in the hands of national authorities, with no joint decisions involving the EU. And while EU integration in general and EU membership of their own country continue to be seen in positive terms by a majority of citizens, a good 53 per cent of them (EU 15) fear that closer integration might result in the loss of social benefits (European Commission 2004c).

These figures indicate a tension, an uneasiness in linking or reconciling 'solidarity' with 'Europe'. Both receive mass public support—but only to the extent that they keep on separate tracks and that solidarity remains a national affair. It is not difficult to explain this preference for separation. Social sharing builds on 'closure'. It presupposes the existence of a clearly demarcated and cohesive community, whose members feel that they belong to the same whole and that they are linked by reciprocity ties vis-à-vis common risks and similar needs. Since the nineteenth century (in some countries since much earlier) the nation state has provided the closure conditions for the development of sharing sentiments and practices within its own territory. European integration, on the contrary, rests on 'opening': on weakening or tearing apart those spatial demarcations and closure practices that nation states have built to protect themselves. Free movement, free (undistorted) competition, and non-discrimination have been the guiding principles of the integration process. This process has undeniably produced a novel social aggregate—the 'Euro-polity'—whose individual members have become 'equals' in respect of economic and (most) civic transactions. But the establishment of an enlarged level playing field in these spheres has not fostered sharing dynamics among the new equals. Based as it is on the logic of economic opening, European integration is programmatically geared towards the expansion of individual options and choices, often challenging those closure conditions that sustain social solidarity. Therefore, it is no surprise that ordinary citizens remain 'nationalist' when asked about the latter and express a preference for keeping the EU away from this sphere.

The problem is, however, that the 'separate tracks' solution—that is, the insulation of national social protection systems from the dynamic of economic integration and from supranational interference—long ago ceased to be viable. When the integration project was launched in the 1950s, the idea was precisely that the European Communities would concentrate on economic opening, while the member states would keep for themselves the sphere of solidarity and welfare. But the compromise was inherently fragile and precarious. Since the 1980s, the division of labour has become increasingly untenable: advances in economic integration prompted the introduction of direct or indirect constraints also in the sphere of domestic sharing arrangements. The establishment of Economic and Monetary Union (EMU) made such constraints very explicit in the course of the

1990s, giving rise to the mass fears that are revealed by opinion surveys. The 2000s have witnessed a growing politicization of the 'opening' issue and, in some countries more than others, of the integration process as a whole. The most evident manifestation of this politicization has occurred in the Spring of 2005, during the campaigns for the French and Dutch referendums which have rejected the ratification of the Treaty establishing a Constitution of Europe, signed in Rome on October 29, 2004. Not surprisingly, questions regarding the social sharing dimension (who shares what, and with whom? is it appropriate for the EU to interfere in such decisions?) are playing a central role in this process of politicization, while national governments find themselves increasingly sandwiched between the growing constraints imposed by the EU on the one hand and the national basis of their political legitimacy on the other—a legitimacy which remains highly dependent on decisions in the social protection domain.

The problematic relationship between the opening pressures linked to European integration and the closure foundations of the nation-based welfare state is the main theme of this book. As suggested by the title, this theme will be framed, analytically, through the concept of *boundary*. Boundaries are sets of norms and rules that define the type and level of closure of a given collectivity vis-à-vis the exterior, gating access to the resources and opportunities of both the in-space and the out-space, and facilitating bonding dynamics among insiders. Historically, the formation of the nation state consisted of a multidimensional process of boundary-building around specific portions of the European territory. The establishment of social sharing schemes (typically through compulsory public insurance) between the end of the nineteenth and the beginning of the twentieth century was an important dimension or step in this process. In its turn, European integration can be understood as a large-scale operation of boundary redrawing: the redefinition or removal of state-national boundaries within the EU space in respect of an increasing number of functional spheres and institutionalized practices, including social sharing. In the wake of the EU's free movement and competition rules, the nation state is no longer the sole and ultimate arbiter of inclusion and exclusion into its own redistributive spaces. The EU constrains not only the scope and content of bounding decisions (who is entitled to share what), but also the very right to bound in the first place, that is, the right of national authorities to enforce social sharing by 'locking' their citizens or residents into compulsory insurance schemes under conditions of state monopoly. Such constraints obviously have enormous economic and financial implications. But their social and political implications may be even greater. Given the importance of social sharing for material life chances, cultural identities, and legitimization dynamics, reshuffling the 'boundaries of welfare' may destabilize the basic architecture of Europe's national societies and political systems.

Addressing the relationship between European integration and national welfare states through the concept of boundary has at least three implications. The first implication is that attention is immediately drawn towards an elementary yet fundamental mechanism through which social solidarity is typically generated: a mechanism which we can term 'internal bonding through external bounding'. As mentioned earlier, solidarity builds on reciprocity expectations: if a space of interaction is confined by boundaries vis-à-vis the exterior (i.e. if insiders cannot easily escape from it and outsiders are not easily admitted), reciprocity expectations can consolidate, stabilize, and generalize over time. The role played by boundaries in group formation and political production is an old theme of classical sociology.[1] The bounding-bonding nexus has not attracted the interest it deserves, however, in the welfare state literature. One obvious reason is that most of this literature has concentrated on intranational developments in the second half of the twentieth century, that is, developments taking place within relatively fixed boundary configurations. The foundational role of such configurations for bonding dynamics and their politics thus remained largely in the background. The chapters of this book will try to demonstrate that a focus on the bounding-bonding nexus can offer novel insights into the overall logic of development and functioning of the European welfare states, and especially into the dilemmas they are now facing in the wake of supranational integration.

The second implication of a focus on boundaries is that it invites the adoption of a long-term historical perspective. From a practical viewpoint, boundaries can be built, redrawn, or taken apart very rapidly, even abruptly (the Berlin Wall was erected and later torn down virtually overnight). But the consequences of bounding and debounding for social interaction and political production take a long time to unfold. From an institutional viewpoint, boundary changes are 'slow moving causal pro-

---

[1] The strong link between boundaries and group formation is effectively captured by the Weberian concept of *Verband* (a word which means both 'association' and 'bandage'), that is a social relationship characterized by closure and guided by its own internal principles and hierarchical rules. According to Weber, if closure has a specific territorial dimension, then it originates a political association, a *politischen Verband* (Weber 1972: para. 17). The term 'political production' refers to those processes through which a territorially closed collectivity arrives at binding rules that stabilize and generalize social cooperation among its members (Stoppino 1994, 2001).

cesses', whose effects can be gauged only over extended temporal periods (Pierson 2004). In this light, the impact of EU-induced boundary redrawing on national social sharing configurations can be fully captured and evaluated only through a detailed understanding of how such configurations were originally forged and subsequently sustained over time, and through the appreciation of the essential role played by closure rules and strategies in these processes.

The third implication has to do with the analytical tool kit. Framing our theme in terms of closing and opening, bounding and debounding requires the elaboration of a vocabulary and conceptual map which are adequate for exploring the spatial dimension of social sharing—and of politics *tout court*. As, again, anticipated by the book title, I suggest that European integration has prompted a new *spatial politics* around social protection, that is, a politics which revolves around spatial issues that were not pertinent or relevant in earlier, pre-integration phases. Now, in its more common usage, spatial means 'territorial'. And to a large extent the argument developed in this book will be, precisely, that European integration has originated a serious double challenge to the established territorial basis of social protection. The first challenge is a direct one and stems from the explicit prohibition of (most) cross-border restrictions regarding access to, and consumption of, social benefits and to some extent also the provision of social services. The nationality filter has been neutralized for admission into domestic sharing spaces, and some core social rights (such as pension or health care rights) have become portable across the territory of the whole EU. The second challenge is indirect and stems from the incentives and support that the EU provides to subnational territories (regions and even municipalities) to emerge as self-contained geographical arenas for certain forms of social sharing: for example, anti-poverty and inclusion measures. This part of the argument is in line with a rich strand of social science debates which have 'brought territory back in' to the analysis of many contemporary political developments and which link this revival of the territorial dimension of politics to the dynamics of European integration and, more generally, globalization.[2]

The concept of space—and in particular 'bounded space'—can be used, however, to designate not only a geographical area but also a membership area, that is, a sphere of social interaction in which insiders share some common traits and/or are subject to a common set of norms and rules. The

---

[2] See for example Keating (1998), Ansell and Di Palma (2004), McEwen and Moreno (2005), and Bartolini (2000, 2005). We survey this debate in Chapter 5.

welfare state is definitely a geographical space, with a recognizable territorial scope demarcated by administrative borders. But at the same time it is a membership space or, more precisely, a bundle of membership spaces: it consists of different functional schemes (for pensions, health care, unemployment, etc.), different 'layers', 'tiers', and 'pillars' of provision (e.g. basic versus supplementary insurance), characterized by their own regulations and surrounded by codified membership boundaries. Seen in this light, the welfare state has always had a 'spatial politics', that is, conflicts on inclusion and exclusion rules and on the relative positioning of different social groups within the bundle of sharing arrangements. But this 'old' spatial politics rested on a stable territorial basis whose boundaries were given and uncontested, and it unfolded in the shadow of a single ultimate hierarchy, that of the nation state. European integration has changed the situation not only by redrawing the territorial boundaries of national welfare states but also by imposing new direct and indirect constraints on its internal membership boundaries, thus casting a new shadow of supranational hierarchy over domestic political interactions. For example, compulsory affiliation to social security schemes is legitimate, under the current EU legal order, only under certain conditions (such as the adoption of pay-as-you-go financing). National actors (workers, employers, insurance companies, etc.) can now challenge their governments on this issue before the European Court of Justice (ECJ), that is, a higher-level hierarchical authority. The impact of integration on the membership (as distinct from the territorial) boundaries of the welfare state is a relatively recent phenomenon. Its visibility is still low also because it is not uniform across the various risk-specific schemes, tiers, and pillars of provision. Nevertheless, as we shall see, it has already prompted dynamics of interest articulation and aggregation at various levels of the Euro-polity. Illustrating this new spatial politics of welfare—its origin, its logic, and its potential consequences—is a major objective of this book.

While until recently the welfare state literature has not directly dealt with the issue of boundaries and the spatial dimension of politics (in both its territorial and its membership senses), this dimension has occupied a central position in another rich strand of social science research, namely, the analysis of long-term processes of state formation and nation-building.[3] This strand of research has been recently revived within EU studies; European integration can be seen, in fact, as a new phase in the

---

[3] See especially Bendix (1964), Eisenstadt and Rokkan (1973), and Tilly (1975a). For a recent discussion, see Spruyt (2002). A survey of this tradition of research is provided in Chapter 1.

development of the European state system (e.g. Bartolini 2005) while the 'Euro-polity' can be interpreted as a novel emergent form of post-state and post-national territorial organization (e.g. Caporaso 1996). The first chapter of this book will therefore start by revisiting the classical 'state-building' debate, in order not only to outline the broader historical context in which welfare institutions were set up from the last decades of the nineteenth century onwards, but also to gain precious conceptual and theoretical insights. This review will focus, in particular, on the works of Rokkan[4] and on two general propositions that this author formulated on state formation as a broad process of spatial (re)configuration. The first proposition interprets state- and nation-building in terms of 'structuring'. This notion connotes the gradual establishment of a hierarchical order and a stable pattern of social interactions around a new territorial centre in a space confined by boundaries—lines of demarcation along the physical/ territorial dimension as well as the social and symbolic dimension. The second proposition connects, in a strong sense, the two elements of the first: structuring implies interdependence between the external closure of a given space and its internal differentiation. Drawing on the famous concepts suggested by Hirschman (1970), Rokkan conceptualized the for-mation of the nation state as a threefold operation: (*a*) the foreclosure of *exit* options for actors and resources in a given territory; (*b*) the establish-ment of 'system maintenance' institutions capable of eliciting domestic *loyalty*; and (*c*) the provision of channels for internal *voice*. The 'locking in' of resources and actors in a bounded space oriented actor strategies to-wards the inside, focused them towards central elites, and promoted the formation of new organizational vehicles for the exercise of voice and the strengthening of loyalty. This threefold process led to the emergence of new highly integrated territorial systems.

The Rokkan–Hirschman 'model' will be extensively discussed in Chap-ter 1 and will provide us with a general theoretical blueprint from which we will derive more specific propositions and hypotheses about the wel-fare state as a spatial organization and about its transformation in the wake of European integration. We have already highlighted the founda-tional role of boundaries in activating sharing dispositions and forging redistributive arrangements. We have also suggested that, by redrawing the boundaries of national welfare states, European integration has prompted novel dynamics of spatial politics: domestic actors can exit

---

[4] For a thorough reconstruction of the theory of Rokkan, see Flora, Kuhnle, and Urwin (1999). A bibliography of Rokkan's main publications is provided in the References.

from national schemes, enter those of other member states, challenge the domestic status quo by appealing to external authorities (such as the ECJ), and so on. If we look at these developments from a 'structuring' perspective, three broad questions spring immediately to the fore—questions that will guide our investigation throughout the book. To what extent can the opening pressures linked to European integration lead to a 'destructuring' of national social sharing, that is, a destabilizing of long-standing patterns of institutionalized solidarity and the ensuing emergence of new lines and forms of distributive conflict? Is a 'restructuring' of social sharing conceivable at the EU level, possibly reproducing—at least partially—the trajectory followed by other federal polities in the past? In the shorter term, can some institutional balance be found between the logic of opening and the logic of closure, between the supranational and the national (and even subnational) levels, a balance capable of sustaining the political production of social solidarity under changed boundary conditions?

Although formulated in abstract language, these are not merely academic questions. They draw the attention towards the deep currents beneath the ongoing transformation of the welfare state and thus may help to elaborate more accurate diagnoses of its problems and prospects. Such diagnoses can in turn facilitate the identification of realistic projects of institutional reform aimed at reconciling 'solidarity' and 'Europe', without either nostalgia for self-contained *patries de fraternité* or a premature embrace of a 'Social Union' that still appears way beyond our reach.

The main findings of the book as regards its three guiding questions can be summarized as follows:

1. European integration has indeed started to exert a destructuring impact on established national configurations of social sharing;
2. The intensity of this impact varies according to country-specific structural profiles and in particular the institutional design of welfare schemes; centre–periphery relations; social and political cleavages;
3. Destructuring pressures have in their turn started to provoke forms of defensive restructuring at the national and subnational levels;
4. Restructuring at the EU level is proceeding at a very low speed, due to institutional blockages and to the heavy resistance of national loyalties and identities:
5. Some (narrow) margins of manoeuvre are however emerging for a possible 'nesting' of nation-based welfare states in a wider EU space, capable of promoting reform and adaptation while upholding, at the same time, the basic preconditions for high levels of social protection.

The book is organized into six chapters. Chapter 1 outlines the theoretical framework, along the lines just illustrated. After presenting the Rokkan–Hirschman model and highlighting its usefulness for studying welfare state developments, the chapter outlines an analytical framework for the exploration of spatial politics, based on a combination of 'locality' and 'vocality' options. It then discusses the emergence and evolution of modern citizenship as a form of spatial closure, and proposes an interpretation of social rights as products of structuring processes. Chapter 2 provides the historical background, summarizing the origins of European welfare states and their development up to the Second World War in terms of external and internal boundary-building. Chapter 3 focuses on the *Trentes Glorieuses* (1945–75) and identifies the first seeds of spatial reconfiguration: the appearance of new membership spaces within national systems (e.g. supplementary pension schemes), the creation of the European Communities, and the establishment of a coordination regime regulating the social entitlements of migrant workers within the EC. This chapter also reinterprets the EC constitutional order as a novel 'law for exits and voice'. Chapter 4 is the central empirical one. It reconstructs developments of EC law (including case law) relating to social protection and traces the differential impact that free movement provisions and competition rules have had on the various functional schemes and tiers or pillars of provision within national welfare states. It also identifies and illustrates the new strategies of spatial politics prompted by the boundary redefinitions operated by the EU, focusing in particular on pensions, health care, and social assistance. Chapter 5 explores another important aspect of spatial reconfiguration: the increasing role of subnational territories (and in particular regions) as new, distinctive, and relatively autonomous 'bounded spaces' in certain areas of social protection, notably health care, active labour market policies, social services, and assistance. The chapter illustrates this new development by reference not only to within-state trends of social protection regionalization but also to novel forms of transnational regional groupings. Finally, Chapter 6 opens by presenting a visual map describing the new spatial configuration of social protection in the EU and then proceeds to highlight its potential consequences in terms of 'destructuring'. The chapter ends with a discussion of how 'solidarity' and 'Europe' might be reconciled through stronger citizenship rights and the development of an intelligent (and more socially-friendly) institutional framework.

I

The Structuring of Social Citizenship:
A Theoretical Framework

Introduction

Since the last decades of the nineteenth century, the social rights of citizenship have played a crucial role in the process of state- and nation-building in Europe. Such rights have given rise to wide 'collectivities of redistribution' that have strengthened cultural identities, enhanced citizen loyalties to public institutions, and promoted a sharing of material resources throughout the social structure, thus enhancing civic and political cohesion. The European nation state has typically become a *welfare state*; the social components of citizenship are no less important than its civil and political components; the right to decide about the forms and substance of social citizenship in its turn has come to be considered a crucial aspect of national sovereignty.

The dynamics of globalization and, more specifically, of European integration have been gradually challenging this institutional configuration. Each state's right to decide on social policy matters has become less comprehensive and 'ultimate' than it used to be. Globalization and European integration have modified the context in which national welfare states operate, imposing new constraints on, and offering new opportunities to, citizens/consumers, producers, and service agencies as well as policymakers (in the widest sense). In the debate, the new challenges to social sovereignty are primarily discussed with reference to highly significant but mainly *indirect* developments: increased cross-country capital flows, the greater volatility of international financial markets and their power to condition domestic choices, the constraints posed by new competitive imperatives and by the rules of new supranational regimes (typically EMU) on fiscal and monetary autonomy, rising migration flows, and so on. While keeping all these developments in serious consideration, this book concentrates on a number of more *direct* challenges to national welfare systems, that is, developments which are weakening two essential traits of social sovereignty in its traditional meaning: (*a*) the capacity of a state to 'lock in' and exercise command over actors and resources which are crucial for the stability of redistributive institutions within the national territory, and (*b*) the capacity of a state to prevent external authority structures from interfering with its own social space and jurisdiction.[1] The direct challenge that interests us is, in other words, the challenge to the *boundaries* of welfare, that is, those institutional demarcations which are essential for solidarity and redistribution.

Boundaries are quintessential components of modern citizenship. Whether understood as 'a status bestowed on those who are full members of a community' (Marshall 1992: 18) or as 'a continuing series of transactions between persons and agents of a given state in which each has enforceable rights and obligations... by virtue of the person's membership in an exclusive category... and [the person's] relation to the state' (Tilly 1996: 8),[2] citizenship rests on boundaries that separate insiders from outsiders. The salience of boundaries has always been particularly high in the case of *social* citizenship, which touches on delicate issues of material redistribution and raises thorny dilemmas of equity, justice, and reciprocity. Originally drawn between the end of the nineteenth century and the first half of the twentieth century, the boundaries of social citizenship have witnessed several changes with the passing of time. But these changes were almost entirely internal to the nation state. The community that Marshall had in mind was the nation, and the citizenship whose history he so effectively traced was 'by definition national' (1992: 9). Tilly's 'exclusive category' comprises in turn 'the native born plus the naturalized' (1996: 8), that is, the legitimate inhabitants of a state's territory, who enjoy a privileged position vis-à-vis the agents of that state. Only with the deepening of European integration has the issue of boundaries started to affect the nation state as such and its

---

[1] I am well aware of the ambiguities inherent in the concept of 'sovereignty'. As highlighted by recent debates in both international relations and comparative politics theory (Biersteker and Weber 1996; Elkins 1995; Krasner 1999; Osiander 2001), such ambiguities concern both the connotation of the concept (many different meanings) and its denotation (various discrepancies between meanings and observed phenomena). But, treated with due caution, the concept remains pertinent and useful, I believe, in capturing the logic of ongoing developments at the interface between member states and EU institutions. A detailed discussion of what I mean by 'social sovereignty' will be offered later.

[2] Tilly's full definition reads as follows: 'a continuous series of transactions between persons and agents of a given state in which each has enforceable rights and obligations uniquely by virtue of 1) the person's membership in an exclusive category, the native born plus the naturalized and 2) the agent's relations to the state rather that any other authority the agent may enjoy'. We will return to the second element of Tilly's definition later.

sovereign capacity to bind not only internally but also externally, that is, in respect of the outside environment.

When and where, exactly, has the nation state started to 'leak'? In what areas, in what dimensions of social citizenship have traditional boundaries become more porous? Or is the process of boundary redrawing more advanced? Are there links between the weakening of external boundaries and the internal configuration of established welfare state arrangements? What are the implications of such developments for the politico-institutional stability and sustainability of social protection? Are new forms of post-state and post-national solidarities, possibly anchored to the EU level, feasible and desirable? These are the fundamental questions that this book sets out to explore. I believe they are important questions both for the welfare state and for Europe. A focus on the 'spatial' challenges to national welfare and its link to territory can cast new light on its increased vulnerability as an institution geared to securing individual life chances and fostering redistribution that is appropriate in the light of both efficiency and social justice criteria. An accurate diagnosis of the multifaceted dimensions of such vulnerability and of its structural roots can assist the identification of remedies capable of reconciling the important traditional objectives of this institution with the transformations in its external environment. A focus on the boundaries of social rights and their ongoing reconfiguration can in its turn contribute to a better understanding of the EU as a polity-in-the-making and thus to identifying a profile and a substance for EU citizenship capable of strengthening its current 'anaemic content' and unclear functions (Follesdal 2001). The 'nature of the beast' (to use Risse-Kappen's (1996) metaphor on the still indefinable profile of the EU as a political entity) is and will definitely remain very different from that of a fully integrated nation state.[3] Yet the institution of citizenship (with its various components) can play a major role in constituting and consolidating the 'polity-ness' of the EU—a prerequisite for its meeting satisfactory standards of legitimacy and performance.[4]

The first task of our exploration is to search for a suitable theoretical framework that can provide us with appropriate concepts and hypotheses. The changing content and institutional contours of citizenship and the role of civil, political, and social rights in the process of state formation and nation-building have long been classical themes of macro-historical sociology and political science: besides Marshall and Tilly, the names of

[3] On the EU as an imperfectly integrated political order, see Olsen (2000).

[4] For an articulate discussion of the legitimacy and performance dilemmas of the EU, see Scharpf (1999).

Bendix, Eisenstadt, and Polanyi (to mention few of the tallest 'giants') come immediately to mind in relation to such themes.[5] Though somewhat overshadowed by the much more cultivated 'power-resources' approach,[6] the 'state-building' tradition (as dubbed by Scarborough 2000) has offered important insights for the analysis of the long-term evolution of welfare states (Alber 1982; Flora and Heidenheimer 1981; Flora 1986), including its problematic encounter with European integration (Leibfried and Pierson 1995). The tradition has also been revived in recent scholarship about the EU (Caporaso 1996; Klausen and Tilly 1997; Marks, Hooghe, and Blank 1996) and, more generally, about processes of territorial restructuring in the wake of globalization and new regional/functional international regimes (e.g. Ansell and Di Palma 2004).

In general terms (and in a nutshell), the notion of state-building designates a set of processes aimed at enabling (or enhancing the capacity of) a state to rule or govern, that is, to stabilize social cooperation and ensure compliance within a given space in the pursuit of broadly defined common goals. Thus, a state-building perspective looks at social rights as 'institutional stabilizers' that bond individuals and groups both with each other and with the state as a distinct entity. Social rights stabilize cooperation because they provide actors with predictable entitlements to material resources, which can be relied upon without engaging in potentially antagonistic negotiations or costly transactions. These rights are institutionalized in at least two senses: they are guaranteed by specialized authority structures and, ultimately, by the coercive power of the state; and, once established, they tend to acquire a 'taken for granted' nature, a feature that reinforces the long-term stability of social cooperation.

But what is the state? In this analytical tradition, the state is not a purely abstract construct or a unitary actor: it is a 'staffed organization', consisting of interested agents performing more or less codified roles (Ikenberry 1986; Stinchcombe 1997). It is through its staff that the state carries out its

---

[5] See especially Bendix (1964), Eisenstadt and Rokkan (1973), Polanyi (1957), Tilly (1975a).

[6] Linked especially with the works of Korpi (1980, 1983, 2000) and Esping-Andersen (1985, 1990), the power resources approach has been the prevailing theoretical framework within the field of comparative welfare state studies. Its main thesis is that welfare state developments must be seen as outcomes of power struggles between organized social classes. In its genetic moment, the establishment of a welfare state critically depended on the capacity of collective organization and mobilization (the first and basic 'power resource') of the workers' movement. Subsequently, the availability of welfare programmes became itself an additional 'power resource', which served to sustain and strengthen the labour movement. For a reconstruction and discussion of this approach and, more generally, of the political theories of the welfare state, see Myles and Quadagno (2002). On the lines of development of welfare state research in recent decades, see Pierson (2000).

basic function of guaranteeing stable and generalized cooperation and compliance. Since their position is ultimately insecure, state agents engage in constant and delicate relations with 'the ruled' (i.e. for our purposes, citizens) with two main (and essentially political) objectives in mind: holding on to office and maintaining or enhancing state capacities as such. In modern democracies, the relationships between rulers and subjects operate in two distinct arenas, the electoral and the corporate, both of which provide opportunities of exchange and bargaining through the deployment of a wide array of resources. From this angle, social rights appear not only as institutional stabilizers but also as a prime currency of state–society relations. Societal actors—from individual voters to organized interest groups—are interested in rights (freedoms, faculties, entitlements), as these guarantee them resources and power. State agents are interested in the support of societal actors for gaining office and holding on to it. These agents produce and police rights by using the capacities attached to their offices. Society's complexion does obviously determine the kind of rights generated; different societies make different demands on their state. But from a state-building perspective the content and distribution of rights throughout society basically reflects the politico-institutional logic of the state as a spatial and staffed organization claiming supremacy over all other organizations within that space.[7] As we shall see, boundary definition is one of the prime instruments used by state agents to achieve their political aims.

The state-building tradition in sociology and political science took its first steps in the 1960s and 1970s with the launch of a substantial research programme on the formation of European states and nations, aimed at identifying the common properties of this process and the main dimensions of variation across countries and through time.[8] This research programme has produced fundamental theoretical insights and empirical knowledge on which it still seems wise and promising to build for an analysis of state developments in the new context of twenty-first-century

[7] These are obviously very crude and sketchy remarks on the concept of 'state' and on the state-building perspective. They are developed and elaborated later. Here we use the term 'state-building' in a very broad sense, to identify a whole strand of debate and school of research. As will become clearer in our discussion, in its more technical connotation state-building is only one step or dimension in the historical process that led to the formation of the European nation states. For an effective historical survey of the development of the state, see Poggi (1978, 1990). For recent discussions and reviews of the literature on the state, see Kahler (2002); Levi (2002); Spruyt (2002).

[8] For an early presentation of the research programme, see Tilly (1975b, 1975c); for a more recent reconstruction, see Flora (1999).

Europe. Thus, our search for appropriate concepts and hypotheses about European integration and national social citizenship will start from here.

This search will proceed in four steps. The first step revisits an often forgotten giant of the state-building school: the Norwegian social scientist Rokkan. He has elaborated powerful arguments about the spatial dimension of political systems and about the crucial role of boundaries in the consolidation of the territorial state and its internal differentiation. Rokkan did not study the welfare state in any depth; and in his late writings he manifested deep scepticism about the possibility of Europe's 'thick' nation states becoming effectively integrated. Yet I find that Rokkan's conceptual map and his basic argument about the interdependence between boundary-building or reduction and internal structuring or destructuring of political space offers a rich analytical framework for interpreting current European political developments, including those affecting the welfare sphere. Rokkan's theoretical framework borrowed important insights from another influential author, Hirschman. Our second step will thus be to revisit Hirschman's well-known 'exit-voice-loyalty' model with a view to enriching and articulating this model and generating a novel conceptual grid of spatial politics. The subsequent two steps will mobilize the analytical framework and theoretical links drawn from these two authors for discussing in general terms the specific object of our interest: the *structuring of citizenship*—and in particular of the social rights of citizenship—and the potentially *destructuring* effects of European integration.

'Bounded Structuring': Rokkan Revisited

In recent years the work of Rokkan has been the object of renewed interest and appreciation in academic debate. The systematic reconstruction of Rokkan's theory so masterfully carried out by Flora with Kuhnle and Urwin (Flora et al. 1999) has contributed to highlighting the remarkable richness and originality of this author in both substantive and methodological terms. The big passion of Rokkan as a social scientist was the political development of Europe and, in particular, of Europe's nation states and their transformation into mass democracies. The conceptual maps, analytical frameworks, and theoretical insights Rokkan elaborated between the 1950s and 1970s not only maintain fully intact their heuristic value in respect of the time span which he explored (the epoch of the national, industrial, and 'democratic' revolutions), but also offer a precious springboard for speculating about the new dynamics of the European state system in the wake of supranational integration and increasing globalization. As with all the classics, the writings of this Norwegian social scientist remain *opera aperta*—permanent points of departure for scientific speculation on old and new research questions.

How were the European states and nations 'built'? How did they come to be pieced together and to form, during the nineteenth century, a novel and relatively orderly 'system' distinct from the pre-existing imperial configurations? Drawing on a wealth of both richly detailed historical literature and conceptually dense social theory, Rokkan laboriously wove together a theoretical framework for addressing such grand questions, a framework in which the notions of *boundaries* and *structuring* occupy a central role. Although he never explicitly used the expression (to my knowledge, at least), his overall interpretation of modern European political development may well be cast in terms of *bounded structuring*. The entire substance of Rokkan's interpretation cannot possibly be summarized here,[9] but a brief presentation of its basic conceptual elements and theoretical links can provide us with the initial building blocks for our analysis.

The road to state- and nation-building was long and winding. Its starting point is to be found way back in history, at the fall of Rome in the fifth century AD. The collapse of the Roman Empire was followed by complex dynamics of functional and territorial differentiation in Europe, which eventually gave rise to two basic sets of structures—centre–periphery and cleavage—each in turn flanked and sustained by a variety of instrumental organizations. Centre–periphery structures are those systems of relationships and transactions linking the dominant loci of command and control, within relatively 'bounded' territories, to their subordinate areas. Centre formation in medieval and modern Europe was a difficult and at times tormented political process, involving the mobilization of coercive, economic, legal-administrative, and cultural-symbolic resources. The process was significantly constrained by historical legacies, pre-existing spatial configurations, and path dependencies. In some contexts centre–periphery relations evolved towards 'monocephalic' structures, that is, territorial systems with a single centre commanding all the crucial resources (economic, cultural, military, administrative). In contrast, other contexts developed 'polycephalic' centre–periphery structures, with a hierarchy of centres commanding different resources. Polycephalic structures typically allowed for the persistence of some substate boundaries around peripheral territories. The great paradox of European development was that the strongest

---

[9] Rokkan's bibliography includes more than 200 writings: see Saelen (1981). Among the most important works are Lipset and Rokkan (1967); Rokkan (1970,1971,1973,1975); Rokkan and Urwin (1981, 1983).

centres—and monocephalic structures—emerged at the periphery of the old Roman Empire (in England, Scandinavia, northern France, a little later in Spain) whereas in its Italian and German heartlands the 'city-belt' which formed itself during the Middle Ages hindered state-building and national unification well into the nineteenth century.

Cleavage structures are those sets of fundamental contrasts, rooted in socio-economic and cultural differences, which have come to systematically divide national communities. Despite the countless objects of contention and lines of social opposition produced by European history, only a very limited number of conflicts developed into obdurate and pervasive cleavages: the church–state and dominant-subject cleavages[10] (both linked to the national revolution), the primary–secondary sector (agricultural vs. industrial–urban interests) and the workers–owners cleavages (both linked to the industrial revolution), and later the socialist-communist cleavage linked to the Russian Revolution (Table 1.1).[11] These cleavages did not automatically give rise to interest or partisan conflicts. In each polity, area-specific configurations, organizational and mobilization dynamics and their temporal sequencing affected the actual translation of cleavages into associational and especially partisan juxtapositions—with implications for both state- and nation-building.

Centre–periphery and cleavage structures rest on a web of instrumental institutions and organizations. Some of these emerged in parallel with structural interactions on the input side, that is, the side of demand

Table 1.1   Critical junctures in European history and main ensuing cleavages

Critical juncture	Historical period	Resulting cleavages
Reformation, counter-reformation, early nation state formation ('national revolution')	Sixteenth–nineteenth centuries	Dominant-subject (centre vs. peripheries; central dominance vs. subject ethnicities and language or religious groups) Church–state
Industrial Revolution	Nineteenth century	Primary vs. secondary sectors (rural vs. industrial and urban interests) Workers–owners
Russian Revolution	Twentieth century	Socialist-communist

[10] The dominant-subject cleavage refes to 'the conflict between the central nation-building culture and the increasing resistance of the ethnically, linguistically, or religiously distinct subject populations in the provinces and the periphery' (cited in Flora et al. (1999: 284)).

[11] A more detailed table drawn by Rokkan himself can be found in Flora et al. (1999: 305).

mobilization—typically interest groups and political parties. Other institutions, however, emerged on the output side, that is, the side of 'system responses' in the face of pressures from below and from outside: typically executive and bureaucratic agencies, whose aim was to secure and maintain the territorial and functional division of labour. The concept of *structuring* (i.e. of structure formation) connotes the stabilization of all these patterns of interaction and institutional-organizational forms through the creation of specific coalitions among actors, of increasingly articulated and codified rules and norms of behaviour, and the establishment of interorganizational links. In the wake of some critical historical junctures, centre–periphery structures and cleavage structures became 'crystallized' or 'frozen', that is, they came to be embedded in, and supported by, a particularly dense network of organizations (especially corporate and partisan organizations, but also service bureaucracies), whose main effect was (and still largely is), precisely, that of reproducing the structures themselves. In his analysis of cleavage structures, Rokkan (1977) used the Dutch term *verzuiling* ('pillarization') to connote an institutional configuration characterized by a high degree of interlocking between cleavage-specific parties (e.g. parties of a given religious denomination) active in the electoral channel of mobilization and the corresponding interest associations active in the functional or 'corporate' channel. An emblematic example of *verzuiling* is the thick constellation of 'cross-channel' (electoral vs. corporate channel) organizations that formed in the Netherlands in the first half of the twentieth century within each subculture. The Roman Catholic, the orthodox Protestant, and the 'general' (*algemene*, i.e. liberal, socialist, and nationalist) segments of Dutch society organized themselves as separate pillars (*zuilen*), resting on cultural organizations such as churches and schools, economic organizations such as trade unions and professional associations, and political organizations such as parties (Daalder 1973; Lijphart 1968). Pillarized (*verzuilt*) configurations are particularly 'sticky': once in place, they display a remarkable degree of institutional inertia.

Structuring processes are typically associated with the presence (introduction, modification, removal) of *boundaries*—the second fundamental concept of Rokkan's framework. This concept has a very abstract connotation, and it identifies virtually any kind of marker of a distinctive condition relevant to the life chances of a territorial collectivity and perceived as such by the collectivity itself. In line with the approach of political geography, the lines of physical demarcation over a territory—for example, borders or frontiers—separating populations from one another can be considered as the emblematic embodiment of boundaries (Anderson 1996; Fouchet 1991;

Taylor 1993). In line with the suggestions of anthropologists, however, boundaries serve not only a physical but also a symbolic function: they possess a constitutive power in respect of individual and group self-perceptions and identities (Cohen 1986). Finally, and perhaps more importantly, in line with the tradition of Weber, boundaries are fundamental mechanisms of social closure and thus sources of group formation, instruments for resource allocation, and at the same time potential objects of contention.

The creation and consolidation of boundaries was a prime ingredient of state formation and nation-building in modern Europe. State boundaries partitioned the continental territory into separate political formations (*politische Verbände*, in Weber's terminology), upheld by the monopolization of coercive resources: these enclosed political formations, 'internalized' pre-existing structures, and gradually nationalized the configuration of actors and institutions. Though operating under the constraints of historical legacies and geography, the different modes of boundary-building offered to centre-forming elites (so masterfully profiled, in their various compositions, by other classical authors such as Moore, Bendix, Eisenstadt, or Tilly)[12] a menu of different strategies, each with different implications for the configuration of social and political resources inside the state territory. It was through boundary-setting that European states and nations were built. Boundaries 'caged' actors into the national terrain and prompted their politicization (Mann 1986). Nationalized structures then provided actors with opportunity spaces and arenas of mobilization (both electoral and corporate) in which those very boundaries could become objects of contention and possibly be modified.

But how precisely did (or does, in general-theoretical terms) *bounded structuring* operate? In order to unravel the internal logic of this process, Rokkan availed himself of the work of Hirschman (1970). The Norwegian social scientist was deeply impressed by Hirschman's exit, voice, and loyalty scheme, which he defined as a 'magic model', provocative and path-breaking (Rokkan 1974a; 1974b). As is well known, Hirschman suggested that, in response to decline in product quality or organizational performance, consumers or members of an organization may react in two possible ways—exit and voice—which interact with a third element, loyalty, that is, a psychological attachment which increases the cost of exit and tends to elicit voice instead. Reading Hirschman encouraged Rokkan to use this author's concepts for the study of spatial politics,

---

[12] See Moore (1967); Bendix (1964); Eisenstadt and Rokkan (1973); Tilly (1975a; 1990). For more recent elaborations, see Ertman (1997); Spruyt (1994); and Te Braake (1997).

problematizing the division territories into units, the dynamics of bound-ary-building, and boundary differentiation, as well as the politics of boundary control: externally, to prevent, permit, or enforce exit or entry; internally, to channel, tolerate, or suppress voice (Rokkan 1974a: 30).

Elaborating on Hirschman's scheme, Rokkan conceptualized the process of bounded structuring in terms of interdependence between the external closure of a given space and its internal differentiation.[13] Historically, state formation (nation-building and later also democratization and redistribution) implied a gradual foreclosure of *exit* options of actors and resources in a given space, the establishment of institutions of 'system maintenance' capable of eliciting domestic *loyalty* (including the consolidation of what Rokkan called the cultural infrastructure: churches, sects, educational institutions, mass media, and other cultural agencies aimed at reproducing ethnic-linguistic communities), and the provision of channels for internal *voice*, that is, claims addressed to national centres from social and geographical peripheries. The locking-in of resources and actors in a bounded space domesticated the latter's strategies, oriented them towards central elites (somehow forcing them, in turn, to become responsive to pressures from below), encouraged the formation of new organizational vehicles for the exercise of voice and the strengthening of loyalty, and, as a consequence of all this, sparked off processes of territorial 'system-building'.[14] Rokkan borrowed this last term from Parsons and used it to connote the emergence of area-specific, functionally integrated constellations of institutions and actors—where 'functional integration' refers to a high degree of coherence, match, or 'good fit' between the economic (adaptive, in Parsons' terminology), the political (goal-attainment), the social (integrative), and cultural (pattern maintenance) realms.[15]

[13] This interdependence between external closure and internal differentiation is the key theoretical link of the Rokkanian framework. This explains why I have coined the concept of 'bounded structuring'. This concept may sound somewhat redundant: after all, almost by definition there can be no internal structuring (or structuring *tout court*) without a spatial demarcation ('bounding') vis-à-vis an 'outside'. But the price of redundancy is compensated, I believe, by the concept's effectiveness in immediately and explicitly evoking the close nexus between the two processes.

[14] Exit options were never totally foreclosed, of course, especially in the economic sphere (see below). In this sphere state-builders had to compromise with the necessity of granting merchants the freedom to practise cross-border trade. The mutual interest in preserving some exit options constrained the potentially predatory instincts of the former and encouraged the latter to support state-builders with money and consensus (North and Thomas 1973).

[15] The influence of Parsons has left a functionalist flavour in a number of Rokkan's writings, which has been the object of some criticism. However, I fully agree with Flora that 'this criticism is justified if we restrict our view to Rokkan's macro-model, but is much less accurate for his more concrete

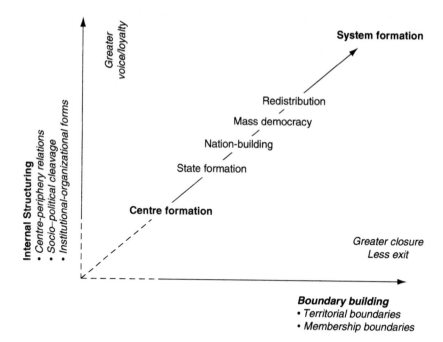

Fig 1.1 Bounded structuring: dimensions and macro-processes

Figure 1.1 summarizes and orders the conceptual elements and theoretical proposition discussed so far. The figure can be used as a grid for reconstructing concrete, historical phases of Europe's political development. But is can also be used as an analytical tool for establishing the hierarchical links on the ladder of abstraction among the basic concepts that we have drawn from Rokkan.[16] Bounded structuring is (on my interpretation, at least) the most general macro-process, connoting the internal differentiation of a given space in the wake of external closure. System-building or system formation[17] is a specific type of differentiation, which

---

historical–comparative studies' (Flora 1999: 16). In his analysis on the advent of mass democracy and of cleavage structuring, Rokkan is very sensitive to the role of actors' choices within opportunity structures linked to available resources and institutional constraints. Flora suggests the concept of *configuration of actors* to capture the interrelationship between the options, alternatives, and choices linked to agency and the distribution of opportunities and resources linked to structures (Flora 1999: 16).

[16] For a parrtially different (and more general) theoretical reformulation of Rokkan's and Hirschman's frameworks, see Bartolini (2005).

[17] 'System-building' and 'system formation' can be considered as synonyms, and Rokkan often used them interchangeably. However, while system-building is essentially a dynamic concept (it connotes a process), system formation has both a dynamic and a static connotation. As a matter of fact, it can designate not only the process of forming a system but also the end result of this

is accompanied by a high (and increasing) degree of internal integration. Centre formation is the initial trigger of bounded structuring—and, potentially, of system-building. It designates the establishment of a new locus of command from which elites advance claims to spatial control. Centre-building already rests on boundary-setting moves and on some instrumental organization (the dotted lines along the horizontal and vertical axes). But boundary-building and internal structuring in the full sense start only when the new centre is actually able to exert some effective spatial control. State-building, nation-building, mass democracy, and redistribution are the four ingredients and at the same time the four time phases of territorial system-building in modern Europe: these are history- and context-bound concepts. The former two were primarily centre-generated thrusts throughout the territory, of a military-economic and of a cultural nature; the latter two were processes of internal restructuring, opening up opportunities for geographical and social peripheries in the symbolic-cultural as well as the economic realms. These four processes both widened and deepened the scope of the modern state (Spruyt 1994). The sequence indicated in the figure is to be read as ideal-typical: as we shall see, in some countries redistributive arrangements were established before the advent of mass democracy based on universal suffrage. System-building and its components are placed within a space delimited by two dimensions: the 'boundary-building' dimension, which connotes the closure of exit opportunities, especially vis-à-vis the outside; and the 'internal structuring dimension', which connotes the domestication of centre–periphery and cleavage constellations and the process of institutional differentiation. 'Voice' and 'loyalty' are placed along this latter dimension, as institutional differentiation provides domesticated actors with channels of communication and contention ('voice') as well as various incentives for mutual and more generally spatial bonding ('loyalty'; see later).

In all the processes/concepts included in Figure 1.1, the spatial element plays a prominent role. Following Rokkan we treat the notion of space as having two distinct components: a territorial component and a 'membership' component, involving socio-political and cultural elements. Thus, boundary-building must be understood in two ways: (a) as the demarcation of physical space through the deployment of effective instruments of territorial defence, primarily of a military and administrative nature; and (b) as the creation of explicit codes and forms of distinction—for example,

---

process, that is, the emergence or creation of a full-blown, integrated system. This is why in Figure 1.1. system formation is placed at the top-right corner.

citizenship rights—between insiders and outsiders, nationals and non-nationals. Membership boundaries are very important, as Rokkan put it:

[They] tend to be much firmer than geographical boundaries: you can cross the border into a territory as a tourist, trader or casual labourer, but you will find it much more difficult to be accepted as a member of the core group claiming pre-eminent rights of control within a territory. (quoted in Flora, Kuhnle, and Urwin 1999: 104)

Membership boundaries can also be used to differentiate within the core group itself, establishing barriers or thresholds for accessing political decisions or socio-economic resources and opportunities. This is an important point. Although Rokkan applied the exit-voice interdependence primarily to dynamics of national differentiation linked to the consolidation of the external boundaries of the state, he also used it for analysing internal differentiation as such, that is, the politics—within the nation state—around the definition of constituencies and spheres of competencies of domestic institutions and organizations, or the struggles over rights of participation or rules of representation. As a general process simply connoting internal differentiation linked to closure vis-à-vis the outside, bounded structuring can take place at different levels—a syndrome that Rokkan himself dubbed the 'Chinese box problem' (Rokkan 1974a: 32). Much of Rokkan's work was actually devoted to analysing in these terms the advent of mass democracy. The differential voting rights across population strata in the nineteenth century created distinct spheres of membership of the political community, which became the object of harsh and prolonged confrontations. Full democratization of the polity implied the modification (and, in many cases, outright removal) of boundaries—in this case, legal barriers—hindering the legitimate organization of certain social groups, their electoral incorporation, and their rights of representation and of executive access. As we shall see, the development of culturally embedded systems of national citizenship, resting on universal civil, political, and social rights, can also be fruitfully analysed in terms of bounded structuring, involving dynamics of both territorial and membership closure. In many respects, national citizenship can be regarded as one of the most significant products of Western-style bounded structuring: the anchoring of people's interaction to an institutionalized system of mutual rights and obligations has allowed a quantum leap in the stabilization and generalization of social cooperation—which is the most fundamental task to be performed by 'politics' as a distinct sphere of action (Panebianco 2004; Stoppino 1994). Though not necessarily the outcome of an 'efficient history' (March and Olsen 1998), the combination of state territorial sovereignty and citizenship rights has proved to be a highly efficient form of organization: it greatly reduced cooperation and coordination problems between rulers and citizens, between citizens themselves, and—last but not least—between states as collective entities (Spruyt 1994, 2002).

Rokkan never systematically used or discussed the concept of sovereignty in his writings. But, if we adopt his perspective (again in line with the Weberian tradition), then sovereignty basically means the capacity of demarcating geographical space and exercising authoritative control on both exit-entries and voice-loyalty dynamics *into* and *within* that space.[18] After consolidation of the centre, the subject of sovereignty thus understood became 'the state' – an organization that differs from all the others by virtue of its territoriality (its being constituted by reference to territory) and by virtue of its claims to legitimacy over and above all temporary bargains struck among the organizations operating in its territory. After the mid-eighteenth century, the consolidation of the sovereign state's twofold ability (demarcating space vis-à-vis the outside and exercising authoritative control inside its territory) was no easy task—not least because of the constant appearance of 'boundary transcending technologies' (from the press to underground movements), requiring the deployment of 'boundary maintaining counter-forces'. The development of world capitalism—or of a world system, to quote Wallerstein's famous concept (1974) that Rokkan took very seriously—brought increasing pressures to tear down boundaries precisely when state-national system-building drove in the opposite direction. Towards the end of the nineteenth century, however, despite the obstacles in its path, in certain parts of Europe the process of bounded structuring gave rise to a novel variant of the sovereign state: that *national, capitalist, democratic*, and *welfare* state which was the most successful political protagonist of the subsequent century.

The fusion between territorial control and identity, mass democracy, and the welfare state produced very solid and highly integrated political systems, functioning according to distinct internal logics. Of course, these

---

[18] If we take Krasner's four meanings of the concept (Krasner 1999), in the Rokkanian perspective two meanings appear as especially pertinent: 'Westphalian sovereignty' (i.e. the exclusion of external actors from authority structures within a given territory: domestic authorities become the sole arbiter of legitimate behaviour) and 'interdependence sovereignty' (i.e. the ability of domestic authorities to control what passes through territorial borders). The other two meanings are: sovereignty as external recognition and sovereignty as the ultimate legal right to decide. As argued by Caporaso and Jupille (2004), Westphalian sovereignty in particular seems to offer greater analytical leverage over the other three meanings for many questions currently being debated about the strains between the authority of the EU and that of member states.

systems maintained several channels of mutual communication, especially in the economic sphere (markets typically rest on the availability
of exit and entry opportunities, especially for goods). Looking at institutional developments from a (very) *longue durée* perspective, Rokkan was
well aware of the tensions inherently building up between processes of
system closure on the one hand and the counter-pressures for 'opening'
brought about by cross-border transactions on the other. While recognizing the importance and to some extent the inevitability of economic
internationalization and even of some forms of economic unification, he
seemed to think that such processes could be managed through the establishment of appropriate legal frameworks: after all, the thriving of commerce in the European city-belt during the Renaissance had been made
possible by the Romanization of customary law; the acceptance of a limited set of principles on the part of merchants for the conduct of cross-
local transactions (the *lex mercatoria*, a 'law for exits') was all that was
needed for a very long time. Writing in the 1960s and 1970s, Rokkan
remained especially sceptical about the prospects for European integration—and in particular about the formation of new cross-system structures 'beyond cooperation between corporate agencies'.

In the last two decades, however, European integration has proceeded
much beyond the stage of a mere open arena of economic transactions
and administrative cooperation. Cross-system boundaries have been
extensively redefined, differentiated, reduced, and in some areas
altogether cancelled. Thus, with hindsight, we can say that Rokkan's
scepticism has been proved wrong.[19] But his theoretical framework does
retain all its heuristic value: in fact it can be 'tested' against the new factual
developments. Following this framework, we should in fact expect that
the ongoing dynamics of boundary redefinition and boundary removal—
occurring along the horizontal axis of Figure 1.1—may have significant
consequences for the vertical dimension as well, that is, on the configuration of internal structures and institutional orders. Is the emergence of
new supranational loci of command and control (the EU centres) generating new forms of peripheralization? And is the access to the new
centre(s) increasing the margins of manoeuvre of old peripheries vis-à-

---

[19] Other scholars of the 'classical' state-building tradition were more far-sighted in this respect. For
example, Tilly, in his conclusion to the edited volume on *The Formation of National States in Western
Europe* (which included a contribution by Rokkan), discussed a number of emerging trends that in his
view threatened almost every single one of the defining features of the state: 'the monopoly of
coercion, the exclusiveness of control within the territory; the autonomy; the centralization; the
formal coordination; *even the differentiation from other organizations begins to fall away in such compacts
as the European Common Market*' (Tilly 1975*b*: 80; emphasis added).

vis national centres?[20] Are we witnessing a gradual transnationalization of the old cleavages or perhaps even the emergence of new 'obdurate and pervasive' lines of (transnational) opposition linked to the very process of European integration? However fascinating in its far-reaching implications, the formulation of general hypotheses about the destructuring effects of cross-system boundary redrawing on deep-seated national centre–periphery and cleavage constellations is a very complex analytical task, which falls way outside the scope of this book.[21] Rokkan's theoretical framework can also be mobilized, however, for raising questions and advancing theoretical expectations about the specific theme which interests us here, namely, the impact of European integration on national systems of social citizenship (Figure 1.2).[22] As noted earlier, national citizenship has been a powerful political invention for underpinning social cooperation on a large scale; and welfare state rights constitute a prime

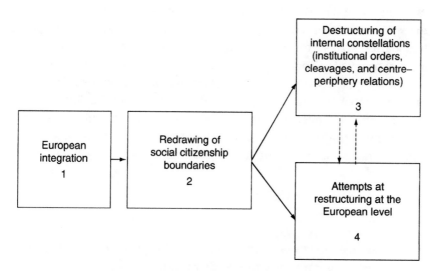

Fig 1.2 The impact of European integration on social citizenship

---

[20] According to the so-called multilevel governance theory, there is ample evidence that this is already happening. European integration has prompted processes of subnational mobilization addressed both towards the EU directly and towards national centres, in order to wrest away from the latter territorial representation vis-à-vis the EU. See Hooghe and Marks (2001). See also Chapter 5.

[21] See Bartolini (1998, 2005) for an extremely insightful and sophisticated exercise in this direction. On the potential transnationalization of functional cleavages, see the interesting discussion by Tarrow (2004).

[22] A more elaborated chart is offered in Chapter 6, at the end of our empirical investigation.

component of citizenship. To what extent (and, again, where precisely) have EU rules affected the territorial and membership boundaries of domestic welfare systems? Is this rebounding likely to undermine the institutional foundations (or prerequisites) of redistribution at the national level? Are there symptoms of wider destructuring dynamics, for example, on cleavages and/or centre–periphery relations—dynamics generated *by* or likely to impact *on* social policy? And if European integration can be looked at as an attempt at 'system-building'—with different ingredients and phases from those which led to the formation of the nation state, but still following the logic of 'bounded structuring'—what are the prospects for a reconfiguration of social citizenship within this new emerging space?

These are obviously very general and very ambitious questions, and we will specify and narrow down their focus in the following chapters in order to manage them on both the analytical and the empirical fronts. But before starting our substantive investigation, we have to elaborate a little more on the general theoretical framework sketched so far. Our next step is to search for a wider range of possible behavioural choices vis-à-vis spatial boundaries. Rokkan made pioneering steps in conceptualizing and theorizing about the political nature of boundaries and in identifying some basic trade-offs between types of social behaviours and between properties of institutional contexts. But I believe that Rokkan did not fully exploit the potential richness of Hirschman's scheme, which can be used for generating a more articulated conceptual map for the macro-analysis of political spaces. After Rokkan, let us then briefly revisit Hirschman.

Locality and Vocality Options in Bounded Spaces: Hirschman Revisited

It is not exaggerated to say that Hirschman's 'magic model' has been one of the most important analytical constructs of contemporary social science. Its influence has spanned disciplines from political science to sociology, from psychology to economics and management, spawning a wealth of theoretical elaborations and empirical investigations (Dowding et al. 2000). Hirschman himself suggested that his scheme could find promising applications in comparative macro-politics, particularly in respect of the dynamics of territorial (state) structuring and restructuring (Hirschman 1974, 1978, 1993). Spatial metaphors and archetypes have always played an important role in this area of inquiry. Compared with such classical and relatively straightforward polarities such as 'in-out', 'flight-fight', 'walk-talk', 'left-right', and so on, the exit-voice-loyalty model has at least two advantages. First, it explicitly and clearly contrasts two distinct dimensions: one involving cross-system movements (from one bounded space to another) and the other involving intrasystem activities (voice in its various manifestations). Second, the model posits an explicit interdependence between the two dimensions, albeit filtered by a third element (loyalty), and develops explicit theoretical expectations about individual choice and behaviour.

One shortcoming of Hirschman's novel imagery, at least in its original and most used formulation, is that the two dimensions are treated and discussed as if offering essentially one option each: exit (on the cross-system dimension) and voice (on the intrasystem dimension). But, as pointed out by several commentators, if all the logical possibilities of the model are unfolded, the repertoire of options can become much richer. To start with, this repertoire should at least include the symmetrical opposite of exit, that is, *staying*, and the symmetrical opposite of voice, that is, *silence*. Exit and voice are not mutual alternatives from a strictly logical point of view. Faced with a perceived performance deficit of a given organization, actors will first confront the dilemma whether to exit or stay put. Only after resolving this dilemma (often based on loyalty considerations) will they decide whether to voice or remain silent (Barry 1974). Silence can in turn signal different reactions: from sheer 'no response' (due to lack of problem perception) to loyal acceptance, from lack of concern to 'frustrated refraining from speaking out' (e.g. for fear of retaliation) (Birch 1974). Moreover, a variety of mixed behaviours can be logically conceived and found in reality: partial exits, threats of exit, boycotts, exit-cum-voice, voice after exit, and so on. While some of these mixed options were already identified and briefly discussed by Hirschman himself in his book, some authors have suggested interesting elaborations on them, which are especially pertinent and useful for the study of territorial politics (Bartolini 1998; Finer 1974). This strand of debate (which includes Rokkan, of course: see Rokkan 1974*a*, *b*) has also made two more general points: first, exit and (especially) voice can be exercised in collective form by aggregate actors (social groups and even whole territorial communities); second, choice dynamics leading to exit and voice are strongly affected by the properties of institutional contexts. In other words, Hirschman's scheme lends itself to be used for the macro-analysis of structures and collective behaviours, and not only for the micro-analysis of individual behaviours. In particular, the scheme can be used for identifying the

Table 1.2 Locality and vocality options: extending Hirschman's model

Vocality	Locality			
	Insiders		Outsiders	
	Exit	Staying in	Staying out	Entry
Hiding	Sneaking out	Hiding underground	Hiding outside	Sneaking in
Silence	Silent exit	Silent staying in	Silent staying out	Silent entry
Voice	Vocal exit	Voice from within	Voice from outside	Vocal entry

options available to actors, given the opportunities offered by the boundary and resource configuration in which they find themselves.

The addition of new concepts has definitely enriched the original model, but the lack of systematic links among the various options and suboptions limits their analytic potential and actually risks subtracting from the model's 'magic'. Is there a way of retaining the most promising enrichments while not losing too much in terms of parsimony and coherence?

My attempt to move in this direction is shown in Table 1.2, which presents a typology of the main behavioural options which seem logically open to the actors of spatial politics. This typology originates in the contrast between a *locality* (or spatial proper) axis and a *vocality* (or confrontational) axis. Locality is a more general concept than exit and it is also spatially neutral; it is meant to connote spatial positioning per se and to identify a range of possible choices and behaviours vis-à-vis boundaries (in a wide sense). In its turn vocality is suggested as a more general and more neutral concept than voice; it connotes modes of 'stance' within a bounded system and identifies a range of visibility and confrontational options vis-à-vis that system.

The locality axis differentiates options according to the 'in' or 'out' position of the actors.[23] Hirschman's scheme was fundamentally conceived for insiders: it is customers who already buy a certain product or actors who are already members of an organization (or citizens of a state) that Hirschman had in mind in his reasoning about cross-system movements and intrasystem operations. This 'insider bias' is linked to the specific phenomenon on which this author focused his attention, namely, quality deterioration. Exit and voice were treated as responses to organizational decline,

---

[23] The recorded positioning is, of course, one that obtains at the time that is pertinent to the research questions addressed.

and thus they have an internal origin and a sort of membership prerequisite: one has to be within the organization in order for one's voice to be more
effective; one obviously has to be located inside the organization prior to
exiting. It is true that the 'outside' does appear here and there in Hirschman's original formulation (e.g. in the guise of 'voice after exit'). But then,
why not incorporate the outside more explicitly and systematically in the
model's core? This incorporation widens the scope of the model not only in
terms of options but also in terms of pertinent actors (outsiders, precisely).
The model becomes more general, and such generalization can provide
useful analytic tools both for a theory of political boundaries and for those
more specific debates which are central to the substantive theme of this
book and which already make use of in-out imageries. Consider the insider-
outsider cleavage in much of the current welfare state debate (e.g. Pierson
2001); or the contrasts between the 'ins' and the 'outs' of various functional
regimes in the EU literature (not to speak of the whole enlargement debate)
(Zielonka 2001); or some recent scholarship on citizenship, in which the
novel categories of 'insiderhood' and 'outsiderhood' have been proposed
for identifying actors and their strategies (Brubaker 1992; Wiener 1999).
Centred as it is on the principle of free cross-border movements of persons,
goods, capital, and services, the process of European integration has
brought to the fore the salience of spatial positionings and of the insider/
outsider divide and strains.

The inclusion of outsiderhood on the locality axis brings immediately to
the fore two new cross-system options: staying out and entering. Faced
with a boundary (territorial and/or social, in Rokkan's sense) that excludes
them, actors can decide to remain outside or they can try to enter, passing
through the filters which are in place to guard that boundary. From a
political perspective, entry is a very interesting option, which I think has
received much less attention than it deserves. Hirschman mentioned it
only as a sort of follow-up to exit: entering a new organization or product
after exiting from an old one; re-entering the old after having left it. In my
scheme, entry is instead a fully autonomous option, which may be chosen
regardless of and without the simultaneous exercise of exit or voice.[24] This
is especially true if the class of events that trigger locality or vocality

---

[24] Entry may be chosen also as a fully rational response to Hirschman's problem, that is, quality
deterioration per se. An activist voter can, for example, choose to become a member of a party in
order to 'improve its quality' (or, more meanly, to participate in the distribution of spoils). The
objection that in this case we are dealing with voice is not convincing. Even in entry-for-voicing
cases one has to distinguish, at least analytically, between two moves: a cross-system or horizontal
move (from outside to inside) and an intrasystem or vertical move (struggling upwards). Likewise,

reactions is not Hirschman's narrow class of 'quality deteriorations' but the more general class of all situations in which actors believe that quality can be improved (Barry 1974) or that gains can be obtained by means of spatial or confrontational moves. Examples abound, especially in the spheres that interest us. Social groups excluded from a given domestic membership space (say, representation rights or welfare entitlements) can decide (and try) to enter this space in search of symbolic or material advantages; or they may prefer to stay out of it in order to defend their own political autonomy or to avoid financial obligations. Cross-system migration (and especially migration from poorer to richer countries) is in its turn an area in which outsiders are the most salient actors and entry the most frequent option—or at least the most sought-after goal.

As mentioned in the previous section, Rokkan did consider entry, but he mainly used this concept in connection with voice. He was interested in entry barriers within membership spaces and their effects on voice structuring; for example, barriers to legitimate organization, group incorporation, rights of representation and of access to executive power—that is, the national government. Rokkan was also aware that in geographical spaces exit options were conditioned not only by the constraints posed by the territory of origin but also by those posed by the territory of destination ('you may well want to exit, but alternative territorial systems are not easily open to entry') (quoted in Flora et al. 1999: 231). But he did not fully develop this line of reasoning and concentrated on entries as crossings of internal membership boundaries. I suggest that a more general reflection on entry options and dynamics—as distinct and partly autonomous from both exit and voice dynamics—may raise interesting theoretical questions. How are entry options distributed across and within territorial systems? How do processes of boundary attenuation affect not only exit flows *from* but also entry flows *into* a given territorial unit? What are the consequences of new entries or threats of entry on exit and voice dynamics? What are the consequences of all this for political structuring (i.e. on centre–periphery relations, cleavage constellations, and the broader institutional order of a given political system)? As we shall see, these are very pertinent and relevant issues for discussing the past and

the objection that in fact there is no entry, because the actor, being concerned with the organization, was already 'inside', does not obtain either. To say the least, it would apply to exit too: after exiting, one may still retain a concern with the organization, to the point that one may opt to voice from outside and/or re-enter if it recuperates. If there is a borderline between an inside and an outside which defines when exit occurs, logic requires that it be a closed line thus allowing for entry gates as well as for exit ones.

present dynamics of social citizenship in Europe. To a large extent, the four freedoms guaranteed by the EU legal order can be considered 'freedom to enter', that is, as faculties of trespassing territorial and membership boundaries on the part of a host of different actors: from workers wishing to access the labour market of another member state to patients seeking treatment abroad; from service providers (such as insurance companies or mutual funds) interested in penetrating the social protection system of a country different from their own to regions forming cross-border associations aimed at integrating their labour markets or welfare systems.[25]

The vocality axis includes three different options: voice proper, its logical opposite (i.e. silence), and hiding. Originally suggested by Laponce (1974), this latter option consists in minimizing one's visibility within a bounded space, avoiding not only any kind of overt confrontation with the other members of the space (and especially its guardians or rulers) but keeping oneself as much as possible in the dark. Hiding 'underground' makes it possible to reduce or even to 'zero' the costs of membership of an organization (e.g. the tax obligations of citizenship) or to waive its formal requirements (e.g. illegal immigration) while continuing to enjoy its advantages. In certain circumstances, hiding can be a fully rational response to quality decline in Hirschman's sense: for example, when there is no belief in quality recuperation or in the efficacy of either exit or voice, or when there is a strong possibility of retaliation. One can hide not only for lack of alternatives, but also for opportunistic reasons. In the former case, hiders will be interested in quality recuperation and/or in the opening up of alternative options. In the latter case, hiders may be interested in the continuation of the status quo. In the words of Laponce (1974: 80):

The Frenchman who under German occupation takes to the woods after having been drafted without taking to the guns; the Poujadist of the pre-Poujade days who hides his profits rather than voice his complaints; the people with no fixed address who from the antiquity to the present...move between here and there and who, wanting to be nowhere, are both here and there; the farmers of the feudal days who invent peasant communes which, because they are collective, continue to live after their members die and thus escape succession duties and reclaims; the trust companies of the Renaissance who apply the farmer's discovery to the urban capitalist setting by hiding the individual within the group: all react to what was, from their point of view, the equivalent of deterioration of an institution; they react by reducing the cost of that institution to them while continuing to draw benefits out of it.

[25] In Rokkan's language we could interpret the move to form a new territorial or membership space on the part of two or more actors as a 'primary entry', followed by the 'secondary entry' of other actors. We discuss the new spatial options and strategies of subnational governments in Chapter 5.

Like exit and voice, hiding has important systemic consequences (think of tax evasion, illegal immigration, or the underground economy in contemporary economies), which in the long run may elicit some sort of response on the part of the concerned organization—or else may precipitate its decay. Moreover, hiding has a certain degree of interdependence with the other behavioural options: the availability of hiding options for some may elicit the voice of others, which in turn may induce the former group of actors to voice for staying in. Think of what is happening in many European countries in the field of migration. The 'sneaking in' and then 'hiding underground' of a growing number of 'third country nationals' is provoking the emergence of anti-immigration movements and parties and at the same time is prompting the mobilization of the immigrants themselves for remaining inside, with legal residence and work permits. Historically, processes of external and internal boundary redefinitions have tended to create, at least transitionally, new hiding opportunities (some of Laponce's examples): a development which seems clearly at work in ongoing processes of financial market integration (e.g. tax havens) or, again, in the Europeanization of migration policies (flows of illegal immigrants exploiting the loopholes of new legislation). Hiding has become an option for collective actors as well and even for 'membership spaces': as we shall see in Chapter 4, some French occupational pension schemes have been able to hide themselves for years exploiting the ambiguity of EU laws on social security and competition, thus preserving their rent as public monopolies.

The cross-cutting of the two axes generates a wide range of behavioural options (see Table 1.2). Silent exit and voice from within are Hirschman's classical options, while silent staying in is the null option originally neglected by this author. Silent staying out and silent entry are the pure options generated by the incorporation of the outside in the model. Hiding underground is also a new pure option, generated by the extension of the vocality axis. Sneaking out (e.g. illegal capital flight), sneaking in (e.g. illegal immigration), vocal exit, voice from outside, and vocal entry are in their turn mixed types generated by a combination of pure options. As can be seen, according to our typology a rich repertoire of acts may be performed on the stage of bounded structuring (to return to the macro-concept discussed in the previous section).

Do we need all these options? Are they all pertinent and observable? These are certainly legitimate questions, and my typology may well appear a cumbersome complication.[26] But, as mentioned earlier, in line with the

---

[26] The construction of typologies is virtually an open-ended process. When two significant dimensions are crossed with each other, one might generate a great number of cells and subcells. The

state-building tradition in this book we want to take boundaries and their reshuffling very seriously. The new institutional topography of the EU, with its increasingly dense stratification of authority structures and membership spaces, calls for a much more varied analytical tool kit than was needed for the study of classical state-building processes. *Nomina sunt numina* (names are like gods): a rich and evocative vocabulary can often pave the way to new ways of seeing things or even to seeing new things altogether. In particular, the typology can provide us with promising dimensions and promising concepts for characterizing the developments occurring in boxes 2 and 3 of Figure 1.2, that is, the new cross-system ('locality') options in the sphere of welfare opened up by European integration, and their confrontational ('vocality') implications on established institutional constellations at the national level. A central argument of this book is, precisely, that European integration has given rise to a new pattern of politics in the sphere of social protection: a new spatial politics in which the widening of locality and vocality options available to actors has generated new interests and new strategies—and thus new patterns of interaction—around the production and maintenance of social rights.

Table 1.2 does not say anything explicit about the notion of loyalty. The latter was the most ambiguous element of Hirschman's original scheme; he saw it as a sort of tax on exit, decreasing the cost of voice. But if exit is properly contrasted with its logical alternative, then what is decreased is simply the cost of staying, not necessarily of voice (Barry 1974). As a matter of fact, in the world of politics loyalty may often put a tax on voice rather than on exit (or in addition to it). A loyal actor does not easily stand up against his or her party or political community—as emblematically suggested by the popular saying 'my country, right or wrong'. However, even before its causality, loyalty has a bigger problem for theory-building (and in particular for macro theories about political boundaries): it is not a behaviour but an attitude. While exit and voice, as well as all the other options of Table 1.2, can be observed in terms of agency and/or relative positioning, loyalty is a state of mind that can be tapped only indirectly, by interrogating actors: a characteristic that induced Barry (1974) to dub loyalty as a 'post hoc equation filler'.[27] However, loyalty is an important

---

real test of a typology is its heuristic plausibility and pertinence *in respect of the empirical facts that a researcher is observing*. Given the complex empirical constellation in which I am interested, I trust that my typology can pass the pertinence test.

[27] If loyalty is assumed to increase the cost of exit and to decrease the cost of voice, and cannot be independently observed as a behaviour, then the observed choice of an agent in favour of exit or of voice can always be explained *ex post* by imputing to him or her the necessary amount of loyalty.

element of bounded structuring: are there ways of remedying the analytic weakness of this concept, which does seem very pertinent to and promising for macro-level investigations also?

Rokkan anchored loyalty to internal structuring, treating it as an essential element for the emergence of a smooth and stable 'centre–periphery balance', that is, a systematic relationship between central rulers and their subjects based on allegiance and diffuse support rather than mere interest-based calculations (Rokkan 1975).[28] Loyalty is generated by institutionalized practices that bond actors to one another in territorial and membership spaces. The exercise of voice—in a context of equalized rights of participation, that is, of political citizenship—is one such practice: this is why in Figure 1.1 we have placed voice and loyalty along the same vertical dimension. But besides voice, there are other practices as well that produce bonding incentives: most prominently experiences of 'sharing', both material and non-material sharing. Think of the practices within society's cultural infrastructure (churches, schools, clubs, etc.), and also the sharing of national symbols after the achievement of a satisfactory degree of national cultural standardization. Or think of the practices of institutionalized solidarity after the establishment of social citizenship. It is true that, even if one adopts a more structural perspective, loyalty ultimately remains a subjective attitude, a psychological ligature that attaches an individual to a certain object (such as a nation and its governing institutions, a local community, a church, an occupational group). But this perspective makes it easier to identify observable *behaviours* based on which loyalty (as an *attitude*) can be plausibly predicated—and thus be brought into the equation without one falling prey to Barry's fallacy.[29] Involvement in bonding practices tends to generate loyalty over time, balancing not only centre–periphery relations but also intergroup relations and contributing, more generally, to system formation. Involvement in bonding practices can be observed in the form of actual behaviour. Thus, participation institutionalized voice activities or other activities involving symbolic or material sharing can be good predictors of the degree of loyalty of a given set of actors. In the course of the last two centuries, many such activities have structured themselves around the institution of citizenship (and social citizenship in particular). It is to such institutions that we now turn our attention.

---

[28] This is also the position of Bartolini (2005), who posits a very close theoretical link between loyalty and system-building as prerequisites for dynamics of political structuring.

[29] For a development of this line of reasoning at the micro-level, partly cast in terms of 'social capital', see Dowding et al. (2000).

Modern Citizenship as a Basic Form of Spatial Closure

In contemporary political systems citizenship has grown to be a highly salient, if not the most salient, space of social interaction. Citizenship is a space, in that boundaries separating insiders (the community of citizens) from outsiders (foreigners or aliens) are a constituent element of the institution. Citizenship affects interaction because its substance disciplines and orients individual and group behaviours within those boundaries. Finally, citizenship has become very salient not only because of its growing 'thickness' (i.e. it entails a significant range of rights and obligations; Tilly 1996) but also because it often operates as a filtering mechanism for other, more specialized spaces of domestic interaction (from the market to the tax system; from social benefits to the military draft). In this sense it is both an object and an instrument of social closure (Brubaker 1992), serving as a sort of ground into which other forms of domestic closure can put down their roots.

Citizenship's boundaries incorporate in almost ideal-typical form the two dimensions of space discussed by Rokkan: the territorial dimension and the membership dimension. Citizenship is linked to territory in two senses: it is a status that can be acquired through various forms of territorial attachment, and its effects unfold fully with reference, again, to a territory. As has been suggested, a basic purpose of contemporary citizenship is that of allocating persons to states (Brubaker 1992; Heater 1990). However, besides being a 'territorial filing' device, citizenship operates also as 'social marking' device, providing persons with rights and obligations (à la Marshall) as well as roles and identities (à la Tilly). Citizenship is the privileged currency of politics (Panebianco 2004; Stoppino 1994, 2001): its filings and markings work to smooth social cooperation and to upgrade significantly the efficiency of this cooperation by fostering trust and attitudes of 'generalized' or 'impersonal' reciprocity (Follesdal 2001; Putnam 1993). As suggested by economic historians (North 1981, 1990; North and Thomas 1973), the legal framework of citizenship greatly contributed to regularizing social and economic life by reducing transaction and information costs, and thus providing incentives for innovation and profit at the micro-level.

In his path breaking historical sketch of this institution, Marshall suggests that the evolution of modern citizenship involved a double process: of fusion and of separation (Marshall 1992: 9). The fusion was geographical and entailed the dismantling of local privileges and immunities, the harmonization of rights and obligations throughout the national territory, and the establishment of a level playing field (the equal status of citizen) within state borders. The separation was functional and it entailed the creation of new sources of nationwide authority and jurisdiction as well as new specialized institutions for the implementation of that authority and that jurisdiction at a decentralized level. As is well known, Marshall had essentially in mind the British experience, where this double process unfolded slowly and smoothly over the centuries and where the building of solid and secure territorial boundaries was achieved very early in history.[30] This is why Marshall concentrated his pioneering analysis on the three internal components of citizenship (civil, political, and social) and neglected the external side of it (what separates citizens from non-citizens), taking for granted that the territorial filing device was in place (or perhaps that it was not even pertinent to his analysis). The early defusing of the territorial boundaries challenge allowed British political developments, including in the sphere of citizenship, to proceed 'swayed by the angel of voice', as Finer (1974: 82) put it—and, one might add, often helped by the 'holy spirit of loyalty' as well.

In other European contexts (and especially in Continental territories), however, the double process of fusion and separation encountered much greater difficulties. State borders remained rather vague and fluctuating, with no univocal and clear-cut implications apart from military ones, well into the early nineteenth century. In part this was due to the institutional complexity of the *ancien régime* and its system of overlapping sovereignties; in part it was due to wars and their territorial disruptions along state borders. War-making did certainly contribute—Tilly's classical argument—to generating a demand for citizenship rights on the part of increasingly tax-ridden populations, subject to mass conscription (Tilly 1975*b*, 1984, 1990). But in much of Continental Europe the territorial dimension of citizenship remained rather confused and contested for a long period of time; and it took the cement of nationalism between the nineteenth and the twentieth centuries to uphold effectively both the geographical fusion of pre-existing institutional spaces and the emergence and concrete functioning of specialized nationwide organizations. It is not a coincidence that the first constitutional proclamation and definition of citizenship per se (i.e. as a status which is preliminary and more funda-

---

[30] In Finer's reconstruction, the Kingdom of England may be considered as having achieved territorial unification as early as 975 AD. Even if stricter criteria are adopted on the meaning of 'territorial unification', by the second half of the eleventh century 'no peripheral elites within the well defined borders of the kingdom ever aspired to its division or tried to secede from it' (Finer 1974: 116).

mental than the rights and obligations attached to it) was made by a nation 'obsessed by the demon of exit' (to cite Finer 1974: 82, once again), revolutionary France. And it is not a coincidence either that, on the other side of the Atlantic, the 'first new nation' (Lipset 1963) formed through voluntary *entries* invented an unprecedented 'contractual' type of citizenship, based on a simple pledge of allegiance to the US Constitution and a minimal set of other requirements.[31]

The nationalization of citizenship (exemplified in the creation of the nineteenth-century synonym 'nationality') wove a *fil rouge* through the various rights and obligations bestowed on all the inhabitants of a state territory and promoted the formal separation between the container (the status of citizen per se, conferring a sort of 'right to have rights') and the content (the specific rights and obligations of citizenship). The two sides remained closely related in symbolic terms, at least in Europe; but this separation produced a gradual problematization of the criteria defining 'insiderhood' as such—the *jus sanguinis* and *the jus soli* being the two opposite poles of various possible empirical combinations (Heater 1990).[32] In parallel with the thickening of rights (especially social rights), the twentieth century witnessed the emergence of a distinct politics of citizenship as an instrument of closure, characterized not only by an explicit spatial vocabulary but also by strategies and behaviours pitting the 'ins' against the 'outs'. Since the 1980s, all European countries have had to respond to increasingly heavy pressures from the outside, manifesting themselves in all the forms indicated in Table 1.2: from the 'voice from outside' of would-be immigrants to the 'silent entries' on the part of qualifying foreign applicants, from the 'sneaking in' of illegal workers to the 'vocal entries' of asylum seekers and refugees. It is true that, in quantitative terms, the new migrations of recent decades have not (yet?) reached the magnitudes of the late nineteenth and early twentieth centuries (Faist 1997). But the institutional context in which these new flows take place makes a great difference: in the presence of thick citizenship spaces, smaller numbers are generating much more complex and 'difficult' politics.

Not surprisingly, Rokkan was much more sensitive than Marshall and the British tradition to the spatial nature of citizenship. In a little-known

---

[31] For a detailed historical reconstruction and discussion, see Heater (1990). On the French experience, see also Brubaker (1992); Noiriel and Offerlé (1997).

[32] According to the *jus sanguinis*, citizenship is acquired by 'blood', that is through family ascendants, regardless of the place of birth; according to the *jus soli*, citizenship is acquired based on the place (country) of birth, regardless of the nationality of one's parents.

passage of his work, he identified two general kinds of rights typically associated with this institution: *rights to roots* and *rights to options*. He defined the former rather narrowly, as 'the right to respect for the community of origin, whatever its language or ethnic composition' and the latter as 'the right of opportunities for the full use of individual abilities within the wider territorial network [of the state]' (quoted in Flora et al. 1999: 172). If we generalize Rokkan's first concept and treat the right to roots as a right (freedom or faculty) to belong to a community, to put down and/or cultivate one's roots on a portion of space (as a preliminary condition to being respected for this), we cut into the deep flesh of citizenship as an object of spatial closure: insiderhood provides unambiguous territorial belongingness, the freedom to establish and/or maintain ligatures that tell you who you are and whom you can trust; but it also provides you with options in the surrounding territorial network, with chances to better your life, and even to uproot or reroot yourself if that suits you. Exactly what options are provided depends on the civil, political, and social rights which are in force in a given nation state. As highlighted by the recent literature on gender and social policy, the range of options for women has been historically much narrower owing to the male bias inherent in the original Marshallian triptych.[33] Civil, political, and social rights in turn give additional substance to people's roots, to their belonging to a community, and—more importantly still—supply powerful procedural and material resources for obtaining respect for these roots and belonging.[34] What makes citizenship so significant in politico-institutional terms is the fact that it allows a well-ordered universal production/distribution of 'guaranteed powers'.[35] Rights are

---

[33] A critical option for women is, for example, in Orloff's well-known formulation, that of 'forming and maintaining autonomous households'—an option which is still short of being effectively provided in most contemporary welfare states (Orloff 1993). On gender, citizenship, and social policy in general, see Daly (2000); Lewis (1992); O'Connor, Orloff, and Shaver (1999); and Sainsbury (1996).

[34] The 'exclusionary' nature of citizenship as a membership space raises, of course, delicate normative issues. What ethical principles can justify the construction of boundaries between 'equal persons' who just happen to be born or to find themselves on different sides of borders? Such boundaries generate disparities of treatment and often huge inequalities in terms of life chances that have extremely shaky normative foundations. For a discussion of such thorny issues, see, among others, McKinnon and Hampsher-Monk (2000).

[35] The idea of citizenship rights as *poteri garantiti* is borrowed from Mario Stoppino's general theory of politics (Stoppino 1994). This author has also highlighted that, contrary to what happens in the economic sphere, in the sphere of politics the function of production always coincides with the function of distribution: rights are inherently linked to actors upon whom they are bestowed and whom they empower.

'powers' in that they bestow upon citizens the faculty to demand that other citizens and/or state officials observe or abstain from observing certain practices. Such powers are 'guaranteed' by the relationship that each citizen has with the state. All the rights of citizenship are 'political' in a large sense: not only 'in that they constitute binding claims on the agents of government, rather than on some other group' (Tilly 1975b: 37) but especially because they serve to stabilize social cooperation and to generalize compliance (Stoppino 1994).

Figure 1.3 summarizes our discussion of modern citizenship as a form of spatial closure. The space of citizenship is demarcated by both territorial boundaries (which identify the geographical reach of the citizen's status) and membership boundaries (which specify the criteria for insiderhood). Within this container, we find the actual substance of citizenship: not only Marshall's classical triptych (civil, political, and social rights) but also Rokkan's more basic duo: roots (belonging) and options. Civil, political, and social rights are placed transversally with respect to the rights to roots and the rights to options because, as already mentioned, the former provide resources for the exercise of the latter. In turn, the rights to roots and the rights to options are placed at the beginning of the table, since they may be considered as the underlying, ultimate purposes of citizenship (and thus normatively superior to the three sets of more instrumental rights). The table also includes the symmetrical counterparts of rights. The duty of

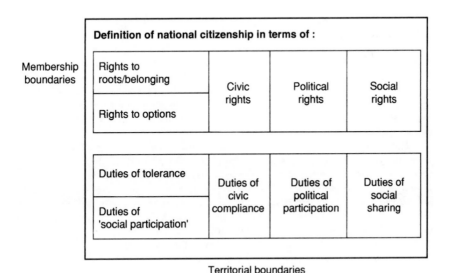

Membership boundaries	Definition of national citizenship in terms of :		
	Rights to roots/belonging	Civic rights	Political rights	Social rights
	Rights to options			
	Duties of tolerance	Duties of civic compliance	Duties of political participation	Duties of social sharing
	Duties of 'social participation'			

Territorial boundaries

Fig 1.3 The boundaries and content of citizenship

tolerance is associated with the rights to roots and belonging. The rights to options must be backed by duties (essentially moral duties) to participate in some way to the life of the community.[36] Civic compliance (essentially respect for the law), political participation, and readiness to share are in their turn the prime counterparts of civil, political, and social rights.

In Europe, the twentieth century marked the apex of national citizenship as a powerful machine for the production, distribution, and maintenance of rights and the forging of cultural identities. But the last decades of the same century also witnessed the emergence of a seemingly contradictory trend: the content of citizenship has continued to thicken while the container has started to thin out. New rights have been added and the old ones have been specified. In the language of the EU Charter of Fundamental Rights think of the explicit clarification of the 'rights to dignity',[37] the addition of new 'freedoms from' (such as the protection of personal data and privacy, or the protection in the event of removal, expulsion, or extradition), of new rights of equal or even preferential treatment (e.g. for children, the elderly, or the disabled), and of course new (or better-defined) rights in the field of solidarity.[38] The substantial catalogue of rights becomes wider and thicker. But at the same time the territorial boundaries of citizenship have become more permeable, while the possession of national roots (the sharing of a distinctive cultural and symbolic heritage or the pledge to do so) has become less important as a marker of insider-

---

[36] Social participation is of course a vague concept, as was Marshall's idea of 'a general obligation to live the life of a good citizen, giving such service as one can to promote the welfare of the community', starting with the duty to work (Marshall 1992: 45). Recent debates on the basic income have addressed squarely the issue of citizen's obligations vis-à-vis the options they enjoy by living in a political community. For a stimulating discussion of such debates, see White (2003). This author puts forward an interesting theory of 'fair reciprocity' as a principle of justice, based on a basket of minimum opportunities that ought to be guaranteed to all members of a political community in return for a 'contributory obligation' under the form of paid work, care work, or, possibly, the provision of a certain amount of capital.

[37] Right to human dignity (art.1), right to life (art. 2), right to the integrity of the person (art. 3), prohibition of torture and inhuman or degrading treatment or punishment (art. 4), prohibition of slavery and forced labour (art. 5) (Chapter 1 of the Charter). The Charter of Fundamental Rights of the EU was signed and jointly proclaimed by the European Parliament, the Council, and the Commission in Nice on December 7, 2000; it was later included in the new Treaty Establishing a Constitution for Europe, part II. The ratification process of this treaty was suspended by the negative results of the referendums held in France and in the Netherlands in May and June 2005.

[38] Workers' right to information and consultation within the undertaking (art. 27); right of collective bargaining and action (art. 28); right of access to placement services (art. 29); protection in the event of unjustified dismissal (art. 30); fair and just working conditions (art. 31); prohibition of child labour and protection of young people at work (art. 32); protection of family and professional life (art. 33); rights to social security and assistance (art. 34); right to health care (art. 35); right of

hood and in particular as a filter for the exercise of many rights. A growing number of immigrants who have alien roots have acquired access to freedoms and entitlements offered by states which are not 'their own' and have been incorporated in legal frameworks that used to be reserved for nationals only (Soysal 1996). The process of European integration has been a major driving force of this double development: the thickening of the content and the thinning out of the container of citizenship. Not only has the EU introduced a distinct EU citizenship superimposed on national ones, but it has also—and especially—promoted a creeping but constant decoupling of rights from national territories. The Europeanization of options through the 'four freedoms' and accompanying measures has entailed a gradual opening up of the distinct citizenship spaces of the member states. A new political figure has emerged on the stage: the *denizen*, that is, an outsider who can enter (and of course re-exit), stay inside, voice, and even 'share', but under certain conditions and for a limited time (Hammar 1990).[39]

Echoing Rokkan, we said earlier that European integration can be looked at as a new, initial form of bounded structuring and as a more or less deliberate project of system-building—even if with different ingredients from those in the past. Now, echoing Marshall, we could look at the development of EU citizenship as a new process of 'fusion and separation': fusion in terms of legal integration, separation in terms of the appearance of new authority structures capable of producing and protecting citizenship rights.[40] However, while this way of seeing things may capture the logic of developments in the sphere of civil and to some extent political rights, in the sphere of social rights the question is much more problematic. In nineteenth-century Europe, social rights emerged out of a *tabula rasa*: there was not much to 'fuse' and a lot to create *ex novo* in terms of institutions. The story of nineteenth-century Britain is emblematic in this

---

access to services of general economic interest (art. 36); right to environmental protection (art. 37) and to consumer protection (art. 38) (see Chapter 6).

[39] The term comes from the old French *denzein* and ultimately from the Latin *de intus* ('being inside'). The Romans were the first to invent different forms of citizenship based on external association and partial incorporation of outsiders (e.g. peripheral populations). Such forms of partial citizenship were used as political instruments and contributed significantly to securing the long-term viability of the Empire (Doyle 1996; Spruyt 2002).

[40] Given the still low degree of 'polity-ness' of the EU, the membership dimension of these two processes remains somewhat vague. What kind of 'community' serves as a marking base for the emerging EU citizenship space? In the words of Caporaso (2001: 23), we might ask: is this community merely a transnational market, an aggregate of those affected by transborder externalities, an authoritative civic proto-space? And what kind of authority is backing EU citizenship rights? Is it

respect: after the collapse of the Speenhamland system and the reform of the Poor Laws in 1834, 'citizens' were virtually abandoned to the newly emerged 'self-regulating' national labour market, with no collective social safety net bar poorhouse internment (Marshall 1992; Polanyi 1957).[41] In today's Europe, not only is the institutional material to be fused very thick and very solid, but *closure* has become a quintessential element in the stability and proper functioning of social rights. These rights rest on *ties* which are both more delicate and more sticky than civil ties and to some extent even than political participation ties.[42] This is what makes an investigation of box 2 of Figure 1.2 (i.e. boundary redrawing of social citizenship) so interesting and also what makes developments in box 3 (institutional destructuring as a consequence of European integration) somewhat alarming for their disintegrative potential and developments in box 4 (i.e. the attempt to restructure social sharing at the EU level) so difficult and unruly. But all these points deserve a closer look.

Bounding for Bonding: The Complex Structuring of Social Rights

Situated as it is at the crossroads between 'liberty' and 'equality', between 'self-interest' and 'altruism', solidarity is a rather elusive concept and a complex social good. On the one hand, it connotes a trait of whole social aggregates, that is, a high degree of 'fusion' or internal union, cohesion, and commonality of purpose of a given group (the noun 'solidarity' comes from the Latin *solidus*, a firm and compact body). On the other hand, it connotes a particular set of ties among the members of such group: *sharing ties*, that is, transactions aimed at pooling (a part of) each member's resources for some common purpose (we might call this the 'brotherhood' side of solidarity). As is well known, modern welfare state programmes pool resources (primarily financial) with the aim of countering the typical

---

'technical authority, the authority of the expert, or legitimate authority deriving from the people'? We return to these thorny issues at the end of our investigation, in Chapter 6 of this book.

[41] As is known, the Speenhamland laws (named after the village in which the Berkshire justices met in 1795) provided that workers' wages should not be allowed to fall below a minimum threshold linked to the price of bread, and thus established a mechanism of public subsidies for low wages. In the economic conditions of the time, this system prompted a spiral of wage reductions and workers' pauperization, which led not only to the abolition of the mechanism but also to a restrictive reform of the poor laws, which abolished outrelief for the 'able-bodied' and envisaged indoor relief (i.e. poorhouse internment) only for those unable to earn a living.

[42] It is true that national voting rights are still a sacred cow and remain strictly restricted to citizens. But, while there exists a supranational political body (the European Parliament (EP)) formed through direct election by all EU citizens, no supranational redistributive scheme targeted

risks and adversities of the life cycle: from sickness to old age, from work accidents to unemployment. Such risks are combated by redistributing pooled resources both horizontally (from the damaged to the non-damaged) and vertically (from the better-off to the worse-off). Looked at from this perspective, the welfare state can be considered a highly articulated and specialized form of institutionalized solidarity, serving both efficiency and social justice objectives (Atkinson 1989; Barr 1993).

Solidarity became slowly institutionalized during the last two centuries in the wider context of territorial system-building. The establishment of redistributive arrangements played a crucial role in stabilizing the new form of political organization (the nation state) that gradually emerged in modern Europe. This stabilization occurred through the anchoring of people's life chances to state-national organizations uniquely dedicated to social protection. The basic duo 'cultural identity cum political participation'—within a demarcated territory—was thus complemented by a novel 'social sharing' component (Flora 2000), reinforcing on the one hand those feelings of 'we-ness' that are a crucial underpinning of the nation state construct and offering on the other hand to national elites new tools for differentiating between insiders and outsiders.

People's life chances were anchored by weaving social rights into the fabric of citizenship. The right to belonging and the right to options ceased to be solely a matter of spontaneous ligatures, individual preferences, and personal abilities and started to be upheld by an entitlement to (a modicum of) material resources. It is true that in some countries civil and political rights were already there when social anchoring took place, supporting people in the defence of their roots and in the exercise of options. But in a context of unfettered markets (and in particular of a purely 'self-regulating' labour market—the destructive utopia described by Polanyi), the safeguards offered by civil and political rights were insufficient. Only the bestowal of certain material entitlements 'not proportionate to the market value of the claimant' (Marshall 1992: 28) could keep ordinary citizens from falling into conditions of need such that neither pre-existing roots nor surrounding opportunities could offer any way out or make any sense at all. The incorporation of social rights into the space of citizenship was no easy task. In the economic sphere, system-building followed the logic of market capitalism and produced a class society inherently built on

to individuals has been created at the EU level so far—and for vast numbers of commentators this absence is a desirable state of affairs.

inequalities, differential rewards, and the 'commodification' of workers (Polanyi 1957; Esping-Andersen 1990). Classes and nations arose together (Bendix 1964; Mann 1986): and even though the virtuous reconciliation between the meritocratic logic of the capitalist market and the egalitarian logic of national citizenship has been one of the greatest achievements of twentieth-century Europe, the itinerary towards this destination was punctuated by marked social and systemic strains and clashes.

Social rights had an enormous impact on social stratification and life chances. Marshall was certainly right when he pitted 'citizenship versus social class', while Korpi and Esping-Andersen are equally right in interpreting these rights as salient 'power resources' for wage-earners and labour movements.[43] But 'decommodification' was not the only issue that shaped the forms and content of social rights in the various countries. Another important front, more pertinent for our line of reasoning, was the issue of *closure*: how far-reaching ought the new redistributive schemes to be? For which collectivities ought the new sharing ties to be defined and introduced? Such 'who' questions were as important as the 'what' questions emphasized by outcome-oriented debates. 'Who' questions typically involve spatial dilemmas, in the terms specified earlier: the degree of spatial closure as such, to begin with, but also the link between rights and territory on the one hand and the link between rights and membership (membership-for-sharing in this case) on the other (see Figure 1.4).

Social rights are more demanding political products than civil and political rights. All rights have costs: enablement costs, to create the conditions for their actual exercise (such as free legal counsel for those people who cannot afford it), and enforcement costs. But, resting as they do on material transfers and services, social rights give rise to 'substance' costs as well. They require the availability of significant amounts of material resources that are not easy to extract from society, and of moral commitments to 'sharing with others' that are not easy to activate at the individual and primary group levels (Offe 1993).[44] The definition of boundaries plays a critical role in the production of these rights. In the first place, boundaries are essential for constructing new 'special purpose communities' ready to pool certain risks. For welfare-state builders, boundary setting was a delicate balancing act between indulgence vis-à-vis the particularistic inclinations of pre-existing social categories and the self-defeating ambitions of redistributive 'stretching', that is, pushing the

---

[43] On the 'power resource' approach to welfare state development see above, n. 6.

[44] For an interesting discussion of social rights as qualitatively different from civil and political rights, see Klausen (1995).

scope of solidarity beyond the limits which could be sustained by available material and moral resources. In the second place, boundaries are essential for enforcing affiliation to a sharing community. Now, compulsion is a prime component of citizenship in all its aspects, a fundamental instrument for assuring a correspondence between rights and duties. But in the sphere of social rights, which have precise, quantifiable costs, the matching of rights (entitlements) and duties (obligations to pay taxes and contributions) must be particularly accurate and stringent if fiscal bankruptcy is to be avoided. At least some civil and political rights can survive even without the full and constant exercise of the corresponding duties (contemporary democracy often functions with voting turnouts closer to 50 per cent than to 100 per cent). But social rights must be sustained by unrelenting sharing acts. This is why they rest on a specialized organizational form: that of compulsory social insurance. In most countries, the establishment of social rights meant the establishment of compulsory insurance schemes: against old age and disability, work injuries and sickness, maternity and unemployment. And, especially in the field of old age, the first implication for the members of such schemes was the payment of contributions (i.e. the exercise of the duty), with benefits arriving only after long 'vesting' periods.[45]

Defining and enforcing closure (in the form of obligatory affiliation and compulsory payments) remained a balancing act politically, but it conferred several economic advantages: less costly protection per insured person (thanks to the large, predictable, and reliable size of the sharing pool), the possibility of charging 'contributions' (flat-rate or proportional payments) rather than premiums (payments differentiated according to individual risk profiles, as in private insurance schemes), and the possibility of granting special treatment (such as lower or credited contributions, or minimum benefits) to categories of disadvantaged members. In contrast to private or voluntary insurance, compulsory (and public) social insurance could thus cover difficult risks such as unemployment or family breakdown,[46] and also produce not only horizontal redistributions (from

---

[45] A 'vesting' period is a temporal prerequirement often envisaged for the actual realization of social benefits: for example, a minimum number of years (months) of insurance, contributions, residence, and so forth.

[46] As demonstrated by welfare economics, the private market can insure only those risks where the following conditions obtain: the probability of risk occurrence for each insured party must be independent of the probability of that of any other insured party; such probability must be lower than 100 per cent; it must be known or estimable; there must be no adverse selection; there must be no moral hazard (Barr 1993).

the healthy to the sick, from the employed to the unemployed, etc.) but also vertical ones (from rich to poor). In this way, social citizenship could bring that 'general enrichment of the concrete substance of civilized life' through an 'equalization between the more and the less fortunate at all levels' that Marshall (1992: 33) saw as its fundamental mission.

Closure matters, then, for social rights, and probably in a more direct and intense way than for the other rights of citizenship. Historically, the *territorial* dimension of closure was important, but it essentially worked to align the boundaries of social rights with those of the nation state. The establishment of compulsory social insurance entailed a nationalization of redistribution, even if in many countries such nationalization remained based on categorical differentiations. Between the nineteenth century and the first half of the twentieth, most European countries introduced codes specifying the criteria for acquiring citizenship, thus putting in place more or less effective 'filing' filters to guard their territorial spaces of redistribution.[47] As we shall see in Chapter 2, the turning point in this process was the inter-war period, during which most European countries started to link rights with nationality and strictly to police their borders (Strikwerda 1997).

The membership dimension of closure was much more controversial and required much heavier political investment than the territorial dimension. Until the 1970s, the 'who' question addressed essentially domestic actors and the definition of internal boundaries for redistribution. Welfare-state-building followed the logic of 'bounded structuring' discussed earlier, and the internal design of European welfare state was significantly shaped by pre-existing or co-evolving structural constellations, in particular cleavage constellations. However problematic and contentious, the drawing of internal membership boundaries gave rise to a web of redistributive collectivities and arrangements which became gradually 'crystallized' through dynamics of institutionalization. If observed from the angle of social citizenship *circa* 1970, the European landscape appeared as a dense forest of compulsory spaces of affiliation, covering virtually 100 per cent of national populations, with very limited

---

[47] In those welfare states that adopted an occupational approach by linking social rights to work status (as originated in Bismarckian Germany), nationality was not required for insurance. However, foreign immigrants (like Polish workers in the Ruhr Valley in the 1880s) did have to fulfil the requirements envisaged by laws concerning the right to abode in the national territory and the right of access to the national labour market. These laws were made more stringent everywhere in Europe after the First World War. Furthermore, the status of migrant workers was precarious: these workers were the object of several forms of discrimination (for instance, in terms of wages, or hiring and firing practices) and their social entitlements were critically dependent on the presence of bilateral treaties (Guerin Gonzales and Strikwerda 1993). For a more detailed discussion, see Chapter 2.

'exit' opportunities (such as in the form of exemption from insurance) and very stringent 'entry' rules for aliens crossing state borders. True, the characteristics and functioning of social insurance programmes were accompanied by a loud 'voice' about the 'whats' and the 'hows' of the various programmes (and by some 'hiding' as well, primarily in the form of tax and contribution evasion). But such dynamics remained essentially a domestic phenomenon: in the vocabulary of Table 1.2, voice from inside (with some occasional hiding underground) was the prevailing game in town.

As noted in the previous section, since the early 1970s the process of European integration has worked to gradually thin out the national boundaries of citizenship, with specific and significant implications for social rights. Through binding regulations and court rulings, social rights (and the corresponding obligations) have been decoupled from national citizenship within the EU and linked merely to work or residence status. The citizens (and, in most cases, more simply the *denizens*, or legal residents) of any member state who move to another member state cannot be discriminated against as 'foreigners' and must receive the same treatment in terms of social rights as do nationals. While residence is still partly a matter of national sovereignty, the freedom to work anywhere in the territory of the EU is protected by the treaties and attentively policed by supranational authorities. On this front, it is clear that European integration has promoted an almost complete cross-local fusion of what Marshall considered the basic civil right in the economic sphere: 'the right to follow the occupation of one's choice in the place of one's choice, subject only to legitimate demands for preliminary technical training' (Marshall 1992: 10). To be sure, the member states still retain very substantial prerogatives over the definition and operation of social rights within their borders. But the underlying and ultimate filtering function performed by national citizenship qua overall and solid container of rights and basic instrument of closure is no longer there. Again, in our spatial vocabulary, this new situation has significantly reshuffled both the locality and the vocality options of the various stakeholders of social citizenship, especially in terms of unprecedented opportunities for entry into foreign redistributive spaces and unprecedented opportunities for challenging from without the authority of domestic social institutions (with acts that, depending on circumstances, can be seen as instances of vocal exit, vocal entry, or voice from outside).[48] Think of the possibility of accessing the ECJ in order to

---

[48] We will illustrate this point in Chapter 3.

enforce rights (freedoms or entitlements) denied by domestic authorities—an opportunity that can be resorted to both by the direct bearers
of social rights (e.g. an unemployed person or a pensioner) and by a wider
set of stakeholders, such as service providers (like insurance companies)
trying to break national monopolies over social insurance.[49] As will be
documented in Chapter 4, claims for (and actual instances of) boundary
transcendence in the sphere of social protection have been rapidly increasing in the last three decades within the EU, prompting a number of (only
partially effective) countermoves on the part of national governments.

Building on the contrast between 'negative' and 'positive' integration,
recent debates have already highlighted the destabilizing effects of all
these developments on national 'social contracts'.[50] The main preoccupation in such debates has to do with the increased power of markets and
market actors to the detriment of long-established redistributive arrangements and their supporting coalitions, laboriously put together through
domestic political channels and resting on territorially bounded balances
of power. Using spatial metaphors, we could say that the main line of
argument found in the literature connects vertical pressures from above
(EU directives and rulings) to horizontal rebalancing between markets
and rights in clear favour of the former. In general terms, both the preoccupation and the argument are well-grounded. But I contend that they
need to be qualified 'horizontally' and developed 'vertically'. Let me
explain.

The institutionalization of solidarity through social rights has effectively combated the disintegrative tendency of the nineteenth century's
greatest social utopia: that of a market entirely capable of self-regulation.
Societies have mobilized in search of protection; states have responded
with the creation of rights. But not all the buffers against market expan-
sionism have served their declared 'emancipatory' objectives, and some
buffers have gone too far. In some moments and in some contexts, the
angel of voice has been hijacked by petty interests, sectional lobbies, and
exclusive groups defending their privileges. Social closure has been used to
serve 'predatory' rather than emancipatory objectives. Contemporary rational choice theories (in both economics and political science) have
unveiled the dynamics which may lead to such undesirable outcomes.[51]
But both the awareness of and the preoccupation about such dynamics

---

[49] The ECJ cannot be directly accessed by individual litigants, but it can be reached via the referrral
of a national court.

[50] For a discussion of such debates, see Ferrera, Hemerijck, and Rhodes (2000).

[51] The classical references are Olson (1965) and Buchanan and Wagner (1977).

were clearly already present in the early and classical debates about social citizenship. Commenting on the upsurge of unofficial strikes at the time he was writing his famous essay, Marshall lamented that an attempt had been made 'to claim the rights of both status and contract while repudiating the duties under both these heads' (Marshall 1992: 42). In his turn, Bendix warned that a fundamental civil right and precondition of voice, the freedom of association or 'right to combine', can be used 'to enforce claims to a share of income and benefits at the expenses of the unorganized and the consumers' (Bendix 1964: 105). Economically inefficient and normatively unjustifiable forms of rights-based closure must be singled out with care and precision, context by context. But to the extent that the vertical and market-oriented pressures of European integration are (or can be) targeted at such forms of closure, then 'destructuring' (i.e. developments in box 3, Figure 1.2) might serve functionally useful and normatively desirable purposes. The challenge on this front is how to single out and how to target correctly.

This brings us to the vertical deepening of mainstream arguments about European integration and national welfare systems. European integration has the potential of prompting changes that are more far-reaching than 'just' a mutual rebalancing of markets and states in response to social needs. What is at stake is the basic spatial architecture of social citizenship, that is, the territorial reach of solidarity, the identity of its constituent communities, and, last but not least, the ultimate source of legitimate authority for the creation and the enforcement of rights. As we have seen, national social citizenship, backed by state authority, has played a crucial integrative role in domestic polities not only as a mechanism of (efficient and equitable) redistribution, but also as a basis for group formation and group persistence, for voice structuring and loyalty generation. By challenging national boundaries and by redrawing these boundaries along different geographical, socio-economic, and institutional lines (EU vs. non-EU citizens, workers vs. non-workers, insurance vs. assistance schemes, first pillar vs. second pillar insurance, etc.), European integration can undermine—and thus *destructure*—deep-seated social and political equilibriums. Although such destructuring may generate gains in terms of both efficiency and equity (as the horizontal argument suggested a moment ago), it may also proceed in the opposite direction. The most obvious alternatives to nationalized structures of redistribution are forms of subnational, transnational, or supranational social protection. In principle, a novel spatial architecture can be imagined, capable of nesting the different social rights within multilevel and multipillar configurations (Faist 2001). To some extent, such a new architecture is already emerging, as we shall see in later chapters of this book. But there are risks involved in this process. A clear institutional strategy is needed to tackle these risks and problems and to promote and sustain a viable restructuring of social rights (and social policies, in a wider sense) in twenty-first-century Europe. But before discussing future scenarios, we have to start our empirical investigation, supported, it is to be hoped, by the analytical framework outlined earlier.

2

From Public Assistance to Social Protection: Welfare State-building in European Nations

Creating Boundaries for Social Sharing: The Territorial Dimension

In the perspective outlined in Chapter 1, welfare state formation can be seen as a lengthy historical process of 'structuring' in the sphere of social protection. This process rested on four distinct, but largely parallel, developments: the drawing of clear territorial and membership boundaries for the identification and the enclosure of redistributive collectivities; the establishment of new institutions for organizing, sustaining, and implementing sharing practices; the emergence of specific patterns of internal voice and of social and political alignments; and the formation of new loyalties and identities in the wake of all these developments. As is well known, entire libraries have been filled with studies of the evolution of social policy in Western countries and on its distinct types of trajectories.[1] In this chapter we will rehearse the story through the analytical lens discussed in Chapter 1. The main questions that will guide our reconstruction can be summarized as follows: How were closure dilemmas solved and redistributive collectivities bounded in different national contexts? Which institutional-organizational forms were created in order to stabilize the new ties of solidarity across social groups? How did such forms interact with the extant cleavage and centre–periphery structures? Let us start with the first question, focusing on the shift from local to state-national spaces of redistribution, that is, boundary setting in its territorial dimension.

A European invention, what has come to be called the 'welfare state' emerged as a result of a slow process of policy experimentation, which began with the 'liberal break' with conservative paternalism around the middle of the nineteenth century and ended with the establishment of

---

[1] For recent reviews of the literature, see Amenta (2003), Myles and Quadagno (2002), and Pierson (2000).

social insurance in most countries by the end of the 1920s (Briggs 1961; Rimlinger 1971). Social insurance was a real institutional breakthrough in the history of the European nation state. Previously, the management of social risks was predominantly in the hands of locally anchored institutions. These operated through occasional, residual, and discretional interventions, considered as dispensations which society granted to persons often considered as undeserving. Beneficiaries were thus severely stigmatized and very often lost their civil and (to the extent they had any) political rights. The actual delivery of assistance took highly differentiated organizational forms, on a very narrow territorial basis.

Social insurance overhauled almost completely this traditional approach (Alber 1982; Ewald 1986; Heclo 1981; Perrin 1969). Its new objective was to provide standardized benefits, in an impartial and automatic form, based on precisely defined rights and obligations, according to highly specialized procedures and *with a national scope*: all individuals falling under state jurisdiction and meeting the given criteria were subject to the new rules. The institutionalization of solidarity through the pooling of certain risks (old age, disability, sickness, work injuries, and unemployment, to name the most important) across the whole population (or designated categories thereof) served in this way to strengthen that link between territories, cultural identities, and participatory institutions on which, as noted earlier, the European nation state ultimately rests. The connection between the establishment of social rights and central elites' objectives in many countries of political integration and nation-building, in the face of an increasingly bitter class conflict under capitalism, has been well documented by empirical research (Alber 1982; Banting 1995; De Swaan 1988; Ferrera 1993a; Friedman 1981; Heclo 1974; Lindert, 2004; Zincone 1992).

One of the core traits of the new technique—social insurance—was its *compulsory* nature. As noted in Chapter 1, it was precisely the obligatory inclusion of wide categories of workers that allowed the new institution to affirm itself as a powerful redistributive machine, capable of affecting the life chances of millions of citizens. The principle of compulsory inclusion lends itself well to being analysed in terms of 'bounded structuring'. The new compulsory insurance schemes can be seen as highly concrete manifestations of that process of institutional differentiation vis-à-vis foreign spaces and parallel internal structuring that characterized the European state system between the end of the nineteenth century and the early twentieth century.

The introduction of nationally differentiated systems of insurance added one extra substantive dimension to the *external boundaries* of the nation state, namely, its demarcation from other territorial systems. From Westphalia (1648) to Vienna (1815), external boundaries were essentially of a military nature and had only a vague administrative-regulatory component. Within state territories there remained numerous internal barriers (e.g. in terms of labour and even physical mobility) as well as a high degree of legal differentiation. The very notion of a uniform legal code (in penal but especially civic law) made its appearance at the doctrinal level only with the Enlightenment towards the end of the eighteenth century and progressed very slowly in practical terms throughout the subsequent century (Tarello 1998). The right to engage in a work activity of one's choosing emerged only with the dismantling of the rigid guild systems and corporatist protections (Alber 1982)—the other side of the coin being, of course, the rapid 'commodification' of workers in the capitalist labour market (Esping-Andersen 1990; Polanyi 1957).

The removal of barriers to free circulation as well as regulatory standardization across the state territory proceeded ever more quickly during the second half of the nineteenth century, and the establishment of social insurance schemes with a national scope constituted a sort of quantum leap for certain countries in this respect. The first country to introduce compulsory insurance was Germany: in 1883 against sickness, in 1884 against work injuries, and in 1889 against old age. Skilled workers of the industrial sectors were covered, regardless of where they worked within the Reich. The Bismarckian reforms had as a prime political objective the taming of an increasingly unruly working class.[2] But they also had 'state-building' objectives in a stricter sense. By transforming itself into a direct and visible source of social protection, the Reich (i.e. the imperial rulers) became much more important for the life of ordinary German citizens and could thus consolidate its position vis-à-vis the federated states, which still operated as gatekeepers of territorial membership through their distinct rules on *Staatsangehörigkeit* (state membership) (Breuilly 1998). The objective of enhancing the loyalty of all German citizens towards the Reich was explicitly mentioned by Bismarck in his parliamentary speech supporting the 1889 pension insurance bill (Eichenhofer 2000: 20).

As highlighted by Manow (2005), the three German social insurance bills of the 1880s were a first significant step towards the strengthening of the

---

[2] In Wilhelmine, Germany, many skilled industrial workers were members of the Second International. Insurance coverage meant not only the provision of benefits but also of opportunities to exercise substantive governance responsibilities in the new boards of the insurance schemes (Steinmetz 1993).

executive powers of the central state: legislative responsibility for social policy (*Arbeiterpolitik*) was allocated to the federal level and a central bureaucracy was created, charged with the oversight of the new schemes. At first, these schemes were internally fragmented along territorial lines that did not, however, coincide with the territorial borders of the various *Länder*. But in 1911 a broad reorganization took place, which promoted administrative concentration and also established a new single national scheme for white-collar employees. When unemployment insurance was introduced in 1927, this scheme was organized on strictly centralist lines.

The German reforms of the 1880s had a vast international echo. Austria–Hungary was the first country to follow suit (in 1887 with insurance for work injuries and in 1888 for sickness). Before the turn of the century came Denmark (means-tested national pensions in 1891), Norway (work injuries in 1894), Finland (work injuries in 1895), and Italy (work injuries in 1898). Other countries began with subsidized voluntary insurance, but shifted to compulsory schemes in the first two decades of the twentieth century. At the outbreak of the First World War, only Belgium was missing from the list (compulsory pension insurance arrived there in 1924). Even Switzerland—where the cantons strenuously opposed federal interference in this field—succeeded in introducing compulsory insurance against work injuries in 1911.[3]

The alignment of redistributive boundaries with the territorial boundaries of the state added one extra spur for the adoption of those strategies of territorial closure and external boundary defence that were accorded priority on the political agendas of many European countries in the wake of 'nationalization' processes. The definition of 'citizenship' and 'nationality' (i.e. who belongs to the national community) and the issue of how to treat 'aliens' became prime objects of public policy and debates at the turn of the century, especially in the larger countries aspiring to consolidate or assert their status as great powers and experiencing at the same time significant immigration flows (Bellamy, Castiglione, and Santoro 2004). France introduced a comprehensive law on citizenship (essentially based on the *jus soli* principle) in 1889.[4] After two decades of discussions and campaigns, the UK passed the first Aliens Act in 1905, and amended it in 1914.[5] The German Reich standardized rules on *Staasangehörigkeit* in 1913,

---

[3] See Alber (1982) for a full picture and discussion of the successive introductions of national compulsory schemes. Alber's analysis does not include Spain, Portugal, and Greece, which also made their first steps in social insurance between the two World Wars (Liakos 1997; Guibentif 1997; and Guillen 1997).

[4] On the French case see especially Weil (1996), Noiriel and Offerle' (1997), and Brubaker (1992).

[5] On the British case, see especially Cesarani (1996)

establishing the *jus sanguinis* as the fundamental criterion for entitlement to German nationality.[6]

Some time elapsed, however, before these new legislative instruments became fully operative and started to be used for purposes of territorial defence. In the two decades before the First World War, the European state system witnessed a period of increasing mutual interpenetration through international trade, foreign investment, and labour migration. The new citizenship codes were not immediately and systematically employed as filtering devices for inclusion or exclusion. Using the concepts discussed in Chapter 1, we can say that the main goal of early citizenship policies was more the identification of nationals per se (citizenship as an object of closure) than the gating of access into domestic membership spaces (citizenship as an instrument of closure). Even the British Aliens Acts of 1905 and 1914 were essentially aimed at empowering state authorities to deport 'undesirable aliens' for public order or national safety reasons rather than at discriminating against foreign workers and residents. In other words, the definition of the 'right to belong' did not have direct and immediate implications for the 'right to options' within the state territory. Nationalist sentiments and doctrines were growing everywhere in Europe at the turn of the century. But, in their early formulations, such doctrines were aimed at furthering claims of autonomy and minority protection rather than claims of national closure. This was especially true in the central empires: Austrian political thinkers engaged in interesting discussions of how the institutions of empire could be modified in order to embrace nationalist aspirations. In Britain too a lively debate developed among 'imperial theorists' on how to reconcile nationalist feelings and transanational loyalties and interests through 'commonwealth' arrangements.[7] In other words, pre-First World War nationalism was still predominantly 'liberal', especially in the economic realm. As noted by Strikwerda (1997), at the turn of the century workers could move freely across borders, passports were almost unknown, residence and work permits were not required, and it was perfectly legitimate to own property and do business in other countries. Each nation was creating distinct arrangements for social sharing that were territorially coterminous with state boundaries; but the latter were easily permeable. In Strikwerda's reconstruction, such a context opened a window of opportunity for 'social internationalism', that is, forms of transnational mobilization for the production of basic rights of

---

[6] On the German case, see especially Brubaker (1992); Breuilly (1998); and Lemke (1997).

[7] For a reconstruction of such debates, see especially Mazower (1998: ch. 2).

protection through a virtuous collaboration between national governments and international organizations.

At the turn of the twentieth century the transnational links between
national unions were surprisingly intense. A sort of advocacy coalition
formed within this network to promote international agreements on
many delicate issues concerning workers' rights: from hours of work to
women's employment, from judicial disputes to child labour and safety
regulations. Frequent conferences on such themes were organized in Berlin, Brussels, and Paris. In 1900 the International Association for Labour
Legislation was set up, which subsequently instituted the International
Labour Organization (ILO) in Geneva. Between 1900 and 1914 more than
200 new international bodies were founded. A few conventions were signed
on minimum labour standards, and national governments entered bilateral agreements guaranteeing reciprocity in the new branch of social insurance that was emerging everywhere, namely, work injuries insurance. Even
without reciprocity agreements, the prevailing legal tradition on labour
disputes applied 'customary international law', so that workers operated de
facto within a relatively homogeneous legal framework. In Strikwerda's
words, in the early twentieth century 'social citizenship was still being
defined, and it could be either national or international or both' (1997: 58).[8]

This period suddenly came to an end during the First World War. The
window of opportunity for any form of social internationalism was closed,
and liberal nationalism (i.e. the readiness and willingness of European
nation states to entangle themselves in a web of mutual socio-economic
relations, resting on a common floor of rights) was replaced by national-
istic protectionism and in some cases outright chauvinist aggressiveness.
It was during the war that the institution of citizenship and the new rules
introduced in the previous decades started to be used as an instrument of
territorial defence. Passports and entry visas became necessary for travel,
residence and work permits were introduced almost everywhere, and the
international mobility of workers and capital became the object of restrictive regulation. For those who had no right to belong, options were dras-
tically narrowed and could be suddenly withdrawn. As noted by Mazower
(1998), the collapse of the central empires and the war settlement at
Versailles brought about the triumph not only of democracy but also—
and more enduringly—of nationalism. In inter-war Europe, the (new)
democracies became exclusionary and antagonistic in their ethnic
relations. During the Great Depression, the expulsion of foreign workers

---

[8] For more historical details, see Guerin-Gonzales and Strikwerda (1993) and Lyons (1963).

became a common practice in many destination countries, like France and Belgium (Cross 1983). In the UK, inter-war legislation temporarily abrogated the *jus soli* principle and explicitly limited the social entitlements of aliens (Cesarani 1996). Racial nationalism grew in Nazi Germany (and to a lesser extent in Fascist Italy), paving the way for odious policies of ethnic purification and minority oppression even within the nation state.

The Great War made the link between social citizenship and national territory more visible also in another way. The territorial annexations that followed the war required difficult operations of institutional surgery as spatial portions of German and Austrian social insurance schemes suddenly found themselves abroad. When Alsace and Lorraine returned to France, both regions had for about three decades been enjoying the schemes introduced by Bismarck in the 1880s, which were much more solid and generous than those in place in the rest of the country. This put pressure on the French government for improvement throughout the 1920s, which led to the establishment of the system of compulsory social insurance in 1928–30 (Baldwin 1990; Hatzfeld 1989; Saint Jours 1982). In its turn, when advancing its claims on the 'unredeemed' provinces of Trento and Trieste (still parts of the Habsburg Empire between 1861 and 1919), the Italian state had already had to promise in 1916 that in case of 'redemption' it would have maintained the more generous sickness insurance introduced by the Austrians in 1888 (Ferrera 1993a). Territories carried social rights, in other words, that could no longer be severed from them.

Originally involving cross-local regulatory standardization and nationwide pooling of certain risks, during the inter-war period social insurance put down deeper territorial roots, increasingly solid external boundaries were built around it, and accurate filtering mechanisms were deployed in order to sort insiders from outsiders. A clear path had been chosen: social protection would be part and parcel of the 'bundle of territoriality'[9]—a territoriality bounded and controled by the authority of the nation state.

Membership Definitions: The Great Divide Between Universalistic and Occupational Welfare States

If the external boundaries of social insurance tended to coincide from the very beginning with the borders of the nation state (at least *de jure*), its

---

[9] Originally suggested by Ruggie (1993), this metaphor refers to the close association between territory and various forms authority structures (including social rights) that emerged with the consolidation of the modern state system. The latter is characterized by 'territorialy defined, fixed and mutually exclusive enclaves of legitimate domination' (Ruggie 1993: 47).

internal boundaries took different forms in different countries and at
different historical moments, oscillating between occupational groups
and the citizenry as a whole. A first fundamental choice in the formation
of modern welfare states concerned the reach of its schemes among the
population: typically a 'who' question, involving closure dilemmas and
spatial strategies in the sense specified in Chapter 1. What criteria of
membership were to be chosen for pooling risks and enforcing sharing
ties? Should the new schemes reproduce the traditional boundaries
between productive sectors and occupational hierarchies? Should they
reflect ethnic and cultural differentiations (if any such existed) within
the nation state? Or should a tabula rasa be created in order to establish
a wide unitary pool of redistribution for the whole population? Such 'who'
questions were highly salient (and controversial) in the early phases of
welfare state formation—more salient than questions regarding benefit
formulas or organizational arrangements. The definition of membership
rules cut deep into interests and identities and demanded explicit and
long-term commitments on the part of both social groups and state elites.
The pre-existing spontaneous sharing ties and the extant identities and
commonalities of experience and even 'fate' among individuals and groups
could perhaps be softened but not ignored in drawing the new lines. And
bounding decisions had to command sufficient and stable support in the
emerging mass political markets, where parties had started to compete
according to a distinct logic, resting on regime-specific rules of the game.
These were the difficult questions facing the welfare state builders in the
last decades of the nineteenth century.[10] Even if this aspect was not clearly
perceived at the time when the early decisions were made, the model of
membership was also going to foreordain the direction of redistributive
flows—with the occupational approach favouring more horizontal redistributions (damaged vs. non-damaged) and the universalistic approach
allowing for more vertical redistribution across income groups.[11]

Gemany's pioneering reforms inaugurated the occupational path by
targeting a narrow category (skilled blue-collar workers) as beneficiaries
of the first compulsory insurance scheme. The 'Bismarckian' approach was

---

[10] These questions quite clearly echo the questions discussed by Rokkan in his analysis of the
political translation of cleavages into partisan alignments. See Flora, Kuhnle, and Urwin (1999: ch. IV).

[11] The occupational approach remained more loyal to the actuarial logic of private insurance,
maintaining a closer link between contributions and benefits and thus containing vertical redistribution. For an interesting argument about the long-term distributional implications of the occupational and the universalistic models, see Lynch (2005). For analysis of the superior redistributive
performance of the universalist model, see Rothstein (1998).

adopted by all Continental countries, originating a long sequence of differentiated group inclusions, typically flowing from industrial employees to agricultural workers, then to the self-employed and finally to other marginal or inactive categories. In certain countries, like Italy, at first only employees earning less than a certain threshold were insured. In contrast to voting rights, social entitlements tended to be extended upwards rather than downwards through the social structure, that is, from lower- to higher-income groups and from manual to non-manual occupations (Flora and Alber 1981).[12] It is important to underline that, even if occupationally fragmented, the Continental schemes rested on a *nationwide* pooling of risks and standardized rules. Only the more traditional forms of social assistance to the poor remained localized and discretionary; and their importance gradually declined.

Table 2.1 offers some illustrative examples of this path in the area of pensions and health insurance. The table lists only the main provisions through time for the largest occupational categories. Especially in some countries of the Continental group (such as France and Italy) membership

Table 2.1 The occupational path in selected Continental countries (pension and health care insurance, private sector)

Country	Pension coverage		Health care coverage	
Germany	1889	industrial blue-collar workers	1883	industrial blue-collar employees
	1899	agricultural workers	1911	agricultural workers
	1911	employees[1]	1930	family dependants
	1938	artisans	1941	pensioners
	1957	farmers	1971	self-employed farmers
	1967	all employees		
Austria	1906	employees[1]	1888	industrial blue-collar workers
	1927	industrial blue-collar workers	1928	agricultural workers
	1928	agricultural workers	1941	pensioners and family dependants
	1957	self-employed	1955	managers
			1965	self-employed farmers
			1966	all self-employed

(Continued)

[12] There were, however, also downwards extensions: for example, towards workers in smaller plants, agricultural workers, and other categories of marginal workers.

Table 2.1 (*Continued*)

Country	Pension coverage		Health care coverage	
Italy	1919	employees[1]	1928	employees[2]
	1950	all employees	1939	family dependants
	1957	farmers	1954	self-employed in agriculture
	1958	artisans	1955	pensioners
	1966	small traders	1956	artisans
	1969	needy elderly	1959	shopkeepers
			1966	unemployed
			1978	all citizens/residents
France	1910	industrial employees[1]	1930	employees of industry and commerce[1]
	1930	employees of industry and commerce[1]	1942	all employees
	1942	all employees	1946	pensioners
	1948	self-employed	1966	self-employed
	1952	farmers		
Belgium	1924	industrial blue-collar workers	1944	employees, pensioners, and dependents
	1925	all industrial employees	1963	self-employed
	1929	all employees		
	1954	self-employed		
	1956	farmers		
Netherlands	1913	employees[1]	1929	employees[1]
	1919	self-employed (voluntary)	1941	family dependants
	1956	all citizens	1951	pensioners
			1964	all employees
Switzerland	1946	all citizens	1916	first cantonal scheme
			1994	subscription to mutual schemes made compulsory for all citizens

[1] Below a certain wage.

[2] Semi-compulsory scheme.

Notes: The French pension scheme of 1910 was never fully implemented. The Dutch pension scheme of 1913 gave pensions based on 'invalidity' and developed as a branch of the work-injury scheme. It became de facto operative only in 1919. Dutch sickness insurance became in its turn de facto compulsory only during the early 1940s.

Source: Flora et al. (1983–87), vol. 1; Flora (1986–87), vol. 4.

fragmentation along occupational lines was much more pronounced than Table 2.1 shows, and reached impressive levels during the period 1945–75 with the establishment of a plethora of micro-sectional schemes with distinct benefit and financing formulas. Domestic bounding through compulsory insurance tended to start earlier in the field of pensions than in the field of health care: poverty among the elderly was historically a more pressing challenge than ill-health. In Switzerland, a federal law enforcing compulsory coverage through categorical or cantonal health funds was passed only in 1994.

It is interesting to note that three of the countries listed in Table 2.1 departed from the occupational track at some point in time. Despite its Bismarckian beginnings (occupational insurance against work accidents in 1911), Switzerland introduced a universal pension in 1946. The Netherlands switched tracks from occupational fragmentation to universal and uniform coverage with a pension reform in 1956. Italy in turn swept away the plethora of occupational health funds in 1978 and established the first universal health care service of Continental Europe. While Switzerland and the Netherlands have remained the only Continental countries with universal 'first pillar' pensions, the Italian example has been followed by the other three south European countries, namely, Spain, Portugal, and Greece, which also established universal health care services (Ferrera 1996; Guillen 2002).

The universalistic path was chosen from the very beginning by the UK and the Nordic countries, despite the echo of Bismarck's reforms. Here the poor law tradition of means-tested relief for the needy oriented both social and state actors towards all-inclusive and uniform coverage, that is, the establishment of sharing ties based on citizenship alone rather than on occupational status. The universalistic path was first adopted in the field of old age protection (see Table 2.2). Initially, the new schemes of 'national' insurance offered benefits only to the needy elderly.[13] Only Sweden inaugurated from the very beginning (1913) a truly universal pension; but its amount was modest and it had to be topped up with either work-related or means-tested benefits. The means test on pensions was subsequently abolished in the UK and the Nordic countries, thus providing a flat-rate pension to all elderly people. After the Second World War, the principle of universal inclusion inspired in the UK and later in Scandinavia the introduction of national health insurances and of other transfer schemes such as child allowances or sickness benefits.

---

[13] In Britain the 'residual' orientation of early pension policy was also in line with trade unions' interest in defending the autonomy and role of their own mutual schemes as well as of collective wage bargaining (Thane 2000).

Table 2.2 The universalistic path in selected European countries (pension and health care insurance)

Country	Pension coverage	Health care coverage
UK	1908 needy elderly	1911 employees[1]
	1925 employees[1]	1946 all citizens
	1946 all the active population	
Denmark	1891 needy elderly	1933 all citizens[2]
	1933 all citizens	1971 all citizens
Sweden	1913 all citizens[3]	1864 all citizens[4]
	1946 all citizens	1954 all citizens
Norway	1936 needy elderly	1909 employees[1]
	1957 all citizens	1953 all employees
		1959 all citizens
Finland	1937 needy elderly	1963 all citizens
	1957 all citizens	

[1] Below a certain wage.

[2] Voluntary coverage for higher incomes.

[3] Very modest flat-rate benefit, with means-tested supplements.

[4] Hospital stays only, with local variations.

Source: See Table 2.1.

The British reforms introduced between 1945 and 1948 designed the first coherent and systematic architecture of a universalistic welfare state, in which membership and territorial boundaries practically coincided. This architecture rested on four distinct but highly coordinated schemes, suggestive also for their official names: the National Health Service (1946), providing health care to the whole population; National Insurance (1946), providing pensions and other short-term cash benefits to the active population; Family Allowances (1945), providing benefits to all households with children; and National Assistance (1948), providing means-tested support to the needy. In the Nordic area, Sweden was the first country fully to implement the universalistic design—with more generous benefit formulas than in the UK and more emphasis on service provision. By the end of the 1960s all the other Nordic countries had followed suit. As has been highlighted by a vast literature,[14] nowhere has the link between 'belonging' and 'sharing' become so strong in institutional as well in symbolic terms as in the Nordic countries: the Swedish metaphor of the welfare state

[14] For a review of this debate and updated discussion of the normative foundations of the Nordic welfare states, see Kildal and Kuhnle (2005).

as 'the people's home' (*folkhemmet*) is the most popular and effective testimony of such a link.

Why Different Paths? The Role of Centre–Periphery and Cleavage Constellations

The original bifurcation between the occupational and the universal paths and its far-reaching subsequent implications for distributional politics and outcomes has been the object of long and articulate debates, which have explored the role of a wide range of causal factors.[15] Particular attention has been devoted to pre-existing employment patterns: the highly differentiated patterns of the Continental countries did not offer, for example, fertile ground for the introduction of universalistic solutions (Baldwin 1990). From our theoretical perspective, however, the interesting link to be highlighted and briefly reconstructed is that between boundary setting for social sharing on the one hand, and national structural profiles on the other hand: that is, centre–periphery and cleavage constellations.

Weaving the *fil rouge* of Rokkan's work, Flora (1986) has already underlined the causal relevance of structural profiles to explaining institutional variations in welfare state development. More particularly, Flora has persuasively discussed the impact of centre–periphery and religious conflicts in determining the degree of *stateness* of the new welfare arrangements, that is, the extent to which the central state was able to affirm itself as a distinct and autonomous agency of redistribution, displacing other local and/or non-state agencies. The early fusion of state and church and the stricter control of peripheries on the part of central elites facilitated in the Scandinavian countries and to a large extent also in the UK a more pronounced public penetration of some spheres that were crucial for processes of nationalization and citizenship-based redistribution: education, health care, poor relief. On the Continent, the persistence of church–state and other religious conflicts on the one hand, and the weaker control of peripheries by the centres on the other, limited the stateness of the new redistributive arrangements and promoted the emergence of an institutional mix consisting of both public and non-public agencies.

Structural profiles played an equally important role in shaping the internal boundaries of sharing collectivities, and thus in determining the institutional fragmentation of welfare states. We noted earlier that social rights are political products in a double sense: they rest on state authority

---

[15] For recent reviews, see n. 1 above.

and they originate from exchanges between politicians interested in state offices and social actors interested in the specific content of state policy. In the four decades (1880–1920) during which most countries made the formative choices, the domestic arenas of political exchange were encumbered by those obdurate and pervasive juxtapositions linked to the national and industrial revolutions and already largely reflected in partisan alignments. Formative choices over sharing boundaries were thus constrained by the character of the arenas that produced them. Choices were ultimately made by agents, acting deliberately and strategically. But in certain arenas certain options were simply not available—given, precisely, the existing structural profiles, which in turn reflected earlier, country-specific historical sequences linked to the national and industrial revolutions.

Requiring the activation of far-reaching material and moral commitments, the establishment of a universalistic scheme was no easy political operation. Take the field of pensions, where universalism first emerged: rather sophisticated state capacities had to be already in place, for example, for the large-scale collection of taxes and contributions or for administering the means tests in reliable and equitable forms. State elites had to be ready and willing to incorporate all societal groups (and not just a selected category) in the new, delicate sphere of public redistribution. All these groups had in turn to be ready and willing to pool resources, based on distributional interests alone, with no mutual prejudice based on other criteria (e.g. ethnic or ideological). A package deal had to be agreed, reconciling the diverse distributional interests; a broad and firm 'majority' had to be put together in the pertinent decision-making bodies, expressed by electoral markets entering the new phase of mass democracy.

The structural profile of Britain's political system at the turn of the twentieth century offered wide opportunities for forging a universalistic pension reform. The pattern of state- and nation-building in this country had defused both the dominant-subject and the church–state cleavage long before the Industrial Revolution took off. Thanks to an early and gradual merger of rural and urban interests, the primary vs. secondary (i.e. farming vs. industry) sector cleavage likewise did not mature in the UK. The only active cleavage in the political arena was the class cleavage (workers vs. owners): territorial, religious, and urban-rural juxtapositions were comparatively weak if not altogether absent. Moreover, the slow unfolding of industrialization and the open and pragmatic attitude of central elites had contained the radicalization of the workers' movement.

A functioning bureaucratic apparatus was available, equipped with tax-collection and client-selection competences (the latter in the wake of the poor law). After the extension of the suffrage, an electoral constituency willing to mobilize for interest-specific rather than ideological issues was also available. In 1901 the Labour Party was officially founded and the issue of social reforms gained political salience. In 1906 the Liberals won a majority in Parliament, with a programme that included pensions legislation. Labour supported this plan and even Conservative opposition subsided. In the aftermath of the election, divisions within the Liberal Party delayed the reform process. But as by-election results indicated that the Liberals were losing to Labour, in 1908 the Asquith cabinet hastened to pass the Pension Act. The dynamic of party competition pushed the Liberals to the left in the attempt to retain the industrial vote that was rapidly deserting it for Labour (Thane 2000).

Also in the Scandinavian countries structural profiles displayed some features that paved the way for universalistic reforms: in particular, the absence of territorial or religious cleavages and the presence of fairly developed state capacities in the social sphere, linked to the early fusion of state and church. In comparison to the UK, however, there was a complication: an urban-rural cleavage was active at the turn of the century and the universalistic compromise had to be forged by lib-lab-green coalitions, including liberals, social democrats, and agrarian parties. The pattern of nation-building and of industrialization followed by Denmark, Sweden, and Norway facilitated the coming together of these three forces: cultural and social distances between blue-collar workers, urban intellectuals, and free farmers were relatively limited in comparison with the rest of the European continent (Alestalo and Kuhnle 1987; Esping-Andersen 1990). Nevertheless, before a distributional agreement could be reached, some ideological prejudices had to be overcome. An alliance between the socialist and the agrarian parties presupposed, for example, that the former accepted the principle of private property: in 1888, three years before the 1891 pension reform, the Danish social democrats removed from their programme the goal of land collectivization (Przeworsky and Sprague 1986). The origins of the Scandinavian model of welfare owe much to the specific orientations of the agrarian interests and parties (Baldwin 1990). The softening of the urban-rural cleavage and of ideological radicalism on the left of the political spectrum played a crucial role in facilitating distributional compromises in a universalistic direction. The experience of Finland confirms the latter point *a contrario*: in this country the radicalization of the workers' movement linked to the civil war of 1917 made the universalistic option unviable well into the 1930s.[16]

The Continental countries lacked the structural preconditions for drawing the internal boundaries of social protection in a universalistic fashion. State- and nation-building processes produced in these countries deep and multiple cleavages, most of which translated themselves into partisan (and even corporate) alignments during the transition towards mass politics. Distributional confrontations between state elites and social groups, and between social groups themselves, took place in political arenas crossed by almost impenetrable barriers of mutual suspicion and rejection that made universalistic options programmatically inconceivable, let alone politically viable.

In Belgium and the Netherlands the ethnic (Belgium) and confessional (Netherlands) juxtapositions produced in the second half of the nineteenth century highly pillarized (*verzuilt*) institutional configurations (see Chapter 1): the state was a sort of 'association of associations', with low autonomous capacities, especially in the social sphere (education and welfare), where subcultural pillars had put down their roots. Political competition between subcultural alignments was oriented in a defensive direction: it was aimed, in other words, at preserving as much as possible the traditional barriers separating societal segments from one another. Against this background, the creation of all-inclusive social rights of protection, resting on citizenship alone, was neither feasible nor convenient for the elites of the various pillars. The economic transformations of the late nineteenth century did create pressures for the establishment of new social protection arrangements. But material and moral resources could be mobilized only within the pillars, not across them. Thus in Belgium different Catholic, liberal, and socialist mutual funds were created, each with internal linguistic subdivisions. A similar process took place in the Netherlands within the Catholic, Protestant, and 'general' (*algemene*: liberal-socialist-national) subcultures. In these two countries the welfare state structured itself from the beginning along two cross-cutting lines (occupational and cultural) of institutional fragmentation. The very principle of compulsory insurance encountered serious obstacles in both Belgium and the Netherlands: pillar elites were more interested in state subsidies for voluntary forms of insurance. Belgium was a true laggard in

---

[16] As Table 2.2 shows, even in Norway compulsory universal pension coverage was introduced only in 1936. But the Norwegian parliament had already enacted a law in this area in 1923, which could not be put into effect due to financial problems (Kuhnle 1986).

this respect: compulsory (pension) insurance arrived in this country only in 1924. In the Netherlands, compulsory insurance was introduced for pensions in 1913, but became effective only in 1919. In the field of health care, compulsory insurance was introduced in 1929 but became effective only during German occupation in 1940–5.

Switzerland is another case in which the presence of a criss-crossing cleavage structure created strong and durable obstacles to boundary setting (and 'bounding' as such) for social sharing (Obinger et al. 2005). In this country there were not only ethnic and religious separations but also deep centre–periphery conflicts—with decision-making rules (such as easy-to-call popular referenda) that virtually gave cantons veto powers over federal policies. The attempt by the federal government to legislate national pensions in 1931 was blocked by a referendum: only after the Second World War did federal legislation become possible. In its turn a federal law imposing compulsory health insurance for all workers was passed only in 1994—leaving wide margins of discretion to the cantons.

Besides ethnic/linguistic, religious, and territorial cleavages, another factor that made the universalistic option unavailable in Continental political arenas was the radicalization of the class cleavage and the ideological polarization between left-wing and right-wing parties. Largely connected with the mode and timing of industrialization, the stark juxtaposition between these two blocs (and especially the anti-system orientations and internal subdivisions of the left) encouraged the creation of fragmented social rights. 'Anarchosyndicalism' and 'ghetto parties' were harsh enemies of universalistic formulas. Oriented as they were towards 'citizens' rather than proletarians, such formulas risked diluting workers' class-consciousness and distorting their objective interest in the revolution—the ultimate programmatic goal of these political formations. Bringing under uniform state coverage also the middle classes (especially farmers) with their conservative inclinations—think of the French *paysans* at the turn of the century—universalism would only have widened the political base of the class enemy, that is, the bourgeoisie and the state as its *comité d'affaires*.[17] Rigorously separatist workers' self-help institutions were thus the privileged strategy of all the socialist parties of Continental Europe. The socialist-communist cleavage linked to the October Revolution generated splits and

---

[17] In the French case, however, it must be noted that the turn of the century witnessed the emergence of a movement in favour of generous social assistance, administered at the local level, based on 'republican solidarity' principles. This institutional project competed for some time with the idea of introducing occupational social insurance—though at the end of the 1920s the latter was finally legislated into existence (Zimmerman, Didry, and Wagner 1999).

competitive incentives within the left that reinforced the strategy of occupational isolationism. In such contexts, moderate and conservative elites in their turn matured political interests that were a mirror image of those of the workers' movement. The concession of state subsidies to and of state controls over the emerging self-help associations and the introduction of occupationally distinct schemes of compulsory insurance (e.g. with different rules for blue-collar and white-collar workers, as in Germany and Austria) could serve as precious instruments for destructuring workers' mobilization and capturing the support (or at least tame the radicalism) of selected categories of workers, so defusing the anti-system threat.

Structural profiles did matter, then, in shaping the formative choices on the internal boundaries of social sharing. In particular, cleavage constellations, as determined by state- and nation-building processes and as reflected in organizational networks and partisan alignments, foreordained the basic options available to actors. Actors did engage in strategic interactions aimed at influencing initial choices. But the context of interaction and the menu of viable alternatives had been pre-defined by earlier, big and slow moving, historical macro processes.[18]

In this section we have treated 'occupationalism' and 'universalism' as very general concepts, behind which a wealth of other significant institutional variations are hidden. For our purposes, however, this grand bifurcation is of great interest, as it had a number of implications for subsequent political and institutional developments.

Once established, compulsory social insurance became an important element in the internal structuring of all European nation states. The creation of the new social membership spaces served to reconfigure (and, generally speaking, to strengthen) the sovereignty of the European nation state, in the sense specified in Chapter 1. In the first place, the production of national social rights enlarged the functional scope of centralized authority; and once the window of opportunity for 'social internationalism' was closed after the First World War, the strategies of domestic actors in the sphere of social protection directed themselves exclusively towards the state: a good illustration of the external closure-internal structuring nexus. In the second place, social insurance largely recast the spatial

---

[18] Adopting Flora's terminology (see Chapter 1, n. 15) we can say that the 'configurations of actors' were historically constrained: structural profiles shaped the overall opportunity space and—to a large extent—the distribution of resources among actors. The latter's agency was however important in determining the specific timing and content of initial choices. On the link between slow moving, macro-historical process and the margins of manoeuvre of actors in time- and area-specific conjuctures, see also Pierson (2004) and Thelen (1999, 2000, 2004).

articulation of national political systems. Various opportunities for entry and exit (or, better, 'staying out') arose for social and political actors, making the system more complex. The new welfare policies soon became the object of increasing voice activity: voice for entry on the part of social groups left uncovered, but also voice *against* entry on the part of social groups that thought they were self-reliant or that regarded social insurance as a 'trap of capitalism'. Besides the activation of voice, the principle of compulsion encouraged in some cases and countries a second type of response: *hiding*, that is, strategies to avoid membership or eschew its costs by operating in the underground economy and/or evading contributions. For example, enforcing social sharing ties among the self-employed and in the agricultural sector was a major challenge, especially in the countries of southern Europe, given their historical deficit of administrative capacities (Ferrera 1996, 2005). Like external boundaries, internal boundaries became the object of increasingly accurate and fine-tuned policies of maintenance and policing.

Institutional Freezing: The Apex of External and Internal Closure after the Second World War

In the wake of their structural consolidation, in the inter-war period but especially after the Second World War public insurance schemes turned into relatively autonomous channels for the shaping of social and political interests—channels that were moved and maintained through their own laws of inertia. The famous 'freezing hypothesis', which Lipset and Rokkan (1967) formulated in respect of the structural consolidation of European party systems, can be fruitfully developed in respect of welfare systems as well. According to these authors, once originally structured around the extant cleavage constellations, European party systems transformed themselves into rigid and self-sustaining mechanisms for the definition of interests, moved and maintained by their own laws of inertia.[19] Partisan alternatives became ossified and remained frozen for a long time; in the 1960s they still largely reflected the cleavage structure of the 1920s. In the sphere of social insurance, which mechanism contributed to the crystallization of initial decisions and the re-enforcement through time of the adopted trajectory?[20] The channeling of interests regarding welfare

---

[19] On this mechanism see also Sartori (1976).

[20] As stressed by Pierson (2004) and Thelen (1999), the precise identification of reproduction mechanisms (that is, those causal chains that stabilize and strengthen over time a given institutional configuration) is a crucial step in all arguments based on path-dependence.

schemes and the ensuing freezing dynamics were driven less by a politico-organizational logic (as in the case of party systems) than by an economic and financial logic. The new membership communities created by social insurance had to safeguard those chains of redistribution activated by the original institutional choices. For a given insurance scheme, structural consolidation meant not only an organizational strengthening and in some cases a growing political interest in self-aggrandizement but also the gradual achievement of actuarial maturation, that is, a self-sustaining equilibrium between contributions and benefits, given the risk profile of the target population. This was especially true for the occupational schemes of Continental Europe, which more or less explicitly rested on actuarial criteria and thus incorporated a natural bias against any 'path shift'; to some extent, it could be said that the adoption of occupational formulas in the design of social protection had a freezing effect similar to that of the adoption of proportional representation in the case of party systems. Both types of formula took snapshots of existing structural constellations and reproduced them in the delicate spheres of political representation and socio-economic redistribution, thus contributing to their long-term persistence.

Needless to say, the material interests of social insurance members were largely exploited by trade unions and political parties in their struggles for power. After the Second World War, for example, in both France and Italy articulate proposals were made to create new highly comprehensive (if not wholly universal) social insurance regimes: but the constellations of material interests around pre-war occupational separatism and the centrifugal logic of 'polarized pluralism' (party systems characterized by high degrees of ideological polarization) effectively blocked such proposals (Ferrera 1993a; Palier 2002).[21] Policy legacies and institutional feedbacks—which have become central notions in current theories about the new politics of welfare (Pierson 2001)—were already at work in the critical juncture crossed by European welfare systems at the time of their post-war reconstruction.

---

[21] The retention of occupational separatism after the Second World War had, of course, far-reaching consequences in these two countries not only for the organization of social protection but, more generally, for wider dynamics of social consensus and political legitimization. In Italy social insurance legislation (often 'micro-legislation') served the purposes of a strategy of 'particularistic attraction' of the middle classes within the social bloc controlled by the Christian Democratic Party (Ferrera 1993a), while in France professional separatism (and especially the separation between *cadres* and *ouvriers*) promoted forms of legitimization based, precisely, on a *differentiation corporatiste* (Castel 1995; Jobert and Muller 1987).

It must be noted, however, that two countries in the Continental cluster were able to switch tracks, as it were, from occupationalism to universalism after the Second World War: Switzerland and the Netherlands (see Table 2.1). A full account of the dynamics that liberated these two countries from the hold of path dependence cannot be offered here. Suffice it to say that the shock of war had an enormous impact on these two small nations and changed the opportunity structure in two important ways: by introducing small but critical 'institutional wedges' that reoriented social policy towards universal coverage, and by softening the traditional lines of conflict and thus allowing the political formation of cross-cleavage distributional compromises.[22]

The *Trente Glorieuses* (1945–75) were the apex of the *national* welfare state. The coverage of its schemes reached its natural limits (i.e. the whole citizenry, at least *de jure*) or got very close to it (see Table 2.3). The more

Table 2.3   Social insurance coverage for pensions and health care 1905–75 (covered workers as a % of the labour force)

Country	Pensions				Health care			
	1905	1925	1945	1975	1905	1925	1945	1975
Austria		5	51*	81	20	47	56*	88
Belgium		29	44	100			46	96
Denmark			100	100			100	100
Finland			100	100			100	100
France		14	52	98			52	94
Germany	51	66	70*	84	41	57	57*	72
Italy		38	39	94			44*	91
Netherlands		53	66	100			42	74
Norway			100			54	90	100
Sweden		100	100	100				100
Swizerland				80				
UK			98	100		79	98	100

*1950

Source: Flora et al. (1983–87), vol. 2.

[22] In Switzerland, the 'wedge' was the introduction in 1939 of a universal subsidy for income replacement to all Swiss citizens serving in the militia. In the Netherlands, the wedge was instead a means-tested universal social pension introduced in 1947 as an 'emergency measure'. The 1946 Swiss reform was voted by all parties and was confirmed by a national referendum in 1948. The war had promoted a rapprochement between the various parties, healing the wounds opened by the 'red week' of 1918 when the country was at risk of sliding into civil war. In the Netherlands, the 1956 pension reform was supported by a 'red roman' coalition, comprising the social democrats and the Catholic party. For a more detailed account of these two cases and a basic bibliography, see Ferrera (1993a).

localized systems of protection were progressively marginalized in their financial size and functional scope. Sophisticated techniques were invented and deployed in order to improve and rationalize the extraction of taxes and contributions, govern redistributive flows from the centre, and deliver benefits and services to the various clienteles. Of particular importance in this respect was the adoption of the 'pay-as-you-go' (PAYGO) system of pension financing whereby the contributions paid by active workers were immediately used to finance the benefits paid to pensioners. This new technique greatly expanded the scope for intergenerational redistribution and in certain countries it allowed for a 'blanketing in' of entire cohorts of pensioners at virtually no financial cost (but with high electoral returns for politicians).[23] Finally, alongside the various insurance schemes for the standard risks, new non-contributory programmes of general social assistance were created, as well as increasingly complex health care systems providing a wide array of medical services. The new programmes of social assistance differed from traditional public charity to the extent that they were based on rights rather than bureaucratic discretion. The most important programmes in this area were social pensions in the Bismarckian systems (i.e. means-tested minimum benefits for those elderly who for various reasons had not acquired an entitlement to a contributory pension) and minimum income schemes, that is, means-tested benefits for any individual or household lacking sufficient resources. Heath care systems shifted in their turn the emphasis of social sharing from the provision of cash transfers to the provision of benefits in kind (pharmaceuticals, medical treatments, etc.). This shift made the institutional profile of the welfare state more complex because it bestowed a new role on service providers as relevant actors. It also made the welfare state more popular in general, and the European welfare state more distinct from its US counterpart, which remained much leaner in terms of public health cover.

Thus, in the first post-war decades the social citizenship attached to state-national institutions achieved full flower and also its greateast degree

---

[23] The establishment of a new PAYGO scheme originates immediate contributive revenues on the side of the active members of the scheme. The logic of this method of financing does not require that such revenues are set aside: on the contrary it encourages their use for immediately paying pensions to inactive members belonging to the same occupational sector, or to active members who reach the age of retirement after very short periods of insurance (e.g. one or two years). This is exactly what happened in countries such as Italy, France, and Belgium between the late 1940s and 1960s, when pension coverage was extended to the self-employed: minimum pensions were almost immediately paid to workers reaching the age of retirement a few years after the creation of the scheme and thus with very low contributory records. See Ferrera (1987) and Palier (2002).

of both external and internal closure. For non-nationals, it was rather difficult to enter the solidarity spaces of other states, especially when it came to deriving benefits from them. Under certain conditions, foreign workers were admitted into the national labour markets and social insurance schemes. Bilateral treaties were agreed between various European countries concerning both the circulation of workers and their social rights.[24] But such treaties were typically designed to favour the labour-importing countries (Romero 1993). Migrant workers were granted only temporary residence and work permits; the presence of 'vesting' rules concerning minimum contributory qualifications often barred them from the actual enjoyment of benefits (typically pensions). Moreover, a number of bilateral treaties maintained direct and indirect obstacles to equal treatment, such as residence clauses (which prevented benefits from being exported) and also displayed gaps in so-called 'material scope', that is, the range of accessible benefits (such as unemployment benefits). Legal migrant workers were thus always obliged to pay contributions; but their chance of actually receiving benefits was far from guaranteed. The 'principle of territoriality'—a central tenet of international labour law (Pennings 2001)—retained control over the most relevant aspects of social security strictly in the hands of national governments, putting non-nationals in conditions of systematic disadvantage in dealing with issues of contribution cumulation, transferability, and the like (Cornelissen 1996; De Matteis and Giubboni 1998; Holloway 1981). More importantly, as a rule non-nationals were excluded from social and medical assistance benefits, either directly through explicit nationality requirements or indirectly via 'gainful residence' requirements (i.e. the possession of legal work permits).

Nationals, on the other hand, were virtually 'locked in', obliged to be members of public schemes. Internally, the level of voice activity and political conflict around welfare policies tended to increase, but the expansion of these programmes contributed substantially to enhancing citizens' 'loyalty' towards their national variant of welfare state. The availability of need-based benefits and 'social minima' linked to citizenship contributed to strengthening such loyalty and enhancing general feelings

---

[24] The first bilateral treaties were already signed before the First World War (e.g. between France and Italy in 1904). The number of such treaties grew rapidly during the 1920s and 1930s. At the end of the Second World War, 133 bilateral agreements were in place, in part thanks to the activism and expertise of the ILO. This net of bilateral agreements, however, had some significant gaps: for example, in the late 1940s no treaty existed between Germany and Luxembourg or between Germany and Belgium. For a detailed reconstruction, see Holloway (1981).

of collective solidarity. Welfare rights, legitimized through the electoral channel, made a fundamental contribution to nation-building, accentuating citizens' territorial identities. As Rokkan noted:

this sets definite limits to any effort of internationalisation and Europeanisation: . . . once broad masses of each territorial population have been mobilised through the electoral . . . channels it will prove very difficult to build up a genuine community of trust across the systems. Once a population has developed some minimum level of trust in the efficiency and fairness of the territorial government, it is unlikely to favour the transfer of substantial authority from this body to agencies beyond direct electoral control. (Cited in Flora, Kuhnle, and Urwin 1999: 265)

Survey data confirm the second part of Rokkan's expectations: public social protection is considered a 'fundamental achievement of modern society' by vast majorities in all European countries; in most countries the majority of people think that decisions regarding this matter should remain the preserve of their own national government (European Commission 2001a; Ferrera 1993b). However, contrary to the first part of Rokkan's quotation, the supposed 'limits to Europeanization' have been massively trespassed in the economic sphere: on this front a substantial transfer of authority has taken place from the nation state to EU agencies. As noted in the Introduction, this situation poses a serious 'destructuring' challenge to the stability of domestic social protection systems. Chapters 3 and 4 will reconstruct the trajectory that has originated this situation and will identify the precise sources of potential destructuring.

3

National Closure During the Golden Age of Welfare Expansion

The First Challenges from Within: Supplementary Pension Schemes

The three decades between the end of the Second World War and the mid-1970s are primarily remembered as the 'golden age' of welfare state expansion, characterized by a widening coverage of social insurance, an increasing generosity of transfer payments, and the greater scope and quality of services. At the beginning of the 1950s social security expenditure was still below 10 per cent of GDP in most European countries. By the early 1970s many countries (such as Belgium, Denmark, France, Germany, Italy, the Netherlands, and Sweden) had passed the 20 per cent mark and most of the remaining ones had already surpassed 15 per cent (Flora et al. 1983–87). The vast majority, if not the totality, of the population was included in social protection schemes for all the standard risks: old age, disability, and bereavement; sickness, maternity, and work injuries; unemployment and family dependants. At least in terms of eligibility, European welfare states had 'grown to limits' (Flora 1986–87): they had reached or were about to reach their widest possible membership boundaries, coinciding with the whole citizenry.

Yet, already during the *Trente Glorieuses*, some first cracks started to appear in these solid institutional compacts, testing the ability of European nation states to maintain monopolistic control over their newly established and far-reaching social sharing spaces. Two main developments were responsible for this. The first development had an endogenous origin, linked to the growing demand for more generous and differentiated welfare protection, especially for old age. The second development had an exogenous origin, linked to the creation of the European Communities. We start with an examination of the first development.

As we saw in Chapter 2, pension schemes had been introduced in all European countries in the pre-war period and broadly restructured after the Second World War. As members of some public (and compulsory) collectivity of redistribution, most workers could thus rely on some form of income protection during old age. The levels of protection, however, were relatively modest: the income replaced by these early public pensions corresponded to only a small percentage (typically less than 30 per cent) of previous earnings. In the new climate of increasing economic prosperity, a demand for more generous arrangements started to articulate itself in many countries, with a view to securing the maintenance of living standards also during retirement.

The issue of an internal differentiation of old age protection, aimed at combining both basic subsistence and income maintenance objectives, arose as early as the first half of the 1950s in the north European countries, which had opted for universal schemes providing relatively low, flat-rate 'minimum' or 'basic' benefits. This type of benefit was regarded as increasingly inadequate to meet the welfare aspirations of many groups of employees (like skilled blue-collar workers and many categories of white-collar employees). These categories thus started to subscribe to various forms of group insurance, sponsored by both unions and employers, in order to top up their public pension with additional benefits. Such initiatives, however, posed a number of regulatory and distributive problems, which prompted state intervention (Whiteside 2003). Not surprisingly, one of the fundamental dilemmas that governments had to face in the wake of group insurance development was the issue of compulsion: was membership of supplementary schemes to be made obligatory, as with the 'first pillar' of state benefit, or should it be left voluntary?[1] Another con-

---

[1] In recent years the increasing institutional articulation of pension systems has prompted the elaboration of a specialized vocabulary. This vocabulary—especially influenced by the World Bank (1994)—distinguishes between: (a) *first pillars*, that is the main public compulsory scheme existing in a given country, regardless of its financing mechanism—but usually based on PAYGO; (b) *second pillars*, that is occupational insurance schemes based on prefunding; (c) *third pillars*, that is private, funded, individual insurance plans. First pillars may be internally subdivided into *basic* or *first tier* benefits/schemes and *second tier* benefits/schemes. Second tier benefits/schemes of the first pillar are not based on prefunding, as in the case of second pillars. Alongside first pillars, there can be means-tested schemes offering benefits to those elderly who are not covered by compulsory insurance or who need additional assistance on top of first tier benefits. While useful for describing developments since the 1970s, this vocabulary is not very accurate for describing the situation of pension systems in earlier historical phases. For example, in many countries 'first pillars' adopted prefunding at their beginning and only shifted to PAYGO in the 1950s or 1960s. In some countries, funded occupational pension schemes ('second pillars' in today's vocabulary) started to operate alongside first pillars before the latter's articulation into first-tier and second-tier schemes. In this and the following

troversial issue was the public versus non-public nature of such schemes. In both cases what was at stake was the degree of 'closure' of this new space for redistribution along the membership axis and the extent of collective control over it. Choices on these critical fronts were doomed to have far-reaching implications in terms of allocative efficiency and, especially, in terms of distributive equity: a purely voluntary solution was in fact likely to widen income differentials among pensioners, limiting the possibilities of vertical solidarity. Less explicit, but equally far-reaching, were to be the 'structuring' implications of choices on this front on the overall national patterns of social sharing. Social democratic parties and trade unions tended to favour, for example, the option of compulsory affiliation into publicly regulated collective schemes (possibly run with the involvement of the social partners), which they saw as promising tools for strengthening traditional class allegiances and alliances. Liberals and conservatives, on the other hand, favoured freedom of choice and market-based solutions.

Different countries made different choices. The UK and Sweden were the first to confront the challenge of a broad spatial reconfiguration of their pension systems through the addition of supplementary schemes alongside basic provision. These two countries also inaugurated two rather different paths of reconfiguration and can thus be regarded as emblematic cases, which deserve a close look.

State Monopoly Over Occupational Pensions? Britain vs. Sweden

In the early 1950s both the UK and Sweden had in place national pension schemes aimed at guaranteeing a minimum income during old age, roughly corresponding to 10–20 per cent of the average wage.[2] But this formula soon proved to be inadequate. To begin with, in order to safeguard the minimum guarantee periodical adjustments had to be made in order to keep up with inflation and real wages. Even though socially equitable

chapters, we will try to stick as much as possible to the recent vocabulary. When discussing historical developments, however, we will use the more general expressions 'supplementary insurance', 'additional benefits', or 'occupational schemes' to denote any form of public (that is second-tier or second pillar) programme aimed at providing additional benefits in respect of those provided by the main public pension scheme that was in place at the beginning of the 1950s.

[2] The reconstruction of Swedish developments is primarily based on Baldwin (1990), Esping-Andersen (1985), Kangas and Palme (1992a), Heclo (1974), Olson (1986, 1990), and Salminen (1993); that of British developments on Baldwin (1990); Heclo (1974); Ogus (1982); Parry (1987); Thane (2000); and Whiteside (2003). More detailed bibliographies on that period can be found in Olson, Salminen, Parry, and Thane.

and politically advantageous, such adjustments posed delicate financial problems. Moreover, in the new context of economic progress and rising expectations, the perspective of a mere minimum income guarantee in old age was no longer considered enough, and growing cohorts of skilled blue-collar and white-collar workers started to resort to voluntary forms of occupational self-protection, financed through contributions and providing additional benefits on top of the basic pension. Around the mid-1950s, about 38 per cent of British employees had joined a supplementary pension scheme (Ogus 1982). In Sweden, the equivalent figure was lower (29 per cent) but still substantial (Heclo 1974).[3] But although they operated as a safety valve for both financial strains on the public budget and individual or group aspirations, the new forms of old age protection threatened to disturb the distributive compromises reached around early pension legislation and its post-war updating, and thus tended to generate intercategorical tensions. A process of social and institutional mobilization began in both countries around the issue of how best to cope with this new challenge.

In 1955 an investigative committee appointed by the Swedish government proposed the establishment of a public and compulsory scheme for all employees, designed to favour employees earning lower wages. This proposal was welcomed by the Social Democratic Party and by the trade unions (closely linked since the 1930s), but it raised doubts in the Agrarian Party, which sat in government with the social democrats, and was strongly contested by the conservatives and the employers. The liberals unsuccessfully tried mediation and declared themselves against a statist solution based on a single, compulsory scheme. Various counter-proposals emerged, aimed at allowing workers who were not interested in the public scheme to opt out of it, and at mitigating the low-wage bias of the committee's project. Supplementary pensions were an important issue at the 1956 election, which witnessed a loss of support for the social democrats (from 46 per cent of the vote to 44.6 per cent) and a rise in support for the conservatives (from 12.3 per cent of the vote to 14.4 per cent). Unable to reach a compromise, political parties promoted a referendum in 1957 on supplementary pensions based on three options: (*a*) a single compulsory and public scheme for all active workers (supported by the social democrats and the trade unions); (*b*) a public but voluntary scheme, with an opting-out clause (supported by the agrarians); and (*c*) voluntary non-

---

[3] In the early 1950s Sweden had a smaller share of employees in the labour force—due to the great number of free farmers—and a smaller share of white-collar workers within employees.

public schemes, run by the social partners (supported by liberals, conservatives, and employers). The results of the referendum were inconclusive. The first option was supported by 46 per cent of the voters, the second by 15 per cent, and the third by 35 per cent (the remaining 4 per cent of ballots were blank). The social democrats interpreted these results as a mandate to go ahead with their plan. The other parties argued, however, that the majority had voted against a compulsory solution. The alliance between the social democrats and the agrarians broke apart and the social democrats formed a new minority government, which in 1958 submitted to parliament a draft bill based on their original plan. The bill was defeated (117 votes were cast against the bill, 111 in favour), the government resigned, and new elections were called. This time the social democrats increased their share of votes (to 46.2 per cent). So the new government submitted a modified version of the previous plan, which treated white-collar workers more favourably.[4] Thanks to the defection of a liberal MP, the plan was approved with 115 votes against 114. The general supplementary pension scheme (known as *allman tillagpension*, ATP) was officially introduced in 1959: this was the first all-inclusive, public, and compulsory supplementary pension scheme to be inaugurated in Europe.

In the UK too the mid-1950s witnessed the appearance of Swedish-style proposals, aimed at contrasting the perspective of 'two nations' of pensioners, one relying only on the basic benefit and the other relying on a more generous combination of basic and occupational benefits. The idea of a compulsory and public form of 'superannuation' (launched by a group of pro-Labour intellectuals such as Richard Titmuss, Brian Abel Smith, and Peter Townsend) was fought by the Conservatives and the employers, but was considered to be not wholly convincing by the Labour Party and the trade unions. Many Labour leaders were more inclined towards a substantial increase in the universal pension rather that 'getting back to Bismarck'. In their turn the unions were not in favour of compulsory coverage in a new public scheme since a great number of their members had already joined industry-wide or company schemes. The Trade Union Congress had just rediscovered its bargaining power and thus preferred occupational schemes subject to collective negotiation and control to a state supplementary scheme that could be easily undermined by the Treasury. Between 1955 and 1957 there was a lively internal debate within

---

[4] The plan also envisaged the possibility of employees already covered by existing schemes staying out of the new scheme. The option had to be exercised once and forever by 1961. The conditions offered by the new ATP scheme were so attractive that only an extremely small number of employees exercised this option.

the British left on the superannuation issue, which culminated in a plan for a supplementary public pension scheme approved by Labour's National Conference in 1957. Contrary to the Swedish social democratic plan, the project of the British left included from the very beginning an opting-out clause, called 'contracting out', for approved private occupational schemes fulfilling certain requirements.

Prompted by Labour's initiative, the Conservatives in their turn launched a serious review of superannuation. The Conservative government concentrated its efforts on forging a plan that was least disturbing of the existing status quo and that could bring at the same time some financial relief to the ailing basic pension scheme. In 1959 a National Insurance Act was passed, which made earnings-related pensions compulsory and introduced, as of 1961, a state 'graduated pension scheme' for employees who wished to contract in. The Act foresaw, in fact, a permanent contracting-out option. The niggardly benefit formulas (strictly linked as they were to contributions) were strongly criticized by the Labour Party which, however, lost the 1959 election and had no chance of implementing its own, more ambitious proposals. The UK thus embarked upon a multipillar path of pension coverage, characterized by a relatively thin first, public pillar and an increasingly strong second pillar, with high internal fragmentation and mostly resting on contracted-out, non-public funded schemes: a spatial configuration which was very different from that put in place in Sweden during the same period.

Why did Sweden and the UK part company at such a critical juncture in the evolution of their pension systems? The literature has correctly highlighted the difference in organizational strength and 'power resources' of the workers' movements in the two countries, in both electoral and corporate spheres.[5] A number of more technical elements, linked to the financing of the basic pension and to the functioning of pre-existing occupational schemes, also worked to mould the different choices by political and social actors. From the perspective of this book, however, it is important to underline the conditioning role played by structural profiles, in Rokkan's sense: that is, cleavage constellations and their political consequences for solidarity-building. In particular, the specific dynamic of party competition in the two countries (linked in its turn to earlier structuring processes in the transition to mass democracy) must be taken into account in order fully to explain the divergence in the paths followed by the UK and Sweden in reconfiguring their pension systems during the

[5] See the references mentioned in n. 1.

1950s. The role played by this dynamic can be illustrated by raising two questions about historical developments that appear particularly import-ant, as they foreordained options or somehow tipped the balance in favour of one option rather than the other. The first question is: why was the British labour movement much more reluctant than its Swedish counterpart to embrace the idea of an all inclusive compulsory public scheme? The second question is: why in Sweden did all the parties which opposed the 'statist' solution fail to join forces in order to block the social democrats after their defeats in the 1957 referendum and in parliament?

To start with the first question: Britain's 'simple' cleavage constellation and smooth democratization bequeathed to the country a bipolar and bipartisan system of electoral competition based on the 'first-past-the-post' and 'winner-take-all' formulas. As noted in Chapter 2, the dynamic of party competition worked in favour of pension universalism at the beginning of the twentieth century, making this option politically reward-ing for both Labour and the Liberals. But the competitive context of the 1950s was very different. The liberals had almost disappeared from the scene, winning less than 3 per cent of the vote in 1951 and 1955. At the 1951 election, the Labour Party lost office: even though it had won a plurality of the popular vote, the electoral formula in fact delivered a majority of seats to the Conservatives.[6] Electoral competition between the two parties remained very harsh throughout the decade: a few 'median' voters in marginal constituencies could decide the result. In such a context, a hardline, Swedish-style proposal for virtually forced inclusion of all em-ployees in a single supplementary public scheme would have been very risky in political terms: the UK median voter was very likely to already be a member of an occupational pension scheme and thus to be afraid of any dramatic change to the status quo. Even though oriented in a more redistributive direction, Labour's plan of 1957 was aimed at reconciling the interests of uncovered (or poorly covered) blue-collar workers with those of already covered white-collar workers interested in the contract-ing-out option. Labour's 1959 electoral manifesto explicitly stated that National Superannuation would not affect those already covered by good superannuation schemes. Despite this, as mentioned earlier, Labour lost the 1959 election. The reform passed by the Conservatives introduced mandatory membership of occupational pension schemes for employees,

---

[6] At the general election of 25 October 1951, Labour got 13,948,883 votes but only 295 seats in parliament; the Conservatives (including the National Liberal and Conservative candidates) got 13,718,199 votes and 321 seats.

but fell short of creating a broad and genuine sharing space at this level. As noted by Heclo (1974: 273), this reform 'not only avoided hindering the development of private occupational pensions but provided a positive fillip to the entire private sector. Pension fund experts and brokers generally seem to have counseled their clients . . . to contract out . . . By the end of 1967, 5.3 million employees had been contracted out.'

The Swedish political context was very different from that of Britain. Although sharing a relatively smooth transition to mass politics, Sweden inherited from her nineteenth-century cleavage constellation a multi-party system and a proportional representation (PR) electoral system. Pension universalism had been introduced in 1913 as a result of a red-green alliance between the social democrats and the agrarians (see Chapter 2). In the 1950s this historical alliance entered a phase of decline and crisis. On the one hand, the rise of white-collar workers was benefiting the liberals and the conservatives in terms of votes. On the other hand, the traditional constituencies of the red-green bloc—blue-collar workers and free farmers—were not only gradually shrinking but also had diverging distributive stakes. In the pension controversy, the blue-collar workers had a strong interest in additional public protection and state redistribution via the proposed ATP scheme; the free farmers had mixed feelings about supplementary pensions and wanted to have the option of 'contracting out'. As mentioned, the alliance between the social democrats and the agrarians fell apart after the 1957 referendum, an event that already reflected the split between the two partners, who had supported different options. As the liberals and the conservatives were arguing, the results of both the 1956 election and of the 1957 referendum would have made it possible to remove the social democrats from the government if only the agrarians had been willing to switch camps. The latter did actually join the bourgeois camp at the end of the decade, but they were not ready to do it at that crucial political moment, which was to have such important implications for the Swedish welfare state. The agrarians' unwillingness abruptly to abandon their historical political allies offered the social democrats a lifeline: they could re-establish their political hegemony and shift pension policy in their preferred direction. Various factors (including personal ones: see Heclo 1974) can be adduced to account for the events of those months of 1957 and 1958. From a longer-term, comparative perspective, however, what mattered were two specific traits of Sweden's political arena during that critical juncture: (a) the fragmentation and internal division of the moderate front, itself a legacy of the historical cleavage constellation and of the PR electoral system, and (b) the stickiness of the pre-war party system, based on social democratic predominance. As argued by Sartori (1976), predominance is not just an arithmetic indicator of the size of the biggest party relative to all the others, but a mechanical property of party systems, which creates rigidities in coalitional dynamics and the electoral stances of parties. If lasting for extended periods of time, predominance originates a situation of 'deep equilibrium', sustained by endogenous forces of inertia.[7] In the 1950s, Swedish society could have possibly accommodated an electoral realignment, which could have had significant implications for the spatial configuration of the welfare state. However, party fragmentation in the non-socialist camp and social democratic predominance stymied such a realignment and allowed Tage Erlander, prime minister and leader of the social democrats, to craft a new sharing space that 'locked' all Swedish workers into the ATP scheme and paved the way for substantial flows of interclass solidarity.

Just like half a century earlier, when early formative choices were made about social insurance, the search for institutional responses to the new sharing issues and solidarity dilemmas that emerged in the 1950s revolved around 'who' questions and boundary-setting. In Britain, the favourable conditions that had promoted a universalistic solution in 1908 were no longer there, and the country embarked upon a new path of fragmented second-pillar provision, leaving ample room for group choice and disparities between categories of beneficiaries. In the long Conservative hegemony under Margaret Thatcher and John Major during the 1980s and 1990s, the state tier of supplementary pension lost most of its salience and the majority of British workers contracted out of it, not only into industry-wide or company schemes but also into heavily tax-subsidized private and funded pension plans (Pemberton 2005). In Sweden by contrast, the political game—embedded in a structural context of social democratic predominance and bourgeois divisions—allowed for the setting of wide-ranging and uniform boundaries around the employed population, strengthening collective sharing ties. The 1959 ATP reform did not have the last word in terms of the spatial boundaries of the Swedish pension system. In fact, during subsequent decades a fully-fledged second pillar of funded occupational group insurance (including life insurance benefits) also developed in Sweden, testing again the principle of state monopoly over pension coverage and old age protection. The fact remains, however, that on the

---

[7] On the notion of 'deep equilibrium', see Pierson (2004). On the role played by social democratic predominance in shaping the Swedish welfare state, see Huber and Stephens (2001).

European landscape the Swedish configuration has represented (and still largely represents) an almost unique instance of 'nationwide, all-inclusive bounding for a strong and effective bonding'—to use the concepts introduced in our earlier discussion.

An Increasingly Variegated Multitier and Multipillar Space

The two different paths inaugurated by Britain and Sweden in the 1950s served as reference points for other countries that had also embarked upon the universalistic track in their formative choices about pensions. Thus, Finland and Norway followed the Swedish example during the 1960s, introducing compulsory public occupational schemes on top of their basic pension pillars (Salminen 1993). Denmark too added a public supplementary scheme in 1964, but not as generous or comprehensive as the Swedish one. This opened the way for the development of employment-based funded private occupational schemes, which have gradually distanced the Danish pension system from those of the other Nordic countries. Two other countries located on the Continent reconfigured their systems in a direction similar to the Danish one: the Netherlands and Switzerland. As illustrated in Chapter 2, these two countries had deviated from the Bismarckian tradition by introducing a citizenship-related basic pension scheme in 1956 and 1946, respectively. Faced with the same demand for more generous protection experienced in the UK and Scandinavia, during the 1960s and 1970s both countries promoted the expansion of a second pillar of industry-wide or company-based funded schemes, run by private providers or by the social partners under state regulation.[8] Thus, the UK, the Netherlands, Switzerland, and Denmark have come to form a common cluster of pension systems, characterized by 'basic security plus private employment-related benefits': a spatial configuration which sets them apart from all the other European systems (Hinrichs 2002; Myles and Pierson 2001). Though with some temporal delay, Ireland has also been moving closer to this cluster during the 1980s and 1990s (Hinrichs 2002).

The issue of supplementary pensions emerged much later and posed quite different challenges in the 'occupationalist' cluster of countries, located in Continental and southern Europe. As mentioned in Chapter 2, these countries undertook broad reconstructions of their schemes

---

[8] Membership of such schemes can be mandatory, depending on contractual norms. In the Netherlands the first supplementary pension schemes had already been established in the late 1940s and were regulated by state law.

dedicated to specific categories after the Second World War and then proceeded to establish new schemes for uncovered categories (typically the self-employed). Between the 1950s and 1970s, these occupationalist countries had to confront two distinct challenges: (*a*) how to guarantee a basic protection to those elderly people who had not accumulated (sufficient) entitlements, and (*b*) how to satisfy the rising expectations and demands of insured workers. The response to the first challenge was the introduction of pension minima and means-tested 'social' pensions—a development which moved them closer to their universalist counterparts, in that it filled the gaps in coverage and established a universal safety net for all the elderly. The response to the second challenge came in two steps. The first and more natural step was that of improving the generosity of the pension formula, typically by shifting from contribution-related to earnings-related benefits, fully indexed to inflation and frequently also to real wages: earnings-related formulas were aimed precisely at guaranteeing a closer correspondence between income from work and transfer income after retirement. The second step was the promotion of a second pillar; but given the wide scope of existing first pillars, the principles of compulsory inclusion and state monopoly were much less of an issue than had been the case in northern Europe.

Germany offers an emblematic example of this two-step strategy: wage-indexed earnings-related benefits were introduced in 1957, in the context of a broad pension reform that also promoted the shift from funding to PAYGO as a system of financing. The demand for additional, supplementary pensions on top of the state pension first emerged within public employees, who in 1967 were able to negotiate a first collective agreement on *Zusatzversorgung* (supplementary provision) (Ebbinghaus 2000; Schmähl 1997). In the private sector, second-pillar benefits continued to be a matter of company initiatives, leading to a plural system of sectoral or local schemes with different organizing principles and methods of financing. In 1974, in the wake of court rulings, a broad framework for the regulation and promotion of all supplementary pensions was adopted, also with a view to securing them against insolvency, termination, and loss of value in a period of crisis and mounting inflation (Alber 1987; Ebbinghaus 2000).

Within the occupational cluster, two countries stand out as relatively anomalous: France and Italy. In France not only did professional separatism reach impressive levels (more than 600 pension funds emerged after the late 1940s), but the answer to the generosity challenge passed through the early establishment of *compulsory* membership to collective

supplementary pension schemes based on PAYGO: the Association Générale de Retraite des Cadres (AGIRC) schemes in 1947 for white-collar
employees (*cadres*) and the Association des Régimes de Retraite Complémentaires (ARRCO) schemes for *non-cadre* employees in 1961. The French
sharing space in the field of pensions thus displays a double internal
fragmentation: a horizontal fragmentation, by professional sector (civil
servants, private employees, farmers, the free professions, etc.) and a
vertical fragmentation, by professional hierarchy (employees vs. *cadres*)
(Guillemard 1986). This design reflects in general the strong corporatist
tradition of French society, but is also the product of the political dynamics of the post-war Fourth Republic, at the time when the reconstruction of
social insurance was undertaken (Palier 2002). Exploiting the fear of communist competition (the French Communist Party had gained 28.6 per
cent of the votes in 1946), the *cadres* were able to obtain from the moderate
parties the establishment of a very favourable *régime complémentaire,* top-
ping up the modest benefits foreseen by the *régime générale* under which
they risked losing ground with respect to the pre-war status quo. The
separate regime allowed them also to reaffirm their special status within
the French stratification system. In 1961 blue-collar workers were able to
catch up with the *cadres*, obtaining the establishment of their own supplementary scheme run by the ARRCO. Other professional groups followed suit and in 1972 a national law regulated the sector, confirming
the national and compulsory character of this level of provision. Though
formally outside the administrative realm of the *sécurité sociale,* these
schemes have played an important role in the French pension system.
On the European continent, France does stand out for the early emergence, the compulsory nature, the wide inclusiveness, and the high economic significance of its *régimes complémentaires* (Lyon Caen and Lyon
Caen 1993). As we shall see in Chapter 4, this peculiar institutional framework has started to clash with EU rules on the free movement of services
that began operation in the 1990s.

The Italian anomaly, by contrast, consists in the outright failure to
develop a second pillar during the second half of the twentieth century.
This country responded very early to the challenge of basic security by
introducing minimum pensions in 1952. When the generosity challenge
emerged in the late 1950s, the National Economic and Social Council
(CNEL) proposed a very ambitious plan that would have somewhat
aligned Italy with the Nordic countries. It foresaw the establishment of a
basic, flat-rate pension topped up by compulsory public professional
schemes. Originally supported by the newly born centre-left government

(the *Centro-Sinistra*, formed out of a strategic alliance between the Christian Democratic Party, DC, and the Socialist Party, PSI), the plan failed to muster the necessary consensus. The Communist Party (PCI) and its trade union wing—the CGIL—were strongly opposed to such a development, favouring instead a strictly 'workerist' approach to social insurance, with pensions treated as deferred wages (Ferrera 1993a; Ferrera and Gualmini 2004). Given the PCI's intransigence, pushing in the direction advocated by the CNEL was politically very risky for the DC and especially for the PSI; the latter suffered heavy electoral losses at the 1968 election, in which the pension issue played a great role. Thus in 1969, under communist and CGIL pressures, a major reform was enacted, which abandoned all universalist ambitions and introduced an extremely generous earnings-related formula for the general scheme (first pillar) covering private employees: 80 per cent of gross wages after forty years of insurance. Workers could add to this generous benefit a lump sum (the so-called *liquidazione*, or end-of-contract payment), roughly equal to one month's wages per year of contract tenure. The combination of these two benefits for a long time satisfied the security aspirations of Italian workers, crowding out any financial and political opportunity for building a second pillar well into the 1990s. In Spain, Portugal, and Greece, too, occupational pensions (in the form of voluntary schemes) took off much later than elsewhere in Europe. But the development of their pension systems was delayed by two or three decades: thus the late take-off of their second pillars is not surprising. By contrast, Italy's failure to develop a second pillar is not merely a temporal lag: it is a developmental anomaly, closely linked to ideological polarization and the internal divisions of the left (Ferrera and Gualmini 2004; Jessoula and Ferrera 2005).

In conclusion, though primarily considered as a period of rapid linear expansion in both quantitative and qualitative terms, the *Trente Glorieuses* were also a period of critical choices for the internal spatial configuration of European pension systems. The state monopoly over social protection and the degree of closure around sharing arrangements started to be called into question. While certain countries (such as Sweden, Norway, Finland, and to a large extent France) were more able than others to preserve these two elements, the general trend was towards more plural configurations, resting on a hierarchy of different tiers and/or pillars, with increasing degrees of openness from bottom (the first pillars) to top. As we have tried to illustrate, the choices regarding the timing and intensity of this shift were moulded by structural profiles and path dependencies, and in particular by the imprint that both left on the dynamic of political competition.

The issue of supplementary insurance (second tiers and second pillars) did not affect the territorial dimension of social sharing. It did, however, affect the nature and contours of domestic social membership spaces, creating new institutions and offering new entry or exit options for the various occupational groups. As we have seen, this in turn had significant implications both for voice (i.e. conflict) dynamics and for redistributive outcomes. Moreover, the spatial reconfigurations of the 1950s and 1960s set the stage for subsequent institutional reform: the margins of manoeuvre that British prime ministers Margaret Thatcher and John Major could exploit to push through their market-oriented pension reforms in 1986 and 1995 can be traced back to earlier decisions taken in the 1950s about the second tier/pillar and contracting out. From a Rokkanian perspective, changes along the membership dimension of boundaries do matter for structuring dynamics, even within a framework of full national sovereignty and territorial closure.

Policy areas other than pensions were less affected by spatial challenges during the period 1945–75: the promotion of a supplementary insurance in health care started to emerge as an issue only during the 1980s and 1990s.[9] But before dealing with this new phase of welfare state development, we must discuss the second source of disturbance of national social closure during the golden age: the creation of the Common Market.

Challenges from Without? Enter the European Communities

It has been argued that the process of European integration was launched in the 1950s with a view to 'rescuing' the nation state after the disastrous upheavals of the Second World War. In the words of Milward (2000: 44), 'the common policies of the European Communities came into being in the attempt to uphold and stabilize the postwar consensus on which the European welfare state was rebuilt. They were a part of the rescue of the nation state.' This interpretation is consistent with archival evidence on policy objectives and diplomatic negotiations for the establishment of the three Communities and then for their subsequent functioning.[10] For the original Six, integration served national interests in two ways: it allowed a more effective management of economic inter-

---

[9] In sectors other than pensions and health care the issue of supplementary insurance has not emerged as a policy or political issue to any significant extent.

[10] For a full methodologial discussion and an illustration of the archival sources, see Milward (2000). For an interpretation of the origins of the EC as the outcome of national interests reflecting domestic coalitions, see also Moravcsik (1998).

dependence and thus greater material prosperity, which could then be exploited for state-national objectives; and it allowed the solution of the German problem, stabilizing intra-European relationships and thus providing a safeguard against external insecurity, at least at the regional level.

The welfare state—and, indeed, its further expansion and improvement—was part and parcel of national post-war settlements. As we have argued and illustrated so far, public social protection typically rests on closure practices, involving both the membership and the territorial dimensions. Territorial closure had gained salience and solidity as a distinctive feature of welfare arrangements during the inter-war period, when precise rules had been introduced in order to sort insiders from outsiders, and socially enfranchised nationals from (largely) disenfranchised aliens. Moreover, especially in the bigger countries, commercial barriers had been extensively used as indirect instruments to shield national distributive patterns from external disturbance. How could a project of supranational integration be reconciled with the closure requirements of social policy? Didn't the surrender of significant degrees of territorial sovereignty pose a threat to a core element of the nation state which needed to be rescued after its wartime crisis or even collapse?

Indeed, the threat was potentially there. With hindsight, we know that since the 1980s the process of European integration has started to exert 'subversive' (though not necessarily negative) effects on national social contracts (Rhodes 1995; Streeck 1995). But, as often happens in the history of institutions, in the genetic phase of the 1950s this threat was neither obvious nor automatic. Milward (2000) is right in suggesting that the European rescue of the nation state worked also to the advantage of welfare arrangements; but this happened at the price of setting in motion a slow institutional dynamic which, in combination with others, was doomed to bring out its long-term destructuring potential for these very arrangements. Let us develop this argument in more detail.

As a consequence of wartime material destruction and social disruption, the European welfare states were in need of fundamental reconstruction. In many countries broad reform projects had already been discussed during the war; in the UK, the Beveridge Report came out in 1942 and had a vast international echo. Tables 2.1 and 2.2 display the great wave of coverage extensions that took place in the aftermath of the war. We have seen in this chapter that the 1950s witnessed a growing demand for income maintenance guarantees, which in some cases led to the establishment of supplementary schemes and/or to an upgrading of extant benefit formulas. Regardless of the country-specific topographies of such spatial reconfigurations, the net effect of this general trend was greater spending commitments, which in turn required the extraction of greater revenues from working populations. Economic recovery was well under way by the early 1950s and growth rates were promising. Such recovery was largely triggered off by the Marshall Plan, but it soon became clear that the only durable engine of growth was trade expansion, especially intra-European trade and most crucially trade with West Germany. The establishment of the European Coal and Steel Community (ECSC) in 1952 and especially of the European Economic Community (EEC) in 1957 served primarily (though obviously not solely) the purpose of securing an effective institutional framework for trade expansion. It also bound the new German state firmly to the West, under French political tutelage, thus eliminating the threat of new military strife in the old continent.

The surrender of significant degrees of 'interdependence sovereignty' in the economic sphere was not seen as a danger to the maintenance of 'Westphalian sovereignty' in the social sphere and, indeed, to a further expansion of its domestic scope.[11] Quite the contrary: historical evidence shows that the founding fathers and, more generally, most of the relevant national elites conceived of European integration as a project capable of creating a virtuous circle between *open* economies and outward-looking economic policies on the on hand, and *closed* welfare states and inward-looking social policy on the other (Milward, Sorensen, and Ranieri 1993; Davies 1996; Deakin 1996; Giubboni 2003). 'Smith abroad, Keynes at home': in Gilpin's famous formulation, this was the motto that inspired the early architects of the Communities (Gilpin 1987). The 'social frigidity' of the Treaties of Paris and (especially) of Rome, lamented by Federico Mancini (1999) and considered in recent debates to be a sort of original sin of the EU template, must be read from a very different perspective (Giubboni 2003). The limited competences assigned to the supranational level in the social policy sphere reflected the explicit objective of a division of labour between national and EC rulers that was seen as virtuous for both the market and the welfare state; it also rested on an implicit bias, a positive orientation (both cognitive and normative) of the founding fathers vis-à-vis social protection, high labour standards, and full employment objectives, whose national scope and closure preconditions were taken for granted and thus assumed to be inherently non-problematic for a project

---

[11] The terms are borrowed from Krasner (1999) (see Chapter 1, n. 18). 'Interdependence sovereignty' is the ability of domestic authorities to control what passes through territorial borders; 'Wesphalian sovereignty' is the ability to exclude external actors from authority structures within a given territory.

essentially aimed at creating a customs union. The EEC did not need to meddle in welfare issues, because these rested at the core of domestic agendas, buttressed by domestic political compromises and legal orders already well tuned in socially protective directions.

The Paris Treaty establishing the ECSC (1951, effective from 1952) clearly stated that social competences were to remain with the member states. National social policy objectives were indirectly endorsed by the Treaty, which not only recognized the right of member states to support the readaptation of workers laid off in the process of adjusting to the new common market, but also provided for the establishment of a supranational fund to support the retraining and resettlement of redundant workers (arts. 56 and 58). Article 68 of the Treaty included one important reserve for the High Authority (i.e. the top managing body of the ECSC): the competence to issue recommendations in case of 'abnormally low' wages set by certain enterprises in certain regions. The rationale behind such a reserve was essentially economic: the norm was meant to avoid distortions of competition through social dumping practices (Lyon Caen and Lyon Caen 1993). But both articles give the flavour of the virtuous circle that the ECSC founders had in mind. The welfare state was seen as a positive institution, it should remain the preserve of national authorities, the common market would generate fresh resources for it, and in no case should it be allowed to weaken social standards through regulatory competition.[12]

This virtuous circle was explicitly spelled out by two reports on the social implications of economic integration that were prepared in the mid-1950s by two groups of experts: one chaired by the economist Bertil Ohlin from the ILO and the other chaired by Paul-Henri Spaak, Belgium's foreign minister (Giubboni 2003). Though with different nuances, both documents recommended that the social policy prerogatives of national governments be left untouched and that precisely these prerogatives could effectively redress and compensate for the imbalances that would flow from increasing market integration. The Spaak report went further and suggested that the EEC, in line with art. 60 of the Paris Treaty, might be given some competence to support member state social policies in easing the unemployment implications of plant closures, and even mentioned the possibility of establishing a European system of unemployment assistance. It too seemed quite confident, however, that national social provisions—and their possible enhancement, indeed in the wake of the greater

---

[12] For an interesting discussion of the 'social vision' of the Treaties of Paris and Rome, see also Sciarra (1999).

prosperity generated by economic integration—were more than adequate to cope with these issues.

The Rome Treaty (signed in 1957, effective from 1958) largely endorsed the philosophy of the two reports. This philosophy is clearly reflected in art. 117 (now 136), which states that the member states agree on the necessity to promote the living and working conditions of the labour force, allowing for the *égalisation dans le progrès* of such conditions. The same article also states that such upgrading is expected to result from the functioning of the Common Market: both from a spontaneous process of harmonization of social protection systems (Germany's expectation) and from Treaty provisions on regulatory *rapprochement* (France's demand). It may perhaps be exaggerated to interpret this article—and the Rome Treaty in general—as 'an external buttress to the welfare state', de facto aimed at improving the level of welfare provision to that of the most generous country (Milward 2000: 216). But it is true that initially the treaties had no 'subversive' intention at all in respect of national sharing practices and redistributive institutions. The rather vague and general content and style of their social provisions and the unanimity rules set for deciding on such matters had the primary objective of preserving, rather than challenging, the 'Westphalian sovereignty' of the state in the realm of solidarity. The EEC's mission was to promote economic growth through increasing intra-European trade flows, and thus indirectly to strengthen the occupational and financial basis (more insured workers, more contributions) for redistributive schemes that were to remain under strict home rule.

In the 1950s the restructured welfare states of France, Italy, Germany, and the Benelux countries were in urgent need of assured revenues in order to honour the new spending commitments created by coverage extensions and benefit upgrading. Domestic solidarity required bounding and closure practices. But the resources of national territories could not be efficiently mobilized—and thus allow for adequate tax revenue—without access to international markets. In the language used in Chapter 1, system (re)building required both economic opening and social closure, a weakening of interdependence sovereignty in order to widen and deepen the scope of the state as an agent of redistribution. As in earlier historical phases, market expansion and internal consolidation seemed to push in opposite directions. The solution to such tensions was found in the establishment of the European Communities, which provided an institutional framework programmatically designed to reconcile transnational and supranational integration in the economic sphere and national autonomy in the social protection sphere. It was not the first time that some form of strictly economic unification was being launched among European states. True, the launching of the EEC was accompanied by a genuine discourse on a federal Europe and by widespread expectations of 'functional spill-overs' from the economic to the political sphere. In this sense the new experiment was different from previous instances of mere customs unions. The new legal framework included from the start some important novel-ties, such as an ECJ, which cast a 'supranationalist' shadow on subsequent developments. But the original treaties were an intergovernmental com-promise, resting on rational state interests (Moravcsik 1998). Indeed, as Rokkan put it in the mid-1960s, the EEC designed by the Rome Treaty was essentially a form—though admittedly a very elaborate one—of cooper-ation between corporate and administrative agencies, not an attempt at building 'a genuine community of trust across the systems'[13] as a prelude to the formation of a fully-fledged supranational state.

Once established, however, institutional orders always tend to acquire a life of their own, which generates new ends and new means, often unin-tended and undesired by their original builders (March and Olsen 1998; Pierson 1996, 2004). The compromise of the 1950s was soon to become an unstable chemical compound (Giubboni 2003). Two endogenous institu-tional developments worked to transform the European Communities from an external buttress—or at least an innocuous presence—for national welfare states into a destructuring wedge: the constitutionalization of the EC order on the one hand and the coordination regime for social security on the other. We examine them in turn.

Law for Exit or Constitution in Disguise? The Shifting EC Legal Order

Medieval Europe offered a first emblematic example of the self-reinforcing mechanism that links trade between local communities or producers and the consolidation of a common legal framework. Commerce along the city-belt extending from Italy and southern France to Germany, Flanders, and the Low Countries was made possible by the revival of Roman law in these territories starting from the tenth century AD. Trade expansion led to the elaboration of a specific set of principles for the conduct of eco-nomic transactions—the *lex mercatoria*—that cut across the congeries of local customs and practices and that disciplined *exits* and *entries*, that is,

---

[13] Citation taken from Flora, Kuhnle, and Urwin (1999: 265). Rokkan's original text was written in 1965.

movements across established territorial boundaries (Milgrom, North, and Weingast 1990). This new set of principles allowed transactions to occur also with more peripheral areas that had developed distinctive national legal systems, such as England and the Scandinavian kingdoms. But the territories of the old central empire always maintained an elective affinity rooted in their adhesion to Roman Law. As noted by Rokkan, it is no accident of history that the Roman law countries were the ones to take the lead, centuries later, in creating a common market (Flora, Kuhnle, and Urwin 1999: 167–8) by removing economic boundaries among themselves and by establishing a supranational legal order for regulating mutual transactions as well as joint transactions vis-à-vis third countries or trading blocs. The institutional mechanism set in motion by the EC treaties, however, had more self-reinforcement incentives than originally intended by its architects and 'principals', namely, the constituent nation states. Rather than merely serving as a law for exits, the new legal order soon started a creeping shift into a de facto constitution through the affirmation of two important principles: the principle of direct effect and the principle of EC law supremacy.

As has been highlighted by a vast literature,[14] the main protagonist of this crucial shift has been the ECJ. This body had been established by the Paris Treaty essentially in order to protect member states and firms from the risk of an excess of power on the part of the new High Authority. The Rome Treaty slightly changed the Court's mandate, assigning to it the task of dispute resolution over EC laws; but one important role of this body remained that of keeping the supranational authorities under check, in a community of states not of individuals (Mancini and Keeler 1994). Manifesting an unexpected activism, the Court soon started to act in a boldly transformative way, developing doctrine through the preliminary ruling system foreseen by art. 177 (now 234).

The first landmark case took place in 1963. In the *van Gend* ruling, the Court affirmed the principle of direct effect, by stating that:

the Community constitutes a new legal order of international law for the benefit of which states have limited their sovereign rights, albeit within limited fields, and the subjects of which comprise not only member states but also their nationals. Independently of the legislation of member states, Community law therefore not only imposes obligations on individuals but it is also intended to confer upon them rights which become part of their legal heritage.[15]

---

[14] See especially Alter (1998); Burley and Mattly (1993); Garret (1995); Garret and Weingast (1993); Golub (1996); Rasmussen (1986); Stone Sweet (2004); and Weiler (1981, 1991, 1994).

[15] Case 26/62, *NV Algemene Transport-en Expeditie Onderneming van Gend & Loos v. Netherlands Inland Revenue Administration* [1963] ECR 1.

The principle of direct effect has substantially altered the nature of the EC institutional order, attributing to individual citizens a firm legal standing resting on judiciable rights and backed by a codified procedure for claiming remedies from the Court itself. This principle has transformed the preliminary ruling system of art.177 (now 234) from a channel for challenging *EC law* into a channel for challenging *national law*, if it is presumed that the latter breaches EC-generated new rights (Alter 1998). In this way the original *law for exit* has became a *law for voice* as well, that is, a set of procedures for the manifestation of grievances and for seeking redress on the part of ordinary citizens vis-à-vis their home authorities. This law for voice serves as a destructuring wedge for domestic legal spaces in that it confers on the subjects of such space the right of appeal (through the mediation of a national court) to a superior source of power that can then coerce domestic rulers from without, though only with the weapons of legal judgment.[16]

A second landmark case came a year later, in 1964. In the *Costa* case, the Court fully affirmed the principle of the supremacy of EC law by stating that:

the transfer by the States from their domestic legal system to the Community legal system of the rights and obligations arising under the Treaty carries with it a permanent limitation of their sovereign rights, against which subsequent unilateral acts incompatible with the concept of the Community cannot prevail.[17]

The principle of the supremacy of EC law was reaffirmed several times after 1964, in respect not only of domestic statutes but also of national constitutions. In 1978 the ECJ specified that supremacy applied not only to primary EC law (the treaties) but also to secondary legislation (such as directives, even if not yet transposed).[18] This principle is of paramount significance, as it has foreclosed the possibility of countering the effects of EC rules by legislating against them at the *national* level. Naturally the member states can change EC rules at the *supranational* level. But acting at this level is difficult: unanimity (but often also qualified majority) requirements render changing the status quo very demanding in terms of political capital- and coalition-building and thus generate 'joint decision traps' which tend to lock actors into the status quo (Scharpf 1988). The external constraint on nation state rule-making has in itself a far reaching 'structuring' potential,

---

[16] An early and innovative interpretation of the effects of 'constitutionalization' in terms of exit and voice was offered by Weiler (1991).

[17] Case 6/64, *Flaminio Costa* v. *E.N.E.L.* [1964] ECR 585.

[18] Case 106/77, *Amministrazione delle Finanze dello Stato* v. *Simmenthal SpA* [1978] ECR 629.

that is, the potential of forming new political arenas or 'venues' and new dynamics of contention. Though it has seldom been the main component of centre-building in European history, the legal element has always backed this process. Thanks to the principle of supremacy, the supra-national duo—Commission and ECJ—has been able to gradually gain, in certain areas, the status of 'ultimate' source of authority for the whole bounded space of the EC, gradually affirming itself as a pole of attraction (and in some cases as a veritable catalyst) for collective actors interested in exploiting the opportunities of the new legal transnational space.

The gradual shift from an essentially international legal order to an integrated and to some extent partially domesticated order has been described by some scholars as 'constitutionalization', that is, a process whereby 'the EC treaties have evolved from a set of legal arrangements binding upon sovereign states into a vertically integrated regime confer-ring judicially enforceable rights and obligations on all legal persons and entities, public and private, within EC territory' (Stone Sweet and Capor-aso 1998: 102).[19] How could such a radical transformation take place in a very short time span (roughly two decades) and with so little resistance from the national member states? It took much longer for US federal authorities to bring about a similar degree of vertical integration in the course of the nineteenth century, countering a veritable parade of defiant acts on the part of the American states (Friedman Goldstein 1997). A great number of explanatory factors have been called into question by the extensive literature that has been addressing this puzzle:[20] the difference of time horizons between politicians and judges, the ability of the latter to balance constitutionalization objectives with the satisfaction of some short-term interests of national governments and with lip service to their persisting sovereignty, coalition-building between EC judges and national judiciaries, institutional obstacles to Court restraint by national governments due to the 'joint decision trap', and yet other factors. As argued by Pierson (2004), judicialization processes tend to be a one-way street: 'you can stir the courts into democratic politics, but you cannot stir them out' (Pierson 2004: 159). A full discussion of such dynamics would divert us from the purposes of this chapter. The relevant issue for us is this: what have been the implications of the creeping constitutionalization of the EC legal order for the historical compromise between external eco-nomic opening and internal social closure that was struck in the 1950s,

---

[19] For a critical view of the EU 'constitutionalization' process, however, see Bartolini (2005).

[20] See n. 14 above.

aimed at creating a viable and indeed virtuous political economy for the reconstructed welfare states? Were the new legal doctrines compatible with that division of labour—trade to EC authorities, welfare to member states—that lay at the foundations of the Paris and Rome Treaties and rested on the assumption of a virtuous circle between the two?

It is clear that the principles of direct effect and of EC law supremacy as well as the transformation of the preliminary ruling system significantly eroded the member states' Westphalian sovereignty, that is, their ability to exclude external authority structures from their jurisdictional space. Their first and thickest firewalls against *potential* external encroachments into their social sovereignty were seriously weakened. But how actual was the danger? To what extent was the ECJ likely to meddle in welfare state issues? And in what direction would it proceed—would it uphold or challenge social closure rules and practices? Along the membership dimension or along the territorial dimension or both? With what consequences? These were the questions posed by the evolution of the EC legal order into a 'law for exit and voice'. Such questions were not at the centre of political debates in the 1960s: actors take their time to perceive new problems and challenges. Moreover, the effects of constitutionalization only became apparent with the passing of time: an emblematic case of slow moving outcome (Pierson 2004). Nevertheless, the chain of institutional developments set itself in motion. Soon after the *Van Gend* and *Costa* cases, litigation began to mount and the transformed preliminary ruling system started to be increasingly used by the bearers of the new EC-generated rights to challenge national provisions. The issue of welfare state closure soon became a prominent object of such litigation, causing some first strains in that delicate balance between open markets and closed social protection systems envisaged by the treaties.

Free Movement of Workers and Social Rights

By conferring justiciable rights on individuals, the constitutionalization of the EC order has gradually encroached on the sphere of citizenship. Tuned as they were towards the creation of a common market, the treaties provided essentially an economic constitution. But modern markets rest on a basket of basic rights which has become increasingly richer since the nineteenth century. In order to exchange commodities in the marketplace, one has to have a right to belong to that marketplace to begin with; second, one has to have a right to options, that is, freedom to exercise choices based on opportunities and preferences. A market citizen is a thin citizen (Caporaso 2003), not necessarily protected by a bill of fundamental rights. But still she is a citizen, bearer of at least a modicum of civil rights.

One of the most fundamental civil rights in the market sphere is the freedom of work: the right to follow the occupation of one's choice in the place of one's choice (Marshall 1992: 10). Art. 48 (now 39) of the Rome Treaty recognized this right, prohibiting all forms of discrimination by the member states regarding employment, starting, of course, with discrimination based on nationality. This article is directly applicable, and already in 1965 the Court found that the free movement of labour was a fundamental pillar of the EC and was to be implemented as fully as possible from legal point of view.[21] By 1961 all intra-European visas had been eliminated and in 1968 Regulation 1612/68[22] and Directive 360/68[23] struck down all remaining restrictions. In 1970 Regulation 1251[24] specified that a worker could rightfully remain in the member state in which she had worked also after retirement. Between 1960 and 1968 migration flows within the Six grew on average 4.7 per cent each year: in 1968 about 830,000 EC workers were living in a member state other than their own.[25] These developments did not go wholly uncontested by national governments. Labour mobility ranked much lower than the other three freedoms (the free movement of goods, capital, and services) in the agendas of the founding member states, except Italy, which was interested in this aspect with a view to solving her chronic unemployment problems, especially in the Mezzogiorno. To a large extent, art. 48 (now 39) can in fact be seen as a political compromise, according to which the Five agreed to gradually absorb the Italian labour surplus (Romero 1993). The economic boom of the 1960s (which affected Italy as well, even more than the other five member states) greatly eased the actual implementation of such commitments: after 1968 migration flows started to slow down, while mobility on

---

[21] Case 44/65, *Hessische Knappschaft* v. *Maison Singer and sons* [1965] ECR 965.

[22] Regulation (EEC) No 1612/68 of the Council of 15 October 1968 on freedom of movement for workers within the Community, *Official Journal L 257*, 19/10/1968, p. 0002–0012, English special edition: Series I Chapter 1968 (II) p. 0475.

[23] Council Directive 68/360/EEC of 15 October 1968 on the abolition of restrictions on movement and residence within the Community for workers of Member States and their families, *Official Journal L 257*, 19/10/1968, p. 0013–0016, English special edition: Series I Chapter 1968(II), p. 0485.

[24] Regulation (EEC) No 1251/70 of the Commission of 29 June 1970 on the right of workers to remain in the territory of a Member State after having been employed in that State, *Official Journal L 142*, 30/06/1970, p. 0024–002, English special edition: Series I, Chapter 1970(II), p. 0402.

[25] Cf. Sindbjerg Martinsen (2004) and Straubhaar (1988). This figure includes only workers in possession of official work permits and is therefore an underestimate.

the part of third country nationals could be kept under the strict control of each member state (Barnard 2004; Van der Mei 2003).

The establishment of an EC-wide freedom to work was a revolutionary achievement, especially in view of the highly restrictive regime that had been put in place in most European countries after the First World War; under that regime, non-nationals could be denied, at any time, the right to belong to a domestic labour market and therefore be barred from or deprived of all options (see Chapter 2). The creation of a common labour market (at least in terms of legal framework) was the first broad and tangible step in that process of 'Europeanization of options' set in motion by the EC treaties.

But what about the social rights of migrant workers? This was certainly not a trivial question. When freedom of work was first established in Europe's national labour markets, typically during the nineteenth century, there were as yet no social rights. The insecurity implications of such freedom did trigger off a demand for social protection, which led to the first wave of public insurance schemes between the 1880s and 1920s, through the process of 'fusion and separation' that was referred to in Chapter 1. But the creation of the EC common labour market during the 1960s took place in a social rights-thick environment. Despite the pledge of the treaties to keep EC hands off national sovereignty in this realm, the issue of introducing at least some form of coordination between the various national sets of rules could not be avoided, in order to solve conflicts of laws.

As a matter of fact, the problem had already arisen in the wake of the Paris Treaty: more than 200,000 migrant workers were active in the steel and coal sectors of the original Six (Lyon Caen and Lyon Caen 1993). In the early 1950s, social entitlements were still not very developed: but the issue of protecting migrant workers (and their family members) through a common supranational regime rather than by multiple and heterogeneous bilateral agreements appeared on the political agenda, also in the wake of a parallel initiative by the Council of Europe. In 1957 a European Convention on the Social Security of Migrant Workers was signed in Rome. Article 51 (now 42) of the Rome Treaty clearly recognized that migrant workers should not be penalized in terms of social protection and in 1958 a Regulation, largely inspired by the Convention, was issued (3/1958)[26] establishing the four basic principles of coordination: (a) non-discrimination and equality of treatment; (b) eligibility of all periods of

---

[26] Règlement n° 3 concernant la sécurité sociale des travailleurs migrants, *Official Journal B 030*, 16/12/1958, p. 0561.

insurance, in whatever country; (c) benefit exportability from one member state to another; and (d) applicability of a single law, the *lex loci laboris* (i.e. the laws of the country of work).

At the time when they were first introduced, these provisions did not seem at odds with the institutional separation between the economic and the social spheres and the division of labour between supranational and national authorities. Coordination did not involve any regulatory standardization (in any case subject to the unanimity requirement of art. 100 of the Rome Treaty, now 94). It was considered a natural corollary of the freedom of work, and protecting migrant workers was seen as a positive goal by socially minded policymakers in the national capitals and in Brussels. The 1958 Regulation explicitly upheld the territoriality principle by recognizing the primacy of the legal rules of the country of work. And in any case EC provisions affected only relations between states. Constitutionalization, however, changed the picture and from the mid-1960s litigation also began to take place in this delicate field.

The first wave of litigation, between the mid-1960s and early 1970s, comprised only a handful of cases, originating in disputes over interpretation: but they put down some important landmarks and immediately set the tone for future developments. The first landmark was established with the *Unger* judgment in 1964[27] which, not surprisingly, concerned the territorial closure of national systems. The Dutch authorities were refusing to reimburse medical expenses incurred in Germany by a person who was no longer working but nevertheless was voluntarily insured in a public scheme of the Netherlands. The Court found that this was discriminatory, ruled in favour of *Unger*, and proposed a common definition of 'employed person' (see later). The lesson was that member states could not keep their social gates closed by manipulating legal definitions, since the ECJ would standardize them. Another case in 1965 confirmed in their turn the principles of direct applicability and EC law supremacy in the specific field of social protection. Thus, in *van der Veen*[28] the Dutch government, again, was forced to grant benefits to a worker returning from France under laws passed after 1958. Member states could not invoke the principle of *lex posterior* to reaffirm their sovereignty.

Two other landmarks laid down in 1966 and 1969 concerned the membership dimension of closure: when does a domestic scheme—a collectivity of

---

[27] Case 75/63, *Mrs M. K. H. Hoekstra (née Unger) v. Bestuur der Bedrijfsvereniging voor Detailhandel en Ambachten (Administration of the Industrial Board for Retail Trades and Businesses)* [1964] ECR 177.

[28] Case 100/63, *J. G. van der Veen, widow of J. Kalsbeek v. Bestuur der Sociale Verzekeringsbank and nine other cases* [1964] ECR 565.

redistribution—fall within the material scope of EC coordination rules?[29] In the *Vaassen Gobbels* case of 1966[30] the Court found that even non-public social schemes (i.e. schemes that were not run by the state) were to be considered social security as long as they were statutory. Almost paradoxically, if a national scheme is compulsory, if it 'locks in' a given group—regardless of management and/or its public or private law status—then it should allow for entries and exits based on EC law provisions; it is also subject to the voice procedures envisaged by art. 177 (now 234). In the *Torreken* case of 1969,[31] on the other hand, the ECJ held that a 'residual', means-tested pension scheme such as the Belgian *révenu garanti d'existence* could be considered part of social security too and thus must be open to non-nationals.

In order to clarify legal ambiguities and take into account the new interpretative jurisprudence of the ECJ, a new Regulation on social security coordination was issued in 1971 (Reg. 1408).[32] This text reaffirmed the four basic principles listed earlier: (*a*) non-discrimination and equality of treatment; (*b*) eligibility of all periods of insurance, in whatever country; (*c*) benefit exportability from one member state to another; and (*d*) applicability of a single law, that of the country of work. Regulation 1408 also offered standardized definitions of the core notions ('worker', 'benefit', etc.) so as to avoid manipulative games on the part of state authorities. The most important move on this front, following *Unger*, was the shift from 'employed persons' to 'insured persons' as the axial concept to define the personal scope of the regulation. While still leaving intact national prerogatives on insurance rules (i.e. boundary setting along the membership dimension), the new approach pre-empted manipulative games based on labour market status: another firewall around Westphalian sovereignty in the social sphere was thus removed. The regulation basically endorsed in this way the 'expansionist' views of the ECJ, regarding not only the

---

[29] The expression 'material scope' refers to the range of benefits—and thus indirectly the range of schemes—to which coordination rules apply; the expression 'personal scope' (used *infra*) refers to the range of social groups or categories.

[30] Case 61/65, *G. Vaassen-Göbbels (a widow)* v. *Management of the Beambtenfonds voor het Mijnbedrijf* [1966] ECR 261.

[31] Case 28/68, *Caisse régionale de sécurité sociale du nord de la France* v. *Achille Torrekens* [1969] ECR 125.

[32] Regulation (EEC) No 1408/71 of the Council of 14 June 1971 on the application of social security schemes to employed persons and their families moving within the Community, *Official Journal* L 149, 05/07/197, p. 0002–005, English special edition: Series I, Chapter 1971(II), p. 0416. A second regulation spelled out the administrative rules for implementing the provisions of the 1971 regulation: Regulation (EEC) No. 574/72 of the Council of 21 March 1972 fixing the procedure for implementing Regulation (EEC) No 1408/71 on the application of social security schemes to employed persons and their families moving within the Community, *Official Journal* L 074, 27/03/197, p. 0001–0083, English special edition: Series I, Chapter 1972(I), p. 0159.

direct and permanent effect of EC coordination rules but also the desirability of wide territorial entry/exit gates linked to domestic sharing spaces. A clear and detailed legislative framework seemed preferable to piecemeal jurisprudence: and in the early 1970s intra-EC migrations were not perceived as a real challenge to the domestic status quo. Despite *Torrekens*, the regulation did not envisage the opening of the gates of the *sancta sanctorum* of national spaces, namely, non-contributory social assistance. As we shall see, this was to become a bone of contention in the years to follow.

One point remained unclear in Regulation 1408: the status of supplementary occupational schemes. As we saw in the first part of the chapter, this type of scheme had been introduced in many countries after the 1950s. Were they to fall within the scope of coordination? The 1971 regulation did not include them explicitly, but neither did it exclude them (Lyon Caen and Lyon Caen 1993). This ambiguity can be explained by the fact that in the original Six supplementary occupational schemes were introduced later than in northern Europe and, except in France, they remained in their first phase more akin to voluntary than to compulsory insurance. The *Vaassen Gobbels* judgement mentioned earlier, however, already gave a flavour of the dispute that was to flare up on this delicate front in subsequent decades.

Golden Achievements, Seeds of Change

We started this chapter by saying that the *Trente Glorieuses* were the apex of welfare state-building in European nations. In subsequent sections, however, we essentially highlighted the cracks that emerged in these new constructs during the same decades.[33] We now wish to recapitulate our argument by vigorously reaffirming the first point. The period between the end of the Second World War and the first OPEC oil crisis was definitely the golden age of national welfare: the buildings created for social sharing were indeed imposing and started to offer widespread security (occasionally, even security cum comfort) to millions of 'little people'—elderly people, poor people, disabled people, and so on—whose life chances had traditionally been modest, haphazard, and subject to uncontrollable forces. Welfare state-building was accompanied by an unpreced-

---

[33] Besides 'spatial' cracks, other social and economic problems started to appear during the 1960s and especially 1970s, but we do not mention or discuss them because they are not pertinent to our argument.

ented political and ideological consensus on the role of the state in society and the economy. This 'social democratic consensus' was important not only for its distributive outcomes but also for its bonding effects: it created strong solidarity bonds (horizontal and vertical) throughout the social structure, as well as strong political bonds between ordinary citizens and politicians through the mediation of interest groups (especially trade unions) and mass parties. The expansion of welfare programmes has consolidated distinct national 'communities of trust', it has contributed to anchoring democracy to society (Morlino 1998) and to feeding a virtuous circle of economic modernization and growth, political legitimization and stability, social cohesion and solidarity. In the words of Fritz Scharpf, the *Trente Glorieuses* led to a veritable 'democratic civilization of capitalism' in Western Europe (Scharpf 1999: 33). The process of European integration that was launched in the 1950s was intended precisely to serve this virtuous circle by taking care of economic interdependence and by facilitating trade flows, thus securing higher rates of growth and higher fiscal dividends. In its initial phase, European integration (as well as the wider international economic order) did not endanger the autonomy of domestic authorities in setting the level and type of taxes and hence the level and type of social protection: national tax bases (including capital) and national consumers were largely 'captive' and thus the distributive and regulatory costs of the welfare states could be easily reflected in prices without jeopardizing the profitability of capitalist production (Scharpf 1999, 2000).

Referring back to the theoretical framework outlined in Chapter 1, we can say that those three decades were also the apex of bounded structuring and system-building around (or, better, inside) the territorial nation state. The space of citizenship became increasingly thick and salient for its legitimate occupants. The meaning and substance of both roots and options grew increasingly significant, the catalogue of civil, political, and social rights grew wider. Opportunities for moving and voicing expanded, but essentially within the national territory and through national channels. Bearing in mind the repertoire of locality and vocality options outlined in Chapter 1 (see Figure 1.3), we can say that the prevailing game in town (at least the game between subjects and rulers, citizens and national authorities) was 'staying in' and 'voicing from inside'. In the realm of social sharing, being a citizen implied having access to a growing range of benefits, but it also meant being 'locked in', that is, in compulsory insurance schemes involving the payment of contributions to the state. Beyond state boundaries, citizenship lost much of its value and practical effectiveness. The coupling of right and territory was very tight.

Yet as that institutional configuration was reaching its zenith, some cracks did emerge. The establishment of supplementary insurance, examined in the first part of this chapter, extended the reach of domestic redistribution, but at the price (in most countries) of weakening the principle of compulsion and thus loosening sharing ties.[34] In its turn, the creeping constitutionalization of the EC legal order and the growing activism of supranational authorities in the area of social security coordination opened some first breaches in the domestic spaces of citizenship. Only the seeds of these two developments were planted in the 1950s and 1960s; their significance for the spatial politics of welfare can be appreciated only with hindsight. Yet both developments presented a challenge to the long-term stability of the established boundaries of social sharing and its underlying politics. They did so by suddenly widening the repertoire of both locality and vocality options. This change is captured in Figures 3.1 and 3.2.

Figure 3.1 visualizes the new intrasystem and cross-system options opened by the two developments mentioned earlier. The horizontal axis refers to the territorial dimension of national social citizenship spaces; the

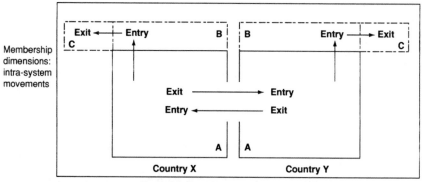

A: Area of compulsory social insurance schemes
B: Area of public supplementary pensions
C: Area of non-public supplementary pensions

Fig 3.1 Spatial reconfigurations in the 1950s and 1960s: locality options

---

[34] As we have mentioned, in a number of countries supplementary pensions adopted funding instead of PAYGO: funding is programmatically less tuned towards intergenerational and interpersonal redistribution.

vertical dimension represents the membership dimension (who is covered for what). Box A represents the space of statutory social insurance in two hypothetical member states X and Y. The establishment of supplementary schemes (box B) opened up various new intrasystem locality options: entry into the new sphere of (compulsory or voluntary, depending on cases) supplementary protection, staying out (no coverage), exit, or 'opting-out' (i.e. choosing an alternative form of coverage: box C). The Swedish struggles around the ATP scheme in the late 1950s (emblematically represented by the three questions of the 1957 referendum); the formation of wide social support for 'contracting out' in Britain during the same period; private employees' demand to obtain their own *régime complémentaire* in France in the early 1960s; and the similar demand for *Zusatzversorgung* from German public employees at the end of that decade: these are all examples of the new spatial politics of social solidarity linked to the emergence of new locality options.

The establishment of coordination rules for migrant workers in its turn opened up new cross-system options: exit from one's original space and entry into the other member state's space. To be sure, exit and entry through foreign migration had always been an option for members of national spaces. But before the 1960s these were typically 'thin' options, as it were. They carried with them a limited range of often precarious social rights. In fact, entitlements (to the extent that they existed) were usually lost in the event of migration. The relevant novelty of the European situation since the 1960s and (more fully) since the 1970s was the maintenance of entitlements during migration. Nationality became an explicitly prohibited criterion and could no longer be used for filtering access into domestic schemes. Furthermore, the principles of the right to accumulate and export entitlements meant that states were obliged to let through their borders 'bundles of entitlements': imports of entitlements acquired under foreign regimes (such as contributing credits) or exports of entitlements to be redeemed in foreign territories (such as claims of payments abroad). Figure 3.1 does not connect boxes B and C between country X and Y. As was mentioned, the 1971 Regulation left the status and coordination rules for this level of social protection temporarily unsettled.

Figure 3.2 visualizes in its turn the new vocality options opened up by EC constitutionalization and the novel role of the EC legal order as a 'law for voice' besides being a law for exit. The continuous arrows depict the traditional channels for articulating political demands and for addressing claims of redress, linking the members of bounded social sharing spaces to their national authorities (governments, parliaments, courts). The dotted

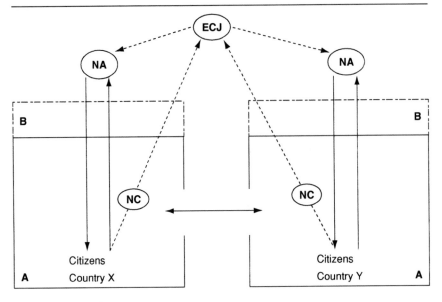

NA: National authorities
ECJ: European Court of Justice
NC: National courts

Fig 3.2 Spatial reconfigurations in the 1950s and 1960s: vocality options

arrows depict the new channel for claims and redress opened up by the transformation of the preliminary ruling system.[35] Since the mid-1960s, insured persons have been able to challenge the national laws of their own country or of another member state in front of the ECJ (through the mediation of national courts). The ECJ can rule against national authorities and, through the mediation of a national court, satisfy the claim addressed to it. In the language of Table 1.2, acts visualized by the dotted arrows can be seen as a special variant of 'voice from outside', which originates from the inside.[36] Typically these acts refer to nationals addressing the ECJ in order to obtain redress from their home authorities via an

---

[35] It must be noted that besides the ECJ the European Commission itself has gradually evolved as a new locus for addressing claims, through ad hoc committes entrusted with the competence of examining individual complaints and questioning national authorities about them. In the field of social security, for example, there exists an Administrative Commission on the Social Security of Migrant Workers that can adopt (non-binding) resolutions on how to settle disputes and conflicts of law.

[36] The locality status of the subject of this act of voice is analytically complex: the subject is physically inside the nation state but is empowered to exercise this type of voice by a supranational legal order that is above the nation state and that creates a new type and layer of membership which is effective also for individual citizens.

ECJ ruling (e.g. the *Unger* case discussed earlier). Vocal entries or vocal exits occur when system boundaries are successfully crossed with the backing of the Court. If a national of country X obtains the Court's backing for a claim on country Y's social protection system within the latter's territory, then we have an act of 'vocal entry' (voice from outside has allowed a successful entry). If the same person obtains from the Court a backing for escaping from his or her home system, then we have a 'vocal exit'. As we shall see in Chapter 4, a growing number of these types of acts started to appear in the 1970s and 1980s.

In the early 1970s, this gradual reconfiguration of the spatial coordinates and politics of welfare attracted very little attention and caused even less concern. On the internal side, the role of supplementary schemes remained circumscribed relative to statutory provision, and even in countries that had opted for non-public and non-compulsory second pillars (or that envisaged wide contracting-out options) state authorities thought that the game was still under their control. For example, in the UK projects were being made to establish a fully-fledged public scheme for supplementary pensions (the State Earnings Related Pension System, or SERPS, to be phased in from 1978). In the Netherlands and Germany private and funded supplementary pensions developed under the umbrella of national contracts, and thus governments could keep an eye on them. Fiscal resources did not seem to be a problem, yet.

On the external side, the constitutionalization of the EC legal order proceeded at a slow pace in an arena—the emerging transnational legal space—that was relatively distant from domestic political arenas. The new vocality options involved only the (then) very small and politically marginal constituency of migrant workers. Voice from outside could be exercised only by individual litigants and thus was much less visible and worrying than the traditional forms of 'voice from inside' exercised by collective actors in relation to domestic welfare programmes. The full significance of 'integration through law' started to be appreciated by academic debates only towards the end of the 1970s and early 1980s (e.g. Weiler 1981).

In sum, at the apex of the golden age the seeds of change were too small to cause concern, and the processes to which they gave birth were slow-moving and thus not very visible or disturbing in their *statu nascenti*. Their destructuring potential in respect of national social closure required additional ingredients to become manifest. The first crucial ingredient was time. But other important ingredients included external economic shocks, the fiscal crisis, the acceleration of migration flows, the internal market, and EMU—to name the most important. The reconstruction and discussion of these developments, however, is the work of the next chapter.

Contested Social Sovereignty: Welfare States Meet the European Union

From Rescue to Subversion? European Integration and the Nation State after the Crisis

The first OPEC oil shock in 1973 brought the golden age to an unexpected end, precipitating the welfare state into a serious crisis and inaugurating a long and difficult transition towards the new, post-Maastricht 'silver' age of permanent austerity (Pierson 2001; Taylor Gooby 2002). As we saw in Chapter 3, some seeds of change and destructuring had already been planted in the 1950s and 1960s. The emergence of supplementary pension schemes and of the European Community had opened some breaches into both the internal and the external boundaries of social sharing, offering new locality and vocality options to their actors. But these first breaches had not substantially compromised what in historical perspective appears to have been a remarkably solid building. European welfare states thus entered the turbulent 1970s while still enjoying a high degree of domestic autonomy, which had hitherto peacefully coexisted with an international economic order resting on 'embedded liberalism' at the global level (Ruggie 1982) and with a deepening market integration, steered by benevolent supranational authorities, at the regional (i.e. European) level.

The oil price crises of the 1970s and the collapse of the Bretton Woods regime suddenly altered the nature of the international economic order. The oil shock gave rise to the unprecedented phenomenon of 'stagflation', a syndrome of simultaneous cost-push inflation, demand-gap unemployment, and economic stagnation. The breakdown of Bretton Woods uncoupled the liberal logic of the international economy from established institutional constraints and traditional practices, and unleashed a new dynamic of escalating capital mobility and acute monetary instability at the global level. This new economic environment started seriously to jeopardize the viability of the Keynesian welfare state. The rapid growth of offshore capital markets beyond the reach of central banks started to weaken governments' control over national tax bases, while floating exchange rates, increasingly driven by speculative currency transactions, started to exert serious disturbances on critical macroeconomic variables such as inflation or export competitiveness (Scharpf 2000). Under such new conditions, the traditional strategies of fiscal and monetary demand management became increasingly ineffective, if not altogether unviable.

In Europe, the initial response was to mobilize all existing capabilities at both the national and the EC levels, without explicitly questioning that division of labour between the two which, as we have seen, lay at the basis of the original treaties. Thus, efforts were made in Brussels to re-establish some degree of monetary stability through the 'snake' experiment, which at the end of the 1970s led to the creation of the European Monetary System (EMS) (Ludlow 1982). Some (blatantly unsuccessful) attempts were also made to put in place a common energy policy for coping with shortage problems (Streeck 1995). At the domestic level, most governments initially resorted to all the classical tools of Keynesian management and pulled the various levers of the welfare state (especially unemployment subsidies and early retirement benefits) to ease industrial adjustment to the new price conditions. In line with the harmonization philosophy of the treaties, the EC largely supported and accompanied these initiatives: following an ambitious (pre-crisis) Social Action Programme launched by the Commission in 1972, in the second half of the 1970s three directives were approved—on collective redundancies (75/129),[1] the transfer of enterprises (77/187),[2] and company insolvency (80/987)[3]—that were aimed, precisely, at facilitating industrial restructuring and at smoothing its social effects in the hope of replicating the virtuous developments in the coal and steel sectors during the 1950s and 1960s. The same period witnessed an attempt to inaugurate a transnational social dialogue between employers and the unions, in accordance with Treaty recommendations on furthering cooperation between management and labour (Streeck 1995).

In the wake of the second OPEC oil shock in 1979, however, these initiatives not only proved to be ineffective in arresting the economic

[1] Council Directive 75/129/EEC of 17 February 1975 on the approximation of the laws of the member states relating to collective redundancies, *Official Journal L 048*, 22/02/1975, pp. 0029–0030.

[2] Council Directive 77/187/EEC of 14 February 1977 on the approximation of the laws of the member states relating to the safeguarding of employees' rights in the event of transfers of undertakings, businesses or parts of businesses, *Official Journal L 061*, 05/03/1977, pp. 0026–0028.

[3] Council Directive 80/987/EEC of 20 October 1980 on the approximation of the laws of the member states relating to the protection of employees in the event of the insolvency of their employer, *Official Journal L 283*, 28/10/1980, pp. 0023–0027.

crisis, but started to be considered as the wrong kind of answer by increasingly influential epistemic communities with neoliberal leanings on both sides of the Atlantic and by the new conservative governments which had gained office in the UK and the USA (Hall 1986). The old institutional compromise of the 1950s ('Smith abroad, Keynes at home'; market-making to the EC, market correcting to the member states) could not rescue the nation state this time around, certainly not its underlying political economy. The rapid and utter failure of Keynesian reflation and welfare state upgrading attempted by the French government in 1982–3 only served to confirm this (Levy 2000). As politicians said then, 'the party is over'. Or, as social scientists said later, 'Polanyi's great transformation is over' (Cerny 1994: 339).

It is largely against this problematic background that one must interpret the ambitious project of a relaunching of Europe that took shape around the mid-1980s. As is well known, the aim of this project was to complete the internal market within the EC and then move towards a fully-fledged EMU. The project had a magic deadline, 1992: this was the year by which the internal market had to be completed, and it also turned out to be the year of the Maastricht Treaty, which established the criteria and the further deadlines for the creation of EMU. The fundamental diagnosis inspiring this grand relaunching of the integration process was that of 'Eurosclerosis': a complex syndrome of economic decline and institutional stalemate linked to ineffective and ill-designed (under the new circumstances) mixed-economy arrangements and welfare state schemes at the domestic level; insufficient and/or distorted competition as well as persisting barriers to the formation of a truly continental market on a scale similar to that of the USA or Japan, and thus able to promote and sustain rapid and incisive innovation; inadequate policymaking and overall steering capabilities at the supranational level, in order to cope with both intra-European and external interdependencies (Keohane and Hoffmann 1991; Sandholtz and Zysman 1989; Sbragia 1992).

The enhancement of the efficiency of the European market(s) was prioritized as the fundamental step on the path to recovery. This resulted from a double compromise: among European governments interested in beating stagflation, lowering unemployment, and revamping growth and fiscal dividends; and between governments and business, interested in obtaining more favourable conditions for their transactions (Sandholtz and Zysman 1989; Streeck 1995). A quantum leap in terms of economic integration and competition rules and discipline was deemed necessary for fighting Eurosclerosis. But how could the leap be achieved at the politico-institutional level? The answer came almost serendipitously (Streeck 1995): the leap could be achieved through a new regulatory device discovered by the EC legal order, namely, the principle of mutual recognition. Originally applied by the ECJ in the *Dassonville* ruling and then again in the famous *Cassis de Dijon* case, this principle was 'constitutionalized' in the Single European Act (SEA) of 1986, offering an Archimedean point for initiating the whole relaunching project. As we shall see, the completion of the internal market and the principle of mutual recognition have had far-reaching implications for the spatial architecture and politics of the national welfare state, offering fertile ground for the seeds of destructuring already planted in the 1950s and 1960s.

Mutual Recognition and the Challenge of Negative Integration

The unification of territorially closed economies can take various forms, entailing the selective removal of different cross-system boundaries. In a free trade area, tariffs and quotas among the participating national economies are removed, but each national government retains the autonomy to regulate transactions with third countries. Customs unions go one step further in that they remove this autonomy from national governments and assign it to a supranational authority entrusted with negotiating and managing transactions with non-members. A customs union is an open space for its members—at least as far as import duties and restrictions are concerned—but a closed space vis-à-vis the outside. In a common market, non-tariff internal barriers too are removed, that is, all those regulations and practices that discriminate against the goods, services, workers, and capital of other participating countries. Finally, an economic and monetary union removes the ultimate barrier to economic transactions, namely, the national currency and its exchange rate, while still allowing some decentralized fiscal and regulatory discretion.

Even if the bulk of the Rome Treaty was concerned with the establishment of a common market, in the early 1980s the EC was still little more than a mere customs union. Non-tariff barriers were legion, entire sectors of domestic economies (such as services of general interest and national monopolies) were left beyond the reach of foreign penetration or competition, and progress towards harmonization was painstakingly slow, even in those areas for which the Treaty envisaged majority voting. As a matter of fact, after the 'empty chair' crisis of the mid-1960s, the notorious Luxembourg compromise (1966) had institutionalized the unanimity rule as the only acceptable procedure for arriving at common decisions. While it had kept together an institutional framework that could have otherwise easily crumbled, the Luxembourg compromise was also largely responsible for Eurosclerosis, at least in terms of supranational capabilities for performing the EC's institutional mission, let alone for effectively steering the new load of problems caused by the oil crisis and the collapse of embedded liberalism.

Eliminating non-tariff barriers through supranational harmonization (the 'high road', as it were) is, however, only one way of creating a common market. Another strategy is that of simply declaring such barriers invalid by rendering all regulations and practices which are lawful in one member state equally and immediately lawful in all the other member states, bar a hard regulative core which is either harmonized or left to national authorities based on some recognized 'public interest' purpose. This alternative strategy (or 'low road', less visible and less demanding) became serendipitously available in the wake of ECJ jurisprudence, buttressed by that constitutionalization of EC law which was illustrated in Chapter 3.

In the course of the 1970s the ECJ started to address squarely the issue of indirect discrimination, that is, barriers to free movement arising from domestic criteria of differentiation whose effect is similar to that of explicit trade restrictions or nationality requirements. In the *Dassonville*[4] landmark judgement of 1974, the Court ruled that all national rules which directly or indirectly, actually or potentially hamper intra-Community trade in goods were prohibited unless they were necessary to satisfy legitimate public purposes or imperative requirements. In the following years, the ECJ made clear that it reserved for itself the right to adjudicate on such legitimate purposes and imperative requirements, and that it would do so with a systematic bias towards integration. In the famous *Cassis de Dijon* ruling[5] of 1979 it also quietly announced the doctrine of mutual recognition: in the absence of public interest reasons (which only the Court itself can define and recognize) and, provided they were not discriminatory, all national rules regarding market transactions must be considered as equally acceptable. Products marketed under such rules in one member state must be automatically admitted into the markets of all the other member states. In the case under review, the French liqueur *Cassis*, lawfully produced according to French rules on alcoholic content, was to be

---

[4] Case 8/74, *Procureur du Roi* v. *Benoît and Gustave Dassonville* [1974] ECR 837.
[5] Case 120/78, *Rewe-Zentral AG* v. *Bundesmonopolverwaltung für Branntwein* [*Cassis de Dijon* case] [1979] ECR 649.

admitted into the German market even if local rules were different. Germany's claim that such admission would pose public health problems was not accepted by the Court.

The principle of mutual recognition was de facto constitutionalized in the SEA adopted in 1986,[6] which was intended to foster the completion of the internal market by 1992 through the removal of all the remaining non-tariff barriers. The SEA did envisage steps along the high road of supranational harmonization, but only a relatively small number of regulatory standards were to be subject to harmonization; moreover, harmonization could be effected by qualified majority voting. In the spheres and matters outside the scope of supranational harmonization, mutual recognition would be the norm.[7]

Backed by ECJ jurisprudence, the SEA unleashed a momentous dynamic of 'market-making' primarily through measures of negative integration (i.e. the removal of national barriers to economic transactions), accompanied by some measures of positive integration (supranational harmonization) aimed at safeguarding minimal standards and a level playing field. To be sure, the 1992 process did also involve some steps in the opposite (market-correcting or at least market-braking) direction. In the field of gender equality, for example, a number of negative integration measures based on Treaty art. 119 (now 141) struck down national rules and practices discriminating against women.[8] In the field of occupational health and safety, a number of positive integration measures adopted by qualified majority did define and improve workplace social standards across the board (Rhodes 1995). Progress on these two fronts has been considered the only genuine example of social policy federalization within the EU. Streeck (1995), for instance, has spoken of 'encapsulated federalism' in this regard. But, apart from these two areas, '1992' was indeed a huge market-building initiative in a double sense: cross-system boundaries were virtually erased, thus transforming the European market into a single, unified space of transactions; and the institutional buttresses of the market *as such* (i.e. as an arena of transactions competing with other institutional arenas)

---

[6] The Single European Act was signed on 17 February 1986 and came into force on 1 July 1987. See *Official Journal L 169, 29/ 6/ 1987*, p. 1.

[7] Article 19 of the Single European Act added art. 110b to the EEC Treaty (later suppressed by the Amsterdam Treaty). This latter article charged the Commission to draw up an inventory by 1992 of all national provisions pertaining to the establishment and functioning of the internal market that had not been harmonized. The Council would then decide that the provisions in force in a given member state must be recognized as equivalent to those applied by another member state.

[8] Based on art. 119 (EEC, 141 EC or TEC), this process started before the single market project, but accelerated after the SEA. See Barnard (1999) and Caporaso (2003).

were significantly strengthened by conferring on free movement provisions (in particular the free movement of goods) and competition law a supreme status in the EC legal order. As has been noted by Poaires Maduro (1999), the higher constitutional status of these two legal principles has made virtually any public regulation of the market subject to judicial scrutiny and has prompted deregulation at the *domestic* level as well. The goal of promoting access to national markets has gradually evolved into the goal of affirming and upholding 'a general right of access to the market' and to conditions of undistorted competition within domestic economies, as strictly defined by the treaties and interpreted by the ECJ.

In 1988 Jacques Delors, then President of the European Commission, tried to launch an ambitious initiative to create the political and institutional space for a 'social dimension' in the internal market, aimed at establishing a platform of guaranteed social rights as a baseline for national systems and as a mandate for future EC legislation. A 'Charter of Fundamental Social Rights of Workers' was adopted by a (non-binding) solemn declaration in 1988, a new Social Action Programme was subsequently issued by the Commission, and talks between management and labour were resumed with the *Val Duchesse* initiative, aimed at institutionalizing that social dialogue already attempted (but substantially aborted) in the 1970s (Gold 1993). The Commission hoped to redress the pro-market constitutional asymmetry of the EC legal order with significant social provisions to be included in the forthcoming Treaty revision. The compromise reached at Maastricht in 1992, however, took only very modest steps in this direction. While the SEA was wholly incorporated in the new European Union Treaty (TEU), social policy was almost entirely relegated to a separate protocol, from which the UK dissociated itself. Unanimity remained the decision-making procedure for all the most important issues, starting of course with 'social security and the social protection of workers'. A new procedure was created for arriving at directives on labour matters, directly involving the social partners. But the reluctance of the employers (and to some extent also the unions themselves) to engage in supranational dialogue severely limited the actual import and effectiveness of such innovations during the 1990s. As is well known, the Maastricht Treaty set in motion a new process that was to lead from the internal market to a fully-fledged EMU. By setting fixed macroeconomic requirements and deadlines for admission, the Maastricht process imposed further constraints on the autonomy of national governments in the welfare state sphere. Delors' ambitions regarding the social dimension were basically defeated by the 1992 constitutional revision.

The post-1986 context was largely considered in the early debate of the 1990s as a subversive factor for national social contracts. Strong and legally binding market compatibility requirements, the new power of business, the hardening of budgetary constraints and pressure to meet the Maastricht criteria, the impossibility of creating some sort of Social Europe due to the institutional obstacles to positive integration: all these elements were expected to unleash regulatory competition between the member states—especially in the realm of labour and welfare standards—whose inevitable outcome would have been a race to the bottom, a drastic reduction of the level and quality of social protection.[9] Rescued in the 1950s, the national welfare state was now in serious danger of being slowly eroded if not entirely taken apart by the new phase of European integration.

More recent discussions, however, have adopted a much more nuanced view. National social contracts have indeed been destabilized, but not necessarily for the worse: the economic, fiscal, and monetary discipline enforced by supranational authorities has prompted or accelerated a dynamic of welfare state recalibration which was anyway appropriate and desirable for coping with a host of endogenous problems (Ferrera and Rhodes 2000; Ferrera and Hemerick 2003; Martin and Ross 2004); after all, Eurosclerosis was not a straw man invented by a conspiring business and its *comités d'affaires*, but a real syndrome of problems that needed to be addressed. Regulatory competition has indeed taken place, but not necessarily towards the bottom (Scharpf 1999). The Court has not always ruled in favour of the market, but has often upheld those social standards which were the norm in a majority of countries (Poaires Maduro 1998, 1999). And, starting with the Amsterdam Treaty of 1997, a novel phase has gradually emerged in which the newborn EMU is becoming increasingly embedded in a new socially protective (or at least social policy-friendly) institutional environment (Martin and Ross 2004).

The focus of this book is not, however, the general relationship between European integration and social policy, but the spatial architecture of social citizenship and, in particular, the subtle nexus between the configuration of boundaries for social sharing and politico-institutional structuring, as defined in Chapter 1. What can be observed on this critical front? Even though they have not led to a crumbling of national welfare systems, the dynamics of the 1980s and 1990s have indeed significantly altered the boundary configuration of national welfare systems. Moreover, in the rather opaque arenas created by the new constitutionalized EC legal

---

[9] For a review of this debate from a labour law perspective, see Bercusson (1999).

order a very interesting and relevant spatial politics has started to unfold, addressing some fundamental issues that closely concern us: who is the ultimate social sovereign? Who bounds whom? With what bonding effects? It is to these developments that we now turn.

Growth Beyond Limits: From Sovereign to Semi-sovereign Welfare States?

Regulation 1408 of 1971 established a rather elaborate set of rules aimed at making national welfare states compatible with the free circulation of workers and thus permeable to cross-border movements. At the beginning, the goal of the Regulation was 'coordination', that is, the definition at the supranational level of some simple rules for solving two basic issues (Pennings 2001): which laws should prevail in case of conflict between different domestic legal orders? How should each domestic order deal with pertinent facts (such as a period of insured employment or residence) outside its own territory? The first issue was solved through the *lex loci laboris* rule: in case of migration, the applicable legislation is that of the country of work. The second issue was solved through benefit accumulation and benefit exportability rules: all the pertinent facts (in particular, periods of contribution) for maturing an entitlement can be aggregated, regardless of the member state in which they have occurred; once obtained, a benefit can be 'carried' from one member state to another. A fourth basic rule of Regulation 1408 addressed equal treatment: any discrimination on nationality grounds is forbidden.

Soon after its adoption, Regulation 1408 started to undergo increasing 'institutionalization' (Stone Sweet, Fligstein, and Sandhotz 1998). This process had both a strictly formal component, involving legal clarification and articulation, and a more informal one, involving de facto compliance with the rules and practices established by the Regulation (and the ensuing jurisprudence) on the part of all pertinent actors, especially national governments and administrations. From a mere technical instrument for managing legal diversity, the Regulation gradually evolved into a powerful wedge for redefining the boundaries of national social sharing spaces. The scope of coordination extended itself along two distinct dimensions: the coverage dimension, that is, the social groups entitled to cross-border rights (personal scope); and the eligibility dimension, that is, the type of benefits to which such groups are entitled when they move (material scope). On both fronts the general trend has been towards expansion. Originally limited to employees, the personal scope was subsequently extended to the self-employed, to part-time workers, students, various categories of non-economically active persons, and eventually, in 2004, to all EU persons regardless of their employment status. The expansion of the material scope has been less comprehensive and more controversial (as will be shown later); but important additions have been made on this front too, with regard not only to statutory social security benefits (such as benefits for civil servants, pre-retirement pensions, or long-term care benefits), but also supplementary ones (such as supplementary pensions).[10]

The development of the EU regime on social security coordination can be read as a new chapter in the long-term process of the expansion of social rights: to rehearse a well-known metaphor (Flora 1986–87), it can be read as a new phase of 'growth beyond limits', that is, of coverage and eligibility extensions beyond the limits of the domestic territory and beyond the reach of the nation state. This new phase has assumed, however, a second and less benevolent face. Interacting with the strengthening of the four freedoms and of EU competition law, the coordination regime has in fact started to pose increasingly serious challenges to the institutional foundations of social protection as such, that is, its underlying 'closure' rules and practices.

In a well-known study on the EU and national social policy, Leibfried and Pierson (1995) have suggested an articulated diagnosis about the declining sovereignty (in their terms, 'legal authority') and autonomy (i.e. de facto capacity to act) of the member states' social protection systems, in the wake of increasingly stringent 'market compatibility requirements'. More specifically, according to these authors the expansion of EU laws and regulations, included Court rulings, has gradually eroded:

1. *National control over beneficiaries.* In compliance with the free movement of workers or persons, member states can no longer restrict welfare state access to their own citizens. Nationals of other EU countries must be automatically admitted too.

2. *Spatial control over consumption.* On the one hand, benefits (such as pensions) paid by each member state have become portable across the whole internal market. On the other hand, the insured of a given national system can increasingly shop around and consume services (like health care) of other EU systems—the so-called passive freedom of service.

---

[10] For a full discussion of developments on the personal and material scope of Regulation 1408, in the wider context of free movement provisions, see especially Sindbjerg Martinsen (2004) (from a mainly political science perspective) and Van der Mei (2003) (from a mainly legal perspective).

3. *Exclusivity of coverage within the national territory.* Member states are increasingly obliged to accept the 'infiltration' into their territory of other countries' regimes. The most emblematic case relates to the so-called posted workers, that is, workers employed in country X who are temporarily sent to work in country Y while remaining under the jurisdiction of the country of employment. The legal position of posted workers was defined by art. 14 of the 1971 Regulation and by a Commission decision of 1996.[11]

4. *Control over access to the status of benefit producer.* In compliance with the active freedom of service, states must grant access to foreign providers into some areas of their national welfare systems (e.g. in the case of supplementary, 'second pillar' insurance, or in the case of health care services.).

5. *Control over administrative case adjudication.* Member states must in fact accept that the determination of beneficiary status (e.g. of being 'sick' or 'disabled') be carried out by the bureaucratic agencies of other member states.

As a consequence of these processes, European welfare states have witnessed an increasing erosion of their external boundaries and of their capacity to control them. On the demand side, exit options from national systems have expanded for an increasing number of social groups, in parallel with new entry options into the systems of other countries. On the supply side, the jurisdiction of a national regime has been extended outside its borders in certain cases, national providers can enter the membership spaces of other states, and, more generally, national authorities have seen their capacity to regulate and control being restricted. All these changes have essentially transformed European welfare states from sovereign to *semi*-sovereign entities, irreversibly embedded in an institutional framework characterized by a systematic pro-market bias and by the opacity of a Court-led decision-making process.

Leibfried and Pierson (1995) have offered a valuable analytical grid for ordering factual developments, and their diagnosis about a growing and unusually tight nexus between the Single European Market and social policy during the 1980s and 1990s can hardly be questioned. But for our purposes the nature and implications of the new 'semi-sovereign'

---

[11] Decision No. 162 of 31 May 1996 concerning the interpretation of Articles 14 and 14b of Council Regulation (EEC) No. 1408/71 on the legislation applicable to posted workers, *Official Journal L 241*, 21/09/1996, pp. 0028–0030. See also n. 50 below.

condition of domestic welfare states need to be further investigated and qualified. The crucial aspect to be assessed is less what national welfare states have surrendered to the internal market (the 'lost half' of semi-sovereignty, as it were) than what they have been able to preserve in terms of boundary control (the remaining half). Has negative integration (and especially the rulings of the ECJ acting as 'market police') structurally undermined the institutional foundations of national social sharing, or do such foundations still underpin member state control? Are there significant variations across different policy areas and across different pillars of provision? And have some areas already reached critical thresholds beyond which boundary maintenance on the part of the state becomes impossible or irrelevant?

As noted by Rokkan, in modern European history the appearance of boundary transcendence options (generally stemming from the expansion of markets) has tended to provoke boundary maintaining countermoves on the part of state-building (or state-keeping) elites. The last thirty years of social policy development have been no exception. Member states have not acquiesced without resistance in the erosion of their social sovereignty flowing from the increasing institutionalization of the four freedoms and competition rules within the EU legal order.[12] National governments and administrations have tried to contain the scope of supranational coordination and to fence off, in general, the public and compulsory nature of their social insurance systems against the forces of competition and the logic of the market.

The tug of war around supranational coordination has affected both the material and the personal scope of Regulation 1408/71 and, more generally, of free movement provisions.[13] Controversies have revolved, in other words, around the crucial issue: which social benefits for whom? This has been the fundamental issue throughout the history of the national welfare state, so it is not at all surprising that it has surfaced again—with all its potential to generate conflict—in the novel evolutionary juncture of this institution, that is, its encounter with European integration.

While basically accepting (after the adoption of the 1971 Regulation) the neutralization of the territoriality principle for employment-related entitlements (as far as the material scope was concerned) and for workers

---

[12] As recognized also by Leibfried and Pierson (2000: 279).

[13] Regulation 1408/71 has given rise to an increasing stream of judicial litigation (338 ECJ rulings between 1971 and 2002) and has witnessed twenty-nine amendments in the same period (Sindbjerg Martinsen 2004).

(personal scope), member states have concentrated their defence efforts in four narrower but crucial aspects of their national social sharing systems: (*a*) the boundaries of their health care systems; (*b*) the boundaries of their social assistance schemes; (*c*) the boundaries of their social protection systems vis-à-vis the so-called 'third country nationals', that is, persons without member state—and thus EU—citizenship; and, last but not least, (*d*) the right of 'bounding' as such in the field of social insurance (and in particular the issues of compulsory membership and public monopoly).[14] Why these four aspects? Health care and social assistance were less directly related to employment and to the free circulation of workers; the maintenance of national prerogatives could be more easily defended on both doctrinal and practical grounds. These two sectors are also very sensitive to free movement, organizationally and/or symbolically. The status of non-EU migrants raised in its turn fundamental questions about belonging, identity, and solidarity: member states were not prepared to delegate to supranational authorities control over such fundamental questions, considering also the weak Treaty base for EC action in the field. Finally, compulsory membership and public monopoly were quintessential ingredients of national social insurance systems: thus, fighting for their preservation was almost a question of survival.

The next sections of this chapter offer a summary reconstruction of developments on these four fronts. We first deal with compulsory health care insurance and show how the four freedoms and subsequently competition law have affected this sector, and how national countermoves have been substantially combated by supranational authorities, paving the way for the formation of an internal market in health care services. We then turn to social assistance; developments in this sector have largely paralleled those of health care, but with more effective countermoves on the part of national governments and the maintenance of at least some 'bounding' prerogatives. The subsequent section reconstructs the challenge of extending the personal scope to third-country nationals: a story that shows the growing boundary-building ambitions of the EU, but also the capacity of national authorities to retain important gate-keeping functions. Finally, we deal with possibly the most crucial issue: the challenge posed by the freedom of service and competition rules on the very 'right to

---

[14] Legal disputes on social security issues have, of course, affected the whole range of benefits, including unemployment benefits, family benefits, and work accident compensation. For an excellent and detailed reconstruction and analytical discussion of the institutionalization of Reg. 1408/71, see Sindbjerg Martinsen (2004).

bound' on the part of the nation state, that is, the extent to which the new EU regulatory regime is still compatible with the maintenance of national (and public) social insurance monopolies. These four factual reconstructions have two main objectives. The first is to trace the most critical changes in the national, cross-national, and supranational components of the new spatial architecture of social citizenship after more than three decades of institutional contention since the approval of Regulation 1408/71 and almost two decades since the SEA came into force. The second objective is to capture the new patterns of politics that have emerged from this process of institutional reconfiguration: a novel spatial politics in which the increased locality and vocality options available to actors have generated new interests and new strategies around the production and maintenance of social rights. The identification of the changed spatial architecture and the emerging politics of social sharing in the EU will provide us with the key empirical information for addressing (Chapter 6) the relationship between 'rebounding' and 'restructuring' European social protection.

Health Care and the Challenge of Cross-border Mobility

Health care systems developed somewhat later than pension systems in most European countries and at a slower pace. Their aggregate economic size has also remained significantly smaller. As shown in Tables 2.1 and 2.2, extensions in health care coverage tended to follow rather than precede pension coverage reforms. And as shown in Table 4.1, public spending on health has grown more slowly and still absorbs a share of GDP that is only about a half of that absorbed by pensions. Nevertheless, health care is the second largest area of European social protection.

In this sector too a great divide can be observed between universalistic and occupational systems. The health care literature (Altenstetter and Björkman 1997; Freeman 2000; Immergut 1992; OECD 1994; Powell and Wessen 1999; Saltman and Figueras 1997) often distinguishes between two basic types of institutional design: (*a*) the national health service (NHS) design, where coverage is universal, all residents are entitled to the same range and type of benefits and services, funding is tax-based, and organization is unified; and (*b*) the social insurance design, where coverage is linked to labour market participation and/or membership of schemes tailored to specific categories, benefits and services can differ from one scheme to the other, funding is based on contributions or premiums, and organization is scheme-specific. Table 4.2 classifies the public health

Table 4.1 Public health and pension expenditures as percentages of GDP, 1980–2000

Country	Health					Pensions [1]				
	1980	1985	1990	1995	2000	1980	1985	1990	1995	2000
Austria	5.3	5.0	5.2	6.2	5.6	13.0	14.1	14.0	15.1	12.1
Belgium	5.4	5.9	6.6	6.1	6.2	11.3	12.1	10.5	11.2	10.6
Denmark	8.0	7.4	7.0	6.8	6.8	7.7	7.3	8.0	9.4	8.1
Finland	5.0	5.6	6.4	5.7	5.0	8.3	10.2	10.4	12.5	9.3
France	5.8	6.4	6.7	7.5	7.2	10.5	11.8	12.0	13.0	12.9
Germany	6.0	6.2	5.9	8.0	8.0	10.3	10.2	9.7	11.7	11.7
Greece	3.7	5.1	4.7	4.8	4.6	7.0	11.5	12.6	11.9	9.8
Ireland	6.8	5.8	4.8	5.3	5.1	5.8	6.3	5.7	5.2	3.0
Italy	5.7	5.4	6.3	5.3	5.9	10.1	12.6	15.1	15.9	14.6
Luxembourg	5.5	5.2	5.7	5.8	5.6	13.0	12.4	11.0	11.7	9.7
Netherlands	5.6	5.6	5.7	6.4	5.5	12.0	11.7	13.0	11.4	12.2
Portugal	3.6	3.4	4.1	5.1	5.8	6.3	7.3	7.1	8.9	11.0
Spain	4.3	4.4	5.2	5.5	5.4	7.4	9.0	9.3	10.4	9.6
Sweden	8.5	7.9	7.6	6.9	6.6	9.2	9.8	9.9	11.0	11.8
UK	4.9	4.9	5.0	5.8	5.9	7.8	8.4	11.0	13.4	11.9
EU 15 Average	5.6	5.6	5.8	6.1	5.9	9.3	10.3	10.6	11.5	10.5

[1]Pension expenditure includes old-age, disability, and survivors' cash benefits.

Source: OECD (2003); OECD, *Social Expenditure Database* (http://www.oecd.org).

Table 4.2 European public health systems: an institutional classification

System type			
National Health Service		Social insurance	
Centralized	Decentralized	Reimbursement	Direct provision
UK	Denmark	France	Germany
Ireland	Sweden	Belgium	Austria
	Finland	Luxembourg	Netherlands
	Italy		
	Spain		

systems of the EU in the two groups, highlighting two further significant distinctions. It subdivides the NHS group into the more centralized systems of the UK and Ireland and the more decentralized Nordic and south European systems.[15] It subdivides the social insurance group into those systems that serve essentially as a 'third party' by reimbursing patients (or hospitals, in case of inpatient services) the expenses they bear directly for their health care needs, and those systems that tend to operate as direct providers by bearing directly the cost of benefits and services.[16]

The territoriality principle (i.e. the tight coupling of 'belonging' with 'options', i.e. the inclusion in a given territorial community, and entitlement to its sharing arrangements) has always played a significant role in the field of health care. Here, sharing involves not impersonal cash transfers but direct relationships between claimants and providers: membership markers not only are a matter of administrative verification but acquire a personal, interactive significance. Hospitals remained primarily local institutions, deeply rooted in the surrounding territory well into the 1950s, and started to be considered as elements of the national welfare state (especially at the symbolic level) only in the 1960s and 1970s. As we shall see in Chapter 5, a trend towards the relocalization of health care institutions can be observed in many countries.

As in transfer schemes, so in health care territorial closure serves to uphold compulsory inclusion and broad risk-sharing—with all the associated advantages. But in this area it serves other important purposes too. Most prominently it allows direct national control over quality and appropriate standards of service—through what Leibfried and Pierson call control over access to the status of provider, or through monitoring procedures—as well as national planning of service capacity. If a pension is 'consumed' abroad, it does not make much of a difference to a national pension scheme, nor does the payment of n additional pensions to non-nationals provided they pay the corresponding contributions or taxes. But a health care system has to organize provision throughout the national territory within constrained budgets that are heavily dependent on medical costs. Planning and managing a national network of medical facilities (hospitals in particular) is no easy task. Free cross-boundary movements of patients and providers (especially if such movements should grow to a

---

[15] The table does not include the health care systems of Portugal and Greece. These countries have formally introduced national health services, but these still co-exist with occupational health funds (Guillen 2002).

[16] In both subgroups, however, health insurance schemes (or 'funds') stipulate contracts with providers (hospitals, the medical professions) regarding the costs, conditions, and even volume of provision.

large size) risk undermining national policies of capacity—and cost-management.

The 1971 Regulation included a chapter on sickness benefits, covering both cash transfers and medical treatment. In this latter field, however, given the risks just mentioned, the coordination regime was tuned in a very conservative way (Bosco 2000; McKee, Mossialos, and Belcher 1996; Mossialos et al. 2001; Van der Mei 2003). Apart from transfrontier workers and emergency care for temporary residents, patients seeking care abroad had to secure prior authorization by competent national authorities (e.g. the relevant health insurance fund or the NHS administration): a filter that had been dismantled by the 1971 Regulation in the case of cash transfers. In the case of authorized cross-border movements of patients, financial burdens would be borne by the home country and treatment would be supplied according to the standards and costs of the providing country. Even if the Regulation was somewhat ambiguous on the point, it was assumed that authorization would be given only for those treatments that were eligible within the authorizing scheme and that the latter could exercise a significant degree of discretion, especially in medical and financial terms.

The principle of authorization was, however, challenged rather early, towards the end of the 1970s. Two rulings of the Court, in 1978 (*Pierik I*)[17] and 1979 (*Pierik II*),[18] opened a serious breach. They found that authorization for treatment abroad was always to be granted when the treatment in question could not be given to the interested party in the territory of the member state in which he or she lived—irrespective, that is, of the coverage rules of any relevant insurance scheme and of financial considerations. This decision risked opening up a syndrome of Continental 'regime shopping' for the best (and most costly) treatments, with uncontrollable consequences for national systems. Thus, the member states reacted swiftly to these judgments and in 1981 forced a restrictive amendment of the Regulation[19] (Bosco 2000; Van der Mei 2003: 256). Despite the 'joint decision trap'—unanimity was required for amendments—national governments were able to agree at the supranational level on blocking a Court-led stream of negative integration, which they saw as potentially undermining their social sovereignty. The amendment not only con-

---

[17] Case 117/77, *Bestuur van het Algemeen Ziekenfonds Drenthe-Platteland* v. *G. Pierik* [1978] ECR 825.

[18] Case 182/78, *Bestuur van het Algemeen Ziekenfonds Drenthe-Platteland* v. *G. Pierik* [1979] ECR 1977.

[19] Council Regulation (EEC) No 2793/81 of 17 September 1981 amending Regulation (EEC) No 1408/71 on the application of social security schemes to employed persons and their families moving within the Community, and Regulation (EEC) No 574/72 fixing the procedure for implementing Regulation (EEC) No 1408/71, *Official Journal L* 275, 29/09/1981, pp. 0001–0014.

firmed the need for discretionary authorization (on both administrative and medical grounds) but reaffirmed the principle that only treatments already included in the health care package of the national system of affiliation could receive such authorization. In other words, national welfare institutions reasserted control over eligible benefits, even if their actual consumption could be authorized abroad.

Thanks to the amended Regulation and its authorization filter, cross-country patient mobility remained a relatively limited phenomenon well into the 1990s. The completion of the single market, however, brought new problems, centred not just on the principle of free movement but rather on the new EU competition regime as a whole.

To begin with, the completion of the single market did affect some 'boundary' aspects of the health care area in general, not only with respect to medical equipment and, to some extent, pharmaceuticals, but most prominently with respect to the free movement of medical professionals (in the wake of the 1989 directive on the mutual recognition of diplomas)[20] and the freedom of all suppliers, including hospitals and private insurers, to provide services in any member state.[21] As we shall see, the liberalization of the insurance market in both the life and the non-life sectors is bound to have a significant destructuring potential for the second and third pillars of national social protection, including health care. But the post-SEA competition regime has offered new leverage for challenging again (and from a different perspective) the authorization prerogatives of national governments, and thus for pursuing new strategies of 'vocal exit' from domestic consumption.[22]

The whole issue of patient mobility was in fact reopened at the end of the 1990s, again as a consequence of supranational jurisprudence. In the *Decker* case,[23] regarding the purchase of a pair of spectacles in Belgium by a person insured in Luxembourg, the Court ruled that the refusal of Mr Decker's fund to reimburse the purchase was in breach of the principle of the free circulation of goods. In the *Kohll* case,[24] regarding orthodontic

---

[20] Council Directive 89/48/EEC of 21 December 1988 on a general system for the recognition of higher-education diplomas awarded on completion of professional education and training of at least three years' duration, *Official Journal L 019*, 24/01/1989, p. 0016–0023.

[21] See Van der Mei (2003) and Mossialos et al. (2001) for a full account and discussion of such developments. For an interesting general discussion on European integration and health policy, see Lamping (2003).

[22] The exit is 'vocal' because it is accompanied and indeed made possible by an act of voice against national authorities; exit is only partial, because financial compensation is paid by home authorities.

[23] Case C-120/95, *Nicolas Decker* v. *Caisse de maladie des employés privés* [1998] ECR I-01831.

[24] Case C-158/96, *Raymond Kohll* v. *Union des caisses de maladie* [1998] ECR I-01931.

treatment sought in Germany, again by a person insured in Luxembourg, the Court ruled that the refusal to reimburse was in breach of the principle of the freedom of service. In both cases the Court argued (*a*) that member states do have the right to organize their health care systems as they like; (*b*) that nonetheless public provisions in this field are not exempt from the basic principle of free movement; (*c*) that the principle of prior authorization to seek treatment in another country under the rules of that country does not prevent reimbursement at the tariffs that apply to the same treatment in the country of insurance; (*d*) that the principle of prior authorization penalizes service providers established in other member states; and (*e*) that the requirement of prior authorization (and a fortiori its denial) can be invoked only when there is a serious threat to the finances of the domestic scheme or for reasons related to public health (AIM 2000).

Since most member states had backed the stance of the Luxembourg government, the *Decker* and *Kohll* rulings provoked harsh and negative reactions around Europe. The implications of the rulings went beyond not only the specific cases in question but also the 1971 Regulation itself. As a matter of fact they have opened an alternative channel of exit to that envisaged by the Regulation: according to the Court, based on EC competition law (and thus the treaties directly), a patient can seek *unauthorized* treatments abroad and then be reimbursed at the rates foreseen by the *home* country (rather than those of the providing country, as laid down by the Regulation) if the treatment in question is covered by the insurance scheme to which the patient belongs. The vocabulary of Figure 1.3 may seem inappropriate to judicial contexts, but it is as if European patients are allowed to 'sneak out' of their schemes of affiliation, without giving notice, and then re-enter them and 'voice' for compensation.

Three subsequent rulings have widened the breach opened by the *Decker* and *Kohll* cases. In the *Smits-Peerbooms* and *Vanbraekel* cases of 2001,[25] the Court made it clear that the alternative channel was not restricted to outpatient benefits and did not concern only those health systems based on *ex post* reimbursement (see Table 4.2): it can apply to inpatient treatments as well (and thus to high-cost hospital care) and does affect all health systems equally. As for the instrument of authorization, the 2001 rulings have further qualified the conditions for its legitimate use by

---

[25] Case C-157/99, *B.S.M. Geraets-Smits v. Stichting Ziekenfonds VGZ and H.T.M. Peerbooms v. Stichting CZ Groep Zorgverzekeringen* [2001] ECR I-05473 ; Case C-368/98, *Abdon Vanbraekel and Others v. Alliance nationale des mutualités chrétiennes (ANMC)* [2001] ECR I-05363.

national authorities. Authorization can be denied only if there are proven reasons of general interests (serious financial imbalances, public health threats, or threats to the maintenance of 'a balanced medical and hospital service open to all'), based on fair, transparent, objective, and justiciable criteria. In the *Vanbrakel* ruling, the ECJ even went so far as to criticize the autonomy and professional discretion of national medical communities as potential barriers to freedom of service, while suggesting (in *Smits-Peerbooms*) that decisions about what is considered usual and appropriate within professional circles must be based on norms that are 'sufficiently tried and tested by international medical science'. The third ruling of 2003 (*Mueller-Fauré* and *Van Riet*)[26] established in its turn that authorization is not necessary for non-hospital treatments, thus paving the way for the creation of an internal market for this type of benefit (Sindbjerg Martinsen 2004).

This last generation of ECJ rulings has not only severely restricted the discretion of national authorities in shaping their authorization policy, but also widened, as mentioned, the range of (vocal) exit options beyond those envisaged by the 1971 coordination regime. Greater cross-border flows of patients are not the only possible effect of this new regulatory context—and possibly not the most disruptive of the status quo. Indeed, the number of 'moving' patients seems to be on the rise in many countries: in Italy since 1997 there has been an annual increase of 4 per cent. But the overall impact on public spending is still very modest: only about 0.5 per cent of total public expenditure is absorbed by treatments abroad (Mossialos et al. 2001). The greater impact of the new rules could be felt on the internal organization and politics of national health services. In most EU countries the 1990s witnessed a trend towards a separation of purchasers and providers, the establishment of contractual relations and quasi-markets even within the sphere of public insurance and provision. The new EC regulatory context could pose two problematic challenges in this respect: a forced opening of national contracting arrangements and quasi-markets to all EU health care providers, and a forced redrawing of the domestic boundaries between state and market in the health sphere, scrapping traditional advantages or protections for non-market actors and institutions.[27] Already in the 1990s private providers in Italy and Belgium challenged the special status of non-profit organization in the

---

[26] Case C-385/99, *V.G. Müller-Fauré v. Onderlinge Waarborgmaatschappij OZ Zorgverzekeringen UA and E.E.M. van Riet v. Onderlinge Waarborgmaatschappij ZAO Zorgverzekeringen* [2003] ECR I-04509.

[27] These issues will be discussed in more depth in Chapter 6.

field of state-funded services for the elderly.[28] The ECJ has ruled against the plaintiffs; but the doctrine might soon develop in a more market-oriented direction (Winterstein 1999).

The member states seem well aware of these challenges and a number of joint initiatives have been launched in the wake of the ECJ rulings with a view to outlining a new strategy of action.[29] Only four countries (Luxembourg, Belgium, Denmark, and Finland) have explicitly modified their administrative rules on authorization and reimbursement to comply with ECJ jurisprudence. The tug of war on boundary control in the health care field is still far from decided.

Social Assistance and the Residence Issue

As mentioned in Chapter 2, the modern welfare state emerged out of a long-standing tradition of localized and discretionary poor relief or 'public/social assistance', codified in northern Europe in specific poor laws. With the birth, consolidation, and expansion of social insurance (whether of the universalistic, 'Beveridgean' sort or the occupational, 'Bismarckian' sort), traditional ad hoc public relief interventions gradually lost functional and financial salience in most European countries, especially during the *Trente Glorieuses*. Between the 1960s and 1970s, however, a new generation of social assistance schemes and benefits made an appearance, with two main objectives: to fill the gaps in coverage at the margins of existing social insurance programmes, in particular for some categories of people and for some (new) types of need; and to establish a safety net of last resort for the whole citizenry, through which nobody would be allowed to fall.

The poor elderly were among the first category to be targeted by this new generation of policies. In most occupational systems social pensions were introduced, open to all the elderly who could not access ordinary, insurance-based benefits. France introduced special old-age pensions for the poor elderly in 1956, Italy and Belgium in 1969, Portugal in 1980, and Spain in 1988.[30] The long-term unemployed, the disabled with special

---

[28] Case C-70/95, *Sodemare SA, Anni Azzurri Holding SpA and Anni Azzurri Rezzato Srl v. Regione Lombardia* [1997] ECR I-03395.

[29] See Mossialos et al. (2001). In 2002 the European Commission circulated a questionnaire among the member states asking what their reactions were to, and what steps they were planning in the wake of, the recent ECJ jurisprudence and the requirement to adjust national laws and practices to single market rules. See EC (2004a).

[30] In all the other Bismarckian countries the challenge of poverty in old age was met via general assistance schemes.

Table 4.3   Minimum income schemes in EU countries

Country	Scheme	Year of introduction/major reform
Austria	Sozialhilfe	Varies according to *Land*
Belgium	Minimex	1974
Denmark	Social Bistand	1974, 1997
Finland	Toimeentulotuki	1997
France	Revenu Minimum d'Insertion	1988,1992
Germany	Sozialhilfe	1961,1996
Ireland	Supplementary Welfare/Allowance	1975,1993
Italy	Reddito Minimo d'Inserimento	1998 (experimental)
Luxembourg	Revenu Minimum Garanti	1986, 1999
Netherlands	Algemeene Bijstand	1996
Portugal	Rendimento Minimo Garantido	1996, 1997
Spain	Ingreso minimo de insercion (renta minima)	Varies according to region
Sweden	Socialbidrag	1982
UK	Income Support	1948, 1978, 1992

Source: MISSOC (2004).

needs, lone mothers, and needy students are other prominent social groups for which schemes of social assistance have been set up in various countries. As for the general safety net, the UK pioneered developments in this area by establishing a so-called National Assistance scheme in 1948 (subsequently renamed Income Support). As shown in Table 4.3, all EU member states except Greece introduced some sort of minimum income guarantee between the 1960s and 1990s.[31]

These 'new' assistance schemes do exhibit some of the traits of social insurance. Claimants have subjective rights, disciplined by codified legislation. Benefit agencies (which in some cases are also the agencies administering social insurance) can exert discretion only within the limits set by laws and administrative decisions that are justiciable. On the other hand, unlike social insurance, such schemes are typically tax-based, there is no explicit link between their levels of benefit and (past) actual financial contributions, they rest on some verification of economic need (through the so-called means test), and, especially in recent years, they have been

---

[31] The Italian minimum income scheme of 1998 was introduced on an experimental basis in a small number of municipalities and extended to a greater number in 2001. The Berlusconi government elected in 2001 has, however, decided to discontinue the experiment, fully devolving responsibility in this field to the regions (Sacchi and Bastagli 2005).

accompanied by some degree of conditionality for those who are able to work and/or participate in 'activation' programmes.

The economic significance of need-based, means-tested, non-contributory, and tax-funded transfers increased in all EU countries throughout the 1980s and 1990s. According Eurostat calculations, means-tested benefits absorbed 9.8 per cent of social protection expenditure in 2000 (EC and Eurostat 2003a). Such a trend has raised awareness in national debates about both the budgetary and the equity implications of this policy area, which in some countries has acquired a novel institutional and symbolic distinctiveness (e.g. as *assistenza sociale* in Italy or *solidarité nationale* in France). Proposals and initiatives were also launched in the 1990s with a view to assigning or relocating to this area some programmes (or hidden functions) traditionally included within social insurance, such as supplements to low contributory pensions.

Article 4 of the 1971 Regulation excluded 'social assistance' from the material scope of the coordination regime. The rationale behind such provision was that the free movement of workers required the portability of work-related entitlements, but not necessarily the neutralization of the territoriality principle for social rights unrelated to work (and contributions). Not surprisingly, member states wanted to reserve these rights to their own citizens. The sphere of 'asymmetrical' solidarity (i.e. public support based purely on need considerations) presupposes in fact those ties of 'we-ness' that typically bind the members of a national community—and them only. As a matter of fact, the 'guest worker' regimes that operated in the 1950s and 1960s (most typically in Germany) envisaged some sort of reverse solidarity: legal immigrants were required to pay taxes on their earnings, and thus partly to contribute to the financing of national assistance programmes; but in case of economic need they had no entitlements and actually faced the risk of expulsion.[32] Besides financial (and political) worries, member states also faced administrative complications regarding free movement in this field of social protection, given the presence of means-test and conditionality requirements and given the sensitivity of benefit levels to national (and even regional) living standards.

Since the 1971 Regulation did not provide a clear-cut definition of social assistance, responsibility for drawing distinctions fell to the ECJ, which from the very beginning adopted an expansionary orientation aimed at

---

[32] Under a 1953 European Convention on social and medical assistance, guest workers could be eligible for medical benefits and also for assistance subsidies—the latter, however, only after a minimum of five years of residence (ten for those above fifty-five years of age) and only as long as they had a valid residence permit, which was always temporary.

subsuming most of the controversial cases under the notion of social security (as opposed to social assistance) and thus within the scope of coordination. The landmark ruling on this front was the *Frilli* case[33] in 1972, in which the Court ruled that, whenever the claimant had a legally defined position which gave him or her an enforceable right to the benefit—with no discretionary powers on the part of the granting administration—the benefit could not be treated as social assistance by national authorities. This ruling gave non-nationals access to most of those 'social minima' linked to citizenship (typically social pensions) mentioned earlier. Other rulings in the 1980s went even further by making these benefits exportable from the country of payment to the country of (new) residence. The *Piscitello* case[34] of 1983 dealt with the refusal of the Italian authorities to pay a social pension to a poor elderly person who had moved to Belgium. The *Giletti et al.* case[35] of 1987 dealt with the refusal of French authorities to pay a means-tested pension to Italian migrants who had returned home. In both cases the ECJ upheld the exportability of benefits. The second case made more impact, since in its wake French taxpayers were de facto subsidizing some poor elderly people in Italy's Mezzogiorno.

Again, the ECJ's activism in striking down national boundaries in such a delicate area provoked member state reactions, especially regarding the link between residence and eligibility. France refused to implement the Court rulings on exportability, and the Commission opened an infringement procedure against it (Van der Mei 2003: 154 ff.). Fearful of having to subsidize foreign elderly people leaving its territory, Germany abandoned a planned establishment of a minimum old-age pension, distinct from its social-assistance guaranteed income (Conant 2001; Leibfried and Pierson 2000). At the same time, the Commission drafted a proposal to amend the 1971 Regulation in this respect. As in the case of health care, supranational agreement was eventually reached—despite the joint-decision trap—in order to regain some national control over territorial boundaries. In 1992, Regulation no. 1247 was adopted,[36] which inserted a specific coordination

---

[33] Case 1–72, *Rita Frilli v. Belgian State* [1972] ECR 457.

[34] Case 139/82, *Paola Piscitello v. Istituto nazionale della previdenza sociale (INPS)* [1983] ECR 1427.

[35] Joined cases 379, 380, 381/85, and 93/86, *Caisse régionale d'assurance maladie Rhône-Alpes v. Anna Giletti, Directeur régional des affaires sanitaires et sociales de Lorraine v. Domenico Giardini, Caisse régionale d'assurance maladie du Nord-Est v. Feliciano Tampan,* and *Severino Severini v. Caisse primaire centrale d'assurance maladie* [1987] ECR 955.

[36] Council Regulation (EEC) No 1247/92 of 30 April 1992 amending Regulation (EEC) No 1408/71 on the application of social security schemes to employed persons, to self-employed persons and to members of their families moving within the Community, *Official Journal L 136,* 19/05/1992, pp. 0001–0006.

mechanism for non-contributory 'mixed' cash benefits into Regulation no. 1408/71. The two main novelties were: (*a*) the principle that such benefits, though regarded as social security benefits, shall be granted exclusively in the territory of the member state in which the beneficiary resides; and (*b*) the inclusion of a positive list (amendable) of benefits for each country as a prerequisite for imposing residence requirements. In other words, nationals of other EU member states can claim the social assistance subsidies included in the list, but in the first place they must be legal residents in the host state; and second, they must 'consume' the benefit in the latter's territory, abiding by the conditionality requirements attached to such benefit (such as work availability). The 1992 Regulation made no reference to in-kind benefits. But when Germany tried to disguise a new benefit for long-term care introduced in 1994 as a benefit in kind, the ECJ promptly intervened to block any manipulatory attempts at legal pre-emption.[37]

In this new regulatory framework, the line of defence by national systems thus shifted to control over rules of residence. While the various European treaties are based on the principle of free circulation of *workers*, member states have maintained some important prerogatives in deciding which *non-workers* can legally reside in their territory. Family members do have residence (and benefit) rights and so do persons looking for a job, but only if these persons are in receipt of an unemployment benefit from the country of last employment and only for up to three months if they move to a different country. Residence eligibility for all other kinds of non-workers (e.g. students, pensioners, and the unsubsidized unemployed) remained highly contentious until the early 1990s. Already in the 1970s the ECJ started to uphold the free movement of persons based on freedom of service, protected by the EC Treaty. In 1979 the Commission presented to the Council a directive proposal for establishing a general right of residence, even though conditional upon proof of sufficient resources. This proposal provoked a veritable avalanche of objections by the member states (Sindbjerg Martinsen 2004). In 1984, however, the ECJ offered a clear and systematic formulation of the doctrine of passive freedom of service in

---

[37] Case C-160/96, *Manfred Molenaar and Barbara Fath-Molenaar v. Allgemeine Ortskrankenkasse Baden-Württemberg* [1998] ECR I-00843. The Court confirmed this doctrine in the subsequent *Jauch* case (Case C-215/99, *Friedrich Jauch v. Pensionsversicherungsanstalt der Arbeiter* [2001] ECR I-01901), concerning the Austrian long-term care allowance. In this latter case (as well as in *Leclere*: Case C-43/99, *Ghislain Leclere and Alina Deaconescu v. Caisse nationale des prestations familiales* [2001] ECR I-04265) the Court has also started to question the criteria used by member states for including special non-contributory benefits in the Regulation Appendix (see Sindbjerg Martinsen 2004 for a more detailed discussion).

Luisi Carbone (1984).[38] According to the Luxembourg judges, all EC nationals have a right to travel with a view to receiving (and not only providing) services. In 1990 three directives (nos. 90/364, 90/365, and 90/336)[39] established the right of residence for students, pensioners, and all 'other' non-economically active persons; but the preamble of all three directives clearly states that claimants must not represent an 'unreasonable burden' on the public finances of the member states. These acts thus allow national authorities to apply a sort of 'affluence test': would-be residents must give evidence that they have resources in excess of the income thresholds for social assistance benefits, so discouraging 'social tourism' in search of benefits.

As it did for the notion of employment, the ECJ has taken steps towards defining a Community concept of residence, directly linked to the treaties and to the principles of EU citizenship (Mabbet and Bolderson 2000). In the *Swaddling* case,[40] for example, the Court said that the meaning of residence could not be adapted to suit the unilateral and uncoordinated preferences of the various national systems, while in the *Martínez Sala* case[41] the Court went very close to recognizing the right of a Spanish citizen to the German tax-financed child allowance based purely on her status as an EU citizen. In the *Grzelczyk* case (2001)[42] the ECJ took two further steps. In the first place, it found that the treaties offered a sufficient basis for prohibiting member states from denying any social assistance benefits to lawfully resident EC nationals; the only power they had was that of performing the 'affluence test' before immigration or not to renew the residence card when it expired. This goes definitely beyond the 1971 and 1992 Regulations to the extent that it recognizes social assistance entitlements directly based on Treaty provisions—a development similar to that witnessed in the field of medical treatments. Second, the *Grzelczyk* ruling interpreted the 1990 directives as if they had established a certain degree of financial solidarity between nationals of a host member state

---

[38] Joined cases 286/82 and 26/83, *Graziana Luisi and Giuseppe Carbone v. Ministero del Tesoro* [1984] ECR 377.

[39] Council Directive 90/364/EEC of 28 June 1990 on the right of residence, *Official Journal L 180*, 13/07/1990, pp. 0026–0027. Council Directive 90/365/EEC of 28 June 1990 on the right of residence for employees and self-employed persons who have ceased their occupational activity, *Official Journal L 180*, 13/07/1990, pp. 0028–0029. Council Directive 90/366/EEC of 28 June 1990 on the right of residence for students, *Official Journal L 180*, 13/07/1990, pp. 0030–0031.

[40] Case C-90/97, *Robin Swaddling v. Adjudication Officer* [1999] ECR I-01075.

[41] Case C-85/96, *María Martínez Sala v. Freistaat Bayern* [1998] ECR I-02691.

[42] Case C-184/99, *Rudy Grzelczyk v. Centre public d'aide sociale d'Ottignies-Louvain-la-Neuve* [2001] ECR I-06193.

and nationals of other member states. If the financial burdens are 'reasonable'—one could argue, following the Court—a single member state has no right to deny help to a needy EU citizen: quite a long way from the old-fashioned guest-worker regimes.[43]

Also in the wake of ECJ jurisprudence, in April 2004 a new directive was adopted 'on the right of citizens of the EU and their family members to move and reside freely within the territory of the Member States'.[44] Making explicit reference to the Charter of Fundamental Rights, this directive treats free movement and free residence as a primary and individual right conferred by EU citizenship and as a fundamental freedom of the internal market. The regime introduced by the directives can be summarized as follows:

- EU citizens have an unconditional right of residence in a host member state for an initial period of three months;
- after this initial period, conditions may be imposed in order to prevent persons exercising their right of residence becoming an unreasonable burden on the social assistance system of the host country; however,
- an expulsion measure should not be the automatic consequence of recourse to the social assistance system. The host member state should examine whether it is only a matter of temporary difficulties, and should take into account the duration of residence and the amount of aid granted;
- after a continuous period of five years without expulsion, an unconditional right of residence should be granted.

The last point is very important: permanent residents will enjoy full social protection rights, including the right to social assistance. In the words of the directive preamble:

Enjoyment of permanent residence by Union citizens who have chosen to settle long term in the host Member State would strengthen the feeling of Union citizenship and is a key element in promoting social cohesion, which is one of the fundamental objectives of the Union.[45]

---

[43] In the recent *Collins* case (C-138-02 Case C-138/02, *Brian Francis Collins* v. *Secretary of State for Work and Pensions* [2004] ECR I-02703) the ECJ has again invited member states to implement the residence requirement for means-tested benefits in a 'proportional' way, that is, only to the extent that it is based on objective considerations that are independent of the applicant's nationality and proportionate to the legitimate aims of the national provision.

[44] Directive 2004/38/EC of the European Parliament and of the Council of 29 April 2004 on the right of citizens of the EU and their family members to move and reside freely within the territory of the member states amending Regulation (EEC) No 1612/68 and repealing Directives 64/221/EEC, 68/360/EEC, 72/194/EEC, 73/148/EEC, 75/34/EEC, 75/35/EEC, 90/364/EEC, 90/365/EEC, and 93/96/EEC (Text with EEA relevance), *Official Journal L 158*, 30/04/2004, pp. 0077–0123.

[45] See n. 43. The cited passage is para. 17 of the directive's preamble.

The implementation of this directive is bound to circumscribe severely not only the legal autonomy of member states in delimiting the sphere of social assistance, but also the actual exercise of this autonomy, through the 'proportionality' qualifications for expulsion measures justified in financial terms. Even though the 'affluence test' has not been formally prohibited, the manipulation of residence requirements for EU nationals has been almost entirely removed from the hands of member state authorities.

Migration and the Status of Third Country Nationals

Europe has a long tradition of cross-country migration, stretching back to the early twentieth century. As we saw in Chapter 2, until the First World War migrant workers could cross borders and enter national bounded spaces (especially the labour market) without difficulty and subject to very little control. It was only after the war that national frontiers started to be policed and that passports, visas, and work permits were introduced. In the inter-war period, citizenship begun to be used as an instrument of closure and as a filter to separate insiders from outsiders, and distinct national immigration policies made their first appearance. These policies had an external side, primarily linked to territorial movements (border controls, exit and entry authorizations, deportation rules, etc.) and an internal side, linked to domestic membership spaces (the rights and duties of legal immigrants vis-à-vis the labour market, the welfare state, etc.).[46]

During the 1950s and 1960s, immigration of foreign workers was encouraged by many countries (such as Germany, France, and Belgium) to fill gaps in their labour markets. Some of these migrant workers came from countries inside the EC (such as Italy), but many were 'third country nationals'— a novel marker of outsiderhood evoking an entitlement differential anchored to a supranational bounded space (the EC) rather than a national one. The substantial waves of immigration of the 1950s and 1960s took place in a social and institutional context that essentially considered foreign workers as guests admitted into the labour market and into employment-related social schemes, but on a temporary and reversible basis. In this phase the entitlement differential between EU and non-EU migrants was not very significant; access rules depended on national authorities, applied to all foreigners, and varied across countries. As we have seen, the common

[46] The literature on migration in Europe and the impact of European integration has been burgeoning over the last decade. See especially Baldwin Edwards and Schain (1994); Geddes (2000); Bommes and Geddes (2000); Geddes and Favell (1999); Hollifield (1992); Martiniello (1995); Miles and Thraenhardt (1995).

labour market started to operate fully only after 1968, and full social security entitlements were guaranteed to migrant workers of the EC member states only with the 1971 Regulation. In 1963 the Association Agreement with Turkey[47] envisaged some special privileges for workers migrating from this country into Europe, introducing the 'mixed' category of a third country national protected by an Association Agreement. But such privileges became operative (though not in full) only in the 1980s.

The economic crisis of the 1970s marked a watershed. European countries suddenly stopped welcoming immigrant workers, especially from third countries (Italian emigration had spontaneously ended in the meanwhile). The general expectation was that most migrants would return to their country of origin. But this did not happen. Many foreign workers had been joined by their families and were interested in permanent settlement. In the wake of national (but also supranational, especially on the part of Turkish citizens) litigation (Guiraudon 2000), large numbers of third country nationals acquired 'denizenship' status, that is, the right legally to reside, work, and 'share' in the country of immigration; some even obtained naturalization. In 1976 the Cooperation Agreements with the Maghrib countries (Morocco, Algeria, and Tunisia)[48] created a second category of special third country nationals. Their privileges were inferior to those envisaged for Turkish nationals, but included equal treatment in work and remuneration conditions within domestic labour markets. All third country nationals, however, remained excluded from the 1971 Regulation on social security coordination. Thus, their welfare rights were entirely dependent on national rules—which obviously reflected strong national preferences on the issue—and cross-border movements were discouraged.

Given the frustration of their re-emigration expectations and objectives, during this second phase (the 1970s and 1980s) European countries started to rein in their immigration rules, but discovered that the EC legal order was imposing unexpected constraints. The ECJ considered the Association and Cooperation Agreements as part of this order, with direct effect and supremacy over national provisions. Some articles of the Rome Treaty itself (such as art. 7a, now 14) could be interpreted as an obligation to create a common market for all persons, regardless of nationality,

[47] Agreement establishing an Association between the European Economic Community and Turkey, *Official Journal P 217, 29/12/1964*, pp. 3687–3688.

[48] Cooperation Agreement between the European Economic Community and the Kingdom of Morocco, *Official Journal L 264, 27/09/1978*, pp. 0002–0118; Cooperation Agreement between the European Economic Community and the People's Democratic Republic of Algeria, *Official Journal L 263, 27/09/1978*, pp. 0002–0118; Cooperation Agreement between the European Economic Community and the Republic of Tunisia, *Official Journal L 265, 27/09/1978*, pp. 0002–0118.

and thus extended to the *extra-comunitari*. And in the mid-1970s this expansionary interpretation started to be voiced by the Commission (later backed by the European Parliament (EP)), which proposed including all migrants within the scope of its ambitious Social Action Plan of 1975. Thus, the 1980s witnessed the emergence of a tug of war between national governments—strenuously affirming their prerogatives on citizenship and denizenship vis-à-vis third country nationals and their policies of differential treatment—and supranational institutions (Commission, Parliament, and ECJ)—typically pushing for equal treatment and the expansion of rights, including in the sphere of social protection (Conant 2001).

Despite the restrictive turn of national policies, the 1980s and 1990s witnessed continuing—and, indeed, for some countries, increasing—flows of migration. New legal entries included especially family members, but also asylum seekers and refugees. Moreover, mounting numbers of illegal migrants started to 'sneak in' across the EU's border, especially via the Mediterranean Sea, and to 'hide inside' the underground economy. Once a major source of emigration, the south European member states in the 1980s and 1990s rapidly turned into receiving countries (Venturini 2004). An interesting syndrome appeared at this time, attesting to the new European interdependencies and the unexpected implications of EU regulations (Baganha 2000; Hunger 1998). Thanks to the rules on 'posting', enabling EU workers to be temporarily employed in other member states under the rules of their home country rather than the host country, increasing numbers of workers from south European countries started to arrive in seasonal sectors in Germany such as building or agriculture. This phenomenon can be considered an example of 'thick entry': it is not only a worker that is admitted, but a worker-cum-rights—the rights (and obligations) of the country of origin. The slots vacated by these same workers in the same sectors in their home countries are filled by immigrants: typically, illegal third country nationals, sneaking into the underground economy with no rights from their country of origin and no rights from the host country. Such 'four corner games' have been taking place for a long time in the backward and segmented labour markets of southern Europe (Ferrera 1996; Perez Diaz and Rodriguez 1994).[49] The EU posting

---

[49] South European labour markets have often been depicted as comprising four subgroups of workers, characterized by different job or earnings and social protection opportunities: (*a*) workers belonging to the core labour market (civil servants, regular employees of the private sector, especially in large enterprises); (*b*) temporary and intermittent workers; (*c*) underground workers; and (*d*) unemployed workers. Most of the workers in this latter group are always ready to jump in and occupy the vacant slots of the other three groups; hence the metaphor of a 'four corner game'.

regime seems to have created the conditions for a sort of Europeanization of these games, with significant implications for the functioning of the highly regulated markets that use posted workers, attracted by their lower labour costs.[50]

During the 1990s, positive net migration became the largest component of population change in the EU, fluctuating around a total of 850,000 immigrants per year. In 2000 third country nationals represented around 3.4 per cent of men and women living inside the EU (Figure 4.1 and Table 4.4).

Given the 'jobless growth' syndrome and indeed rising unemployment levels, the member states tried to respond to this upsurge of new migration with a policy of closure, accompanied by stricter enforcement rules and more closely linked to security policy in general (Bommes and Geddes 2000; Conant 2001). Migration suddenly became a contentious issue in national politics, with some old and new parties voicing against undesired entries as well as calling for the preservation of domestic public order (and

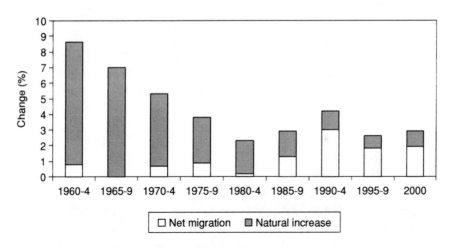

Source: Eurostat (2004).

Fig 4.1 Average annual rate of population change by component, EU-15, 1960–2000

[50] In 1996 a Directive (96/71/EC) severely restricted the 'home country principle' for posted workers and allowed member states to enact legislation applying to posted workers certain key labour rules concerning minimum wages, working time, and equal treatment, even in the case of temporary posting. In recent years the ECJ has however started to challenge national constraints on posting (Barnard, 2004, pp. 343–6). A new directive proposal—known as the 'Bolkestein directive'—contains a limitative reformulation of the scope and content of the posting regime, with a view to promoting an internal market of services. (EC 2004b).

Table 4.4   Non-EU nationals as a percentage of total population, 1985–2000

Country	Percentage of non-EU nationals			
	1985	1990	1995	2000[1]
Austria	*n.a.*	*n.a.*	7.4	7.9
Belgium	2.5	3.5	3.5	3.3
Denmark	1.2	1.6	1.8	3.8
Finland	*n.a.*	*n.a.*	0.6	1.4
France	4.7	4.3	3.9	3.5
Germany	4.5	5.6	6.0	6.7
Greece	0.6	0.5	1.1	1.1
Ireland	0.4	0.5	0.6	0.9
Italy	*n.a.*	*n.a.*	1.3	1.9
Luxembourg	1.4	2.1	3.0	3.8
Netherlands	2.6	2.9	3.4	2.9
Portugal	0.4	0.5	0.3	1.4
Spain	0.2	0.1	0.4	1.2
Sweden	*n.a.*	*n.a.*	2.9	3.5
United Kingdom	*n.a.*	1.8	1.9	2.5
Eu (15)[2]	2.9	3.0	3.0	3.4

[1]2000 data refer to 1999 for Denmark, France, Luxembourg, and the UK; to 1997 for Greece.
[2]Weighted average. Missing values for 1985 and 1990: Austria. Finland, Italy, and Sweden.
Source: own elaboration on data in: European Commission and Eurostat (2003); Eurostat database (http://epp.eurostat.cec.eu.int).

often for protection of domestic labour markets and sharing arrangements as well). Thus, during the 1990s virtually all member states legislated for major restrictive changes to their migration regimes (EC 2003*a*). They also engaged, however, in joint policy efforts, aware that the challenge of migration required at least some common responses to be more effective, especially within the framework of the new single market and of weakening internal frontiers. How to reconcile the implementation of common measures with the maintenance of national sovereignty on citizenship and denizenship? The solution was found in keeping this area of cooperation strictly outside the EC institutional order. The Schengen Agreement of 1985 was an intergovernmental treaty. The Maastricht Treaty established a separate third pillar, for justice and home affairs (covering also immigration, visa, and asylum policies), wholly outside the Community framework and thus immune from ECJ interference. The new EU citizenship remained strictly complementary to member state citizenship, despite proposals from the Commission to grant it also to third country nationals after five years of legal residence. And the new Association Agreements of the 1990s with the countries of the former Soviet bloc were carefully worded so as to exclude legal direct effects (Conant 2001).

This phase of 'thin Europeanization' (Geddes 2000) came to an end with the Amsterdam Treaty of 1997. The emergence of a transnational advocacy coalition for the rights of third country nationals, and the activism of supranational actors such as the Commission and Parliament, prepared the ground for a new phase of gradual communitarization of immigration and asylum policy. The new Treaty brought virtually all issues concerning these two areas within the first pillar. Article 61 (*ex.* 73I) of the Amsterdam Treaty formulates the goal of progressively establishing an area of freedom, security, and justice within the EU; and art. 62 (*ex.* 73J) explicitly recognizes that this will apply to all persons, including the nationals of third countries. Despite its innovative character, however, the Amsterdam Treaty confirmed the exclusionary nature of EU citizenship in respect of third country nationals, raising both practical and normative dilemmas for millions of permanently resident non-nationals (Follesdal 1999).

Progress was made, however, in subsequent years. The Tampere European Council of 1999 explicitly requested a more vigorous integration policy, aimed at granting legally resident third country nationals rights and obligations comparable to those of EU citizens. In their turn, most of the provisions of the Charter of Fundamental Rights proclaimed at Nice in 2000 are applicable to all persons, irrespective of their nationality. Following a first proposal launched by the Commission in 1997, the 1971 Regulation has been extended to all third country nationals in 2003, thus equalizing their status with that of EU migrants relating to social security rights.[51] The new regulation will affect about 13 million people legally residing in the EU. It must be stressed, however, that third country nationals still do not enjoy full free movement rights from one member state to another—this making their assimilation to the legal status of EU migrants merely symbolic. With a view to implementing the provisions of the Amsterdam Treaty, the Commission has recently proposed a number of directives aimed at introducing a 'civic citizenship' (or denizenship) for immigrants, defined as guaranteeing certain core rights and obligations which they would acquire gradually over a period of years, including that

---

[51] Council Regulation (EC) No 859/2003 of 14 May 2003 extending the provisions of Regulation (EEC) No 1408/71 and Regulation (EEC) No 574/72 to nationals of third countries who are not already covered by those provisions solely on the ground of their nationality, *Official Journal L 124*, 20/05/2003, pp. 0001–0003.

of moving to other member states for employment or study purposes (EC 2003a).

All the steps of this last phase have substantially curbed (and are likely to further curb in the coming years) domestic discretion over the treatment of third country nationals. In this respect, it must be recognized that EU institutions have gradually emerged as highly salient boundary-setters in the delicate area of citizenship, understood as both an instrument and an object of social closure. In the employment and welfare areas, once they have acquired a legal residence in any member state, third country nationals now enjoy virtually the same rights and obligations as nationals. But free movement across the member states is not included in the basket of rights not a trivial exclusion. And of course, legal residence rules for non-EU nationals are still in the hands of the member states. This is a critical buffer that remains to protect national civic sovereignty vis-à-vis entries from outside the EU; and, as one would expect, unanimity is required for removing it.

Compulsory Membership and Public Insurance Monopolies Contested

As highlighted several times in this book, the core element of the modern welfare state is the principle of compulsory membership of public schemes for the nationals (or residents) of a given territory. It is this principle that gives a solid institutional and financial foundation to domestic social insurance as a key tool for redistribution. How have things evolved on this critical front in the context of EU market-making? Has the boundary reconfiguration linked to free movement and competition rules jeopardized the sovereign right of national authorities to enforce compulsory membership of sharing collectivities? We noted earlier that the single market project prompted a gradual and subtle shift from the goal of promoting access to national markets for other EU economic actors towards the goal of affirming and upholding a general right of access to the market *as such* for the widest number of providers within domestic economies and a general right of choice between competing providers for the widest number of consumers. A possible corollary of these rights in the sphere that interests us is a general right of entry *into* (for providers) and exit *from* (for consumers or members) national 'bounded sharing' spaces, that is, public and compulsory social insurance schemes. We have seen that the freedom of services and the gradual Europeanization of the market for health care have indeed prompted instances of vocal entry and exit that have challenged some national prerogatives of boundary control in this sphere. We now have to examine more closely the extent to which EU market-making has actually challenged two of the most fundamental institutional tenets of the modern welfare state, namely, the principles of compulsory membership and public insurance monopoly. Important and complex developments have indeed been taking place on this crucial battleground since the 1970s, involving both national and thus largely endogenous dynamics and supranational and exogenous ones. In order to unravel the complexity, we need to proceed step by step, separately addressing the various issues and their evolution through time. We first summarize national developments in the direction of a new multitier, multipillar form of welfare state. Then we briefly describe the liberalization process of the insurance market in Europe. Third, we discuss the challenges to the principles of compulsory affiliation and public insurance monopoly in relation to first and second pillars. Although we focus mainly on pensions, when discussing second pillars we briefly return to health care as well. Finally, we say something about third pillars, that is, private, voluntary insurance plans.

The Rise of Multitier and Multipillar Configurations at the National Level

With the passing of time, European welfare states have become increasingly plural in their mix of welfare provision, with significant implications in terms of 'closure' for their sharing spaces. A significant second level of supplementary insurance has emerged, offering additional benefits and coverage to selected occupational categories. Some countries have maintained the principle of compulsory membership within supplementary insurance; in the case of pensions, this is most notably the case of the Nordic countries, France, and Greece. Many countries, however, have adopted a softer approach: membership rules (including obligatory cover) can be drawn up by collective agreements, which may in turn be backed by national legislative provisions (as in the Netherlands); in some cases, membership is instead voluntary, but encouraged and subsidized by the state (as in Ireland or the Iberian countries). Even if not (always) formally compulsory, this second level of provision still tends to retain a 'collective' nature, in that it rests on group insurance principles and agreements with particular categories of citizens, thus allowing for many of the redistributive and solidaristic effects typically linked to compulsory social insurance. Alongside this second level of provision, a third pillar has in its turn developed, essentially based on individual choice and market criteria. Here there is no compulsion, and the distance from solidarity principles is much greater; but even at this level public regulation plays a role justified on both efficiency and equity grounds.

In the field of pensions, the second level of supplementary provision had already developed by the 1970s in most EU countries (see Chapter 2). This second level included both 'second tier' schemes—based on PAYGO financing and defined-benefit formulas—and 'second pillar' schemes proper, that is, schemes based on prefunding. During the 1980s and 1990s the latter schemes further consolidated, following deliberate policies of encouragement pursued by national authorities. The increasing strain on public pension programmes due to demographic ageing, system maturation, budgetary constraints, and the new competitive imperatives have in fact induced governments (as well as the European Commission) to look at funded supplementary schemes as a promising instrument for relieving the pressure on first-pillar schemes, and thus (in part) on labour costs. Favourable regulatory and especially tax frameworks have been introduced in order to induce both workers and enterprises to earmark resources for funded supplementary pensions. A corollary objective of such initiatives has also been to promote capital accumulation within the economy and to support and enlarge domestic financial markets. Against this background, by the early 1990s a fairly substantial 'market' for second-pillar pensions had developed in several EU member states (EC 1994). This was particularly the case in those countries that form the 'basic security plus employment related benefits' cluster (see Chapter 2), namely, the UK, the Netherlands, Denmark, and Ireland (as well as Switzerland outside the EU). As Table 4.5 shows, in 1993 in these countries the assets of pension funds already displayed very high values in relation to GDP, with substantial coverage rates (Table 4.6). During the 1990s regulatory reforms opened new spaces for funded supplementary pensions also in Austria, Belgium, France, Germany, Portugal, and especially Sweden (which also displays high coverage rates). Though with less institutional and financial significance, third pillars have also become more important over the last two decades—especially, again, in the first cluster of countries.

A novel development of the 1980s and 1990s has been the formation in many countries of collective and individual forms of supplementary insurance also in the field of health care. Collective schemes typically cover the gaps in public health insurance: elective treatments, reimbursement of patient charges for pharmaceuticals, consultations or hospital stays, nursing care, and so on. Some of these collective schemes, however,

Table 4.5 Pension fund assets as percentage of GDP, selected years

Country	1993	1997	1999
Austria	—	11.5	12.3
Belgium	3.4	4.8	6.4
Denmark	20.1	20.4	24.5
Finland	—	8.6	10.1
France	3.4	6.9	6.0
Germany	5.8	14.5	16.0
Greece	—	4.4	4.3
Ireland	40.1	53.8	57.1
Italy	1.2	2.1	2.4
Luxembourg	—	0.2	0.3
Netherlands	88.5	113.0	115.4
Portugal	—	10.9	11.9
Spain	2.2	4.0	3.9
Sweden	—	47.5	54.1
UK	79.4	79.1	92.6
EU-15	20.3	26.1	30.1

Sources: EC (1997: Table II); EFRP (2001).

Table 4.6 Coverage of second-pillar pension schemes, 1993–2001

Country	Estimated coverage for employees in the private sector (%)	
	1993	2001
Belgium	31	35
Denmark	80	82
Germany	46	50
Ireland	40	47
Italy	5	15
Netherlands	85	91
Sweden	—	90
UK*	48	57

*Estimated coverage of personal and occupational plans for those employed in the public and private sectors.

Sources: Elaboration by the author on EC (1997); Irish Department of Social and Family Affairs (2002); British Department for Work and Pensions (2002); EC and Council (2003).

provide alternative channels of care to the first pillar, either through contracts with specific providers or through *ex post* reimbursement of individual expenses. The latter is the typical mode of functioning of third-pillar schemes, that is, private health insurance.

A number of factors are responsible for the building of supplementary insurance in European health care, whose aggregate financial size has come to absorb about 25 per cent of average total health spending in 1999 (EC 2001c): cost containment and rationing policies within public systems, linked to demographic ageing and medical inflation; rising consumption standards and choice aspirations, due to higher incomes but also to the growing health care expectations of both patients and practitioners; fast progress in medical technology and treatment, which makes available a growing amount of expensive new equipment and procedures. From an organizational viewpoint, the articulation of supplementary insurance in health care is extremely varied, including company-based schemes, provident funds, and mutual aid societies alongside private insurance carriers.

While the first pillar remains everywhere the main source of provision in both the pension and health care spheres, it is equally true that the institutional architecture of European welfare states has undergone a significant transformation in recent decades. A growing number of people now rely on supplementary and private provision to satisfy a substantial share of their retirement and/or health care needs. The degree to which this actually happens in each country is a function of national configurations and path dependencies. But, however diverse from a cross-sectional perspective, all national trajectories along the new road of multipillar social protection have been affected by the exogenous wave of European integration. And, as can be easily imagined, integration—and in particular the increasing pressures of free movement and of the EU competition regime—has had different implications and effects on each of the three pillars of provision.

The Internal Market for Insurance

In order to specify more precisely the link between EU market-making and national 'bounded sharing' spaces, we have to consider developments in an economic sector which lies very close to these spaces, namely, insurance services. A single market has in fact been gradually created in this sector, through the elaboration of a common legal framework aimed at stimulating competition and increasing consumer choice. The exogenous challenges to compulsory membership and public insurance monopoly have primarily stemmed from this specific process.

The first step in the creation of an internal market for insurance was taken in the 1970s. During that decade a first generation of directives set the conditions for the freedom of establishment, that is, the opening of branch offices and agencies in any member state: this was achieved by

Directive 73/239 [52] for non-life insurance and by Directive 79/267[53] for life insurance. A second generation of directives was adopted after the SEA, as part of the 1992 project: Directive 88/357 (non-life)[54] and Directive 90/619 (life)[55] set the conditions for actual freedom of service, allowing insurance carriers to cover a risk located in the territory of another member state without having to set up a branch office or agency. The application of such freedom, however, remained limited to policyholders who did not require special protection by virtue of their size, status, or risk (such as transport risk or fire). Finally, a third generation of directives (92/49 for non-life[56] and 92/96 for life insurance)[57] completed market liberalization by extending the principle of free movement of services to all risks and all policyholders (including the 'mass risks' typically covered by social protection) in a common framework of basic consumer protection. The second and third waves of EU regulation have relied heavily on the principle of mutual recognition of those authorization and prudential rules operating in the state of solvency (home country control).

Market liberalization has prompted a massive wave of cross-border takeovers and mergers in Europe's insurance industry, with a clear trend towards concentration. National regulatory regimes have been substantially modified under the two-pronged pressure from the rules on free movement and on undistorted competition. While this has unquestionably produced efficiency gains, there are also signs of some perverse side effects, especially in terms of cream-skimming practices by carriers, that is,

---

[52] Council Directive 73/239/EEC of 24 July 1973 on the coordination of laws, regulations and administrative provisions relating to the taking-up and pursuit of the business of direct insurance other than life assurance, *Official Journal L 228*, 16/08/1973, pp. 0003–0019.

[53] Council Directive 79/267/EEC of 5 March 1979 on the coordination of laws, regulations and administrative provisions relating to the taking-up and pursuit of the business of direct life assurance, *Official Journal L 063*, 13/03/1979, pp. 0001–0018.

[54] Council Directive 88/357/EEC of 22 June 1988 on the coordination of laws, regulations and administrative provisions relating to direct insurance other than life assurance and laying down provisions to facilitate the effective exercise of freedom to provide services and amending Directive 73/239/EEC, *Official Journal L 172*, 04/07/1988, pp 0001–0014.

[55] Council Directive 90/619/EEC of 8 November 1990 on the coordination of laws, regulations and administrative provisions relating to direct life assurance, laying down provisions to facilitate the effective exercise of freedom to provide services and amending Directive 79/267/EEC, *Official Journal L 330*, 29/11/1990, pp. 0050–0061.

[56] Council Directive 92/49/EEC of 18 June 1992 on the coordination of laws, regulations and administrative provisions relating to direct insurance other than life assurance and amending Directives 73/239/EEC and 88/357/EEC, *Official Journal L 228*, 11/08/1992, pp. 0001–0023.

[57] Council Directive 92/96/EEC of 10 November 1992 on the coordination of laws, regulations and administrative provisions relating to direct life assurance and amending Directives 79/267/EEC and 90/619/EEC, *Official Journal L 360*, 09/12/1992, pp. 0001–0027.

the selection (or preferential treatment) of good risks at the expenses of the bad ones—as typically predicted by market failure theories. This seems to be primarily connected with the fact that, by prohibiting public price controls and prior authorization of insurance products, the new EU regulatory regime has increased the opportunities for carriers to differentiate their offers with a view to attracting less risky consumers, while at the same time it has restricted the scope of application of 'open enrolment' rules (i.e. the obligation to accept business regardless of individual risk profiles) (Mabbet 2000; Rees et al. 1999).

Ever since the first generation of directives, the field of national 'statutory social security' (the notion used by the 1971 Regulation, adopted by the first non-life directive) has been exempted from the liberalization process, which legally affects only insurance 'undertakings'. Thus, compulsory membership of public insurance monopolies—and with it the central institutional foundations of national welfare states—did not seem to be in question. Although this exemption is rather firmly rooted in the treaties, since the early 1990s a mounting stream of litigation has emerged, witnessing several attempts at 'vocal exit' from domestic sharing spaces by invoking, precisely, the newly established freedoms of insurance in the internal market. These attempts have tended to fail as far as first-pillar schemes are concerned, but have tended to be more successful in the grey area of supplementary schemes, which, given their nature, functioning, and organization, are not automatically protected by the exemption clauses envisaged in both the treaties and secondary legislation.

Failed Challenges to First-Pillar Schemes

The first attempts at vocal exit from basic compulsory social insurance that reached the ECJ came from France in the early 1990s. In this country the second and third insurance directives prompted an articulate debate on the status and future perspectives of the so-called *monopoles sociaux*, that is, precisely, the collective compulsory schemes falling under the social security code.[58] Given the high fragmentation, the mode of functioning (e.g. through *ex post* reimbursement in health care; see Table 4.5), and the relative autonomy from the state of these schemes, some concerns emerged during the liberalization process about their exemption from competition rules and from rules on the free movement of services. In order to strengthen their position, in 1991 the French government added

---

[58] The source used here for French developments is a report by the French Senate (Sénat 1999).

an article to its social security code (art. L-652-4), which nullified all insurance contracts in the field of social protection that were intended wholly to substitute for public social security cover (the so-called '100 per cent contracts' or *contracts au premier franc*). In 1993 the implementation decree made violations of this new provision subject to serious penalties. These moves on the part of the national authorities were partly aimed at reassuring the social partners, who were fearful of an exogenous destabilization of the *monopoles sociaux*, which they largely controlled. But these moves were also aimed at discouraging other actors in the domestic arena that did indeed see in the liberalization of the EU insurance market a chance to break these public monopolies through acts of vocal entry (by private providers) or vocal exit (by members and/or consumers). The federation of private insurers (*Fédération Française des Sociétés d'Assurance*) had started to bring cases in national courts against the supposed privileges of social security schemes for certain risks and professions. The thesis that the EU insurance directives were de facto prescribing the dismantling of the *monopoles* was vigorously defended by various commentators (e.g. Mouly 1996) and even welcomed by the conservative press, such as *Le Figaro*. Taking this thesis seriously, a group of right-wing politicians formally initiated legislation in parliament to suppress the public social insurance monopoly and replace it with free choice among providers. At the same time, some self-employed workers were starting to withhold contributions to the *monopoles*: the *Confédération de Défense des Commerçants et Artisans* (a movement of neo-Poujadiste orientations) was waging a campaign of non-payment against compulsory membership, arguing that EU liberalization was conferring on all Frenchmen the ability to shop around outside the *sécurité sociale* (including abroad).

Litigation soon reached the ECJ, which had thus to establish whether public social insurance monopolies were indeed compatible with the norms on competition and free movement. The landmark ruling came in 1993 (*Poucet-Pistre*).[59] In these joined cases the Court established that the freedom of service and the rules on competition could not be invoked to justify exit from compulsory national insurance schemes (in these cases pension and medical insurance). The Court's ruling rested on the recognition of the solidaristic purposes of such schemes, symbolized by such features as the absence of risk selection and the redistribution between income groups (from the better-off to the worse-off: distributive solidar-

---

[59] Joined cases C-159/91 and C-160/91, *Christian Poucet v. Assurances Générales de France and Caisse Mutuelle Régionale du Languedoc-Roussillon* [1993] ECR I-00637.

ity), between different risk branches (financial solidarity), and especially between different age groups (intergenerational solidarity). The Court viewed the adoption of the PAYGO method of financing as a particularly important factor: only by 'locking in' subsequent generations was it possible to sustain such a system of financing, which served critical redistributive functions. In view of all these features, public social insurance schemes could not be considered as undertakings engaged in economic activity, and the principles of obligatory coverage and public monopoly did not violate Treaty norms. It is interesting to note that in the Court reasoning the legal status of the providing institution (public or private) did not matter; what mattered rather was whether the agency under scrutiny was an undertaking engaged in economic activity. The French authorities fought hard in the supranational legal arena to defend the position of their *régimes legaux* against the threat of competition (Coron 2003*a*, 2003*b*).

This Court's doctrine about the social purposes of public insurance monopolies and their exemption from competition rules has been upheld in various other rulings,[60] with some interpretive restrictions (Giubboni 2003). Though always stressing the importance of intergenerational solidarity, in the *Cisal* case of 2002[61]—an attempt at vocal exit from the public work injuries scheme run by INAIL in Italy—the Luxembourg judges have again placed emphasis on the other solidaristic elements as well, and in particular on the element of distributive solidarity guaranteed by a non-profit agency operating under state supervision. Moreover, in *Cisal* the Court has explicitly found that 'the principle of compulsory affiliation which characterises such an insurance scheme is essential for the financial balance of the scheme and for application of the principle of solidarity, which means that the benefits paid to insured persons are not strictly proportionate to the contributions paid by them' (para. 44).

It can thus be concluded that, as far as first-pillar public insurance schemes are concerned, the strategies of vocal exit pursued so far by domestic actors have not been supported by the supranational court. Boundary setting and boundary control remain firmly in the hands of the national authorities, within the free movement of workers constraints imposed by the 1971 Regulation. The strategies of vocal entry attempted by

---

[60] See for example Case C-238/94, *José García and others* v. *Mutuelle de Prévoyance Sociale d'Aquitaine and others* [1996] ECR I-01673.

[61] Case C-218/00, *Cisal di Battistello Venanzio & C. Sas* v. *Istituto nazionale per l'assicurazione contro gli infortuni sul lavoro (INAIL)* [2002] ECR I-00691.

providers, with a view to opening up the *monopoles sociaux* and thus creating new market opportunities for non-public carriers, have also failed, even before reaching supranational litigation. Social insurance remains a realm of public service that is immune from the EU competition regime. Under ECJ jurisprudence, however, this immunity is strictly conditional upon the presence of solidaristic indicators. For example, the principle of compulsory affiliation and the statutory character of first-pillar schemes are not by themselves sufficient conditions for immunity. In Belgium, where social insurance against work accidents is statutory but run by non-public for-profit agencies at their own risk, the government's attempt to keep this sector outside the scope of the third non-life directive has failed. In *Commission* v. *Belgium*[62] the Court has in fact ruled that the solidaristic requirements for such an exemption are absent. The maintenance of boundary control powers weakens as the internal organization of public social protection approaches market principles - a point that receives clear confirmation if we move from the first to the second (and, obviously, third) pillars of welfare provision.

Second Pillars: Towards a Europeanization of Supplementary Pensions?

In the early 1970s supplementary pensions were not a big issue, at least in the original Six. This explains why neither the coordination regime for social security (Reg. 71/1408) nor the first generation of insurance directives (73/239 and 79/267) explicitly and specifically dealt with this form of provision. Only France had a significant second tier of supplementary pensions: the *régimes complémentaires* (see Chapter 3). French authorities could have easily brought such schemes within the material scope of the Regulation. But the social partners, who controlled them, were afraid that this might jeopardize the special autonomy that the *régimes* enjoyed under the social security code. Thus, legally, they remained *ni souris ni oiseax* well into the 1990s (Lyon Caen and Lyon Caen 1993): neither statutory schemes subject to coordination rules nor private insurance schemes under competition rules. In fact, deliberately pursuing a 'hiding' strategy in respect of the EC legal order, they engaged in an expansionary programme, offering their members not only supplementary benefits linked to compulsory affiliation (and PAYGO financing) but also voluntary and funded additional benefits, the so-called *prestations sur-complémentaires*, largely crowding out private insurance companies from the nascent second and third pillars.

[62] Case C-206/98, *Commission of the European Communities* v. *Kingdom of Belgium* [2000] ECR I-03509.

During the 1980s, however, the ambiguous status of supplementary pensions (not only in France) vis-à-vis EC rules as well as their function in old age protection started to attract increasing attention. The first enlargement had brought into the Community three new countries (the UK, Ireland, and Denmark) in which this type of pension—primarily resting on the prefunding method of financing—played an important role. The single market project included the goals of enhancing labour mobility and promoting an internal capital market. Achieving the former required, *inter alia*, an effective coordination of all employment-related benefits; achieving the latter required, *inter alia*, a common regulatory framework for such important financial institutions as pension funds. In the second half of the 1980s, supplementary pensions had, moreover, come under the gaze of the ECJ because of the *Barber* case, involving the legality of higher ages of retirement for men than for women set by an occupational pension fund in the UK. In *Barber*[63] the Court ruled that second-pillar pensions must be treated as remuneration, and thus no gender discrimination was permissible under art. 141 (*ex.* 119). The ruling provoked a small earthquake in many EU pension systems; it forced member states to equalize the retirement age in all second-pillar schemes and risked opening a Pandora's box of retroactive financial litigation—a threat that was neutralized through a special protocol to the Maastricht Treaty in 1992. Apart from its specific merit, the *Barber* case reverberated across Europe and served to focus attention on second-pillar pensions.

In the context of the single market project and EMU, the Commission started to take legislative initiatives in the early 1990s both on the cross-border coordination of supplementary schemes and on the free circulation of the capital and services of occupational pension funds. Despite initial obstacles, the first steps towards a coordination regime were finally taken in 1998 through a directive (98/49)[64] establishing basic criteria for safeguarding supplementary pension rights: acquired rights must be maintained in the case of cross-border movement by workers, all EU nationals must be equally treated, and benefits are exportable to the territory of other member states.[65] Progress has been slower and more controversial

---

[63] Case C-262/88, *Douglas Harvey Barber* v. *Guardian Royal Exchange Assurance Group* [1990] ECR I-01889.

[64] Council Directive 98/49/EC of 29 June 1998 on safeguarding the supplementary pension rights of employed and self-employed persons moving within the Community, *Official Journal L 209*, 25/07/1998, pp. 0046–0049.

[65] The framework for the coordination of supplementary pensions, however, remains incomplete, and in 2001 the Commission issued a new communication on the portability of supplementary pension rights (EC 2001*b*).

along the second dimension, that is, the creation of a European market for supplementary pension funds.

A first proposal made by the Commission in 1991, largely inspired by British doctrines and practices, failed to win unanimous support in the Council, mainly due to French opposition to its potentially destabilizing effects on the *régimes complémentaires*. The Commission tried to issue the text at least as a Communication in 1993, but France (backed by Spain) challenged the legality of the act and won its appeal to the ECJ.[66] The Commission was thus forced to adopt a softer approach; it prepared a Green Paper on supplementary pensions and the single market whose main purpose was to encourage a broad debate on how to exploit the growth of pension funds and the creation of a capital market in the forthcoming EMU context for responding to the challenge of maintaining high levels of retirement income, without jeopardizing the soundness of public budgets (EC 1997). The generally positive results of this broad consultation were summarized in a Communication two years later (EC 1999a), which outlined the possible contours of a common regulatory framework in this area.

Parallel to these legislative steps, however, the 1990s witnessed judicial steps that addressed many of the legal ambiguities concerning second-pillar provision in pensions and in particular the two issues that are most important for our analysis, namely, those of compulsory affiliation and public insurance monopoly. Not surprisingly, the first landmark case originated again in France, in the wake of the turbulent developments around the *monopoles sociaux* mentioned earlier. The *Fédération Française des Sociétés d'Assurance* pressed a case against the tax privileges granted by the French government to a voluntary second-pillar pension scheme for farmers, named COREVA (*Complément de Retraite Volontaire Agricole*), arguing that such privileges violated EC competition rules. The case reached the ECJ, which in 1995 ruled against the French government.[67] The COREVA scheme did not operate based on a PAYGO basis but on prefunding rules: intergenerational solidarity was absent. A funded scheme is inherently more geared towards investment than to redistribution; consumers should be free to choose and providers free to sell 'the best investment opportunities' in a context of undistorted competition. Preferential treatment by national governments of a state-sponsored scheme is therefore not allowed under EC law. Strictly speaking, the *COREVA* judgement had

---

[66] Case C-57/95, *French Republic* v. *Commission of the European Communities* [1997] ECR I-01627.

[67] Case C-244/94, *Fédération Française des Sociétés d'Assurance, Société Paternelle-Vie, Union des Assurances de Paris-Vie and Caisse d'Assurance et de Prévoyance Mutuelle des Agriculteurs* v. *Ministère de l'Agriculture et de la Pêche* [COREVA] [1995] ECR I-04013.

BOX 4.1   France's *régimes complémentaires*
and the EU legal order: a summary

The second and third insurance directives and the 1991 draft directive on pension funds prompted the national management of the *régimes complémentaires* (AGIRC and ARRCO) to mobilize in defence of their peculiar position. They could no longer 'hide outside' both the coordination regime and the competition regime of the EC, shielded by the loopholes and the *non-dit* of ambiguous legislation. They were forced to make themselves visible to regulators and to explicitly voice for 'staying out'. In a common motion made public in September 1991 the two organizations expressed a double refusal: a refusal to enter into the coordination regime (which could put at risk their legal autonomy in France) and a refusal to move within the scope of EC competition (which would jeopardize their *monopole social*). The Commission, as a result of pressure on its president, Jacques Delors, modified its proposal so as to exclude these regimes from its material scope. However, this exclusion affected only the compulsory part of the schemes, leaving their voluntary part, that is, the *prestations sur-complémentaires*, at risk. Moreover, the domestic transposition of the insurance directives forced the regimes into a corner: the laws of 27 January 1993 and 1 July 1994 made a clear distinction between compulsory schemes offering supplementary pensions based on PAYGO and voluntary schemes offering additional benefits, subjecting them to quite different rules. The mixed character of AGIRC and ARRCO did not suit either the domestic or the EC legal orders, and this anomaly was increasingly visible. The two schemes also became a target of protest by the French insurance industry which, alarmed by the incipient EU-wide restructuring of the sector in the wake of market liberalization, lamented the narrow margin of manoeuvre left to it because of the *prestations sur-complémentaires*. The attack continued throughout the decade, in connection with both the ECJ rulings and the EU legislation on pension funds. AGIRC and ARRCO, realizing that 'staying out' was no longer a viable option, decided to phase out their third pillar supplementary benefits and to retreat into the safer waters of compulsory second-tier supplementary schemes, based on PAYGO. The institutional reforms of *la sécu* (the social security sector) during the second half of the 1990s had in any case redefined their legal status vis-à-vis the French state. In 2000 they finally engaged in a 'vocal entry' strategy and formally asked the French government to include them in the EU coordination regime (by amending Reg. 1408/71), as an additional articulation of France's first pillar. Under this shield, they will not be affected by the 2003 directive on European pension funds.

Source: Coron (2003a, 2003b).

no implication for the *régimes complémentaires*, which operated according to PAYGO. But, as Box 4.1 shows, the developments of the 1990s did bring substantial institutional changes to these peculiar French schemes, first uncovering and then ending their 'hiding' strategies and forcing them to comply with EC law.

The prohibition of preferential treatment on grounds of distorted competition has affected not only domestic providers (as in *COREVA*) but also national providers vis-à-vis other EU providers. In a number of other rulings[68] the ECJ has strictly limited member state powers to applying different tax rules to pension funds established elsewhere in the EU. And in 2003 the European Commission formally asked Denmark, Belgium, France, Spain, Portugal, and Italy to modify their national regulations granting special tax treatment to national institutions, following a Communication of 2001 on the elimination of tax obstacles to the cross-border provision of occupational pensions (EC 2001b).

According to the doctrine developed by the ECJ in the mid-1990s, voluntary second-pillar schemes based on prefunding are not exempt from competition rules, while compulsory second-tier schemes based on PAYGO are exempt. In many EU countries, however, supplementary pensions are indeed funded, but they are also compulsory under contractual agreements. The Netherlands is a typical case in point: here, supplementary pensions are normally organized through collective schemes covering a particular sector of the economy, a profession, or the employees of a given undertaking; such schemes are managed by pension funds based on capitalization; membership is compulsory based not only on contractual agreements but also on the law (Clark 2003; Van Riehl, Hemerijck, and Visser 2003). In the context of a broad process of welfare state reform that was launched in the 1990s by successive Dutch governments, the issue of 'exit' by individual companies from compulsory affiliation to industry-wide schemes came to the fore. A textile company (Albany International BV), followed by others, refused to pay contributions to its industry pension fund, arguing that this obligation violated EC competition law. The case reached the ECJ, which did recognize both the nature of 'undertaking' of the fund and the absence of intergenerational solidarity. This notwithstanding, in *Albany* (1999)[69] the Court ruled in favour of the pension fund,

---

[68] Case C-196/98, *Regina Virginia Hepple v. Adjudication Officer and Adjudication Officer v. Anna Stec.* [2000] ECR I-03701 and Case C-136/00, *Rolf Dieter Danner* [2002] ECR I-08147.

[69] Case C-67/96, *Albany International BV v. Stichting Bedrijfspensioenfonds Textielindustrie* [1999] ECR I-05751.

based on two main elements: the presence, in the scheme under scrutiny, of distributive solidarity arrangements and its nature as an outcome of collective bargaining, a practice that could not be considered as violating antitrust norms under treaty rules (especially after the Amsterdam Treaty and its new employment chapter).

Increased litigation, transnational lobbying by business and pension funds,[70] and Commission activism revamped the legislative strategy for arriving at a common and coherent regulatory framework. In 2000 the Commission issued a draft directive on pension funds, which, after lengthy negotiations, was formally adopted in 2003 (Directive 2003/41/EC).[71] This directive regulates the activities and supervision of all 'institutions for occupational retirement provisions' (IORP), including pension funds and superannuation schemes. The text contains detailed 'prudential' rules on both the operation and the investment strategies of IORPs. It also sets out a regulatory framework for cross-border activities aimed at liberalizing the provision of second-pillar benefits across the EU; para. 5 of the preamble explicitly states that the directive is 'a first step on the way to an internal market for occupational retirement provision organized on a European scale'. And para. 33 specifies the core elements of the regulatory strategy that will make this possible:

Without prejudice to national social and labour legislation on the organisation of pension systems, including compulsory membership and the outcomes of collective bargaining agreements, institutions should have the possibility to provide their services in other Member States. They should be allowed to accept sponsorship from undertakings located in other Member States and to operate pension schemes with members in more than one Member State. This would potentially lead to significant economies of scale for these institutions, improve the competitiveness of the Community industry and facilitate labour mobility...

The underlying rationale, in other words, seems that of reconciling national prerogatives and practices on compulsory affiliation and scheme profiles with an EU market of competing providers (the IORPs), abiding by detailed prudential rules and subject to supervision. The directive explicitly excludes from its scope of application both first-pillar schemes ('social security schemes which are covered by Regulation no. 1408/71') and in general institutions which operate on a PAYGO basis. It also lists a

---

[70] A European association of institutions run by the social partners (AIEP), linking most second-pillar pension providers, was established in 1996.

[71] Directive 2003/41/EC of the European Parliament and of the Council of 3 June 2003 on the activities and supervision of institutions for occupational retirement provision, *Official Journal L 235*, 23/09/2003, pp. 0010–0021.

number of specific national exceptions. Nevertheless, this directive opens up an enormous space for the dynamics of 'Europeanization' of social protection: the institutions affected by the directive cover about 25 per cent of the EU labour force (with peaks above 80 per cent in a few member states: see Table 4.6) and manage assets worth about 30 per cent of the EU's GDP (see Table 4.5). The directive's provisions on cross-border activities are very complex and envisage various national filters (authorizations, information, consultations, etc.). Based on regulatory experience of this kind at the EU level, we expect that the emergence of pan-European pension funds will not be a rapid and uncontroversial process—and the legislative text appropriately speaks of 'a first step', as mentioned earlier. But there is no question that a novel—though slow moving—institutional dynamics has been unleashed, which might lead to a significant reconfiguration of European pension systems in the years to come, along both the membership and the territorial dimensions.

The Grey Area of Supplementary Health Care

Supplementary health care schemes are a more recent phenomenon than supplementary pensions, and are smaller in terms of both coverage and cost. But the importance of this sector is increasing, and regulatory dilemmas and conflicts have already emerged in both the judicial and legislative arenas of the EU. To a large extent, developments have paralleled those observed in the field of pensions.

The third non-life directive (92/49) allowed member states to adopt or maintain special requirements for health insurers offering contracts that partially or wholly substitute for statutory cover (the first pillar), on 'public good' grounds. This provision was mainly aimed at safeguarding the German and Dutch status quo; in these two countries higher-income groups are not subject to compulsory affiliation, but the two governments have traditionally encouraged insurance membership through open enrolment, community rating, lifetime cover, and fixed standards requirements on insurers. Substitutive health care does not play a great role in other EU countries. France explicitly prohibits it. In other countries (such as Italy) proposals to introduce an 'opt out' from statutory cover have indeed come to the fore, but with no practical effect (Ferrera 1995).

However, the typical second-pillar scheme in health care is not substitutive but complementary to statutory coverage. It fills the gaps in the first pillar by offering additional benefits or alternative channels of provision alongside those envisaged by the compulsory schemes (or the NHS). This second pillar is typically collectively organized, in order to avoid market failures, through group insurance contracts with private providers or through mutual associations. The latter are non-profit bodies providing social services and protection, are democratically managed by their members, and are committed to solidarity and cohesion. They were very active in the early phases of the welfare state's expansion (Van der Mei 1993). Membership of supplementary health schemes can be voluntary or it can be envisaged by collective agreements, backed by the law, as in the case of supplementary pensions.

Not surprisingly, during the 1990s two contentious issues emerged: must collectively organized supplementary health care schemes comply with EC competition rules? And can they be made compulsory? Some countries have regulatory frameworks that recognize special advantages for, and impose special requirements on, such schemes, implicitly or explicitly relying on the 'public good' exemption (e.g. Ireland or Italy). France has a long tradition of state preferential treatment of *la mutualité*, which plays a substantial role in supplementary health care. Belgium and the Netherlands tend to include supplementary health benefits in their collective agreements, often on a compulsory basis. The provisions of the third non-life insurance directive do not offer a sufficient basis for determining the legality of these diverse national practices. It must also be noted that no coordination rules exist (as they do in the field of supplementary pensions) for supplementary health insurance.

Despite increasing complaints from the insurance industry, ECJ jurisprudence has been rather conservative and has not challenged domestic protection of second-pillar health care schemes from competition. In *Van der Woude*[72] the Court has even accepted, as in *Albany*, that membership can be made compulsory if such schemes originate in collective agreements, as happens in the Netherlands. However, the Commission has recently started to object to the tax advantages that France accords to its mutual funds, even though, following an infringement procedure,[73] the French government was forced to modify the mutuality code to make it compatible with the third non-life directive (Mossialos et al. 2001).

All these regulatory dilemmas and conflicts have already prompted some legislative steps. Following its clash with the Commission on mutual funds, the French government set up a task force led by Michel Rocard,

---

[72] Case C-222/98, *Hendrik van der Woude v. Stichting Beatrixoord* [2000] ECR I-07111.
[73] Infringement Procedure IP/02/742.

who advocated the establishment at the EU level of common rules safeguarding the public good by preserving solidarity and accessibility, applicable to all operators in the field of voluntary health insurance. Mainly on
Rocard's initiative, the European Parliament adopted a resolution on supplementary health insurance in 2000, calling for a common regulatory
framework based on the principles of no risk selection based on genetic
typing or medical screening, lifelong insurance (with portability),
transparency of premiums, and so forth (EP 2000). However, no legislative
proposal has originated from this resolution.

The insurance industry is actively seeking to enter the potentially prof-
itable field of supplementary medical benefits. Some governments are
seriously exploring the possibility of moving some limited functions of
their first pillars (such as long-term care) to this pillar of provision, with
the involvement of mutual funds and private insurers.[74] Existing EC laws
however, contain many ambiguities about what can actually be done and
how in this area. Some commentators recommend a fourth generation of
insurance directives (Mossialos et al. 2001), setting out effective and prudential rules for an internal market for supplementary health care benefits, clearly distinguishing the space of collective insurance schemes—
where national social and labour standards might play a bigger role, as
in the case of pensions—from that of individual plans.

Third Pillars: Only Regulatory Fine-Tuning of the Internal Market

While in the case of second-pillar provision national governments have
maintained at least some boundary control and regulatory prerogatives,
third-pillar schemes fall squarely within the scope of the insurance directives, and thus must fully abide by free movement and competition rules,
bar a few exceptions in the name of public purposes. We mentioned earlier
that the three waves of EU regulations prompted in the 1990s a dynamic of
mergers and industry concentration and that the directives were interpreted in a minimalist fashion, generating some perverse side effects. The
supranational regulatory framework in this area, however, is still in flux.
Various legislative acts were adopted in the 1990s to fill gaps and close
loopholes. In the life sector, the overall framework became so complex
that in 2000 the Commission proposed the adoption of a single coherent
text. The Council decided, however, to wait until June 2002 so that it could

---

[74] A proposal in this direction was launched by the Italian Minister of Health in the Spring of 2003.

incorporate the provisions of Directive 02/12[75] on solvency margin requirements. The new, simplified directive on life insurance was finally adopted at the end of 2002 (02/87).[76]

Insurance is part of the broader area of financial services for which the Commission outlined a detailed action plan of legislative interventions in 1999 with a view to removing the remaining obstacles and fine-tuning the internal market (EC 1999b). This plan is inspired by a 'consumer-oriented' perspective and stresses questions of accessibility, security, prudential behaviour, and oversight. Some of the foreseen measures apply to insurance companies and the coverage of 'social risks'. The full implementation of this plan will require several years: the exact balance between efficiency and equity can be assessed only after the process is completed.

Capped Social Sovereignty and the New Spatial Politics of Solidarity

What conclusions can we draw from our analysis on the boundary-setting powers of national welfare states? In short, we can say that, as far as the internal boundaries of social insurance are concerned, the interplay between national and supranational authorities has so far resulted in the maintenance and protection of the central tenet of domestic social sovereignty, namely, compulsory membership of public insurance monopolies, but has posed a 'cap' on it: residents can be locked in to secure a proper functioning of domestic sharing arrangements, but no further than the extent of their existing basic or first-pillar schemes, where solidaristic elements are more evident. The Regulations of 1971 and 1992 (as well as the 1998 directive on supplementary pension rights) provide for coordination rules that make these capped territorial or membership spaces compatible with the free movement of persons, while the ECJ doctrine on solidarity (as developed especially in *Poucet-Pistre*) shields these spaces from competition rules. Outside the cap, however, member states have witnessed a substantial loss of boundary-setting prerogatives, along both the territorial and the

---

[75] Directive 2002/12/EC of the European Parliament and of the Council of 5 March 2002 amending Council Directive 79/267/EEC as regards the solvency margin requirements for life assurance undertakings, *Official Journal L 077*, 20/03/2002, pp. 0011–0016.

[76] Directive 2002/87/EC of the European Parliament and of the Council of 16 December 2002 on the supplementary supervision of credit institutions, insurance undertakings and investment firms in a financial conglomerate and amending Council Directives 73/239/EEC, 79/267/EEC, 92/49/EEC, 92/96/EEC, 93/6/EEC, and 93/22/EEC, and Directives 98/78/EC and 2000/12/EC of the European Parliament and of the Council, *Official Journal L 035*, 11/02/2003, pp. 0001–0027.

membership dimensions. Second pillars are subject to competition rules and to provisions on freedom of service. Member states do retain some boundary-setting and regulatory powers, but under the new limits set by supranational authorities. Third pillars are, by contrast, almost fully integrated into a single market. This three-layered regulatory regime applies in full to EU nationals. Third country nationals enjoy virtually equal treatment in the member state where they have legal residence and if they are legally allowed to move. But entry and residence requirements still depend on national decisions, based on economic and political considerations.

Some additional conclusions can be drawn from the four surveys of case law and regulatory developments presented earlier. The first is that, far from being a linear and unilateral, top-down process of erosion, the redrawing of cross-state boundaries in the social sphere since the 1970s has resulted from a tug of war between the national and the supranational levels, in which the member states have been able in various cases to assert their interests and to claw back prerogatives regarded as critical for their sovereignty. As predicted by the theory of 'bounded structuring', boundary transcendence dynamics that reflect market transactions have provoked countermoves to maintain boundaries on the part of state authorities, with a view to defending the 'bundle of territoriality' and re-establishing the traditional link between rights and obligations on the one hand and territory on the other. Since the 1970s, such countermoves have basically followed five strategies.

1. *Constitutional protection*, centred on formally shielding in the treaties certain areas from EU competence (e.g. citizenship and residence rules) and/or maintaining unanimity requirements as much as possible for decisions regarding social security. The most emblematic example of this strategy is perhaps the choice of creating an altogether separate pillar in 1992 for immigration policy, in the hope of avoiding the interference of the Commission, Parliament, and especially the ECJ in the setting of boundaries vis-à-vis third country nationals.

2. *Legislative amendment*, aimed at modifying supranational rules that were proving to be threatening to the status quo, especially in the wake of ECJ judgements. For example, despite the joint decision trap, governments have been able to agree on two significant amendments of the 1971 Regulation: once in 1981, to block off an attempt to deprive them of authorization powers in the field of health care; and again in 1992, to reaffirm the link between residence and eligibility for social assistance benefits.

3. *Legislative pre-emption*, aimed at incorporating ad hoc protective clauses in new EU acts directly or potentially affecting domestic arrangements. The preambles of the third insurance directives and of the pension fund directives are telling examples of such clauses, inserted with the clear goal of safeguarding national islands of social sovereignty. This strategy has also had some domestic parallels, such as Germany's attempts to tailor social legislation on minimum pensions and long-term care so as to avoid supranational interference.

4. *Proactive political mobilization* in the EU legal and legislative arenas in order to influence the substance of the proceedings and to orient them towards general principles and rules in favour of domestic social sovereignty. As mentioned earlier, the French government worked hard to turn the *Poucet Pistre* judgment in its favour. In many cases, national governments have formed coalitions in both the judicial and legislative arenas to neutralize a potential threat to their social sovereignty. And in general the Council has offered an effective arena in which to block, modify, or delay legislation in sensitive areas. The story of the pension fund directive, summarized earlier, clearly illustrates this point.

5. *Non-compliance* and *hiding*, aimed at delaying or distorting the domestic transposition of EU legislation potentially disruptive of the national status quo. French resistance to complying with the ECJ rulings on the exportability of social pensions or the controversy on preferential tax treatment of domestic pension funds and mutual societies illustrated earlier constitute emblematic examples of this strategy—which of course can operate only as a temporary countermove, perhaps to gain time to organize one of the other strategies.[77]

The second conclusion that can be drawn from our reconstruction is that, far from ruling systematically in favour of the market, the ECJ has in some critical instances defended essential prerequisites for national solidarity (e.g. in the *Poucet-Pistre* or *Albany* cases) or struck down national impediments, not to the *market*, but to cross-border *redistribution* (e.g. the *Giletti* case). In this light, the view of the Court as 'market police' ought to be partly reconsidered: the issue of reconciling the principle of social protection with those of free movement and competition in a widening market has been taken more seriously by the Court than usually acknowledged.

---

[77] For a more detailed discussion of the various strategies of influence and adaptation of national authorities to supranational law, see Conant (2001, 2004) and Sindbjerg Martinsen (2004), which also contains exhaustive reviews of the relevant literature.

The third conclusion is that case law and regulatory developments have had a differential impact on distinct areas of national social protection. With pensions, member states have been able to preserve effective barriers around the principle of compulsory membership of public schemes in their first pillars (an essential bulwark for domestic redistribution), but have lost considerable ground at the second pillar level. The pension fund directive of 2003 has created the conditions for a gradual Europeanization of this level of provision. In the field of social assistance, the reassertion of the territoriality principle after 1992 has given back to the member states important prerogatives in determining who can enter the 'inner circle' of need-based solidarity. The critical fault line on this front is constituted by residence rules: the formalization of a 'Community concept' of residence is gradually undermining national control over entries into this pillar of provision. The balance has tilted further away from national control in the case of health care; together with supplementary pensions, health care currently appears the sector most exposed to destructuring dynamics.

The final and more general conclusion is this. As the encounter between national welfare states and European integration has become more intense, a distinctive new spatial politics has emerged, structured around locality interests and vocality strategies. As discussed in Chapter 3, the seeds of this development had already been planted during the *Trente Glorieuses*, with the appearance of supplementary schemes on the one hand and the establishment of the common market on the other. Between the 1970s and 2000s these seeds have come to maturity in the wake of four distinct dynamics: the endogenous transformation of national welfare states and their shift towards a multitier and multipillar reconfiguration; the relaunching of European integration with the single market project and EMU, as well as the further institutionalization of the EC legal order; rising migration flows, both within the EU and across the EU's external borders; and the interaction of the first three dynamics.

The new spatial politics of welfare is obviously not coterminous with the (new) politics of welfare *tout court*, but it is an increasingly important part of it. In this politics, actors define their interests in terms of their position in arenas crossed by boundaries that confer (different) rights and impose (different) obligations to the membership or territorial spaces created by them. Being 'in' or 'out', being able to enter or exit from these spaces, makes a substantial difference for actors. Spatial positioning per se thus becomes a salient goal and a distinct object of voice activities. The multilevel character of the EU polity (and especially the EC institutional order as a new 'law for exit-and-voice') offers in its turn to actors a rich repertoire of strategies and venues for pursuing their novel spatial interests. In our reconstruction of events, virtually all the locality and vocality options listed in Figure 1.3 have turned out to be pertinent to and useful for describing different situations and behaviours.

We discuss at more length the functioning logic and the practical implications of this new institutional and political configuration in Chapter 6. Before doing so one important building block must be added to the picture: the rise of regions and local governments as new actors and/or arenas for welfare provision and thus as new relevant coordinates for the spatial architecture and politics of solidarity. Chapter 5 is entirely devoted to this important and novel development.

5

From Welfare States to Welfare Regions

Local, National, Regional? The Long Territorial Parabola of European Social Protection

Social protection emerged in Europe as a highly localized sphere of activity. Parishes, municipalities, charities, and, somewhat later, mutual societies were its firstz protagonists, all operating with decisional discretion and territorial particularism. As highlighted by T. H. Marshall, the building of citizenship entailed a slow and delicate process of institutional 'fusion' of previously circumscribed ambits of social interaction, regulated by their own formal and informal codes of conduct. The existence of strong peripheries, that is, areas characterized by a tradition of cultural distinctiveness, political autonomy, and economic independence, tended to disturb the consolidation of the central state and internal standardization. In such contexts, the removal of local boundaries and especially the fusion of pre-existing sharing ties and practices into a single 'national pot' encountered severe difficulties: the administrative integration of the state territory based on principles of equal citizenship could proceed only at a very slow pace. The most emblematic example of this syndrome is certainly offered by Switzerland, where the tradition of cantonal solidarities based on associative self-help, coupled with high levels of local political participation and direct democracy, slowed the development of the national welfare state to an extraordinary degree in both qualitative and quantitative terms (Flora 1986; Obinger, Armingeon, Bonoli, and Bertozzi; 2005). As is well known, federalism delayed welfare state formation also in the North American context, in both Canada and the USA (Banting 1995; Flora and Heidenheimer 1981; Obinger, Leibfried, and Castles 2005).

Variations in the centre–periphery and church–state cleavage linked to the national revolution (in Rokkan's sense) were especially relevant for the early structuring of 'social services' (education, health, poor relief) (Flora 1986). Strong peripheries and/or strong subcultures (in particular, religious ones) had often already developed solid institutional structures and practices in these sectors, with entrenched links to the surrounding territory in terms of cultural norms, funding, management, and so forth. The margins of manoeuvre enjoyed by such structures and practices long delayed the penetration of these spheres by public authorities, and even in those countries where full (or quasi-full) state control and nationalization did finally occur (as in Italy, Germany, Belgium, or the Netherlands) peripheral and localist traditions left an institutional residue that resurfaced when the state-national parabola of social protection started to show—as we shall see—the first signs of reversal.

Centre–periphery and church–state cleavages played a much smaller role in the field of transfer payments. Public and compulsory social insurance was a new invention; there was nothing to fuse across subnational territories when the first schemes were introduced in the late nineteenth and early twentieth centuries. Peripheral opposition did delay introduction in some countries: subnational and or subcultural elites were conscious of the role that the new schemes could play in central state consolidation and thus strove to defend their prerogatives in this field. But even the Dutch pillars (the *zuilen*) accepted state pension insurance after the First World War, and the Swiss cantons did so after the Second World War. The new technique could offer unprecedented material advantages to various social groups, but it required a wide reach in terms of membership. This in turn presupposed the mobilization of administrative and coercive resources that only the central state could muster. Even though Bismarck's reforms responded primarily to the political threats of the new social question linked to capitalist industrialization, they also served clear state-building purposes: they were aimed at consolidating the position of the Reich vis-à-vis the federated states, which in the 1880s still operated as gatekeepers of territorial membership through their citizenship laws (see Chapter 2).

With the advent of public compulsory insurance, social rights acquired both a standardized content and an individualized nature, as subjective entitlements to certain forms of public protection—originally and typically cash transfers. The source of such new rights was the nation state, even in those countries which opted for an occupationalist rather than a universalistic approach. Soon after its inception (but especially during the *Trente Glorieuses*), social insurance became not only a factor of national closure and an important dimension of external boundary-building, but also a powerful engine of centralization, increasing the concentration of authoritative, administrative, and fiscal resources at the national centre. The engine also worked in the direction of further domestic standardization, that is, greater uniformity among localities and a gradual ironing out of territorial diversity in institutional structures and practices. Though typically affecting the social transfer component of the welfare state, these two trends eventually had a spill-over effect also on social services: their staff became part of the public bureaucracy, national standards of performance were defined (and sometimes imposed on recalcitrant peripheries, especially in education and health care), and in a few cases national organizations run by the central state were set up to cater for the social needs of special categories such as orphans or the disabled.

To be sure, the nationalization of social protection and its massive expansion in the first decades after the Second World War did have significant implications for territorial redistribution. Centre–periphery strains over the allocative and distributive choices of fiscal policy as a whole did not subside, and even tended to increase with the rise of 'big government'. However, the territorial redistribution brought about by the welfare state followed indirectly from interpersonal transfers based on standard risk definitions and eligibility criteria. Thus areas with high proportions of elderly people could receive higher transfers from the central administration, but only to the extent that the elderly qualified for old age pensions. Class positions were regarded as the prime source of social need, and class conflicts were the driving force of welfare state politics. In most European countries territorial redistribution per se remained a much less salient political issue than interclass redistribution, and could be dealt with through a separate set of policies explicitly devoted to regional aid and development by means of territorially earmarked fiscal transfers (La Spina 2003).

The ascending phase of this parabola of welfare state nationalization started to slow down during the 1960s, with a renewed emphasis on local government in the sphere of social services (e.g. in the Nordic area) and the launching of grand debates on decentralization and its merits. The first wave of decentralizing reforms arrived, however, during the 1970s and 1980s. Almost everywhere local governments were rationalized and reinforced as service providers; 'meso-governments' (i.e. units of government immediately below the national level, typically 'regions') were established in many countries, including hyper-centralist France (Le Galès and Lequesne 1998; Sharpe 1993; Moreno 2003). Italy, Spain, and Belgium became regional states, creating the basis for a gradual process of federalization. In those states that were already federal (Germany, Austria, Switzerland) a new pattern of intergovernmental relationship emerged, involving *Politikverflechtung* (the interlocking of policy competences and policymaking across levels of government) and greater activism on the part of subnational units in a context of more cooperative, even if occasionally gridlocked, federalism (Baldi 2003; Klatt 1989; Manow 2005; Scharpf 1988).

This first wave of decentralization (and in particular regionalization) was partly a response to functional pressures originating in the administrative overload of the central state and the ensuing search for more effective management of public services and a better implementation of national policies (Le Galès 2002). But it was also partly the result of politico-institutional dynamics: the implementation of specific constitutional prescriptions (as in Italy, Spain, and Belgium), growing demands for democratic participation and control (also on sectoral activities of the state, such as education, health care, and social services), and the gradual defreezing of traditional cleavage structures and party systems. It was in the 1970s and 1980s that regionalist parties made their first vocal appearance in many European countries, promoting or exploiting the revival of peripheral identities and interregional rivalries (De Winter and Türsan 1988). Once established as directly elected levels of government, regions naturally acquired an interest in self-aggrandizement, elaborating more or less deliberate strategies of 'competitive region-building',[1] that is, institutional strengthening at the expense of both other regions (a strategy that might be called *horizontal* region-building) and other levels of government (*vertical* region-building). The rise of this new regionalism can be seen as a significant endogenous brake, if not a threatening and destructuring wedge, for the wider process of bounded structuring around the nation state that had peaked in Europe during the 1950s and 1960s.

The trend towards decentralization and regionalism was also linked to the internal logic of development of the welfare state proper, for at least two reasons. The first has to do with the expansion of social services, in a broad sense. Even though transfers (and especially pensions) were indeed the most dynamic component of social expenditure, from the 1960s social services also began to grow significantly in terms of spending, infrastructures, staff, and users. The Nordic countries were the pioneers on this front (Fargion 2000). Having embarked upon this course when economic resources were readily available, these countries were able to reconfigure the overall profile of their welfare state in a 'service-rich' direction. As Figure 5.1 shows, in the mid-1980s services for families, the elderly, and

---

[1] The notion of competitive region-building borrows from Banting's idea of a 'competitive state-building' process, pitting the federal state against the provinces in Canada during the historical formation of the Canadian welfare state (Banting 1995).

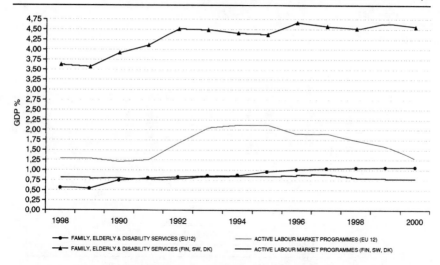

Notes: expenditure trends have been calculated for two clusters of EU countries: EU-12 includes Austria, Belgium, Germany, Spain, Greece, France, Italy, Ireland, Luxembourg, Netherlands, Portugal, and United Kingdom; the other cluster comprises three Nordic countries: Finland, Sweden, and Denmark.

Statistics are in the form of averages of OECD expenditure data. Missing values: Austria 1981–4 and 1986–9 for family and elderly and disability services; Greece 1980–9 for elderly and disability services; Austria 1986–9, Italy 1985–1990, and Portugal 1985 for active labour market programmes.

Total expenditure for active labour market programmes, as defined by OECD, corresponds to the sum of expenditures on: public employment services and administration, labour market training, youth measures, employment subsidies, and disability services.

Source: OECD (2004)

Fig 5.1 Expenditure trends for social services and active labour market programmes in the European Union, 1980–2000

the disabled already absorbed more than 3 per cent of GDP on average in Finland, Sweden, and Denmark, and grew to exceed 4.5 per cent of GDP during the 1990s. Active labour policies started from about 1 per cent in 1985 and peaked at above 2 per cent in the mid-1990s. Other European countries moved later, under increasingly severe resource constraints. But in the early 1990s the resources spent on services started to grow on average also outside the Nordic context. As shown by Figure 5.2 health care spending also grew significantly between the 1970s and 2000s.

This recalibration towards services is largely related to the changing structure of needs in European societies (Esping-Andersen 2002). Demographic ageing, the gender revolution, and changes in family patterns and

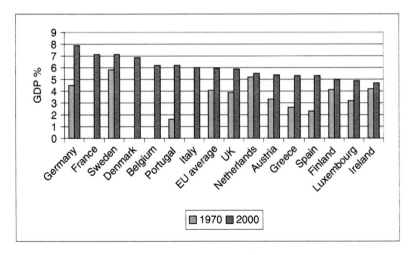

EU-15 average has been calculated with available data for the 15 EU member states. Missing values: Belgium, Denmark, France, Italy for 1970.
Source: OECD (2003).

Fig 5.2 Public expenditure on health in the European Union, 1970–2000

behaviour have brought to the fore 'care' needs that can no longer be absorbed by households or individuals (Saraceno 2002). The transition to post-Fordist labour markets has in turn created the need for individually tailored job placement, training, and retraining opportunities that were not foreseen by traditional unemployment insurance schemes or national labour exchanges (Crouch, Finegold, and Sako 1999). While still relevant, class positions have become less important than 'life situations' in originating social needs (Alber 1995). Life situations are determined not only by age, gender, and physical and educational status, but also by the concrete opportunities and supports offered by the surrounding territory, in particular the local availability of adequate social and labour market services. The place of residence and its endowment of social infrastructures do affect people's life chances to a very significant degree. Take one of the most pressing 'new' social risks which is rapidly spreading throughout European ageing societies, namely, 'dependency', the loss of personal physical autonomy due to illness or disability. The ability to cope with this risk is critically linked to the local availability of appropriate 'care packages' consisting of home help, community initiatives, organized transport, targeted health services, and so on. National standards can still play a significant role in the area of new social risks, for instance in safeguarding basic equity across localities, supporting and promoting territorial mobility, and providing benchmarking and evaluation standards. But local and especially regional contexts have increasingly affirmed themselves as optimal areas for the planning and management of new forms of service provision. Activism in these sectors can also serve competitive region-building strategies, offering subnational elites a promising and rewarding basis for differentiating their policies in search of legitimization and votes. As highlighted by Banting, when different levels of government engage in politico-institutional competition, the locus of initiative and command of social policy programmes can play a crucial role: 'social programmes designed and controlled at the regional level can become instruments for strengthening regional cultures and enhancing the significance of local communities in the lives of citizens, thereby reinforcing differentiation and centrifugal tendencies at the national level' (Banting 1995: 271). Given the pre-emption of 'old' welfare programmes (i.e. traditional social insurance schemes) by central state institutions, it is not surprising that regional governments have striven to move first in the promotion and control of the 'new' programmes, remobilizing (where available) all the historical residues of social and institutional capital in this realm (such as a vibrant local tradition of voluntary work and organizations and/or of firm-based apprenticeship or vocational training practices).

The second direct link between the welfare state proper and the new regionalism has to do with fiscal imperatives and the so-called new politics of welfare (Pierson 2001). The pressing need to contain costs in order to reduce deficits and debt has prompted central governments to try to regain control over subnational spending. The first wave of decentralization typically transferred to regions and local governments spending powers in service provision, while keeping most taxation powers at the central level. During the 1990s a second wave of reforms took place in many countries, aimed at reconfiguring centre–periphery financial relations with a view to increasing the fiscal responsibility of subnational units. Rigid institutional constraints have been imposed on the expenditure side, sometimes (as in Italy, Belgium, and Germany) by stipulating an internal 'stability pact' for complying with EMU requirements (Maino 2003). Financial transfers from the central government have been reduced, forcing subnational governments to raise local resources in order to finance their own social programmes. This 'decentralization of penury' (Keating 1998) has been driven not only by functional pressures but also by political calculations. 'Passing the buck' to subnational governments had the obvious advantage of shifting on to local government the blame for unpopular policies of retrenchment.

The effect of this new phase of centre–periphery relations has been the growing politicization of the issue of interterritorial transfers and solidarity. Subnational governments have become much more sensitive and alert to their net financial balances vis-à-vis central governments, punctiliously comparing the revenues generated by their own tax base but appropriated by the central state with the transfers received from the central state. Such comparison has been extended beyond tax revenues and territorially earmarked grants to include interpersonal transfers (like pensions) financed by social security contributions. In this way, the politico-institutional separation between policies for regional aid and development on the one hand and welfare policies on the other has started to erode. The new politics of austerity has acquired a salient territorial dimension, pitting richer areas against poorer ones, and winning areas against losing ones, while regions have become important and vocal 'entrenched interests' in the difficult game of welfare state recalibration. To use Börzel's effective metaphor, more 'pay' (i.e. financial responsibilities) has prompted more 'say' (Börzel 2000), encouraging regions to mobilize in all the relevant policymaking arenas and occasionally to act as powerful veto players. To the extent that regional mobilization has succeeded in blocking, influencing, or even disobeying national decisions (as in Catalonia or Lombardy during the 1990s), the decentralization of penury has fostered and accelerated, rather than contained, vertical region-building dynamics. Instead of leading to regained control over the peripheries by the centre, the second wave of centre–periphery reforms has ended up by strengthening regions both politically and institutionally. This is especially true in those countries that had already taken significant regionalizing steps in the 1970s and early 1980s: devolution (i.e. the transfer of exclusive competences to meso-governments) has taken place in Belgium (which officially became a federal state in 1993), Italy, and Spain. But a similar development has occurred in the UK, especially with the Scottish devolution of 1998 (McEwen 2002, McEwen and Parry 2005). In the Nordic countries too during the 1990s important competences were transferred to regional governments in the field of social and employment services, especially in Denmark (Persson 2003).

The twenty-first century has thus begun with a marked revival of 'peripheries' within European nation states and with visible symptoms of a regionalization of social protection, especially of policies targeted at new

social needs. Regions have increasingly become the spatial units of reference for organizing a collective response to such needs. Regional governments have become important political and institutional actors and have
increasingly engaged themselves in voice activities, both horizontally (vis-
à-vis other regions) and vertically (vis-à-vis local governments below them
and national governments above them). They are also protagonists in, and
focal points for, the emergence and functioning of those governance
networks, extended to non-public actors, which are becoming more and
more important for the design and implementation of many social and
economic programmes aimed at territorial growth and development. As is
well-known, theorists of multilevel governance explicitly consider the
regions as the 'third level' of the new composite EU polity (Jeffery 1997;
Hooghe and Marks 2001), characterized by a clearly recognizable institutional autonomy and logic of development. Given the size of 'old' social
schemes, it would be misleading and definitely premature to speak of a
momentous process of denationalization of European social protection.
But the regional third level is likely to have very significant consequences
for European 'system-building' in general and for the future configuration
of social protection in particular.

European Integration, neo-regionalism, and the Rise of Competitive Solidarities

The revival of peripheries and the appearance of competitive region-building have been promoted not only by the endogenous elements and developments illustrated earlier but also by two exogenous factors: economic
internationalization and European integration. A brief discussion of the
role played by these two factors will allow us to highlight more clearly the
link between changes in territorial boundaries (and boundary-building
strategies) on the one hand and the new spatial politics of solidarity on
the other.

Starting in the 1980s, the growing openness of domestic economies and
the creation of the single market, coupled with improvements in technology and communication as well as the rise of multinational corporations,
have fundamentally altered the nature of territorial competition. During
the *Trente Glorieuses*, national economies essentially functioned as 'black
boxes' connected to each other by flexible exchange rates (Gilpin 1987). The
metaphor of the black box is meant to highlight the self-contained nature
of national territories and the relatively high degree of domestic sovereignty of their central governments. As part and parcel of the black box,

regional (i.e. within-state) territories were not directly or autonomously exposed to foreign competition. National boundaries carefully filtered their external transactions, locking them in to a robustly bounded regulatory space. The public budget took care directly or indirectly of regional disparities and imbalances within the black box. In the new liberalized context that has been emerging gradually since the 1980s, regional territories have come to find themselves into a completely different situation. The removal of boundaries has opened up unprecedented opportunities (and/ or risks) of direct and autonomous cross-border transactions based on a logic of 'naked' competition, that is, competition no longer (or more weakly) mediated by national regulatory regimes and flexible exchange rates. The objects of this competition are basically markets, investments, and technology (Keating 1998). In order to survive and succeed in the new environment, regional territories must be skilled in exploiting all available assets and comparative advantages: the logic of economically integrated areas is precisely that of promoting competitive specializations. Territorial differentiation is linked not only to economic assets and advantages *stricto sensu* but also to social and institutional assets which can make a difference in attracting desirable mobile resources. Thus, a region's development is increasingly dependent on the overall 'quality' of its territory: not surprisingly, quality enhancement (e.g. of local infrastructures, public services and administration, or human capital) is one of the leading themes of the new region-building process and politics. As noted by Bartolini (2004), the strategies of competitive differentiation pursued by regional governments during the last two decades can be fruitfully interpreted as boundary-building, that is, the creation of novel spaces with increasingly distinctive public policy profiles aimed at favouring insiders and attracting groups of outsiders that can bring advantages to the regional community. To a certain extent, these regional boundary-building strategies echo the traditional strategies already experimented with by national state-builders of different ideological leanings. In his survey of new regionalisms, Keating (1998) identifies, for example, both 'bourgeois' and 'social democratic' types of neo-regionalism, promoted by specific developmental coalitions, that is, 'place-based interclass alliances' devoted to economic growth.[2] But Keating also discusses more innovative strategies: for example, a 'sweatshop

---

[2] A 'bourgeois' strategy is centred on technology, productivity, and added value; economic and social policies are weakly connected; the local labour market is flexibly organized. A 'social democratic' strategy is centred on labour reskilling, active employment services, and quality of life issues. In the Italian context, an example of the first strategy can be found in Lombardy; an example of the second in Emilia-Romagna (Gualmini and Alti 2001; Ferrera et al. 2001).

economy' strategy aimed at offering to foreign investors a low-wage and regulation-lean productive context, or an explicit 'nation-building' strategy emphasizing internal unity and cohesion based on cultural distinctiveness and geared towards neo-mercantilist goals.

European integration has fostered peripheral revival and neo-regionalism not only indirectly through market-making but also directly through cohesion policies. In contrast with the experience of individual nation states, EU system-building could not proceed to establish supranational sharing arrangements based on interpersonal transfers and individual social entitlements. It did, however, establish mechanisms for territorial redistribution through regional grants (Anderson 1995; Bache 1998; Christiansen 1999; Hooghe and Keating 1994). Given the meagreness of the EU budget compared with national budgets, the real size of these grants is relatively modest. However, it has been constantly increasing through time: in the mid-1970s structural funds absorbed about 5 per cent of the EU budget; in 2000 they had come to absorb about 35 per cent, or about 0.4 per cent of the EU's GDP. For regions that fully qualify for aid, EU support from the structural funds can represent several percentage points of the region's GDP. Not surprisingly, the EU's cohesion policy was incisively reformed and greatly strengthened in line with the acceleration of the internal market project after the SEA. The 1988 reform was explicitly aimed at counterbalancing the potentially adverse effects of the single market on the poorer regions and at smoothing the dynamic of territorial differentiation that was to be expected from deeper economic integration (Bailey and De Propris 2002). The magnitude of EU financial support for the average region actually grew from 0.4 per cent of GDP in 1985–7 to 0.6–0.7 per cent in 1989–93, with an upward trend in following years (Cappelen et al. 2003). It must also be noted that the stricter enforcement of competition rules during the 1980s and 1990s led to the elimination of many national programmes of direct and indirect regional aid (typically territorially earmarked social security contribution exemptions or rebates), thus further enhancing the salience and attractiveness of EU funds.

The net impact of the structural funds on regional growth and in particular on pan-European territorial cohesion is a highly controversial issue (Bailey and De Propris 2002; Fagerberg and Verspagen 1996; Hooghe 1998; Viesti and Prota 2004). Without denying some positive effects on growth and cohesion (as vigorously argued by the Commission), recent debates tend to stress the importance of mediating factors and in particular the availability at the regional level of appropriate capacities to compete for grants in the first place and then to actually take advantage of them, in combination with other local resources (Bailey and De Propris 2002). For our purposes, the issue of how effective the structural funds actually are is less important than the overall reconfiguration of centre–periphery relations that their very existence has brought about, qua novel source of authoritative decisions and resource allocation/distribution, with all its system-building implications. In a nutshell, it can be said that the emergence of a distinctive supranational policy of regional support and cohesion has had the following main effects:

- it has contributed to the repoliticization of territorial cleavages and in particular of the issue of interregional redistribution;
- it has enhanced the salience and visibility of meso-governments as both membership spaces and as institutional and political actors;[3]
- it has made available new and increasingly substantial resources (primarily, but not exclusively, financial) both from the EU budget and from national budgets (through co-financing rules);
- it has provided further incentives to both horizontal and vertical region-building dynamics, often acting as a catalyst for the formation of local developmental coalitions and of institutional capabilities; and
- it has established and institutionalized a direct channel of access to supranational authorities on the part of such coalitions and thus direct means of communication between EC institutions (in particular the Commission) and the 'third level' of governance. In the early 1990s this dynamic spilled over into the wider EU institutional framework: the Maastricht Treaty in fact established a new Committee of the Regions in which the interests of the third level are officially represented at the EU centre.

All these developments have brought about a significant recalibration of Europe's centre–periphery relations. If the debate on the economic impact of structural funds has produced conflicting findings, the literature on the politico-institutional consequences of EU cohesion policy tends to agree that its net effect has been to substantially empower subnational governments vis-à-vis national ones. True, there are some sceptical or nuanced views in this literature: empowerment is significantly mediated by national institutional traditions and constellations (e.g. Börzel 2000) and by local dynamics of political agency (Bukowsky, Piattoni, and Smyrl 2003; Graziano 2004). Such empowerment has affected to a much greater extent those regions in which favourable preconditions already existed, and it leaves much to be desired on equity grounds

---

[3] Countries such as Portugal, Greece, and Ireland have virtually created regional subunits *de novo* in order more effectively to exploit the opportunities offered by the EU cohesion policy.

(e.g. Bailey and De Propris 2002). The strengthening of subnational governments has sometimes been paradoxically weakened or nullified by the complexity of EU rules and their constraints (e.g. Le Galès 2002). In some cases and some moments European integration has undermined rather than strengthened regional political power (e.g. Bourne 2003). But—in my reading at least and that of the burgeoning research on multilevel governance—the overall balance sheet of the debate is positive (i.e. increasing empowerment). The new dynamics of territorial competition and regional empowerment unleashed by European integration has intertwined with and reinforced most of the endogenous trends towards subnationalization discussed earlier. More fundamentally, however, it has inserted a new configuration of actors and opportunity structures in the sphere of territorial politics. As far as actors are concerned, the main novelty is not regional empowerment per se but the complex web of different coalitions that can emerge from the proliferation of levels of governance. Horizontal interregional coalitions (possibly cutting across national boundaries) and vertical regional–supranational coalitions are the most innovative combinations that can be registered on this front. As far as opportunity structures are concerned, the main novelty is a significant expansion of both 'locality' and 'vocality' options for all actors, but in particular for the regions.

As illustrated in Chapter 1, locality options have to do with spatial positionings: choices regarding exit or entry, 'staying in' or 'staying out' of a bounded space. On the locality front, the big change brought about by European integration is the substantial increase in both exit and entry options for subnational governments. In a first and more obvious sense, options expand for regional actors (especially the members of local developmental coalitions) to move freely across the geographical space of the EU (and even further) in the pursuit of regional goals: this is a direct consequence of boundary removal dynamics, especially in the wake of EMU. In a second and deeper sense, locality options expand for the regions qua territories or, more precisely, qua membership spaces. The new institutional context allows unprecedented opportunities for a region to opt out of certain existing domestic regulatory regimes, to stay out of newly established ones, and to join interregional or EU-wide programmes: in other words, regions can increasingly constitute themselves as distinctive localities, bounding or debounding themselves according to their own region-building strategies.[4]

---

[4] Illustrative examples will be given later in respect of the Italian experience.

Vocality options are in their turn choices about whether and how to manifest one's voice (claims, demands, and protest) vis-à-vis the central authorities of a given space. On the vocality front, European integration has expanded options in at least three directions. First, regions have gained a right to voice at the new centre, that is, at the supranational level (Marks, Haesly, and Mbaye 2002). Borrowing Rokkan's famous distinction (Rokkan 1970), we might say that, in the new Euro-polity, regions have passed at least two of the four classical thresholds for an effective expression of voice:

- *legitimate organization*: regions are now recognized actors that can freely and officially organize at the supranational level (individually and/or collectively) for expressing their interests;
- *incorporation*: regions have gained formal rights of participation through a dedicated supranational body (the Committee of the Regions) in which they have suffrage and eligibility rights.

Sub-national governments have made less progress along the other two dimensions: 'representation' and 'executive' power, which have to do with access to and control of the core representative and executive bodies of the political system. Some steps have however been made along these dimensions. Sub-national governments are often formally included in many committees for EU policy-making and implementation. Moreover, the regions of certain countries (e.g. Belgium or Germany) have gained the right to sit on the Council of Ministers when the agenda includes issues that fall within their competence. But of course the basis for territorial representation in the core EU institutions remains clearly national.

The second direction of expansion of vocality options concerns the domestic arena. Thanks to their novel exit potential, regions have increased their bargaining power vis-à-vis the central state and have tended to gain new institutionalized opportunities for voicing their interests and influencing policymaking at the domestic level, for example through the establishment of new specialist bodies for intergovernmental bargaining and concertation. Regional voicing can often take the form of voice for exit (at the limit, through separatism and secession) or partial exit (e.g. through

---

[5] Rokkan distinguished between four distinct 'thresholds' in the historical development of voice channels, that is, mechanisms for the transmission of claims from territorial and social peripheries towards central authorities: (*a*) the threshold of legitimate organization; (*b*) the threshold of incorporation; (*c*) the threshold of representation; and (*d*) the threshold of executive access (Flora, Kuhnle, and Urwin 1999: 231 ff.)

devolution), especially by the more prosperous regions and/or the historical peripheries (such as Scotland or Catalonia). But it can also take the form of voice against exit by poorer regions for which separatism, devolution, or federalism might imply fewer fiscal transfers (Bartolini 2004).

Third, regions have acquired new opportunities for exerting mixed, cross-level forms of voice, in particular 'voice from outside' vis-à-vis other regions or national governments, either through political channels (especially forming alliances with the Commission) or through judicial litigation before the ECJ.[6] The multilevel governance literature has discussed a number of emblematic examples of successful alliances between regions and the Commission to impose their will or point of view vis-à-vis national authorities (see e.g. Ansell, Parsons, and Darden 1997).[7]

According to Bartolini, this new configuration is likely to confer on the emerging EU political system a 'stratarchic' imprint, that is, to orient it towards a pattern of political transactions less structured on cross-local functional conflicts and alliances than on cross-level territorial ones. In a stratarchy the predominant mode of representation and political production will be 'based on the interaction between substate territorial coalitions of social groups and their territorial rulers, the national rulers and the centre-builders and central claimants at the EU level' (Bartolini 2004: 21). Cross-territorial patterns of interaction, functional conflicts, and alliances (both within the nation state and in the EU system as whole) will obviously not disappear, but they will tend to be disturbed and destructured by the increasingly salient territorial issues of contestation and channels of representation. To the extent that they actually take place, supranational polity- and state-building are likely to follow from strategies of 'central consolidation', that is, alliances and political exchanges be-

---

[6] Subnational governments do not formally have a right of appeal to the ECJ. However, the issue has started to be hotly debated, especially by those European regions that have legislative powers. The Court of First Instance has begun to admit appeals from the regions in the late 1990s: e.g. Judgement of the Court of First Instance (Fifth Chamber, extended composition) of 30 April 1998, Case T-214/95, *Het Vlaamse Gewest (Flemish Region)* v. *Commission of the European Communities* [1998] ECR II-00717 and Judgement of the Court of First Instance (Fourth Chamber, extended composition) of 4 April 2001, Case T-288/97, *Regione Friuli-Venezia Giulia* v. *Commission of the European Communities* [2001] ECR II-01169, both related to state aid controversies.

[7] One of the best-known episodes of subnational–supranational alliance against a national government is the Scottish coalfields case, in which Scotland allied with the Commission to force the UK government to revise its financial plans and procedures so that Scotland could obtain EU funds from a Community Initiative called RECHAR (McAleavy 1993). For a discussion and further examples, see Ansell, Parsons, and Darden (1997).

tween central claimants (EU politico-administrative elites) and subnational communities, at the expense of national rulers.[8]

If Bartolini and much of the new regionalism and multilevel governance literature are correct, what are the implications for solidarity and sharing ties? Will the dynamics of competitive region-building, stratarchic representation, and EU central consolidation push in the direction of a significant subnationalization of social protection? Welfare policy does offer fertile ground and precious resources for processes of politico-institutional structuring and restructuring. As mentioned earlier, European societies are changing in a direction that renders place-based differences in life situations a relatively more important source of needs than traditional class-based inequalities. Conditions may thus be ripe for evolution towards a model of 'competitive solidarities' constituted around subnational communities (Streeck 2000), often backed by symbolic, financial, and other resources provided by EU supranational authorities. Research on the new regionalism has underlined that the actual content and flavour of such territorial systems of solidarity may vary greatly, ranging from an exclusive-xenophobic extreme to an inclusive-cosmopolitan one (e.g. Longo 2003). But a precise characterization of empirical types and a discussion of their institutional and distributive implications must await more reliable and systematic fact finding.

In the next the two sections we take a preliminary step in this direction by discussing some illustrative examples of social protection subnationalization. We first deal with cases of cross-border regional association for social policy cooperation as well as EU-prompted region-building in the field of employment and social services. In the final section, we discuss in more depth subnationalization trends in Italy, a country which in many respects has recently become a laboratory in Europe for experimentation with welfare regionalization.

Social Policy Activism and Innovation at the 'Third Level'

If we look at grass-roots movements and institutional innovation in the sphere of regional social policy during the last two decades, we detect at least three developments which point in the direction of subnational

---

[8] Bartolini borrows the notion of 'central consolidation' from Te Brake's analysis of historical state formation in medieval and modern Europe (see Te Brake 1997). For a discussion of territorial vs. functional representation in the EU political system (and an alternative view in respect of Bartolini's), see Tarrow (2004).

experimentation and restructuring, backed or even prompted by the supranational level:

1. the formation of cross-border interregional or transregional aggregations addressing social policy issues and experimenting with some first forms of 'fusion' of welfare practices and infrastructures;
2. growing institutional and financial links between such initiatives and EU authorities; and
3. the emergence of a deliberate EU strategy (especially on the part of the Commission) for strengthening the 'third level' and enhancing its involvement in social policy, especially employment and social inclusion.

Cross-border Experimentation

Interregional or intermunicipal associationism is not a new phenomenon in Europe: the first 'historical' association of this kind was founded in 1951 with the name of Council of European Municipalities and Regions (CEMR), which has grown to include more than 100,000 subnational units from twenty-nine countries. The 1970s witnessed the creation of organisms dedicated to EU regions sharing certain geo-economic characteristics or of associations grouping smaller numbers of regions based on a common project of policy cooperation. These smaller aggregations have often adopted the name and legal formula of a 'Euro-region', officially recognized by both the Council of Europe and the EU, and envisaging a relatively standardized institutional format. A Euro-region is typically a transfrontier legal association aimed at easing communication and at providing common services to a socio-economic and/or socio-cultural basin crossed by a state border.[9]

Border regions occupy 50 per cent of EU territory and contain 10 per cent of its population. They also tend to be physically located along the two historical axes of trade and communication in Europe: the northern Italy–North Sea axis (via the Rhine basin) and the Catalonia–Carinthia axis (via the French *Midi*, the Po Valley, Switzerland, and Bavaria). These two corridors structure transactions across the core of the European continent: an area of outstanding global economic integration defined by the cities of Barcelona, Milan, and Munich to the south, and Paris, London, Hamburg, and Copenhagen to the north. It is precisely this heptagon that has witnessed the formation of the stronger and more active interregional associations since the 1970s (see Table 5.1). In some cases the creation of an interregional association has prompted the creation of other

[9] Several different labels can be used to establish a Euro-region: for example, Euregio, Euregion, Euroregion, Europaregion, Grand Region, Regio.

Table 5.1 Main regional associations in Europe dealing with social policy: some basic facts

Association name	Founding year	Member states included	Cooperation in social policy
Council of European Municipalities and regions (CCRE)	1951	29 European countries	Ad hoc working group on employment
Conseil des Communes et Régions d'Europe (CCRE)	1951	29 European countries	Ad hoc working group on employment
SaarLorLux	1970	France Germany Luxembourg	EURES*
Association of European Border Regions (AEBR)	1971	85 border regions	Health care
Euroregio Rhein-Waal	—	Germany Netherlands	EURES Heath care
Euroregio Schleswig-Sønderjylland	—	Denmark Germany	EURES Health care
Euroregio Oberrhein/ Rhein supérieur	1971	France Germany Switzerland	EURES
Argealp	1972	Switzerland Germany Italy	Employment policies Vocational training
Euroregio Mass-Rijn/Meuse-Rhein	1976	Germany Belgium Netherlands	EURES Health care
Alpe Adria	1978	Italy Germany Slovenia Croatia Austria	Health and social affairs
COTRAO	1982	Italy, France, Switzerland	Social affairs
Assembly of European Regions (AER)	1985	25 European countries, 300 regional governments	Social cohesion, social services, public health

Table 5.1 (*Continued*)

Association name	Founding year	Member states included	Cooperation in social policy
Eurocities	1986	26 European countries, 97 cities	Social welfare
Four Motors for Europe	1988	Italy France Germany Spain	Social affairs
European network of cities and Regions for the social economy (Reves)	1998	12 Countries	Projects in the field of employment, social economy, social inclusion

*EURES ('EURopean Employment Services') is a Community programme launched by the Commission in 1994 that fosters the integration of cross-border labour markets through partnerships between public and non-public actors (see later in the text).

transregional functional associations. For example, the foundation in 1988 of 'The Four Motors of Europe'—an interregional association between Baden-Württemberg, Lombardy, Catalonia, and Rhônes-Alpes—prompted the major trade unions of the same regions to establish in 1990 their own association with a view to furthering workers' interests and prioritizing social issues on the institutional agenda of cooperation. More than forty Interregional Trade Union Councils were active in 2003 (Ciampani and Clari 2005). Transregional (or translocal) initiatives on the side of trade unions have started to emerge also in response to the new pan-European or global strategies of multinational corporations, building on the organizational opportunities offered by the establishment of European Work Councils.[10]

Not much systematic research has been carried out on the actual activities and achievements of these experiences of interregional and transregional aggregation.[11] However, to judge from the scattered available information,

[10] European Works Councils (EWCs), comprising employee representatives from all the subsidiaries of a firm operating in different member states, were established in the wake of an EU directive adopted in 1994. Various other cross-border networking activities have been launched in parallel with the formation of EWCs, involving not only the social partners but also regional and municipal institutions (Kristensen and Zeitlin 2005).

[11] For a discussion and short review of early debates, see Conzelman (1995); Goldsmith (1993); Ansell, Parsons, and Darden (1997). For a more general discussion on cross-border cooperation in Europe, see Deschouwer et al. (2002).

three factual elements seem especially pertinent and relevant to our purposes.[12] First, virtually all the initiatives include a social policy component,
typically in the field of health care, employment, or care services. Second,
all associations have set up permanent institutional structures for the management and monitoring of such cooperation. These are not ephemeral or
'paper' structures but tend to be serious bodies, with dedicated staff engaged
in administrative, data gathering, and reporting work. Third, many associations have actually taken some steps towards a 'fusion' of service provision
and consumption across localities, promoting a transregionalization of
both demand and supply. The most advanced experimentation on this
front has involved health care services. At least six Euro-regions have established procedures for the sharing of patients and hospitals, also exploiting
the new EU rules on cross-border mobility in health care discussed in
Chapter 4.[13] The figures involved are not great, but mobility trends are
increasing and a growing diversification of demand (i.e. of patients) is
noticeable, as are intensifying dynamics of gzzrass-roots networking and
administrative cooperation on the part of providers (Busse 2002; Coheur
2001). It may be risky to draw conclusions from scattered data and impres-
sions. But what can be noticed on the ground is, at a minimum, not incon-
sistent with the expectation that new subnational processes of 'bounding'
should be at work in the most active territories of Europe, partly aimed at
cross-border 'bonding' of populations sharing similar needs and increasingly common interests.

Stronger Links Between the Subnational and the Supranational Levels

The second interesting development that can be observed is the formation
of a direct and specific link between subnational mobilization in cross-
border welfare activities and the supranational level. Since their inception,
interregional associations and transregional projects have sought and
received the support of the European Commission, especially through
the structural funds. At the beginning of the 1990s the INTERREG initiative
was launched by the EU, explicitly dedicated to supporting and encour-

---

[12] These conclusions have been drawn from an analysis of the information contained in the
associations' websites.

[13] Meuse-Rhine (Belgium, Germany, and the Netherlands), Rhine-Waal (Germany and the Netherlands), Scheldemond (Belgium and the Netherlands), Hinaut/Nord-Pas de Calais (Belgium and
France), Schleswig/Suedjuetland (Denmark and Germany), Eems-Dollart and Rhine-Eems-Ijssel (Germany and the Netherlands).

aging the cooperation of border territories (regions but also other units of local government). The original initiative had a time horizon of four years (1990–3), but was subsequently renewed as INTERREG II for the period 1994–9. Given the success of the first two initiatives, in 2000 INTERREG III was launched for the period 2000–6 and placed on a broader footing by widening the range of eligible actions and areas and by a substantially larger budget than the two previous rounds. Compared with the other cohesion funds, the budget remains certainly modest (just below €5 million). But the relevance of this initiative lies less in its financial size than in its being a first explicit attempt to implement a supranational policy of spatial reconfiguration which largely ignores state boundaries and actually aims at rebordering the EU space according to broad geoeconomic and geosocial considerations and objectives. This rebordering exercise also has a recognizable symbolic (and thus possibly identity-forming) component: the EU space is subdivided into distinct macroregions cutting across state borders, for which novel evocative labels or acronyms have been created (such as 'Alpine space', 'Medocc', or 'Archi-Med').[14]

The INTERREG initiative has a rather wide thematic scope: from territorial development to transport, from environmental protection to energy policy, from natural resources to cultural heritage. Social policy objectives do, however, feature prominently, especially within the largest section of the initiative devoted to transfrontier cooperation, with a particular focus on the integration of regional labour markets, vocational training and lifelong learning, and social integration of vulnerable groups, that is, those fields where both the pressure of problems and subnational discretion are greater. Virtually all the new cross-border projects funded by INTERREG III have a job-training and employment-policy component; many also have a social service and health component. A recent analysis of INTERREG III-funded projects involving at least one Italian subnational unit has shown that social services are always included in the cooperation projects (Mantino 2002). In the field of health care, an important initiative had already been funded by INTERREG II—namely, PAMINA, involving a number of regions of the Alpine space—aimed at promoting the reduction of excess capacity in the field of medical care, joint procurement and

---

[14] The Alpine space macroregion includes territories in south-eastern France, the Po Valley, southern Germany, the whole of Austria, and Slovenia; the Medocc macroregion includes all the territories along the Mediterranean coast from Spain to Sicily, with connections to the Maghrib countries; the Archi-Med macroregion includes southern Italy, Greece, Malta, Cyprus, and western Turkey, with connections to Egypt.

utilization of technical medical facilities, and steps towards the procedural harmonization of social insurance systems.[15]

Besides INTERREG, another interesting programme linking the subnational and the supranational level in the social sphere is EURopean Employment Services (EURES), launched in 1994 by the Commission and aimed at fostering the integration of cross-border labour markets through partnerships between public institutions (especially employment services) and non-public actors (especially the social partners) at the local level. More than twenty cross-border partnerships have emerged since 1994, involving actors from thirteen member states. As shown in Table 5.1, many interregional associations have established formal links with the EURES network.

Again, no systematic study is available on the content and consequences of the INTERREG or EURES initiatives from social and institutional points of view. The paucity of the financial resources involved might induce one to discount the relevance of this programme as simply a drop in the ocean of EU cohesion policy. But even sceptics cannot deny that we are confronted with an undisputable example of 'stratarchic' interaction directly linking supranational rulers pursuing deliberate and distinctive spatial objectives, and subnational developmental coalitions interested in responding to new local needs and at the same time seeking resources for strengthening the institutional foundations of their communities.

Subnational Empowerment Through the EU

Interregional and transregional aggregations can be regarded as examples of 'horizontal' territorial mobilizations, with a 'bottom up' interest in support from higher levels. The INTERREG and EURES initiatives can in turn be seen as a mixed process through which supranational authorities reach down, as it were, to establish contact with a mobilizing third level and thus to exploit an opportunity for central consolidation. In both processes, the enhancement of 'new' social services features as a salient ingredient of spatial differentiation. However, a third development is observable, characterized by a clear top-down direction: the emergence of a deliberate EU strategy of regional and local empowerment in the fields of employment and social inclusion through a greater involvement of the third level per se (i.e. independently of aggregative dynamics) in all the phases of policy processes addressing new social and economic problems.

Although the first steps of this strategy had already been taken during the 1980s, within the wider cohesion policy, it was in the early 1990s that the Commission started to call explicitly for a regional and local

---

[15] Detailed information on the INTERREG initiatives and on all the funded projects can be found on the website of the Commission (http://europa.eu.int/comm/regional_policy/).

dimension of employment policy, in particular with the 1993 *White Paper on Growth, Competitiveness and Employment* (EC 1993). The major steps in this direction, however, were taken in 1997, with the inclusion of the employment chapter in the Amsterdam Treaty. A first step was the launching of the Territorial Employment Pacts (TEPS) in selected European regions, providing financial incentives (mainly through the structural funds) for encouraging multi-actor partnerships and innovative measures aimed at job creation in a given local area (Regalia 2003, 2005). Eighty-nine TEPs were supported in the 1997–2001 period, with an average grant of about €250,000 each. This initiative constitutes an almost emblematic example of the role that the EU can play in the formation of subnational developmental coalitions and in prompting territorial mobilization for socio-economic 'bounding' and policy differentiation.

A second and more important step in 1997 was the launching of the so-called Luxembourg process, which offered just the right institutional opportunity for casting the issue of subnational social policy activism into a larger and more legitimate framework. The new employment chapter of the EU Treaty, agreed at the Amsterdam European Council in 1997, laid down the principles and procedures of a coordinated European Employment Strategy (EES), encouraging all the member states to work within a common framework (later to be known as the 'open method of coordination', OMC) to increase their capacity to create more and better jobs and provide workers with the skills to fill them (Trubek and Mosher 2003; Zeitlin and Pochet 2005). Since its inception, the EES has emphasized the need to explore job creation potential at the local level, and the employment guidelines have repeatedly asked the member states to enhance the territorial (and in particular, regional) dimension of their employment policies. In early 2000 a Communication was issued on 'Acting locally for employment' (EC 2000), around which the Commission launched a broad process of consulting relevant 'local players': not only public authorities but also the social partners, firms, voluntary associations, and specialist agencies operating in the field of employment, education, and vocational training. The consultation was flanked by a host of other initiatives providing financial incentives to local actors willing to mobilize for employment creation and active labour market measures: the so-called preparatory measures for local commitment for employment (2000 and 2001), the third system and employment pilot action (1997–2001), the local social capital pilot projects (1999–2001), the creation of a European network for the identification, dissemination, and exchange of good practices in local and regional employment development (IDELE), as well as the wider initiatives EQUAL (equal employment opportunities), URBAN (urban renewal), LEADER (rural development), and LEDA (local economic development).[16] The main instrument used by the Commission to underpin the regionalization of the EES has been the European Social Fund (ESF). Since 2000 the ESF has offered considerable support for subnational action, including the so-called innovative measures introduced by art. 6 of the ESF Regulation 1784 of 1999, aimed at stimulating innovative partnership-based local projects involving cross-level (for example, regional-provincial or regional-municipal) cooperation. The ESF provides around €9 million a year for employment creation initiatives.

Though entrusted only with advisory powers, the Committee of the Regions has actively backed the Commission's strategy of regional and local empowerment within the EES (COR 2003). In particular it has called for increased involvement of local and regional authorities not only in the implementation but especially the formulation of the National Action Plans for employment. In a number of countries (such as Belgium, Spain, Italy, Denmark, Sweden, and Finland) some regions and municipalities have started to formulate their own Regional or Local Action Plans (Council of the European Union 2002; Zeitlin 2005a).

In addition to employment, the Commission has actively sought subnational empowerment in social inclusion, a broad area including not only traditional anti-poverty programmes but most of the measures linked with new social needs: childcare, elderly care, access to decent housing, education, and health on the part of vulnerable categories (such as immigrants). A social inclusion process based on the open method of coordination (OMC) was officially launched in 2000, with a biannual cycle of dedicated National Action Plans (NAPs) (Ferrera, Matsaganis, and Sacchi 2002). Many of the financial instruments which underpin the regional dimension of the EES can also support this dimension within the social inclusion process. A dedicated Community action programme to combat social exclusion (2002–6) has provided additional grants to support pilot reconnaissance activities of existing challenges and potential responses.

It is too early to evaluate the actual impact of all these initiatives in both institutional terms (the development of greater policy capabilities at the subnational level) and substantive terms (the degree of territorial policy differentiation and innovation). According to the annual Joint

---

[16] Basic information on these programmes can be found on the website of the Commission (see n. 15 above).

Employment Reports, which monitor and evaluate EES progresses, an increasing involvement of the third level in the phase of NAP formulation and independent Regional Action Plans (RAPs) or Local Action Plans (LAPs) production is indeed noticeable.[17] A similar finding emerges from the second Joint Inclusion Report (Council of the European Union 2004), though with significant cross-national and cross-regional variations. It is true that so far third-level empowerment through the OMC has been essentially a top-down affair (Smisman 2004), but in due course vertical, top-down dynamics can encourage horizontal mobilizations as well. The launching of the social inclusion process has, for example, prompted the formation of a European Trans-regional Network for Social Inclusion (RETIS), including thirty regions and local governments from twelve member states. If these indications are reliable, then it must be recognized that the Commission's strategy is definitely more than a simple rhetorical smokescreen or merely symbolic policy.

In sum, the three empirical developments briefly discussed so far do signal that a certain degree of spatial reconfiguration is taking place in Europe, resting on a general empowerment of the third level, on cross-local forms of mobilization, and on increasingly stronger links between subnational communities and EU authorities. Whether these dynamics are deemed to accelerate and snowball into something of systemic significance for the territorial structuring of European social protection remains at this stage an open question. National arrangements of social sharing, centred on the 'old' and heavy schemes of compulsory social insurance, are still alive and well. The emergence of stratarchic patterns of political and institutional interaction in the outer circles of welfare provision may be theoretically interesting, but may well prove factually irrelevant in the long run. However, as highlighted at the start of this chapter, several dynamics which are endogenous to domestic systems of both centre–periphery relations and social protection also push in the direction of welfare subnationalization. More transformations are taking place than can possibly be captured by a pan-European point of view. It is beyond the scope of this chapter and book to offer a comparative overview of national developments; but it may be interesting to take a closer look at one of the EU countries which has been walking faster down the road of competitive region-building in the last two decades, namely, Italy.

---

[17] For illustrations taken from Italy's experience, see later.

Welfare Regionalism at Work: The Case of Italy

Italy's welfare state followed rather closely the historical parabola of 'nationalization' which was described at the beginning of this chapter. The first compulsory social insurance schemes were introduced between 1898 and 1919, breaking with the tradition of localized and discretional assistance offered by religious charities and (later) friendly societies (Ferrera 1987). The system of national social insurance was completed and consolidated during the 1950s and 1960s. Starting in the 1970s, however, a thoroughgoing process of regionalization took off, increasingly affecting the welfare state sphere.

The Constitution which came into force in 1948 defined the Italian Republic as a unitary state divided into regions. The latter were to exercise a list of competences laid down by art. 117, including health care and social assistance. The actual establishment of regions was a very slow process. Given their special geoeconomic or geocultural situation, five autonomous regions were created in the 1950s and early 1960s,[18] but the other fifteen ordinary regions became fully operative only in the late 1970s. The post-war economic miracle had promoted generalized progress, but regional disparities were still wide, especially between the north and the south. Territorial cleavages and the issue of interregional redistributions were kept under control by political parties through forms of central brokerage and local clientelistic practices, largely involving social benefits (Della Porta 1999).

The first wave of decentralization in the 1970s essentially created an administrative regionalism with direct political legitimization. Regulatory competences in the spheres envisaged by the Constitution were indeed transferred to the regions, together with earmarked fiscal transfers. But regional action remained formally constrained from above (every act needed *ex ante* approval from the centre) and also from below, given the strong powers of subregional units of government, directly protected from the national level. Autonomous taxing powers were in their turn extremely limited.

The reforms of the 1970s did, however, prompt a gradual dynamic of competitive region-building. Not surprisingly, the main protagonists were northern regions which, capitalizing on their historical legacy of civic culture and institutional capacities (Putnam 1993), were able rapidly to exploit all the margins of manoeuvre opened by the new context,

[18] The autonomous regions are the two islands of Sicily and Sardinia and the three regions with ethnic/linguistic minorities, namely, Valle d'Aosta (French-speaking minority), Trentino-Alto Adige (German-speaking minority), and Friuli-Venezia Giulia (Slovene-speaking minority).

especially in the relevant spending sectors of health and social assistance (Fargion 2000). The 1980s also witnessed the emergence of regionalist parties in this area of the country in the form of local leagues or *Leghe* (Biorcio 1997; Diamanti 1993; Diani 1996). Striking ethno-regionalist and populist chords, these movements started to call for more autonomy, for barriers against foreign immigrants and even against southern Italians, for less taxation, and especially for less redistribution towards the south. In the field of welfare, they advocated a localistic closure of sharing schemes, including the regionalization of social insurance and the recognition of special privileges (e.g. in education, housing, or civil service jobs) for 'regionals' as opposed to non-regionals. In the 1983 election, the Liga Veneta won 4.3 per cent of the regional vote and similar percentages were won by the Lombard and Piedmontese leagues in 1987. The various leagues joined forces in 1989 under the name of Lega Nord, which organized itself as a mass party with various collateral organizations. In 1992 the new formation gained 8.8 per cent of the national vote, with peaks of well over 20 per cent in the north.

Besides witnessing the appearance of ethno-regionalism, the 1980s were also a decade of economic growth for the north (especially the north-east) and increasing internationalization, in particular by small and medium-sized enterprises grouped in industrial districts (Ferrera and Gualmini 2004). Even though still mediated by national boundaries, competitive pressures stimulated territorial differentiation in terms not only of productive specialization but also of policy profiles (e.g. in vocational training, one of the competences transferred to the regions in the 1970s). Economic and political interests combined to intensify regional voice for more powers vis-à-vis the central state, and also in EU affairs. In 1988 a State-Regions Conference was formally established for intergovernmental concertation and for greater participation by the regions in European policy. Some regions started to operate directly in Brussels, even though this became fully legal only in 1996 (Baldi 2002). Many northern regions also joined, and contributed to the founding of, active interregional associations such as Alpe Adria, The Four Motors of Europe, and COTRAO.[19] As summarized in Box 5.1, regional exits have prompted reactions ('voice against exit') on the part of the central government. The

---

[19] Alpe Adria was founded in 1978 in Venice and includes Veneto, Lombardy, Trentino-Alto Adige, and Friuli-Venezia Giulia for Italy and a number of other regions from Switzerland, Germany, Austria, Slovenia, Croatia, and Hungary. 'The Four Motors of Europe' was founded in 1988 by Lombardy, Baden-Württemberg, Catalonia, and Rhône-Alpes. COTRAO (Western Alps' Working Community) was founded in 1982 between the alpine regions of France, western Italy, and western Switzerland.

Box 5.1   INTERREG III—The controversy between Italian
regions and the national government

On 15 January 2002 the Italian regions of Veneto, Friuli-Venezia Giulia, and the Italian Autonomous Province of Bolzano signed a cross-border cooperation agreement with the Austrian *Länder* of Carinthia, Tyrol, and Salzburg in the framework of the EU initiative INTERREG III A. The envisaged cooperation was to cover various policy areas, including education and the labour market (e.g. training, promotion of transfrontier economic activities, and student and apprentice exchanges), health care, and 'system harmonization' in order to promote interregional mobility and to exploit the human resources and the overall attractiveness of the six-region area, with an eye on the possible upheaval following forthcoming eastern enlargement. Promoting a better implementation of the European Employment Strategy was also mentioned in the initiative's programme document.

On 31 May 2002 the Italian Government, through its Ministry for Regional Affairs, brought a case to the Constitutional Court, arguing that the cooperation agreement violated the foreign policy prerogatives of the state as defined by art. 117 of the Constitution. In particular, in its appeal the Ministry objected to the establishment of common decision-making bodies among the Italian regions and their Austrian counterparts, arguing that such bodies might interfere with the foreign policy orientations of the national government.

On 22 July 2004 the Court ruled against the appeal. The Court found that the agreement in question could not conceivably interfere with the national foreign policy and the constitutional prerogatives of the state in this field. In addition, the creation of common decision-making bodies between the Italian and the Austrian regions could not possibly be contested, as this was required by the regulations of the INTERREG initiative. Having been established by an EU Regulation (no. 1260/99), the provisions of the initiative are directly applicable to the internal law of the member states.

Sources: On the INTERREG initiative: http://www.interreg.net/index_i.asp; for the ruling of the Italian Constitutional Court (no. 258/2004):
http://www.cortecostituzionale.it/ita/attivitacorte/novita/
Elenco_decisioni_22_07_2004.pdf

Italian Constitutional Court has, however, ruled in favour of the regions, based on EC law.

The 1990s witnessed two new waves of regionalization and the launching of a process of federalization. The crisis of the First Republic and the Maastricht process constituted the general frameworks for change in centre–periphery relations (Ferrera and Gualmini 2004). The severe fiscal crisis of Italy's welfare state prompted the executive to decentralize both penury and blame to the regions by transferring to them in 1992 and 1993 greater financing responsibilities. In 1995 the Lega Nord endorsed an explicitly separatist political programme, threatening secession in case of an Italian exclusion from EMU. Opinion surveys showed that almost a quarter of northern voters considered secession not only advantageous but also desirable (Diamanti 1996). In 1997 the Olive Tree Coalition government headed by Romano Prodi launched two far-reaching initiatives. The first was an immediate reform aimed at introducing the highest possible degree of decentralization without changing the Constitution. This entailed: (a) full administrative decentralization (no more *ex ante* controls from the centre or regional oversight of provinces and communes); (b) substantial autonomous taxing powers for the regions; (c) the phasing out of earmarked fiscal transfers and their replacement with a system of general revenue sharing, with much greater spending discretion for the regions; and (d) the establishment of a new Solidarity Fund within the Treasury for interregional redistribution. The second initiative was the elaboration of a broad project of constitutional change to establish a true federal system. In 1999 the direct election of regional 'governors' was introduced, as well as a constitutional change that allowed each region to adopt its own regional statute, defining the organizational design of the regional government. In 2001 Title V of the Republic's Constitution was changed, devolving to the regions exclusive competences in a wide range of fields—basically all those not explicitly listed as prerogatives of the centre or as shared national-regional competences. The new Title also envisaged the central government sharing foreign economic policy with the regions, and allowed the regions to sign agreements with foreign, central, or local governments.

What have been the specific consequences of this incisive reconfiguration of centre–periphery relations for Italy's welfare state? In spite of the Lega's early demands, national compulsory transfer schemes (i.e. pensions and sickness, work injuries, and unemployment insurance) have not been affected by regionalization. But the latter has had an increasing impact on virtually all other welfare programmes, in particular health care, social assistance and services, labour market policies, and at least to some extent supplementary pensions. We consider these sectors in turn.

Health Care

In 1978 Italy introduced the first universal national health service (NHS) of Continental Europe, suppressing all the pre-existing occupational health funds. In line with constitutional prescriptions, the regions were given some competences, but mainly at the level of planning and framework-setting. All important decisions were taken at the centre, while the actual management was undertaken at the municipal level. During the 1980s increasing fiscal strains prompted the national government to involve the regions more directly in cost control. But the real turning point came with the 1992–3 reforms, which introduced managed competition between purchasers and providers (Maino 2001). These reforms devolved to the regions both explicit financial responsibilities for 'their' portion of the NHS and significant autonomy in determining the specific model of managed competition. A process of gradual policy differentiation thus emerged, with substantial implications for ordinary citizens. This process was clearly driven by competitive region-building dynamics. On the vertical front, a real tug of war started between all regions and the centre over 'who pays what' and 'who decides what'; most regions also engaged a downward battle against the municipal level in order to claw back those prerogatives that had been transferred to it in the early NHS phases. On the horizontal front, many regions engaged in a deliberate strategy of institutional differentiation. The extreme case is constituted by Lombardy, a region governed by a centre-right coalition, which in 1997 gave its own regional health service a strong pro-market profile, centred on competition between public and private providers and free patient choice. A national reform of 1999 tried to rein in centrifugal dynamics and to encourage a general reorientation from managed competition to managed cooperation. But the reform was only partially successful. While still concerned about cost containment, the Berlusconi government (elected in 2001) has looked favourably on both regional autonomy and market-oriented experimentation.

Competitive region-building dynamics increasingly brought to the fore the issue of interregional solidarity. The 'federalist' reforms of the late 1990s and early 2000s have phased out earmarked transfers for health care based on population and past spending and replaced them with a system of financing resting on three sources: (a) revenue sharing: each region will decide how much of its share will be used to finance public health care; (b) regional taxes, including user fees; and (c) transfers from richer to poorer regions through a central solidarity fund. The new system is generating wide interregional differences, especially in taxes and fees. It is also generating growing strains between richer and poorer regions. While a number of northern regions are virtually self-sufficient in financial terms, in many southern regions external transfers cover as much as 80 or even 90 per cent of regional health expenditure.

Following the 1999 reform, in 2001 the central government defined the so-called *livelli essenziali di assistenza* (LEA) or 'essential levels of care', that is, a basket of treatments which must be offered by all regions and which cannot be denied to any Italian resident. Above this basic floor, however, regions are free to do what they want. They can guarantee a wider range of treatments by using more of their own resources or imposing higher taxes or charges; they can establish a 'second pillar' of supplementary insurance; or they can just leave patients to purchase uncovered treatment out of their own pockets. Processes of regional differentiation are starting to manifest themselves on this front too. For example, in 2003 the Autonomous Provinces of Trento and Bolzano announced the establishment of a compulsory insurance scheme for dependency and long-term care, modelled on the German long-term care insurance (*Pflegeversicherung*). This is the first example of a new 'hard' boundary for social sharing established at the subnational level.

The 2001 reform of Title V of the Italian Constitution lists health care among the competences shared between the national and the regional governments. The setting of national standards for financing rules and essential levels of care is in line with this approach. However, the Berlusconi government, under pressure from the Lega Nord, has submitted to parliament a new project of constitutional change, under which health care would shift from a 'shared' to an 'exclusive' competence of the regions. Such a change might well unleash a disintegrative response in which individual regions might conceivably 'exit' from the national health service and establish, for example, a system of occupational health funds.

Social Assistance

Local governments (the *comuni*) have traditionally been the main loci of (public) response to social needs not covered by national insurance schemes. The establishment of ordinary regions in the 1970s did not substantially alter this situation: in 1977 a law specified that social assistance and services were to be a municipal competence, backed by direct central government transfers. However, during the 1980s and 1990s regional governments became increasingly active in this sphere and adopted framework laws setting regional goals, standards, and guidelines of action for the *comuni*. A dynamic of rapid territorial differentiation ensued. Northern and central regions promoted a thorough modernization of types and forms of provision, trying to give an impulse especially to social services in response to new needs. The southern regions remained more anchored to traditional approaches, based on emergency cash transfers, institutionalized care, and heavy reliance on religious charitable institutions (Fargion 2000). Even in modernizing regions financial constraints prevented the establishment of comprehensive public assistance and service systems. The 1990s witnessed instead the emergence of various regional 'welfare mixes' including various types of non-public providers, typically social cooperatives (Pavolini 2003). The specific ingredients of such mixes (types of actor, modes of financing, forms of regulation, nature of intergovernmental relations, etc.) have actually become a major dimension of territorial differentiation. Even if operating within legislated regional institutional frameworks, local governments have maintained a fair number of spending and organizational prerogatives. As Table 5.2 shows, substantial differences are noticeable in terms of per capita spending on various types of services, not only between north and south but also between emblematic municipalities within each macroregion.

In 2000 a broad national framework law was passed with the aim of rationalizing and homogenizing this policy area, especially through establishing clear planning procedures and national standards. One of the main ambitions of the law was to define a basket of 'essential levels' of assistance and services (LIVEAS), similar to those defined for health care. Standard setting is, however, a more difficult and controversial operation in social

Table 5.2 Per capita spending by Italian municipalities for selected social care functions, 2000 (in euros)

Macroregion/municipality	Nursery care	Residential elderly care	Other personal social care benefits/services
North	43.8	31.2	98.0
Turin	41.8	32.2	151.2
Milan	75.2	56.6	86.8
Centre	32.7	13.0	63.7
Bologna	57.1	n.a.	119.3
Florence	69.7	43.7	81.8
South	22.6	7.5	56.6
Naples	26.7	7.1	65.7
Palermo	28.3	6.7	63.7
Italy	35.7	20.6	77.8

Notes: Data refer to a sample of sixty municipalities scattered throughout Italy.
Source: CGIL-SPI (2003).

assistance than in health care. Moreover, the reform of Title V of the Constitution in 2001 classified social assistance as an exclusive competence of subnational governments, thus delegitimizing attempts at national standardization.

Since the 1980s Italian regions and municipalities have slowly learned to use EU funding opportunities for their social assistance policies. The launching of the social inclusion process has prompted in its turn some grass-roots mobilization of stakeholder groups and has supplied further incentives for the definition (and institutional defence vis-à-vis the central government) of distinctive local models of social care (Sacchi and Bastagli 2005).

Labour Market Policies

As elsewhere in Europe, the shift from a passive to an active approach to employment problems in Italy has promoted an increasing territorial embedding of public policy in this sector since the 1980s. This trend has been reinforced and accelerated by the parallel process of regionalization and, in the 1990s, of federalization of the Italian state. Vocational training was the first substantial competence transferred to the regions in 1978. During the 1980s some first steps were taken for the regionalization of employment services, while many regions were developing the new institutional capabilities for steering their own labour markets. In the course of the 1990s, also in the wake of the EU cohesion and employment strategy, a new generation of active labour market policies was introduced, inspired by a 'partnership' approach aimed at mobilizing all pertinent local actors, both public and private (Graziano 2004; Gualmini 1998; Sestito 2002). Specific financial incentives were provided for drafting territorial pacts (even beyond the above-mentioned EU regulatory framework) and 'area contracts' between the social partners, tailored to local productive conditions. In 1997 a broad 'flexibility' package was adopted, which substantially widened the menu of employment forms and contracts; in the same year the traditional state monopoly on job placement was abolished and the decentralization of employment services to regions and provinces was completed. Subnational prerogatives over labour market policies (except for insurance schemes) were confirmed by the Constitutional reform of 2001. These developments have prompted the formation of quite distinct regional labour market regimes, often with internal submarkets as well. To some extent, cross-regional variations are linked to pre-existing and long-standing differences in regional economic profiles. Two new factors, however, are increasingly important for such variations: the wider menu of policy instruments which is now available for the main labour market actors, and the much greater autonomy of subnational governments in regulating their employment systems.

As in the case of regional social care models, so in the labour market sphere the most noticeable contrasts run from north to south. Promoting job creation and economic development in the Mezzogiorno is admittedly a very difficult task, given the historical legacy of marginality and backwardness. In this area of the country regional governments and local developmental coalitions face a challenge that is not only greater than but altogether different from that of their northern counterparts. The interesting development for our purposes, however, is the emergence of cross-regional differentiations within the north and within the south, linked to the different strategies pursued by local actors and in particular by politico-administrative elites. In the northern context, for example, a growing divergence is noticeable between 'neoliberal' Lombardy, which relies primarily on flexibility measures, and 'neocorporatist' Emila-Romagna, which places more emphasis on training and reskilling, with greater involvement by the social partners. Within the south, Apulia has been able to embark upon a relatively successful proactive strategy of economy and employment, emphasizing vocational training, while Calabria has remained largely trapped in the tradition of passivity and policy immobilism (Ferrera et al. 2001; Graziano 2004).

Supplementary Pensions

The promotion of a second pillar in pension insurance reached the national agenda in the early 1990s. The Amato and Ciampi governments introduced a new regulatory framework allowing for the creation of two types of pension funds: 'open' funds, based on individual membership and managed by financial institutions, and 'closed' funds, based on contractual agreements and involving contributions from both employers and employees. The 1993 law envisaged the possibility of establishing closed funds also on a territorial basis, following local agreements between the social partners. The expansion of supplementary pensions during the 1990s was very slow and modest at first, due to a number of legal and financial disincentives (Jessoula and Ferrera 2005), but picked up in the second half of the decade, as also did the expansion of territorial funds. Not surprisingly, the first movers on this front were a number of northern regions: Valle d'Aosta, Trentino-Alto Adige, Veneto, and Friuli-Venezia

Giulia. These regions passed regional laws regulating the establishment of territorial funds, whereupon regional social partners signed contractual agreements setting up closed funds for selected categories of workers, backed by regional support.

The most comprehensive initiative was launched by Trentino-Alto Adige. The regional law passed in 1997 provided for the creation of an ad hoc institution (*Centrum Pensplan*) for the promotion of supplementary pensions in the area. Sponsored by local banks and insurance companies, the institution was to offer legal, administrative, and marketing support to newly established funds and to set up a Guarantee Fund with two aims: providing a safety net against bad investment decisions of the funds and paying the contributions of members who found themselves in situations of temporary economic hardship. Besides a number of 'open' funds, *Centrum Pensplan* was to support also a territorial 'closed' fund. This was created in 1998 (called *Laborfonds*), based on an agreement between the regional social partners. Membership is voluntary and strictly territorial; only employees of participating enterprises registered in the region can join, and only if their jobs are physically located in the region. In 2004 *Laborfonds* had a membership of 67,000, or 15 per cent of the region's labour force.

The experience of Veneto is also interesting. A regional solidarity fund (*Solidarietà Veneto*) to promote individual retirement savings had been active in Venice since 1990. In 1997 the regional employer associations and the CISL union agreed to set up a closed pension fund with defined contributions and individual capitalization, reserved to industrial employees of participating enterprises. The fund started to operate in 1999, building on the experience of the existing *Solidarietà Veneto* scheme. Its membership is much more limited (about 13,000 employees) than that of *Laborfonds*. The other regional unions (and especially the CGIL) were not keen on the initiative, which they thought could weaken efforts to negotiate centrally on supplementary pensions. But, siding with the employers on this issue, CISL argued that Veneto's workers and enterprises needed a territorial scheme tailored to their profile—a profile not adequately represented in industrial relations at the national level. During the 1990s Veneto witnessed impressive economic growth, mainly connected to the internationalization of small firms, often in sectors (such as leather working) without a national industrial agreement. Veneto's experience can thus be interpreted in terms of a strong link between productive specialization in a new international context and innovative sharing arrangements based on territorial membership and regional social pacts.

A closed territorial fund has been operative in Valle d'Aosta since 1999, while in the same year Friuli-Venezia Giulia passed its own regional law in the field. The constitutional reform of 2001 mentions supplementary pensions as a shared competence between the central state and the regions. In 2003 the national conference of regional 'governors' adopted a resolution in which they called for regional consultation on any matter regarding this policy field, requesting direct representation on the national supervisory body for all types of supplementary pension funds.[20]

Conclusion

As these four brief surveys show, the Italian welfare state is witnessing a clear dynamic of regional differentiation in important policy areas. While social insurance *stricto sensu* is still controlled from the centre, health and social care, active labour market policies, and, to some extent at least, supplementary pensions are increasingly falling within subnational competence, with significant implications for people's life chances: not only the quality but the accessibility, intensity, and scope of protection in these fields have started to display a great deal of variation across Italian regions. Virtually all the factors discussed in the first part of this chapter have played a role in this process, from 'neo-regionalism' dynamics to the pressure of new social needs, from the 'decentralization of penury' to European integration. A new round of constitutional reform might easily push this process of welfare state regionalization one step further, from subnational autonomy to fully-fledged 'semi-sovereignty'.

To what extent do Italian developments represent a more general European trend? In the first part of this chapter we mentioned a number of examples from the experience of other countries. Although comparative systematic evidence is lacking, several signs in several countries do point in a direction of greater social policy regionalization. In Italy this trend has accelerated owing to the temporal coincidence of three distinct developments: the transition to a regional (and possibly even federal) state in the wake of both constitutional norms and endogenous politico-institutional changes; the reorganization of the welfare state in the wake of both new needs and mounting fiscal pressures; and the post-Maastricht acceleration of the EU integration process, including developments on the cohesion and social policy fronts. At least two other countries in the EU—Spain and

---

[20] Resolution adopted by the Conferenza dei Presidenti delle Regioni e delle Province Autonome in its meeting of 15 April 2003.

Belgium—have been moving in a similar direction. In the last two decades both countries have embarked upon a path of thoroughgoing federalization linked to endogenous politico-institutional dynamics, while having to cope at the same time with the challenges of welfare state reorganization and of European integration (Moreno 2001; Boudewyns and Dandoy 2005; Gallego, Gomà, and Subirats 2005). It is not surprising that Spanish and Belgian regions have come to acquire an extremely salient role in social policies such as health care and social services, in close parallel with Italian developments. As in Italy, the issue of 'secession' has explicitly and repeatedly surfaced in Spanish and Belgian public debates during the 1990s and early 2000s, even though political and financial considerations have eventually worked to contain centrifugal tendencies.

For a long time the welfare state has operated as an instrument and symbol of national unity, while European integration was seen as a gentle force for the pacific and gradual fusion of selective ingredients of national economies and administrations. At least for some countries, the situation has recently become less reassuring; a far-reaching process of territorial destructuring of social protection seems to be gaining momentum, with an as yet unknown final destination.

6

New Boundaries, New Structuring?
On the Future of Social Protection
in the European Union

Boundary Changes in European Welfare: A Summary

This book set out to explore two basic factual questions: to what extent and in what ways has the process of European integration redrawn the boundaries of national welfare states? What are the effects of such redrawing? These questions are interesting and relevant because boundaries 'count': they are a prerequisite for bonding individuals, groups, and territorial units, and for activating or strengthening their dispositions to share. If the profile of boundaries changes over time, we might expect significant consequences for bonding dynamics, that is, for the way solidarity is structured in a given political community.

As we saw in Chapter 2, historically welfare state formation can largely be read as a process of boundary-building. The watershed in this process was the establishment between the nineteenth and twentieth centuries of compulsory public social insurance, an innovative technique that allowed the pooling of risks among wide social collectivities and thus made redistribution towards the less fortunate enormously more efficient than all prior forms of social protection. Compulsory insurance operates as a boundary because it 'locks' entire segments of the population (or in certain cases the whole population) into redistributive schemes resting on the authority of the state, which impose obligations and confer entitlements on those who are 'in' while rigorously keeping out all those who do not qualify, those who do not meet the requirements for admission. Compulsory insurance is a form of bounding that has both a social and a territorial component: it typically rests on rules of affiliation linked to individual status (e.g. employees, the unemployed, or the elderly); such rules are binding within a given territory, normally the entire national territory. Social protection schemes are thus 'bounded spaces', with clearly defined memberships and territorial scope. Boundaries and compulsory affiliation play a fundamental role in securing and stabilizing redistribution over time, especially vertical redistribution from stronger to weaker groups and individuals.

Based as it is on legal rights and obligations, social insurance has become a prime component of a broader institution that emerged in the wake of the boundary-building interests of the nation state: the institution of citizenship. The twentieth century marked the apex of 'national citizenship' as a powerful machine for the production and distribution of rights and the forging of cultural identities. The 1950s and 1960s saw the full blossoming of this institution as both an object and an instrument of national closure. Being a citizen entailed a wide range of civic, political, and social rights (the *objects* of closure); but the space of national citizenship was not easy to enter for outsiders and not easy to exit for insiders, at least on a permanent basis and with full access to rights. Citizenship operated as a filtering device vis-à-vis the exterior, as an *instrument* of closure. But within the boundaries citizens were 'captives' of their nation states: they had guaranteed rights but also the corresponding set of obligations and constraints. Cross-system movements were indeed possible, but at the risk of suffering significant losses of protected freedoms, faculties, and entitlements. This state of captivity did not only affect the sphere of citizenship. Thick boundaries existed in those decades around most of the other functional spheres of each nation (including the market), and most of these closures reinforced the welfare state not only as a mechanism of redistribution but also as an instrument of social integration, territorial cohesion, voice structuring, and loyalty generation.

As the various chapters of the book have shown, the process of European integration has indeed gradually altered this relatively compact institutional configuration. Cross-system boundaries have been extensively redefined, differentiated, reduced, or altogether cancelled. An internal market has been established, resting on the free circulation of goods, persons, capital, and services. A common currency has been introduced, accompanied by rather rigid constraints on domestic fiscal policies. A tightly monitored competition regime forbids national closure practices that are judged to be market distortions by supranational authorities. Firms, capital, and, more generally, 'tax bases' are no longer captive of the nation state, thus weakening the traditional economic foundations of redistributive arrangements. European integration has, moreover, affected in a direct way the boundaries of national citizenship spaces and of the institutional core of the welfare state, namely, compulsory social insurance. The traditional link between rights and territory has become much looser: for most civic and social rights, the filtering role of nationality has been neutralized. A new political figure has emerged on the stage: the *denizen*, an outsider (in respect of the national space) who can enter (and of course re-exit), stay inside, voice, and even 'share' under certain conditions. In the field of social protection proper, coordination rules on the one hand (essentially, Regulation 1408/71) and competition rules on the other have severely restricted the exclusionary or discriminatory prerogatives of national governments vis-à-vis outsiders and have even launched an attack on the very 'sovereignty to bound' of the nation state in the social sphere. Thanks to the principles of benefit cumulability and exportability, national welfare states now must let in and out of their borders entire 'bundles of entitlements': import of entitlements matured under foreign schemes (as in the case of claims for the recognition of contributions paid abroad) or exports of entitlements to be redeemed in foreign territories (as in the case of claims to payments abroad). Although work-related insurance schemes had always envisaged the possibility of non-nationals participating as long as they enjoyed the status of legal immigrants, the institutional framework put in place by the 1971 Regulation represents a quantum leap in terms of opening, not only in its extremely wide personal and material scope but also in its degree of juridification, emblematically represented by the powers of a supranational court enjoying supremacy over domestic courts. The sovereign 'right to bound' is still there, but it is no longer an absolute right, subject as it is to the limits imposed by EU competition and coordination regimes— which specify the conditions under which it can be legitimately exercised—and by the judicial review of the ECJ.

The redefinition of the boundaries of social sharing has unquestionably increased the range of alternatives available to the various actors in the welfare arena: a new opportunity structure has emerged. Insured people and service consumers, providers, financing institutions, and, more generally, political and corporate actors can choose from a much wider repertoire of 'locality' options, that is, choices about where to locate within the EU space: staying inside the original space of affiliation, exiting from it, entering into other spaces, staying out selectively from localities they dislike. Moreover, actors can pursue such options through a wide range of 'vocality' strategies, that is, strategies that exploit all the possible confrontational opportunities offered by the EU multilevel institutional system. Above all, the new EU legal order increasingly serves as a 'law for exit and voice', that is, a set of norms and venues which actors can use in order to pursue their novel spatial interests. The wider menu of locality options and vocality strategies has prompted a new spatial politics of solidarity in which the territorial dimension (in its purely geographical but also geo-hierarchical aspects) has become increasingly salient.

European integration, however, has not been the only source of boundary redefinition in the sphere of social protection. As we have seen, at least two other endogenous developments have played a role as well, by promoting a more diversified landscape of solidarity spaces within the member states. The first development is the gradual shift from single-pillar or single-tier configurations (i.e. a structure of provision based on a unitary sector of statutory schemes) to more plural configurations, resting on a hierarchy of different schemes characterized by higher degrees of openness. Alongside public first pillar schemes, a significant second pillar of supplementary insurance has emerged (typically in pensions but also in health care), offering additional coverage and benefits to selected occupational categories. A few countries have maintained the principle of compulsory membership also at this level. But most countries have adopted a softer approach: membership rules are set through collective agreements, which in turn can envisage obligatory cover for whole industries or just optional affiliation. Alongside second pillars, a third pillar has in its turn developed, essentially based on individual choice and market criteria. Here there is no compulsion, and the distance from solidaristic principles is greater; but public regulation maintains some role also in third pillars, on both efficiency and equity grounds. This pluralization of pillars has given rise to complex social sharing constellations, characterized by multiple memberships in redistributive spaces with different rules, scopes, and objectives.

The second endogenous development is the revival of subnational territorial units (especially regions) as new, distinctive, and relatively autonomous "bounded spaces" in certain areas of social policy, in particular health care, active labour market policies, social services, and assistance. This trend is the result of many factors that were discussed in Chapter 5: the functional overload of central governments, new cost containment imperatives, the need to tailor provision to the specific needs of territorial contexts, and the resurgence of ethnic regionalisms. Once introduced, the decentralization of functions to subnational governments has set in motion a dynamic of 'competitive region-building', that is, strategies of politico-institutional strengthening of these territorial units at the expense of both other units and/or the central state. Given their salience for people's concrete life chances and their potential for generating loyalty, social policies have become central instruments for this new type of territorial competition. As shown in Chapter 5, there are visible signs of social protection subnationalization in certain countries and, to some extent, also experiments with new transnational regional groupings. These developments have further complicated the internal articulation of national sharing spaces. The menu of locality and vocality options has widened not only above the nation state, but also below it.

Figure 6.1 summarizes the main elements of our diagnosis of the ongoing spatial reconfiguration of social protection within the EU.[1] In panel 1, European integration is indicated as the prime factor of change, impinging on the boundary configuration of social sharing through the four freedoms and competition rules. Panel 2, however, points to the aforementioned endogenous developments, which have exerted an autonomous impact on such configuration. A dotted line connects panel 1 with panel 2. As a matter of fact, to some extent at least, the endogenous developments towards a multipillar configuration and—especially—towards welfare subnationalization have found positive reinforcement in the dynamics of integration and in supranational rules and actors. Panel 3 contains "state of the art" social protection within the EU, reflecting the spatial changes prompted by the first two panels.

The previous chapters have already cast light on the nature, direction, and intensity of boundary reconfiguration and on its destructuring effects, namely, the destabilizing of institutional arrangements for *nationwide* redistributions and of the social and political equilibriums that have traditionally supported them (panel 4). Although the opening up of domes-

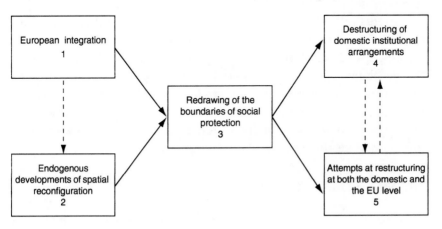

Fig 6.1 The spatial reconfiguration of social protection in the EU

[1] This figure is a new version of Figure 1.2 , slightly revised through the addition of a new panel (panel 2) containing endogenous developments.

tic citizenship and solidarity spaces does increase the options for those who are in need of social protection, the process entails risks. Too much emphasis on competition may jeopardize the delicate compromises between efficiency and equity, between the market and the solidarity logics, which have been laboriously arrived at through the long historical process of welfare state-building. Narrowing the scope of solidarity towards subnational communities may revive a world of local particularisms pitted against each other. Especially after the 2004 enlargement, stretching the scope of solidarity beyond the reach of individual member states by opening of wide exit and entry gates can raise fears of 'social tourism', trigger undesirable dynamics of xenophobia, and create new strains between social groups instead of new ties. Such stretching can also raise delicate issues of legitimacy and democratic accountability, at least in so far as important societal actors, large sections of national public opinions, and some national governments perceive the EU's low 'polity-ness' as a problem.

Besides destructuring signs we can also expect, in principle, the new boundary configuration to prompt a number of restructuring processes at both the domestic and the supranational level. At the domestic level restructuring might take the form of defensive mobilizations on the part of social or political actors aimed at restoring some mechanism of internal closure compatible with the EU legal order. At the EU level restructuring would imply dynamics of institutional reform or experimentation aimed at stabilizing the complex web of spatial interactions which is emerging in the wider and reconfigured EU space, with a view to gradually 'Europeanizing' the sphere of social sharing.

The remainder of this chapter focuses on panels 3, 4, and 5 of Fig 6.1, and on the links between them. The next section presents a map for visualizing the new spatial architecture of social protection in the EU resulting from the developments analysed so far in the book. The subsequent three sections discuss the destructuring implications of the new architecture, highlighting some examples of defensive restructuring at the domestic level, while the final section discusses the margins of manoeuvre and the prospects for restructuring at the European level.

The New Spatial Architecture of Social Citizenship in the EU

Boundary redrawing has affected the various components of the welfare state in different ways and with different degrees of intensity. Is there a way of capturing the nature and direction of change in a systematic fashion? We try to do this with the help of Figure 6.2. This figure outlines a space defined by two dimensions:

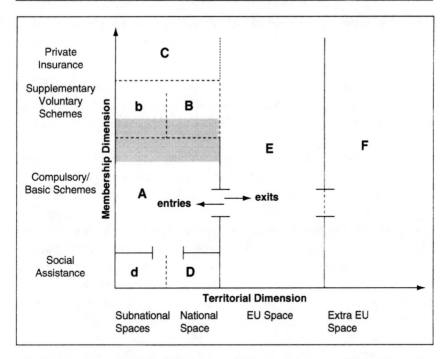

Notes: The grey area signals the existence of compulsory second-tier schemes in space A and compulsory second-pillar schemes in space B.

Fig 6.2 The new configuration of boundaries for social sharing in the European Union

- a territorial dimension, on which geographical movements occur, physical borders between systems are located, and rules defining what can pass through such borders are of prime importance. On this dimension the main novelty vis-à-vis the past is the formation of a new space, the EU, next to (or, better, underneath) the traditional space occupied by national systems. Through the four freedoms, competition rules, and the coordination regime, the EU can now legitimately encroach on national social citizenships; this new space is in turn increasingly demarcated by its own external borders, set against foreign territorial units and 'third country nationals';
- a membership dimension, on which 'movements' across the various layers or pillars of social sharing occur, institutional boundaries between schemes are defined, and rules governing who is eligible to what benefits and who can provide such benefits are of prime importance. On this dimension, the main novelty is the 'cap' imposed on statutory, first pillar schemes and the emergence of an increasingly salient space occupied by

supplementary (second pillar) and private (third pillar) schemes; a space which extends beyond the reach of obligatory affiliation and public monopoly provision.

The intersection between the two dimensions and their internal partitions generate a number of different subspaces, characterized by different kinds of boundaries and exit/entry options. Let us briefly summarize the characteristics of each space.

Space A is the historical core of social sharing systems: it includes those compulsory and public insurance schemes which still constitute the fundamental pillars of national welfare, as well as a prime source of domestic legitimization for the member states. The continuous lines surrounding this space are intended to signal the persistence of a good degree of closure along both the membership and the territorial dimension. This space remains in fact relatively protected from external encroachments as far as its internal organization is concerned: as discussed in Chapters 3 and 4, the EU regulatory framework rests on the *lex loci laboris* principle and recognizes that the features of national legislation must be respected, while the ECJ has so far upheld the principle of compulsory affiliation and public monopoly as prerequisites for social solidarity, thus shielding this space from EU competition laws. The novelty for this particular space has been the opening of a relatively wide gate along the territorial dimension through which eligible persons can enter and exit according to the rules set by the coordination regime, constantly monitored (and often reinterpreted) by the ECJ.

In April 2004 a new Regulation on 'the coordination of social security regimes' (883/2004)[2] was adopted by the EP and the Council, replacing the old Regulation 1408, taking into account all the amendments, Court rulings, and changes in national legislation that had been introduced since 1971. This new regulation is now the fundamental text setting the rules for entries and exits of persons through the two gates of space A. The personal scope of 883 is very wide and covers all 'nationals of a member state, stateless persons and refugees residing in a Member State who are or have been subject to the legislation of one or more Member States, as well as to the members of their families and to their survivors' (art. 2, para. 1). As for the material scope, the regulation applies to social security legislation, defined as all laws and regulations which establish obligatory cover or insurance for the whole range of social protection benefits, namely, (*a*) sickness benefits, (*b*) maternity or equivalent paternity bene-

---

[2] Regulation (EC) No 883/2004 of the European Parliament and of the Council of 29 April 2004 on the coordination of social security systems, *Official Journal L 166*, 30/04/2004, pp. 0001–0123.

fits, (*c*) invalidity benefits, (*d*) old-age benefits, (*e*) survivors' benefits, (*f*) benefits in respect of accidents at work and occupational diseases, (*g*) death grants, (*h*) unemployment benefits, (*i*) pre-retirement benefits, (*j*) family benefits. The new Regulation is still based on the four principles of its predecessor, namely, equal treatment, *lex loci laboris*, cumulability, and exportability, but it is simpler and internally more coherent. It includes new provisions on civil servants benefits, pre-retirement benefits, long-term care benefits, and unemployment benefits, and is generally in line with the jurisprudence in this field discussed in Chapters 3 and 4, with the exception of health care. In this latter area, the situation is still in flux. The Regulation does cover access to benefits in kind in case of sickness, but it maintains the authorization regime that has been challenged by the ECJ in the cases discussed in Chapter 4. In a 2004 Communication (EC 2004*a*: 7), the Commission has formulated three general principles which should inspire the regulatory framework on health care services:

- 'Any non hospital care to which you are entitled in your own member state you may also seek in any other member state without prior authorization, and be reimbursed up to the level of reimbursement provided by your own system.
- Any hospital care to which you are entitled in your own member state you may also seek in any other member state provided you first have the authorization of your own system. This authorization must be given if your system cannot provide your care within a medically acceptable time limit, considering your condition. Again, you will be reimbursed up to at least the level of reimbursement provided by your own system.
- If you wish to seek treatment abroad, your health authorities can provide you with information on how you can seek authorization for care in another Member State, the reimbursement levels that will apply and how you can appeal against decisions if you wish to.'

The first two principles clearly reflect the recent case law of the ECJ, which has opened up a second channel of exit/entry in the area of health services (even at the level of basic compulsory insurance, that is, space A), directly based on Treaty provisions. National governments are for the moment quite reluctant to accept this interpretation and to codify it in secondary legislation, but have allowed the Commission to establish a so-called High Level Group on Health Services and Medical Care to outline policy proposals (EC 2004*a*). The Commission has also prepared a directive proposal on services in the internal market (EC 2004*b*) aimed at eliminating the obstacles to the freedom to establish services and free movement of services, including health care services. If adopted, this directive will take full effect by 2010. It is thus plausible to expect that the next few years will continue to witness political controversies and judicial litigation in this delicate area, based on the locality interests of patients, providers, national governments, and administrations.

Within space A, Figure. 6.2 includes a grey area, which crosses over into space B. This is the area of a particular type of supplementary pensions: those which are mandatory and are run by specific institutions under conditions of monopoly. The French *régimes complémentaires* (see Box 4.1) are the typical example of supplementary pensions falling within space 'A'. Originally set up as separate schemes of pension provision financed through the PAYGO system and resting on defined-benefit formulas, these schemes have ended up within the scope of statutory social insurance, thus becoming de facto incorporated into the first pillar. The Swedish ATP scheme (now superseded by the 1998 pension reform) or the Finnish occupational pension schemes are other examples of supplementary PAYGO schemes which have been gradually merged into the first pillar. These schemes enjoy protection from EU competition rules, but are subject to the coordination regime to the extent that they are statutory.

Space B is the new area of second pillar schemes—particularly important in old age pensions and health care. Here, as we have seen, endogenous and European pressures have combined to weaken the degree of both membership and territorial closure: hence the broken lines used in the figure to demarcate this space from both third pillars (space C) and the larger EU space. The primacy of funding as a method of financing, the much stronger link between contributions and benefits, and the high importance of investment decisions have prompted a growing 'tight coupling' between this sector and the single market. Member states can still maintain some internal and external bounding prerogatives (as confirmed, e.g. by the *Albany* ruling discussed in Chapter 4); but the creation of an internal market for pension funds (and possibly for health care supplementary funds) has already taken its first steps.

The regulatory status quo is defined by the pension fund directive of 2003 (41/03 EC),[3] regulating the activities of all 'institutions for occupational retirement provisions' (IORPs), that is, collective funds and superannuation schemes based on prefunding. The text contains detailed

---

[3] Directive 2003/41/EC of the European Parliament and of the Council of 3 June 2003 on the activities and supervision of institutions for occupational retirement provision, *Official Journal L* 235, 23/09/2003, pp. 0010–0021.

'prudential' rules on the operative, procedural, and investment strategies of the IORPs, but its most innovative part is the set of provisions relating to cross-border activities, that is, pension funds seeking sponsoring undertakings (potential members) in other member states and corresponding faculty of undertakings to sponsor funds located anywhere in the EU. The directive explicitly excludes social security schemes that are covered by Regulation 1408/71 (now 883/2004) and, in general, schemes operating on a PAYGO basis (space A). Moreover the directive does not put in question national prerogatives in defining membership rules and their binding character. In line with the *Albany* jurisprudence illustrated in Chapter 4, occupational pension funds that are based on compulsory membership, resting on statutory outcomes of collective agreements, remain fully legitimate. This is why space B in Figure 6.2 contains part of the grey area: here are located those supplementary schemes that are funded but still based on closure practices by virtue of their origin in contracts between management and labour, made binding by the state. The novelty introduced by the directive as regards this grey area is the obligation eventually to separate fund ownership from asset management and to liberalize the latter, that is, to expose this activity to market competition within the whole EU.

Space B also contains occupational supplementary schemes for health care benefits. In this field the situation is still in flux. Despite the initiative of the EP aimed at promoting the definition of prudential rules and consumer safeguards, and despite ECJ case law (see Chapter 4), a common regulatory framework is still missing, leaving the floor open for both experimentation and contention.[4] As mentioned in Chapter 5, some experimental initiatives in cross-border cooperation in health care services (especially among transfrontier regions) are already under way. An internal market already exists for third pillar schemes (space C in Figure. 6.2) in the wake of the liberalization of the insurance sector. As we have seen, at this level only fine tuning is needed (primarily in the field of taxation) to strike down the remaining impediments to a fully free circulation of customers and providers throughout the whole EU.

Space D is that of means-tested benefits. Here the external wall surrounding national systems of social assistance is still buffered by member state prerogatives on rules of residence. The gate opened at the bottom of space A does allow non-nationals to access social assistance benefits 'from above': a

---

[4] The proposed directive on services in the internal market could provide this new common framework. See EC (2004*b*).

foreign person with residence permit can, for example, claim means-tested non-contributory benefits if he or she meets the requirements set by the host country for its own nationals. But lateral access is still barred. In this respect, the EU is not (yet) like the USA or other federal polities, whose citizens are free to settle where they choose.[5] Regulation 883/2004 specifies in an Annex the list of 'special non-contributory benefits' which are subject to residence requirements and are thus not exportable. Unlike its predecessor, the new regulation includes important innovations. Para. 16 of the preamble states, for example: 'Within the Community there is in principle no justification for making social security rights dependent on the place of residence of the person concerned'; and para. 37 adds: 'As the Court of Justice has repeatedly stated, provisions which derogate from the principle of exportability must be interpreted strictly. This means that they can apply only to benefits which satisfy certain conditions.' But para. 16 ends thus: 'nevertheless, in specific cases, in particular as regards special benefits linked to the economic and social context of the person involved, the place of residence could also be taken into account.' In April 2004 a directive laid down uniform rules on the freedom of residence which, while not prohibiting an 'affluence test' for non-nationals, severely circumscribes the autonomy of national authorities in this field.[6] In its turn, the new Charter of Fundamental Rights signed in 2000 lists social assistance as a fundamental right of persons in the EU. As in the case of health care, space D is very likely to be the object of institutional strains and litigation in the years to come.

In Figure. 6.2, space D and space B are crossed by (incomplete) dotted lines that give rise to internal subspaces (*d* and *b*). These lines are meant to signal the emergence, within many national systems, of some internal differentiations based on territory rather than (or on top of) categorical membership. As illustrated in Chapter 5, regional and even municipal responsibilities in the area of social assistance and services have been growing everywhere in Europe. In some countries (such as Italy) regions are becoming the most active level of government for the regulation and even the creation of region-specific supplementary pension and health funds. Decentralization trends are (re)creating infranational boundaries which, though much weaker than cross-national ones, could lead to new

---

[5] This freedom is typically expected to generate 'welfare magnet effects', that is, incentives on the part of 'the poor' to shop around for those subfederal units that offer more generous benefits. For a discussion of these issues, see Mabbet and Bolderson (2000).

[6] Directive 2004/38/EC of the European Parliament and the Council. See the summary and discussion in Chapter 4.

forms of fragmentation and may thus represent a threat *from within* to the maintenance of nationally bounded (standardized and integrated) social rights. In a few countries (e.g. Italy, Belgium, and Spain) this trend is affecting health care systems as a whole. In these cases, the dotted line of boundary 'infranationalization' cuts across space A as well, to the extent that the latter includes compulsory sickness insurance.

Space E corresponds to the 'near abroad' of national welfare systems, that is, the EU space from which entries and exits are legitimized by either rights of free movement (especially of workers and services) or by port-ability rules. The figure visualizes this space at the same level as the national space. In reality, what we find next to the latter are all the other EU national spaces. The EU space as such should be considered as a floor on which national spaces rest. The formation of this space has been primarily treated in terms of 'market-making' and therefore as a source of disturbance and erosion of national solidarity. The ability of the EU to engage in activist social policy (i.e. affirming itself as a source of 'market braking' social rights) is limited by those inherent obstacles of positive integration that a vast literature has identified and analysed.[7] From our perspective, however, in the midst of its negative and positive rule-making the EU has slowly started to perform two tasks with at least some degree of 'structuring' potential. Along the membership axis, it has started to point towards the existence of possible pan-European solidarity publics. EC law has indeed attenuated or even eliminated many boundaries between the member states in the sphere of social protection, but in many cases it has done so by invoking the existence (at least in normative terms) of a new pan-European solidarity space. Especially in the field of social assistance (the sancta sanctorum of national welfare, under the symbolic profile), the orientation of the ECJ has been very clear: its jurisprudence has tended to restrict the scope of the discretion exercised by member states, challenging their closure tactics by appealing not only to the principle of non-discrimination but often by referring also to the need to promote trans-national solidarity flows at the individual level.

In other words, the EU has played not only a market-making role but also a 'solidarity-making' role. Moreover, it has started to perform an additional important function of spatial structuring: that of building a single (or at least more homogeneous) boundary vis-à-vis third countries and their

---

[7] On the concept of 'negative' and 'positive' integration and their application to the analysis of the process of European integration, see Tinbergen (1965); Scharpf (1996); Leibfried and Pierson (2000). See also our discussion in Chapters 1,3, and 4.

nationals. For this reason our map identifies a space F (extra-EU) in respect of which the EU is increasingly affirming itself as the legitimate authority for defining and guarding the borders of citizenship—and not only social citizenship. As discussed in Chapter 4, the Amsterdam Treaty has paved the way for a gradual communitarization of immigration and asylum policy within the EU. If it is true that one of the main external objectives of communitarization is the containment or control of entry flows (and thus the construction of recognizable EU boundaries along both territorial and membership dimensions), among the internal objectives we find that of legal assimilation, that is, non-discrimination of third-country nationals in terms of rights, starting with social rights. It is not by chance that the Nice Charter of Fundamental Rights speaks of 'persons', not of 'EU citizens'. The principle of non-discrimination on the grounds of social rights was eventually introduced for third-country nationals in May 2003 through an amendment of Regulation 1408/71. Thus, as far as employment and social protection are concerned, the 13 million or so third-country nationals who find themselves within the EU now enjoy the same rights (and obligations, of course) as EU nationals, so long as they are legally resident in one of the member states. It should be noted, however, that third-country nationals do not enjoy the right of free circulation: they cannot be discriminated against in the hosting country if they have entered it from another member state, but they cannot freely move for employment purposes from one member state to another as EU nationals can. Member states are still in full control of the rules of residence on their own territory as these apply to third-country nationals (as noted earlier, some discretion on this ground still exists also in relation to other EU nationals, but has been significantly limited by ECJ jurisprudence). In other words third-country nationals largely remain second-class *denizens*: the EU has become an important source of external boundary-building, but the nation state still retains important prerogatives over who can put down roots within its territory.[8]

In sum, there can be no doubt that the process of European integration has significantly altered the spatial architecture of social citizenship. This change has impacted on the scope of solidarity along the territorial dimension and the membership dimension, has created the basis for the formation of new sharing collectivities (especially at the level of supplementary pensions), and has transferred to the EU certain important

---

[8] This state of affairs has not been challenged by the 2005 Green Paper on economic migration, even though its text calls for more supranational coordination in this area (EC 2005).

boundary-control prerogatives—with all the 'structuring' potential that such prerogatives always carry with them. Far from being a mere question of the 'transnationalization' of rights, the construction of a new EU space for the exercise of social citizenship has rested on distinct and salient dynamics of supranationalization: not only the elaboration of common definitions of old and new rights, but also the codification of jurisdictional protection of such rights. The EU certainly does not have (and perhaps never will have) its own social protection budget, fed by autonomous taxing powers, through which direct interpersonal flows of redistributions can be financed (Sbragia 2004). But it has gradually equipped itself with regulatory competences which are able to discipline the sharing spaces of the member states and thus to orient their distributive outcomes.

If Figure 6.2 does provide an accurate picture of the new boundary configuration of social citizenship in Europe today, what further speculations can be offered about its 'destructuring' and 'restructuring' implications? It is to these questions that we now turn.

What Kind of Destructuring?

In the theoretical perspective outlined in Chapter 1, destructuring should be conceived as a causal chain typically operating through the following steps:

1. boundary opening alters the spatial options available to actors and thus the value of the resources they control. Therefore:
2. a novel opportunity structure gradually emerges, prompting actors to reconsider their spatial positioning, their confrontational strategies, and their traditional loyalties, and to experiment with new forms of spatial politics;
3. the internal order of the pre-existing bounded space is subject to increasing challenges and is gradually destabilized; significant resources are withdrawn from old institutions, undermining their individual performance or mutual complementarity; traditional actor alignments and organizational networks weaken or possibly break apart; new lines of conflict emerge and the overall process of domestic political production is disturbed, even jeopardized, by the interference of external and competing authority structures.

This causal chain unfolds incrementally over time through small but cumulative effects. The existing internal order may be able to absorb the challenges and contain destabilization dynamics through various forms of adjustment, including explicit defensive restructuring along the old boundary lines (or what remains of them). Destructuring is not a one-way street to social and systemic disintegration. The wider space generated by boundary opening may in its turn become an arena for a novel process of restructuring and system-building. After all, this was precisely the historical experience of the nation state itself, especially in federal polities. System formation was achieved in these polities through complex and lengthy processes of internal boundary removal and the building of new common external boundaries. Destructuring, defensive restructuring along the old boundaries, and restructuring along new, wider boundary lines are three processes that can coexist and proceed in parallel for long periods of time, maintaining some sort of mutual equilibrium. This seems to be, to a large extent, the current state of affairs in the EU: the Euro-polity can be seen as a widening and deepening bundle of 'member spaces' (an expression that is becoming increasingly more appropriate than 'member states') constantly engaged in balancing acts between opening and closing, with a yet unknown destination in terms of the eventual 'structuring' pattern.

Chapters 4 and 5 gave several illustrations of the destructuring sequence in the field of social sharing since the 1970s, a sequence prompted by the new boundary configuration generated by free-movement provisions and competition rules. Individual and collective actors (including subnational territorial systems) have learned how to take advantage of the new locality opportunities offered to them. And the increase of cross-boundary movements has been accompanied by a parallel intensification of voice dynamics: typically, voice against entry (e.g. the entry of foreign migrants), voice against exit (e.g. the exit of domestic firms seeking lower labour costs or the exit of domestic capital), voice for entry (e.g. on the part of foreign providers of social protection benefits and services), or voice for exit (e.g. on the part of the wealthier insured who want to opt out of existing compulsory schemes). The institutional status quo has been explicitly and directly challenged in some of its foundational properties: for example, the link between legal residence and the fruition of means-tested social assistance, the public monopoly over compulsory insurance, or the very right to impose compulsory affiliation to social sharing schemes. These challenges have been overcome, so far, either by successful defensive reactions of national governments—through the various strategies outlined at the end of Chapter 4—or by benevolent rulings from the ECJ. But one wonders what might have happened if the Court had ruled in favour of *Poucet-Pistre* or *Albany*: the whole French system of *monopoles sociaux* and the Dutch sector of second pillar pensions would have been seriously destabilized, with a likely domino effect on the social protection systems of other member states as well. The very presence of such 'foundational' challenges must be interpreted as a sign of the deep tension which is building up in the relationship between nation-based forms of social protection and the logic of European integration.

The *Poucet-Pistre* and *Albany* cases are interesting for our purposes not only for the critical legal issues that were at stake in the two litigations (the legitimacy of public monopoly and the very right to bound), but also for the context in which these two litigations emerged. During the 1990s in France and the Netherlands a new line of conflict made its appearance precisely around the new locality options generated by the integration process. As illustrated in Chapter 4, the EU-induced liberalization of the insurance market prompted in these two countries a dynamic of social and political mobilization on the part of certain collective actors (the self-employed, some groups of employers, private insurance companies) interested in changing the existing rules of social sharing. The self-employed and employers 'voiced for exit', that is, for exempting themselves from the obligation to insure with predetermined public or collective schemes. Private insurance companies in their turn 'voiced for entry', that is, for gaining access to a new potential market and for meeting the demands for alternative forms of social protection on the part of the other two actors. Trade unions, left-wing parties, social insurance funds, national bureaucracies, and, ultimately, national governments counter-mobilized in both countries in defence of traditional closure rules. By upholding the status quo, the ECJ rulings blocked destructuring developments, re-establishing the equilibrium between domestic sharing orders and the EU single market. Nonetheless, these two episodes remain important as they cast valuable light on the cleavage-generation potential of the new boundary configuration, on specific interest alignments, and on the forms of mobilization through which such new cleavages might actually emerge, and—last but not least—on the precarious state of national–supranational equilibriums.

French and Dutch developments during the 1990s are instructive for another reason. Why did they take place, precisely, in France and the Netherlands? In part, the answer may well lie in local conjunctures, which should not concern us here. But to some extent at least the answer must be sought in some distinctive feature of the French and Dutch welfare states that made them especially sensitive to the destabilizing potential of market liberalization in the insurance sector. A punctual discussion of such features would divert us from our main line of argument.[9] The general point that is worth making is this: destructuring does or will not affect national welfare states in a uniform way. In such an abstract formulation the point may sound trivial and thus needs some elaboration.

In Figure 6.2 the internal design of each national space is a mere stylized representation. In reality, each individual welfare state has its own mix of layers and pillars of different sizes and different internal designs. Using the language of Chapter 1, we can say that each national welfare state has a distinct structural profile consisting of institutional forms which are embedded in nation-specific cleavage and centre–periphery constellations, linked to historical 'bounded structuring' dynamics (i.e. the formation, precisely, of those constellations and those institutional forms in the wake of the boundary-building processes of the past). Given the wide variation in structural profiles, we should expect that the potential destructuring (and reconfiguration) of European welfare systems will take place in different ways and with different degrees of intensity. This expectation is very much in line with the perspective of Rokkan and his constant effort to contextualize general trends and hypotheses according to specific 'typological–topological' factors.[10] A detailed case-centred contextualization of the general hypotheses on destructuring stemming from the sequence charted in Figure 6.2 would be beyond the scope of this book. We can, however, advance the suggestion that destructuring pressures on national systems will be filtered by the two main components of structural profiles: (a) the institutional status quo at the domestic level in the sphere of social protection, and (b) cleavage and centre–periphery constellations (see Figure 6.3). In the next section we illustrate how the first filter may operate, focusing on the issue of supplementary pensions. The subsequent section discusses the filtering role of the second factor, addressing the more general—and increasingly thorny—theme of migration and welfare.

---

[9] As mentioned in Chapter 4, the problematic feature of the French system is likely to have been the complex architecture of its first pillar, characterized by a very pronounced fragmentation and by the ambiguous role of the *régimes complémentaires*. The problematic feature of the Dutch pension system may in its turn be connected to the Janus-like character of its second pillar, resting on a plurality of funded schemes and on affiliation rules negotiated by the social partners and then enforced through national laws. We return briefly to these aspects in the next section.

[10] Typological factors are those linked to social and institutional variables; topological factors are those linked to the territorial dimension, that is, the geographical location of a given 'case' (a country, a region) and its internal territorial organization.

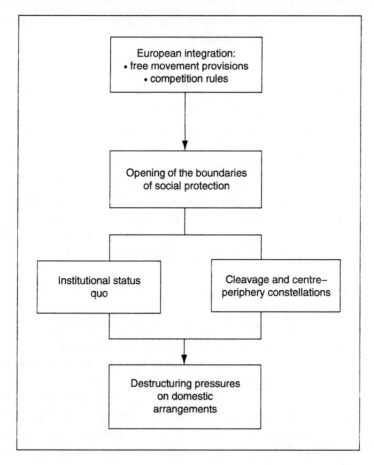

Fig 6.3 European integration and destructuring pressures on domestic arrangements for social sharing

Institutional Legacies and Boundary Redefinitions: The Case of Pensions

As we have seen, since the mid-1990s both the law and the jurisprudence of the EC have promoted market-making and upheld competition rules at the level of second and third pillars, with a view to developing a big European space for occupational and private pensions. This sector is thus likely to be exposed in future years to increasing destructuring challenges. The social reach and economic salience of occupational and private pensions is quite considerable. It is estimated that around 25 per cent of the

EU's population is now covered by occupational schemes (see Chapter 4). The value of funded pension assets as a percentage of the EU's GDP is also substantial: about 30 per cent for second pillar schemes and nearly 15 per cent for third pillar schemes (EC 1997, 1999a; EFRP 2001). At this level of provision there is a fertile ground for interest articulation and aggregation in the wake of boundary opening, especially in terms of increasing 'voice for exit' on the part of wealthier groups in search of more individualized forms of protection, and of 'voice for entry' on the part of foreign providers in search of new customers. Economic and political pressures are likely to build up for changing existing institutions, for creating new ones, and perhaps, in the future, for challenging the traditional mix of statutory and supplementary, mandatory and voluntary, collective and individual forms of provision. At least as regards its second pillars, European social protection is likely gradually to veer towards the North American model, which rests more heavily on market forces and actors and leaves no room for the 'social dialogue' between employers and trade unions.

The expansion of the second pillar and the creation of a single market for pension funds (in the wider context of financial internationalization) have an additional implication, of no secondary importance: the establishment of direct links between the domestic resources allocated to retirement security and global finance (Bonoli 2003). From a purely economic perspective, this link may generate various advantages (such as the possibility of higher returns on contributions) and disadvantages (such as higher risks on investments). But in politico-institutional terms this development is likely to be a significant source of potential destructuring: pension funds will be uncoupled from the national political economies that they have traditionally served. For a number of EU countries this uncoupling may disturb established practices and interest constellations, and even prompt some first dynamics of 'voice against exit'.

Which institutional configurations are more exposed to destructuring challenges? As has been stressed and illustrated several times in this volume, Europe has experienced a wide variety of developmental trajectories that have moulded in different ways the relative size and the internal design of pension systems. What seems especially important for our discussion is the extant division of labour between basic, first pillar schemes and supplementary, second pillar schemes, as well as the internal organization of the latter. The great divide in the EU pension system is between two distinct models: (a) a model resting on limited first pillars offering basic security, complemented by extended, non-public second and third pillars providing employment-related benefits; and (b) a model resting on extended first pillars offering more substantial security, complemented by more limited second and third pillars. The first model prevails in the UK, Denmark, the Netherlands, and, increasingly, Ireland (as well as, outside the EU, Switzerland). The second model characterizes—with internal variations—the other Nordic and Continental countries.[11]

The pensions systems of the first cluster are unlikely to suffer significant destructuring pressures as a result of the emerging EU regulatory framework on free movement and competition in general and pension funds in particular. The institutional architecture of these systems is already largely in line with the EU framework. It already in fact envisages wide options for 'consumers' (active workers) and wide margins of manoeuvre for the providers of supplementary benefits; moreover, pension funds operating in these countries are already well integrated with international finance. The most emblematic case in this respect is certainly the UK. The formation of a pan-European market of 'institutions of retirement provision', as foreseen by Directive 41/03, is unlikely to affect the UK pension situation to any significant extent. Given its size and sophistication, the UK market will be the largest exporter of financial services for retirement (especially asset management) rather than an importer of foreign products: London is already the gateway for accessing global financial markets and is thus the likeliest candidate to become the hub of European pension fund trading (Clark 2003; Emmerson 2003). In this respect we could hypothesize further that European integration in the field of retirement policy will probably work to reinforce the distinctive features of the British pension system: its high degree of fragmentation, its basis in competing plans offering diverse formulas and guarantees, and its low degree of interpersonal redistribution.[12]

The Dutch (and to some extent the Danish) situation is somewhat more exposed to destructuring threats. The Dutch second pillar is in fact much more structured than its UK counterpart: it is based on mandatory plans organized at the company, sector, or professional level; it is tightly coupled with the system of collective bargaining; it is run by the social partners under close state regulation; and it incorporates elements of both horizontal (cross-firm) and vertical (cross-salary level) redistribution (Clark 2003; Van Riehl, Hemerijck, and Visser 2003). The *Albany* controversy has

---

[11] We discussed these two models and their historical genesis in Chapter 3. For an analysis of the distinctive features and developmental problems of the pension systems of the new member states of central and eastern Europe, see Natali (2004).

[12] The new 'pension process' of the EU might, however, exert a different kind of influence on the UK pension system, encouraging it to improve the adequacy of basic benefits. See later the discussion of the potential impact of the OMC.

already shown that the Dutch configuration may collide with the EU competition regime. In that controversy the ECJ has upheld the status quo, while the EU pension fund directive does take into account the existence of distinct national provisions on mandatory affiliation, including those linked to collective bargaining. Thus no immediate earthquake is looming beneath the architecture of the Dutch pension system. It may, however, be difficult in the future for Dutch funds fully to maintain their monopolistic prerogatives, especially in respect of the actual management of assets: the separation between ownership and management of the pension funds and the full liberalization of the latter in the emerging EU market might pose some destructuring challenges for the Dutch model, with uncertain implications for the role of the trade unions and the dynamics of industrial relations (Clark 2003).

Destructuring challenges will be much more serious in the second cluster of pension systems. Here public first pillars based on the PAYGO mechanism are still the cornerstone of retirement provision; but, in response to demographic and financial pressures, during the 1990s various reforms promoted a transition towards new 'multipillar' configurations, widening the scope of second and third pillars. Such transitions will have to abide by the rules set by the EU, forcing national actors to accept more opening than they are accustomed to, and disturbing established social practices and political equilibriums. In France, for example, during the 1990s a consensus gradually emerged on the need to complement the first pillar (now including the AGIRC and ARRCO regimes) with a second funded pillar. But most social and political actors assumed that the design of such a pillar would reflect some typical features of the French social security tradition, in particular management by the social partners. They also assumed that the assets of this new pillar would be invested in the domestic economy (Palier 2003). As mentioned in Chapter 4, the French government was among the fiercest opponents of supranational activism in the field of supplementary pensions. Now that the pension fund directive has been adopted, the margins for a nationally distinct and 'closed' trajectory of pension funds *à la française* have become much narrower, strengthening the position of certain actors (such as the employers and the *Fédération Française de Sociétés d'Assurance*, FFSA) and weakening the position of the unions and left-wing parties. The opportunity structure of the French pension system has been altered by the new boundary configuration: destructuring seems to have entered the second stage of the sequence outlined in the previous section.

Another interesting experience is that of Sweden. In this country a pension reform adopted in 1998 established a new funded second pillar financed by mandatory contributions (Box 6.1). In accordance with EU law, not only will this novel 'space' of Sweden's retirement provision be open to other European providers, but it will be possible to invest the funds collected from Swedish workers in foreign financial markets. This break with an entrenched tradition of national closure has been accompanied by a lively political debate: the trade unions above all (but also some sectors of business) have clearly recognized the potential destructuring effect of this break. For example, the unions have complained that 'the new openness is diverting Swedish capital and is . . . lowering investment in Sweden with implications for employment growth' (Palme 2003: 158). Concerns have also been raised about the macroeconomic implications of the new framework, for example in relation to exchange rate stability. Emerging signs of the 'politicization' of the pension boundary issue in a country such as Sweden are an interesting development, fully in line with our theoretical framework: debounding tends to disturb established social and political compromises and to elicit voice—in this case, 'voice against exit'. It must be noted that this politicization of the boundary issue is taking place against the background of wider policy and academic debates in recent years on the resilience of the Scandinavian model of welfare state in the face of internationalization and Europeanization. Such debates recognize that the institutional balance is gradually shifting away from the Nordic tradition of full universalism towards a more plural landscape in which non-public and non-national options will play a greater role in the social protection of citizens. Where this might lead in terms of institutional design and—more importantly—in terms of distributive outcomes can only be the object of speculation, which seems to range from the seriously pessimistic (Hagen 1999) to the moderately optimistic (Alestalo and Kuhnle 2000; Palme 2003; Steinmo 2002).

While the Scandinavian countries seem to be the most exposed, at least potentially, to destructuring threats linked to European integration, the south European countries find themselves at the other extreme. Their pension systems are overwhelmingly centred on the first pillar, which still provides the largest share of retirement income. During the 1990s a series of reforms reduced the generosity of the pension formulas and tried to promote the development of a funded second pillar (Ferrera and Gualmini 2004). Partly anticipating EU developments, the south European reforms have already adopted regulatory frameworks geared towards choice and competition. One might thus expect a gradual and soft transi-

---

BOX 6.1   The Swedish pension system in transition

The pension system introduced with the 1998 reform rests on a universal public scheme which provides for a basic 'guaranteed pension' and for an income pension based on a 'notional defined contribution' (NDC) formula.[13] The scheme is still financed through PAYGO and therefore is entirely located within space A of Figure 6.2. The reform has, however, introduced an important innovation: fully funded individual accounts, financed by mandatory contributions equal to 2.5 per cent of earnings, which are paid into a single Premium Pension Authority (PPM) and managed by independent specialist institutions (individual contributors can choose up to five different managers). These accounts belong to space B, together with a number of pre-existing voluntary and funded occupational funds established between the 1960s and 1990s.

In contrast to their UK and Dutch counterparts, Swedish pension funds have never pursued a strategy of internationalization. On the contrary, they have traditionally maintained a strong national orientation, investing predominantly in the Swedish capital market and serving social objectives (such as the development of public housing). Fund assets were, in other words, seen as part and parcel of the 'nation-based welfare state'. Public restrictions on the investment strategies of voluntary pension funds were relaxed during the 1990s. But the 1998 reform marked a turning point in the Swedish tradition of national closure at this level of pension provision. The newly established mandatory funded component has in fact embarked on a course of gradual integration into global finance. In the first place, foreign firms are allowed to manage the assets of the PPA, and a sizeable number of contributors have actually chosen them. This development has been partly the result of EU pressures. The pre-existing occupational pension funds are not (yet) open to external fund managers (the Dutch situation). But this is likely to change after the EU pension fund directive, thus widening the entrance foreign players into the Swedish market of occupational retirement services. In the second place, fund managers are free to invest wherever they deem appropriate, even beyond Swedish borders. This freedom has been accorded also to the pre-existing voluntary pension funds. Thus, at least as regards the investment activity of the second pillar, national closure has been superseded.

Source: Palme (2003).

---

[13] A notional defined contribution formula (NDC) links the pension amount to the total amount of contributions that have been paid into the scheme, adjusted by some index linked to interest rates, inflation, and economic growth. The adjusted total is then divided by some 'transformation coefficient' linked to average life expectancy at the age of retirement, to determine the actual pension amount. The link between contributions and benefits is 'notional' because there is no actual account into which individual contributions are paid, as is the case with genuine defined contribution formulas.

tion from closure to openness, in the wider context of the creation of a pan-European market for pension funds. But, as the Italian developments summarized in Box 6.2 illustrate, such smooth scenarios cannot be taken for granted.

We cannot offer here a systematic and contextualized analysis of each national case (Clark and Whiteside 2003). The general point that we want to make should, however, be sufficiently clear: national programmatic configurations do make a difference to the way in which pension systems are responding to boundary redrawing linked to European integration, thus confirming the filtering role of institutional legacies highlighted in Figure 6.3. We can now turn to discuss briefly the second 'filter', that is, cleavage and centre–periphery constellations.

Old and New Cleavage Lines: The Case of Migration

The second critical factor that will filter national dynamics of destructuring and restructuring is the changing constellation of cleavages and centre–periphery relations. We have already emphasized that the original architecture of European welfare states closely reflected the cleavage and centre–periphery structures that existed when mass social insurance was introduced. Based on the analysis in previous chapters, we may suggest that these original architectures have now begun a process of (partial) unfreezing as a result of both exogenous and endogenous pressures. There seems to be room, in other words, for the formation of new sharing alliances, challenging the existing redistributive configurations. We also know that national cleavage and centre–periphery structures have in their turn been subjected to a process of transformation, with the emergence of new interest organizations and partisan formations (Bartolini 2000, 2005; Franklin et al. 1992). It is therefore plausible to expect a 'mutual attraction' between the two processes, that is, a reconfiguration of social protection in which sharing arrangements will tend to match with the new, emerging social and political alignments.

One of the most powerful potential catalysts for developments in this direction is the immigration issue. The presence (and especially the rapid increase in a relatively short period of time) of foreign immigrants in a given national community tends to disturb the existing distribution of material resources and life chances among natives, and often challenges (or is perceived as a challenge to) the prevailing cultural norms and symbolic codes. Thus, the entry of outsiders is very likely to catalyse the voice of insiders. In the field of social protection, immigration allows

---

BOX 6.2   The winding road to the second pillar in Italy

Since the early 1990s, various Italian governments have tried to encourage a second pillar to take off by diverting towards occupational funded plans the mandatory contributions that Italian employers have to pay for the so-called end-of-contract payment (TFR): a lump sum that employees receive when their contract with an employer ends, typically at the age of retirement. TFR benefits are no trivial component of Italy's income maintenance system, in particular for retirees: mandatory contributions are set at around 7 per cent of gross earnings; annual expenditure on such benefits amounts to around 1.5 per cent of GDP.

In 1993 the government introduced a new regulatory framework for second pillar schemes. This framework envisaged voluntary affiliation, encouraged the formation of 'closed' funds (at the sectoral level) on the part of the social partners, but also foresaw the possibility of 'open' funds set up by financial intermediaries. In the case of closed funds, the 1993 law envisaged the separation of ownership and control functions from asset management functions, making the latter subject to competition rules. To a large extent, the 1993 law anticipated the EU approach. Yet the transformation of the TFR into a proper second pillar has proved much more difficult than expected.

The social partners have, in fact, a strong vested interest in keeping TFR resources firmly under their control. For employers, TFR contributions are a significant source of cheap credit; they are set aside only notionally in the company's budget, and the interest which must be paid on them (eventually accruing to the final payment to the employee) is much lower than the interest that employers would have to pay to financial institutions if they borrowed money from them. The trade unions in their turn consider TFR benefits as 'deferred wages' and are not keen to make them available to 'third parties' (e.g. open funds) or to weaken the significance of such benefits in wage bargaining. The 1990s witnessed a long tug of war between the government and the social partners about the reform of the TFR and its mobilization for the take-off of second pillar plans. Looming in the background of this controversy is the issue of openness: if moved into the second pillar, the substantial resources of the TFR would be 'liberated' from Italy's industrial relations system and domestic economy, and would be open to offers from other players (insurance companies and other financial institutions) and from global financial markets. This scenario might be good for the sustainability of Italian pensions and the security of future cohorts of retirees, but for the present it would deprive important social actors of crucial financial resources.

In July 2004 the Berlusconi government passed a reform that will hasten the transformation of the TFR into a supplementary occupational pension. Thus in the coming years a mass of financial resources (all or part of the TFR mandatory contributions) is likely to flow into a second pillar, which will in turn rapidly integrate with global finance. Italy might even leapfrog Sweden in denationalizing pension fund assets—with domestic actors much less prepared than their Scandinavian counterparts to manage proactively this delicate transition. The implications of such a 'big bang' may be far-reaching, not only for the Italy's welfare state but for Italian capitalism in general.

Source: Jessoula and Ferrera (2005).

non-natives to penetrate (at least partially) the national sharing space and raises thorny questions of reciprocity and fairness which may prompt defensive mobilizations on the part of (certain groups of) natives. Even though the member states still have the last word in regulating the inflow of third-country nationals, the EU has gained increasing powers in this area, especially over the rights of immigrants once they have entered EU territory.[14] Moreover, the eastern enlargement has transformed the citizens of ten new countries from 'third-country nationals' into EU citizens, though with a period of transition that will last until 2011. Symptoms of a growing politicization of the immigration issue are clearly visible today in all European countries. The likelihood that this issue will actually work as a catalyst for explicit and tangible defensive restructurings of sharing institutions is closely linked, however, to national cleavage and centre–periphery configurations—that is, the second filter indicated in Figure 6.3.

The question of who pays for the welfare benefits of migrants has become increasingly salient in many of the 'old' member states. From a strictly financial point of view, it is difficult to determine precisely the impact of migration on the welfare state of the hosting country. The entry of foreign workers into national sharing spaces implies new contributions, not only new outlays. Much depends on the actual pattern of migrations (which jobs, what kind of workers, with what kind of demographic profiles and family backgrounds, etc.). From a broader perspective, there can be little doubt that migration plays a positive and not a negative role for the longer-term sustainability of European welfare states, given adverse demographic trends. But 'local' disturbances do occur—to a particular national programme, for example, or to the welfare system of a given region—and are difficult to avoid. And even small disturbances may have big consequences in the wake of specific 'framing' dynamics and domino effects.

The 1971 Regulation was designed to contain as far as possible the disruptive effects of growing flows of exits and entries. Intra-EU cross-border flows (of migrant workers, pensioners, patients, etc.) have remained relatively modest so far, even if constantly growing. But migration from outside the EU has been rapidly increasing in the last two decades. As noted in Chapter 4, during the 1990s, annual entries of third-country nationals fluctuated around 850,000 immigrants. Even if not formally assimilated as EU citizens, third-country nationals have come

---

[14] See our reconstruction of events in Chapter 4.

to enjoy virtually full access to social benefits in the member states where they legally reside.

The financial impact of migration has become a very pressing issue with the eastern enlargement of the EU. The rules on social security coordination were extended to nationals of the countries of central and eastern Europe immediately after accession. However, the free circulation of workers will be phased in over seven years.[15] According to recent estimates (Boeri and Brückner 2001; Brückner and Boeri 2003), in the next twenty-five years between 3 million and 4 million workers are likely to migrate from the new eastern member states. These workers will be primarily attracted by better job opportunities and not necessarily by more generous social benefits. Expert studies demonstrate that there is no cause for concern about the consequences of labour mobility; indeed, full free circulation is likely to bring significant advantages to both sending and receiving countries.[16] Nevertheless, tensions are rising in anticipation of the 2011 deadline and of possible 'welfare magnet effects', in the above-mentioned context of growing politicization of the immigration issue in most countries.

Even if the factual answer to the 'who pays' question is that migrant workers themselves bear the burden of the benefits and services which they consume (at the aggregate level and usually also at the individual level), public perceptions are highly sensitive to cases of opportunistic behaviour which may take place at the margin. Kvist (2004) has coined the term 'social raids' to designate such behaviour (in their ideal-typical form) and the alarms that they originate in public debates. A social raid is 'a surprise attack on national social security by a small or large group of people from abroad' (Kvist 2004: 306). Its protagonists are able-bodied workers and their families who strategically obtain a work permit (not necessarily a genuine one) in order to capture social benefits with minimum effort, possibly exporting them to their home country.[17] The fear of

---

[15] The Accession Treaty envisages for the new eight central and eastern European member states (Cyprus and Malta are excepted) a transitional period of up to seven years, with a $2 + 3 + 2$ formula. Between 2004 and 2006 each of the old member states will be allowed to impose national restrictions on labour mobility. In the subsequent period (2006–9) they will be able to choose whether to apply national rules or EU rules: in the latter case they will be allowed to reintroduce temporary restrictions in the event of unexpected disturbances in their labour markets. Between 2009 and 2011 all member states will apply EU rules unless they can demonstrate 'serious disturbances'. After 2011 only EU rules of free circulation will apply.

[16] For a full discussion and a review of the literature, see Boeri and Brücker (2001).

[17] According to studies cited in Kvist (2004), in Denmark or Sweden a migrant's work of ten hours per week is sufficient to qualify for benefits also for his or her partner, children, and parents; and work could even be fictitious.

social raids has already prompted forms of pre-emptive, defensive reform of national schemes on the part of many EU-15 countries in anticipation of the new flow of immigration from central and eastern Europe.[18]

The enlargement has moreover promoted various forms of 'sneaking in' which are not entirely illegal, but exploit the loopholes of the existing EU rules on free movement and competition. The most emblematic example is the increasing flow of the Polish, Baltic, Czeckh, Slovak, and Hungarian self-employed who enter the German or Austrian labour markets as 'service providers'. The Accession Treaty envisaged a seven year transition for the free movement of workers, but allowed from the beginning (i.e. from June 2004) the free circulation of services. Workers from the new member states can thus register themselves as (individual) service enterprises in Germany, and then compete for jobs in the low-wage sectors of the economy (hotels and catering, social services etc.). This dynamics has already prompted 'voice against sneaking in' on the side of various German actors.[19] The German government (supported by most of the other EU-15 governments) has mobilized to block the Commission proposal for a directive on the internal market for services, which may further increase the competitive advantage of low-wage member states vis-à-vis the high-wage ones.[20] The so-called 'Bolkestein directive' and its expected negative implications for national workers has been a major target of the front opposing the constitutional Treaty in France in view of the referendum of May 29, 2005.

To be sure, defensive restructuring of national welfare schemes based on boundary manipulation has occurred in earlier phases of European integration. When Denmark joined the EC, for example, it changed its pension regulations, making access to the full basic pension conditional on residence (forty years) rather than mere citizenship. But the pre-emptive moves that the EU-15 member states are undertaking in response to the eastern enlargement are a novel phenomenon, in at least two respects. First, they are often accompanied by the presence, in national debates, of new anti-immigrant and xenophobic voices (a point to which I return later), which use the 'social raid' caricature as an argument for eliciting or exacerbating popular fear of foreigners and opposition to the dynamics of economic and social opening. Second, a pre-emptive move in one country triggers a chain reaction in other countries: no country wants to remain the only one with an unprotected national welfare state. In other words, the intensification of labour mobility and the anticipation of

[18] For a review and discussion, see Kvist (2004).

[19] See *Der Spiegel* (2005).

[20] See note 50, chapter 4.

high migration flows from the new member states tend to generate a policy dynamic of social protectionism, based on strategic cross-national interactions, less concerned with actual trends than with the advantages that can be seized by countries that move first in closing their welfare systems. Such a syndrome may well subside if actual developments prove that the fear of social tourism and 'social raids' is unwarranted. But it may also maintain its momentum owing to the surge of 'ethno-regionalism' and 'new right populism' in an increasing number of European countries. The immigration issue may, in other words, transform itself into a basis for cleavage formation: an insider–outsider (natives/non natives) cleavage or a fully–fledged pro-integration–anti-integration cleavage. The destructuring implications of such a development would obviously be far-reaching. One might even imagine a scenario of nationalistic/xenophobic 'offensive restructuring', based on an explicit and large-scale attack to the opening obligations imposed by the EU institutional order.[21] The negative results of the French and Dutch referendums on the Constitutional Treaty held in May and June 2005 demonstrate that this scenario may prove to be something more tangible than a mere academic speculation.

The fear of a destabilization of domestic sharing spaces has become so intense in recent years that the new Constitutional Treaty includes a 'clause of appeal' in respect of EU legislation on the social security entitlements of migrant workers. In fact, Art. III-136 states that in this field 'where a member of the Council considers that a draft European law or framework law...would affect fundamental aspects of its social security system, including its scope, cost or financial structure, or would affect the financial balance of that system, it may request that the matter be referred to the European Council' (TECE, art. III-136, para. 2). Referral to the European Council may result in a request to the Commission to abandon the proposed legislative act and submit a new proposal.

In which national contexts is the new insider–outsider opposition more likely to build up, destabilizing the institutional status quo and paving the way for dynamics of defensive restructuring, based on exclusionary measures and new demands for closure? Here is where the filter of domestic centre–periphery and cleavage constellations (and thus party system configurations) comes into play. Such constellations play a crucial role in

---

[21] In this scenario, the demand for closure may go beyond the national labour market and extend to the product markets (e.g. through the reintroduction of tariffs vis-à-vis the goods and services of low cost countries, especially China and India, as well as the introduction of penalties for national firms that relocate to these countries). Such demands have already started to be voiced in some countries, especially in relation to the end of restrictions on textile imports into the EU.

defining, within each national context, the structure of opportunities for crafting rebounding operations in a defensive direction. The legacy of an unresolved territorial cleavage, signalled by the presence of weak centres and/or strong peripheries, is a first crucial factor in creating margins of manoeuvre for this kind of operation. In Chapter 5 we argued that the loosening of state-national boundaries has prompted the rise of a 'new regionalism', that is, a growing protagonism on the side of subnational territories in the economic and social spheres, often encouraged and supported by supranational initiatives and incentives. This new regionalism may aim in several directions, ranging from an inclusive-cosmopolitan extreme to an exclusive-xenophobic one (Keating 1998; Longo 2003). The latter takes the form of an inward-looking process of region-building, resting on 'ethnic or cultural magnification in the face of "otherness" through historical manipulation, and mythologizing of local cultural forms' (Longo 2003: 479). The local *Gemeinschaft* is typically presented in this context as the natural place for identity-based forms of sharing. Not surprisingly, this form of region-building tends to be accompanied by explicit proposals/demands to gain regional control over 'entries'—in particular, control over the territorial entry of foreign immigrants and/or their access to welfare benefits and services. This mode of region-building is more likely to occur in territories already characterized by cultural distinctiveness and is typically promoted by locally strong ethno-regionalist parties. The presence and strength of such parties is in turn linked to historical patterns of centre–periphery relations.[22] Not all ethno-regionalist parties have developed marked anti-immigration profiles. But it is within this family that we do find some of the most explicit xenophobic policy platforms in contemporary Europe: think of the Vlaams Blok in Belgium or the Lega Nord in Italy.[23] In other words, strained centre–periphery relations in general and the presence of ethno-regionalist formations in particular offer a fertile ground for the immigration issue to catalyse defensive restructurings of social solidarity at the subnational level.

---

[22] According to Rokkan and Urwin (1983) ethno-regional mobilizations build on the availability within 'peripheries' of substantial cultural, economic, or political resources, but are actually prompted by specific 'catalysts' that worked during two historical junctures: the advent of mass democracy (in the wider context of nation-building) and the expansion of the welfare state (in the wider context of the 'second industrialization' that took place after the Second World War). European integration and rising foreign migration flows may well be seen as a third historical juncture which may re-enforce or catalyze ethno-regional mobilizations.

[23] For an illustration of the Lega Nord policy platform, see Chapter 5.

A second important element which opens up opportunities for the politicization of the natives/non-natives cleavage is the presence of 'new right' populist movements, emerged in the wake of the unfreezing of national party systems which started a few decades ago. This type of movements can be observed in many European countries: in a few of them, they have become active and vocal actors of the party system (Betz 1994; Ignazi 2003; Mény and Surel 2000; Mair 1998; Sabel and Zeitlin 2003). Right-wing populism made an early appearance in the 1970s and 1980s, taking the form of anti-tax and anti-bureaucratic campaigns mainly addressed to a petite bourgeoisie of self-employed and small business people this is for instance the experience of the National Front in France or the Progress Parties in Norway and Denmark. Once established as organized political parties, however, these populist movements have gradually soft-pedalled their anti-welfare state profile, playing to other themes such as the fight against privilege and corruption, opposition to spending cuts (for native male insiders), and foreign immigration. The evolution of the Danish People's Party (DFP), the Austrian Freedom Party (FPÖ), or more recently the Swiss People's Party (SVP) and the Dutch "Liveable Netherlands" party (LN) founded by Pim Fortuyn well represents this ideological turn, which has attracted the support of working-class voters, made anxious by globalization trends, economic shocks, and occupational upheavals. Rising migration flows and intercultural relations have brought new fuel to new-right populism, making 'the defence against immigrants' a top priority of their policy agenda. At the domestic level further strengthening of new right populist parties (and especially their access to executive power) is likely to spur an exclusionary reorientation of existing welfare state schemes, creating a sharper divide between nationals and denizens, let alone illegal immigrants. In Denmark, for example, the DFP has strongly voiced in recent years for a reform of immigration laws and for restricting the access to welfare of foreign workers. Partly in the wake of such voice, the Danish conservative government did introduce in 2004 restrictive measures on the fruition abroad of childcare leave and sickness benefits and has withdrawn the right to social benefits and of residence renewal to unemployed migrants (Kvist 2004). At the European level, the rise of new right populism is bound in its turn to disturb and hinder institutional attempts at entrusting the EU with greater social policy powers and more generally, at furthering the integration process as a whole. Not surprisingly, parties of this family (together with many ethno-regionalist parties) are among the most vocal opponents of the new Treaty Establishing a Constitution for Europe, signed in October 2004. The mobilization of the French

National Front and Dutch LN party greatly contributed to the victory of the 'no' in the popular referendums on the Treaty held in May and June 2005.

Restructuring at the EU Level? Some Cautious Conclusions

All the described trends towards *national* destructuring and (at least in part) defensive restructuring will interact with developments at the *supranational* level, that is, the further evolution of the EU institutional order. So far we have primarily regarded European integration as a source of strains and problems for domestic welfare states. To what extent and in what ways can European integration also work in the opposite direction, that is, providing solutions to at least those problems for which it can itself be held responsible? Can the EU conceivably transform itself into an arena capable of eliciting forms of virtuous 'structuring' in the delicate field of social sharing? After all, this transformation did take place in historical federations (Obinger, Leibfried, and Castles 2005). A scenario of virtuous structuring at the EU level would entail the emergence of institutional arrangements and political dynamics capable of stabilizing the complex web of spatial interactions prompted by the new boundary configuration, with a view to gradually Europeanizing the sphere of social sharing. By 'Europeanization' we do not mean a supranational fusion of existing domestic arrangements: a totally unrealistic development. What we mean is rather the 'nesting' of such arrangements in a wider, multilevel bounded space, within which the production of social security is not programmatically sacrificed to the advantage of market promotion and unfettered competition. Is such a nesting scenario viable? Do any empirical signs already point in this direction? These questions need to be addressed from a broad perspective, briefly discussing 'systemic' developments and challenges.

Especially after the quantum leaps of the 1990s, there can be little doubt that European integration has embarked upon an ambitious attempt at system-building. In the language introduced in Chapter 1, system-building refers to a process of institutional growth and political differentiation of the EU qua distinctive territorial polity demarcated by its own increasingly recognizable external boundaries and by increasingly weaker (or dismantled) internal boundaries. This process is extremely complex and extremely variegated, but has already promoted some initial structuring dynamics in a general sense: a new territorial centre has consolidated itself in the economic sphere, closely interacting with national and subnational 'peripheries', a common membership space (mainly consisting of economic and non-discrimination rights) has put down roots under the authority of the ECJ, and new voice channels have formed for the representation of interests, operating in a framework of 'multilevel pluralism' and 'composite democracy' (Ansell and Di Palma 2004; Fabbrini 2004; Sbragia 2004). The EU has made much slower progress in terms of loyalty generation; on this front the resistance of the national cultural infrastructures (languages, historical traditions, educational and other identity-forming institutions, etc.) is enormous. At least for the foreseeable future, the EU is bound to remain a large-scale experiment state-building (at least partially democratic), with very limited nation-building (Flora 1993, 1999, 2000). 'We-feeling' attitudes among European citizens will form at only a very low and probably oscillating pace, leaving little space for supranational forms of large-scale social sharing (Mau 2005; Van Kersbergen 2000). As mentioned above, the 'fusion' scenario appears today as entirely unrealistic.

The low degree of systemic loyalty (and thus legitimacy) is not the only constraint to EU system-building. Progress in this direction is made more difficult by the simultaneous presence of at least three other macro challenges, which directly impinge on social protection and its relations with other salient institutional spheres:[24]

1. *system adaptation* in the EU-15 member states, in the wake of deep endogenous transformations of their socio-economic structures (demographic ageing, the transition to a service economy, new gender relationships, etc.);

2. *system restructuring* in the new central and eastern European member states, which have to cope not only with socio-economic change but also with politico-institutional change in the wake of their post-Communist transitions and their recent EU accession; and

3. *system competition*, especially regulatory competition (largely centred on tax and social policy regulations), both within the EU and between the EU and the other regional blocs of the world.

To judge from this background, it may well be that any effort to Europeanize (even in the weak sense specified earlier) social protection is doomed to confront virtually insurmountable barriers. We can call this perspective the 'supranational social stalemate' scenario: that is, a scenario in which there is no progress in the structuring of a Social Europe. In this case, the only 'hard' powers of the EU in the social sphere will remain of a regulatory nature and essentially geared towards solving coordination problems

---

[24] For an early formulation of these challenges, see Flora (1993).

and safeguarding a limited range of minimum standards around the 'temple of competition' (Lamy and Pisani-Ferry 2002). The only supranational sharing institutions endowed with their own financial resources will continue to be the structural funds, aimed at limited (and, after the 2004 enlargement, increasingly contentious) interregional redistributions. In this scenario the destructuring trends outlined above are likely to build up, posing increasing problems to the welfare state as a political institution. The clash between on the one hand EU free movement and competition rules ('opening'), and on the other legitimization dynamics deeply rooted in the national sharing practices and cultural infrastructures, is in fact likely to disturb or even undermine the political production of security and solidarity and thus to generate strains in terms of social and systemic integration. National (and subnational) moves of defensive restructuring may partly contain such strains; but, as we have argued, a possible outcome of this scenario is the activation of 'offensive restructuring' dynamics, that is, a full-blown politicization of the opening versus closure issue and the growth of anti-integration oppositions, launching a heavy-handed attack to the whole EU edifice and its 'ever closer union' objectives.[25] The French and Dutch referendums on the Constitutional Treaty, held in the Spring of 2005, have opened an alarming window on such scenario.

If we observe the situation through a more focused lens and from a dynamic perspective, other elements come to the fore, allowing us to outline a second, less pessimistic scenario. This scenario might be called 'incremental social supranationalism'. Since the late 1990s the institutional architecture of the EU has in fact witnessed a number of important changes that may open a narrow but promising path through the blockages which have so far hindered the development of Social Europe and which may pave the way for virtuous forms of structuring. The margins of manoeuvre of this second scenario have probably become narrower after the French and Dutch 'no' to the Constitutional Treaty: it nevertheless remains useful to highlight its possible contours.

As observed in Chapter 3, in its early phase the integration project rested on the assumption that it was not only possible but indeed desirable to separate market-making functions from social sharing functions, assigning the former to the supranational level and leaving the latter under the control of national governments. In the wake of the world economic crisis triggered by the two oil shocks, during the 1980s this division of labour ceased to be viable. The EC responded to the crisis by stepping up market-

---

[25] For a general elaboration of this scenario see especially Bartolini (2005: ch. 7).

making and monetary unification, de facto inaugurating a 'subversive' phase in respect of national welfare state institutions, with all the destabilizing implications that have been highlighted. Towards the end of the 1980s the pendulum started to swing: the idea of a social dimension of the internal market made its appearance in the wake of the SEA, and some significant measures of positive integration were adopted establishing common social standards in a number of spheres (health and safety at work, gender equality, contractual relationships, etc.) (Hine and Kassim 1998; Rhodes 1998). In the second half of the 1990s the reconciliation of economic and social policy objectives *at the EU level* started to appear explicitly on the agenda. While remaining aloof from any suggestion of regulatory harmonization from above (let alone the promotion of supranational redistributive schemes), the new approach inaugurated with the Amsterdam Treaty goes beyond the traditional mix of cohesion measures and the setting of minimum social standards (Szyszczak 2001). The emerging approach aims at embedding national (and subnational) systems of social protection within a two-pronged institutional framework: fundamental social rights on the one hand and open policy coordination on the other. The first element is aimed at supplying a positive list of enumerated social freedoms and entitlements recognized and upheld by the EU legal order: the general but common content of EU citizenship in its social dimension. The second element (the open method of coordination or OMC) is aimed at supplying in its turn both a common set of routinized procedures and a common set of policy goals and targets capable of encouraging and supporting reforms at the domestic level while orienting such reforms in a convergent direction—a direction possibly capable of responding to the whole set of systemic challenges mentioned earlier. These two elements can trigger politico-institutional dynamics moving along the lines of the 'incremental social supranationalism' scenario. Let us consider them in turn.

A catalogue of social rights recognized by the EU has been included within the Charter of Fundamental Rights, first proclaimed by the European Council at the Nice summit of 2000 and subsequently included as Part II of the Treaty Establishing a Constitution for Europe signed in October 2004.[26] As can be seen from Table 6.1, the rights listed under Title IV (devoted to 'Solidarity') are nothing new in respect of what already

[26] At the time of writing, the ratification of this Treaty and thus its actual entry into force are under question in the wake of the negative results of the French and Dutch referendums; the Nice Charter of Fundamental Rights will remain in force, however, even if the Treaty should fail to be eventually ratified.

Table 6.1 The Charter of Fundamental Rights: Title IV on 'Solidarity'

Article	Content
Article 27 Workers' right to information and consultation within the undertaking	Workers or their representatives must, at the appropriate levels, be guaranteed information and consultation in good time in the cases and under the conditions provided for by Community law and national laws and practices.
Article 28 Right of collective bargaining and action	Workers and employers, or their respective organizations, have, in accordance with Community law and national laws and practices, the right to negotiate and conclude collective agreements at the appropriate levels and, in cases of conflicts of interest, to take collective action to defend their interests, including strike action.
Article 29 Right of access to placement services	Everyone has the right of access to a free placement service.
Article 30 Protection in the event of unjustified dismissal	Every worker has the right to protection against unjustified dismissal, in accordance with Community law and national laws and practices.
Article 31 Fair and just working conditions	1. Every worker has the right to working conditions which respect his or her health, safety, and dignity. 2. Every worker has the right to limitation of maximum working hours, to daily and weekly rest periods and to an annual period of paid leave.
Article 32 Prohibition of child labour and protection of young people at work	The employment of children is prohibited. The minimum age of admission to employment may not be lower than the minimum school-leaving age, without prejudice to such rules as may be more favourable to young people and except for limited derogations. Young people admitted to work must have working conditions appropriate to their age and be protected against economic exploitation and any work likely to harm their safety, health or physical, mental, moral or social development or to interfere with their education.
Article 33 Family and professional life	1. The family shall enjoy legal, economic, and social protection. 2. To reconcile family and professional life, everyone shall have the right to protection from dismissal for a reason

Table 6.1   *(Continued).*

Article	Content
	connected with maternity and the right to paid maternity leave and to parental leave following the birth or adoption of a child.
Article 34 Social security and social assistance	1. The EU recognizes and respects the entitlement to social security benefits and social services providing protection in cases such as maternity, illness, industrial accidents, dependency or old age, and in the case of loss of employment, in accordance with the rules laid down by Community law and national laws and practices. 2. Everyone residing and moving legally within the EU is entitled to social security benefits and social advantages in accordance with Community law and national laws and practices. 3. In order to combat social exclusion and poverty, the EU recognizes and respects the right to social and housing assistance so as to ensure a decent existence for all those who lack sufficient resources, in accordance with the rules laid down by Community law and national laws and practices.
Article 35 Health care	Everyone has the right of access to preventive health care and the right to benefit from medical treatment under the conditions established by national laws and practices. A high level of human health protection shall be ensured in the definition and implementation of all EU policies and activities.

Notes: Title IV—Solidarity—includes three more articles, which respectively refer to access to services of general economic interest (art. 36), environmental protection (art. 37) and consumer protection (art. 38). The articles listed in the table have been included in the new Treaty establishing a Constitution for Europe signed in Rome on 29 October 2004 (from art. II – 87 to art. II – 95).
Source: European Parliament (http://www.europarl.eu.int/topics/default_en.htm).

exists in the member states. Moreover, in strictly legal terms the recognition of such rights in the new Treaty does not make them directly enforceable rights; rather, they have the status of 'programmatic principles' or 'aspirational rights', and are thus endowed with a much lesser binding character than other civic or political rights such as free movement or non-discrimination (Giubboni 2004).[27] Looked at from a 'perfectionist' angle, the social dimension of EU citizenship thus remains conspicuously 'thin', even in the wake of an eventual constitutional reform. But perfectionism is seldom an appropriate yardstick for assessing the nature and especially the structuring potential of a new institution. The sheer fact that something akin to a bill of rights—including social rights—has been the object of formal codification must be regarded as a very significant (some have said 'spectacular': Ziller 2003) innovation, which effects a normative and symbolic rebalancing of the EU's overall mission and thus might prompt a gradual redress of the asymmetry between the economic and social dimensions of the integration process. The subjects of the new rights are not merely economic actors, but 'persons'. Thus the social aggregate which is taken as an implicit point of reference is no longer a transnational market, but a civic collectivity. The ECJ may soon start to make reference to fundamental rights in its jurisprudence. So far the Court has not yet directly used the Charter for its case law, in view of the 'aspirational' character of its provisions; but according to many commentators the weaker enforceability of constitutional 'principles' is very controversial from a legal point of view and it may reasonably be expected that the ECJ will sooner or later change its orientation,[28] thus attributing to EU (social) citizenship a denser and more authoritative status and turning it into a potential magnet for both voice and loyalty dynamics. Throughout the book we have noted the important role already played in the past on several occasions by the ECJ in upholding social sharing objectives—sometimes by confirming the legitimacy of closure (e.g. as regards compulsory affiliation), sometimes by confirming the legitimacy of opening (e.g. as regards non-discrimination of immigrants within social protection). The codification of fundamental rights will allow the Court to exercise this function in a more consistent, firm, and continuous way. More generally, this codification can contribute to shifting gradually the centre of gravity of the EU political production towards some middle point between the safeguard of 'freedoms' and the

---

[27] The Treaty establishing a Constitution for Europe signed in Rome on 29 October 2004 treats most of the social provisions of the Charter of Fundamental Rights as 'principles'. In art. II-112.5 it specifies that 'The provisions of the Charter which contain principles *may* be implemented by legislative and executive acts taken by institutions, bodies, offices and agencies of the EU, and by acts of Member States when they are implementing EU law, in the exercise of their respective powers. *They shall be judicially cognizable only in the interpretation of such acts and in the ruling on their legality'* (emphasis added). This article (and in particular the emphasized passages) confers on social rights a weaker binding character, subject to the mediation of other law-making bodies.

[28] See the debate illustrated in Giubboni (2004).

stabilization of 'entitlements'—the two sides of life chances in the European tradition.

The second prong of the new institutional framework is the OMC, a new instrument of multilevel governance in the social policy sphere, initially inaugurated in the field of labour policy with the European Employment Strategy (EES) in 1997 (Ferrera, Hemerijck, and Rhodes 2000). In the context of the Lisbon strategy launched in 2000, the OMC has been subsequently extended to the field of social inclusion (2001), pensions (2003), and more recently health care (due to start in 2006). From our perspective, the OMC is promising, from both a procedural and a substantive point of view: as we shall see, both dimensions can have important 'structuring' implications. Procedurally, the OMC is centred on the following steps: (*a*) the setting of broad objectives and guidelines for each sector of intervention; (*b*) the translation of these objectives into national action plans periodically prepared by member state governments; (*c*) the monitoring

Table 6.2 The employment, social inclusion, pension, and health care 'processes': main substantive objectives

Employment: overarching objectives

- full employment
- quality and productivity at work
- social cohesion
- inclusion

Social inclusion: common objectives

- to facilitate participation in employment and access by all to the resources, rights, goods, and services
- to prevent the risks of exclusion
- to help the most vulnerable
- to mobilize all relevant bodies

Pensions: common objectives (broad headings)

- safeguarding the capacity of systems to meet their social objectives
- maintaining their financial sustainability
- meeting changing social needs

Health care and care for the elderly: long-term objectives

- accessibility
- quality
- financial viability

and evaluation of such plans through peer review and benchmarking exercises; and (*d*) a comparative assessment (with the possibility of issuing recommendations, in the case of employment policies) performed jointly by the Commission and the Council, feeding back into the first step at each subsequent round. From a substantive point of view, the OMC specifies for each sector the priorities for action with a view to orienting the content and direction of policy change. The substantive priorities for employment, social inclusion, pensions, and health care are set out in Table 6.2. While a few of these priorities reflect the economic and financial preoccupations typical of EMU discourse, most of them do speak a different language. This is particularly the case with the social inclusion objectives. As noted by Daly (2004: 9), in the social inclusion process 'there is a vision of the good society... one where people have access to a range of social goods, where family solidarity prevails, where life is not blighted by life crises and where, politically, all relevant bodies (and especially those experiencing poverty and social exclusion) are mobilized. Hence the community is seen as political community.' Though primarily considered a procedural innovation, the OMC does have an important substantive dimension, which can work in the same rebalancing direction as the Charter of Fundamental Rights.

The introduction of the OMC and its diffusion throughout various policy sectors has prompted an increasingly articulate political and academic debate, in which optimistic and sceptical views about the significance and actual impact of the new method seem to balance each other out.[29] A serious and systematic evaluation of the OMC requires sound empirical evidence, which is not yet fully available; however, some empirically grounded indications are now beginning to emerge from research projects on both the employment and the social inclusion processes, that is, the two areas in which the OMC has been applied for some time (since 1998 and 2001 respectively). The following indications can be inferred from one of the best projects to date[30] (Zeitlin 2005a):

---

[29] For a comprehensive online bibliography on the OMC, see the website of the EU Centre at the University of Wisconsin at Madison: http://eucenter.wisc.edu/OMC/index.htm.

[30] See the research project on 'The Open Method of Coordination in Action: the European Employment and Social Inclusion Strategies', coordinated by the University of Wisconsin-Madison, the Observatoire Social Européen, and the SALTSA Joint Programme for Working Life in Europe, comprising a combination of national and comparative studies covering seven countries (Denmark, France, Germany, Ireland, Italy, the Netherlands, and Sweden) and four themes (activation, participation, gender equality, hard law and soft law). The results of the project are contained in Zeitlin and Pochet (2005).

1. Both the employment and the social inclusion processes have indeed contributed to a number of substantive changes in the member states, prompting broad shifts in policy orientation and thinking and in some cases inspiring and/or facilitating the introduction of specific reform measures.

2. Participation in the OMC has induced procedural shifts in social policy governance, for example through administrative reorganization and institutional capacity-building for overall policy steering.

3. A growing mobilization of subnational and non-state actors is clearly visible around both processes: regions, municipalities, the social partners, and various advocacy networks from civil society, representing the views and interests of stakeholder groups, are increasingly directing their attention and efforts towards both processes with a view to exerting influence.

4. Through the OMC some (admittedly still limited) mutual learning dynamics have emerged whereby domestic actors and in particular political and administrative elites have become aware of foreign practices and programmes and have started to take them into account in elaborating domestic reforms.

If it is true that fundamental social rights on the one hand and the various OMC processes on the other form the two main pillars of the new institutional architecture for Social Europe inaugurated by the Amsterdam Treaty and now formalized by the Constitutional Treaty, then one of the most interesting developments in years to come will be the dynamics of interaction between these two pillars (Smisman 2004).[31] This interaction may in fact generate two parallel trends: (*a*) a gradual 'hardening' of the OMC objectives which, through the mediation of fundamental rights and ECJ jurisprudence, may acquire a more binding character vis-à-vis domestic policy environments and choices; and (*b*) the establishment of systematic

---

[31] Despite proposals and pressure for its explicit and full constitutionalization (Giubboni 2004; Zeitlin 2005*b*), the Open Method of Coordination has not been officially incorporated into the new Treaty establishing a Constitution for Europe. However, in Part III the Treaty does provide for the application of key elements of the OMC in some policy areas, among them social policy: for example, art. III-210, which deals with social policy, states that 'European laws may establish measures designed to encourage cooperation between the Member States through initiatives aimed at improving knowledge, developing exchanges of information and best practices, promoting innovative approaches and evaluating experiences, excluding any harmonisation of the laws and regulations of the Member States' (TECE, art. III-210, para. 2(a)). In different passages of the Treaty one does find reference to the main substantive objectives of the various processes as well as to the main procedural features, including the full right of participation on the part of the social partners and civil society actors.

procedures for the actual implementation and monitoring of fundamental rights at the domestic level through the mediation of the employment, social inclusion, and (to a lesser extent) the pension and health care processes (Sciarra 2004).

The first testing ground for both developments could be the sphere of social inclusion and in particular the 'right to sufficient resources', which features explicitly in the catalogue of fundamental rights and is at least indirectly evoked by the broad objectives of the social inclusion process (see Table 6.2). The establishment of a common guarantee of sufficient resources appeared on the EU agenda in the early 1990s (Ferrera, Matsaganis, and Sacchi 2002). The Commission's proposal was blocked but has since remained part of policy and academic debates (e.g. Boeri and Brücker 2001; Schmitter and Bauer 2001). If the narrow path resting on fundamental rights and the OMC remains open or possibly gets wider, then the adoption of an EU minimum income guarantee for 'the most vulnerable' might be its first tangible institutional achievement. Such a move might also find adequate support from public opinion. We said in the Introduction that ordinary citizens are jealous of the decision-making prerogatives of their national governments in the core sectors of social protection. But, according to the Eurobarometer, in the field of poverty and social exclusion a majority of 62 per cent would indeed favour joint national–EU decision-making.[32]

The OMC is a relatively young mode of governance and much can be done to improve its effectiveness and accountability (Radaelli 2003; Scharpf 2001; Zeitlin 2005a). But if the first indications emerging from empirical research are confirmed, there are good reasons to expect that this method may prove to be a viable counterweight to at least some destabilizing pressures that European integration is exerting on national welfare states. More generally, the OMC may prove to be an effective strategy for coping simultaneously with the whole set of systemic challenges mentioned at the beginning of this section. By stimulating the search for innovative policy goals and measures, and by promoting mutual learning dynamics, the OMC can support 'system adaptation' in the more mature member states: that is, a transformation of their social protection arrangements capable of responding to the most compelling endogenous challenges. This is especially important for the challenges linked to population ageing, to changed gender relationships, and to the rapid transformation of labour markets and production systems in the

---

[32] Only in Denmark and Sweden do slight majorities prefer exclusively national decision-making. See EC (2000a).

wake of the transition to the knowledge-based economy.[33] With some procedural refinements, the OMC lends itself well to serving as a flexible vehicle for supporting the broad restructuring of the still fragile welfare states of the new central and eastern European member states in the wider context of complex economic and politico-institutional transitions (Brusse and Hemerijck 2002; Guillen and Palier 2004; Vaughan-Whitehead 2003). At the same time, the various OMC processes can discipline regulatory competition within the EU so that it does not degenerate into a 'race to the bottom'. Finally, nested as it is within the Lisbon strategy—a broad and multidimensional strategy geared towards enhancing the overall competitiveness of the European social model vis-à-vis other regions of the world, and the USA and Japan in particular—the OMC can contribute to meeting the challenge of 'system competition' on its external side.

In a structuring perspective, the OMC is an important innovation not only in institutional but also in political terms. One of the indications arising from empirical research is, precisely, that this mode of governance is mobilizing a wide range of state and non-state, national and subnational actors around the objectives of the various processes and around their procedural junctures (such as the preparation of periodic National Action Plans). For some countries there seems to be evidence that the European Employment Strategy and, even more so, the social inclusion processes have started to break with entrenched policymaking practices and to empower traditionally weaker actors, such as local communities or representatives of stakeholder groups (a development already noted in Chapter 5). In Sweden, for example, the OMC has allowed local communities and NGOs to open a participatory breach in national policymaking, breaking the monopolistic control of the social partners over both sectors (Jacobson 2005). In various member states (and especially the UK) NGO networks have been empowered to voice in the field of anti-poverty policy, breaking the traditional bureaucratic monopoly in decision-making (De la Porte and Pochet 2005). Admittedly, these are only seeds of change: in most cases traditional actors and practices still manage to keep the social policy game in their hands. But through the OMC the various EU arenas are indeed becoming increasingly important venues for the exercise of voice, for the expression but also the solution of distributive conflicts, while national governments seem to be losing their role as gatekeepers

---

[33] As is well known, the discussion of these challenges and of the possible strategies of reform and adaptation is a central theme of current welfare state debates. For a well grounded and persuasive argument about 'why we need a new welfare state', see Esping-Andersen (2002).

between the domestic and the EU social policy arenas. With the passing of time, these seeds may mature, gradually altering patterns of social interaction and political production by shifting their focus towards transnational and supranational arenas.[34]

It would be naïve and certainly premature to interpret fundamental rights and the OMC as unequivocal signs of the activation of the 'incremental social supranationalism' scenario. As shown by Rokkan, structuring in the full sense involves a deep entrenchment of both voice and loyalty dynamics in the basic social, cultural, and political fabric of a territorial system. But, as suggested by the term itself, structuring is a process which may originate from small changes at the margin of the status quo, which never starts in a vacuum, and which builds up through a recombination of pre-existing actor configurations. Of course, we do not know whether fundamental rights and the OMC can work as catalysts of such a recombination. The eastern enlargement and the 'anti-Europe' oppositions (of right-wing neo-populist, but also left-wing neo-radical leanings) unleashed or strengthened by the national referendums on the Constitutional Treaty may pose insurmountable obstacles for the incremental social supranationalism scenario. But the European Union has already crossed troubled waters several times since its inception in the 1950s. Options and trajectories of development that seemed irremediably 'lost' during a period of sudden crisis have resurrected later—and sometimes with a vengeance (let us think of the monetary union). The possibility of setting up 'enhanced cooperations' can facilitate in the future the launch of institutional experimentations among a smaller number of countries, also in the field of social protection. It is in this perspective that we think it useful to end this section by outlining a concrete institutional framework within which the political production of solidarity might restructure itself within the EU—or at least a pioneering portion of the EU. This framework can be visualized through Figure 6.3. At the centre of the figure we still find the national welfare state (space A): a reformed and 'modernized' welfare state, possibly reconfigured in a decentralized fashion and complemented by a number of novel transnational forms of sharing, such as cross-border 'institutions of retirement provision' covering certain occupational groups, transfrontier health care or labour market programmes, and so on. Each national welfare state is nested, however, within two wider and common regulatory spaces.

---

[34] As already mentioned, this shift will also be encouraged by developments outside the OMC processes. For example, the establishment of cross-border pension funds in the wake of the 2003 Directive is likely to spur structuring dynamics, through institutional innovation and the formation of new transnational coalitions and conflicts around the new institutions.

Space B is already in place: it is the single market, resting on free-movement provisions and competition rules—and, in the EMU countries, on a common currency, a common monetary policy, and common budgetary rules. Space C is the novelty and can be called the emerging 'EU citizenship area', resting on a common (and adequately 'hardened') catalogue of fundamental civic, political, and social rights—including, if it should prove feasible, an EU 'guarantee to sufficient resources', possibly funded directly by the EU budget. Space C also includes the various OMC processes, in both their substantive and governance dimensions. Space B and space C overlap underneath space A. This overlap is meant to signal two facts: first, some civic rights (typically the four freedoms) by their nature belong to both spaces; second, the economic and budgetary policies of space B are (or ought to be) programmatically linked to the social policies of space C.[35] There may be other, more sophisticated forms of visualizing the overall institutional framework needed for overcoming the current predicament of

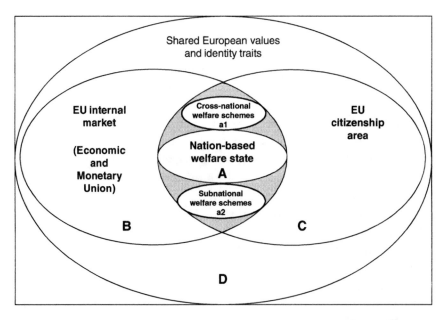

Fig 6.4 A virtuous 'nesting' of the welfare state in the EU institutional framework

[35] From a substantive viewpoint, space C should also include the EU fiscal equalization and cohesion policies; from a political and procedural point of view, it should include the various 'social dialogue' institutions. On the concept and theory of "nesting", see Aggarwal (1998).

the national welfare state and for countering the destructuring scenario outlined at the beginning of this section. The purpose of Figure 6.4 is purely illustrative: the important message is its focus on spatial nesting as a precondition for a virtuous structuring process—if such a process actually is able to gain momentum.

Figure 6.4 includes a third, outer (and thinner) circle: a sociocultural space consisting of a (limited) 'core' of values, symbols, and identity traits shared by all EU citizens. This space should underpin the other three spaces and provide a basic reservoir of systemic loyalty for the functioning of the whole Euro-polity and the strengthening of its legitimacy. There is little need to repeat how crucial the availability of such a space would be for virtuous structuring and yet how difficult and problematic its formation will be, given the 'deep equilibrium' of state-national cultural infrastructures.[36] But, again, loyalty-building is a process, which—to the extent that it actually happens—rests on the build-up of incremental changes: in particular the gradual increase in mutual relevance and mutual trust among the various European nationalities, in the wake of denser transactions and contacts (Delhey 2004). Generational replacement is likely to accelerate such a process. If we look for them we do find some empirical signs that already point in this direction. For example, a Eurobarometer survey of 1999 asked respondents the following question: 'Is there a European cultural identity shared by all Europeans?' (EC 2001a). On average (EU-15), 49 per cent of respondents answered negatively and only 38 per cent positively. But, interestingly, the percentage of agreement was higher among educated and especially among young people.[37] The young are also much more likely to feel 'national and European' than the average population.[38] This suggests that generational replacement may indeed work in favour of greater 'we-feelingness'. It must also be noted that 49 per cent on average is not an absolute majority and, more importantly, 38 per cent agreement is not negligible at all. There seems to be, in other words, a sizeable 'capital' on which to build.

[36] I borrow this notion from Pierson (2004: 157–60) who argues that a deep equilibrium 'occurs when the various factors contributing to the resilience of a particular institution or sets of institutions are so considerable that once arrangements settle on that point they are highly likely to endure for an extended period of time'. One mechanism through which a deep equilibrium can be reconfigured is generational replacement: old members of the existing actor configuration die off and are replaced by new ones who lack the old attachments.

[37] Among young people under the age of twenty-four, the percentage of agreement reaches 44 per cent, while disagreement declines to 43 per cent (EU-15 averages).

[38] Among young people under twenty-four, the percentage of respondents that define themselves as 'nationals and European' increases to 51 per cent (total EU-15 average is 43 per cent (EC 2004c)).

The prospects and—especially—the pace of advance on the delicate front of a common floor of identity traits should not be overestimated. Loyalty generation results from boundary-building and its effects on internal structuring. The multilayered, undefined, and relatively open European boundaries will continue to militate against the formation of strong links between the identities and loyalties of Europeans and the new EU territorial system. Though favourably viewed by the majority of Eurobarometer respondents, the eastern enlargement is very likely to have added further brakes to the formation of such links. But, as argued in a rich debate, the discourse and practice of EU citizenship—with all its identity-forming potential—may work its way through the maze of cultural diversities and actually build on them to forge a common basis of distinctively European 'liberal interculturalism', capable of balancing the right to roots with the obligation of tolerance, the right to options with the duty of participation.[39]

It is now time to conclude. I started this book by highlighting the difficulty in reconciling 'solidarity' and 'Europe', the logic of closure which underpins national dispositions and practices of social sharing, and the logic of opening which typically inspires the European integration project. It is certainly not easy for the EU to find a balance between these two opposite logics: a balance (to repeat the words of the Introduction) capable of sustaining under changed boundary conditions the political production of social solidarity. But if the analysis of this last section is correct, then finding this balance is not impossible. The nation state still is, and probably will remain for a long time, the ultimate guarantor of entitlements and the prime legitimate space for the exercise of social citizenship and for the delicate balancing of rights and obligations. But in the wider space of the EU some institutional elements are emerging—citizenship rights, regulatory instruments, seeds of a core of shared values and identity traits—which if carefully cultivated may provide a fertile ground for the 'nesting' of national sharing traditions within wider membership spaces, thus containing destructuring pressures and possibly activating cross-national bonding dynamics. In any case, what are the alternatives? As I said at the beginning of the book, the time of the *patries de fraternité* (that is, of self-contained islands of national social sovereignty) is long gone and cannot be resurrected; the establishment of a fully-fledged Social Union is in its turn still totally unrealistic. The perspective of 'national de-structuring with no supranational restructuring'

---

[39] For an updated discussion (with Eurobarometer data also on the enlargement countries) and literature review of the issue of a European cultural identity, see Ruiz Jiménez et al. (2004).

cannot be ruled out. This gloomy spiral must be counted as one of the possible outcomes of the delicate juncture created by the negative results of the French and Dutch referendums on the constitutional Treaty, held in the Spring of 2005. But there are possible ways of solving the institutional tension between 'solidarity' and 'Europe': the two spheres are not set on an irremediable course of mutual collision. Scenarios are still open; and, as Rokkan noted, if structures do count, it is actors who ultimately decide.

References

AIM (Association Internationale de la Mutualité) (2000). *Implication of Recent Jurisprudence on the Co-ordination of Health Care Protection Systems*. Summary Report for the European Commission, May. www.aim-mutual.org

Aggarwal, V. (1998). *Institutional Designs for a Complex World*. Ithaca: Cornell University Press.

Alber, J. (1982). *Von Armenhaus zum Wohlfahrtsstaat*. Frankfurt: Campus.

—— (1987). 'Germany', in P. Flora (1986–87) (ed.), *Growth to limits: The European Welfare States Since World War II*, vol. 2. Berlin/New York: De Gruyter.

—— (1995). 'A Framework for the Comparative Study of Social Services', *Journal of European Social Policy*, 5/2: 131–49.

Alestalo, M. and Kuhnle, S. (1987). 'The Scandinavian Route: Economic, Social and Political Developments in Denmark, Finland, Norway and Sweden,' in R. Erikson, E. J. Hansen., S. Ringen, and H. Uusitalo (eds.), *The Scandinavian Model*. New York: M. E. Sharpe.

—— (2000). 'Introduction: Growth, Adjustments and Survival of the European Welfare State', in M. Alestalo and S. Kuhnle (eds.), *Survival of the Welfare State*. Oxford: Routledge.

Alston, P. (ed.) (1999). *The EU and Human Rights*. Oxford: Oxford University Press.

Altenstetter, C. and Björkman, J. (eds.) (1997). *Health Policy Reform, National Variations and Globalization*. London: Macmillan.

Alter, K. J. (1998). 'Who Are the Masters of the Treaty? European Governments and the European Court of Justice', *International Organization*, 52/1: 121–47.

Amenta, E. (2003). 'What We Know about the Development of Social Policy: Comparative and Historical Research in Comparative and Historical Perspective', in J. Mahoney and D. Rueschemeyer (eds.), *Comparative Historical Analysis in the Social Sciences: Achievements and Agenda*. Cambridge: Cambridge University Press.

Anderson, J. (1995). 'Structural Funds and the Social Dimension of EU Policy: Springboard or Strumbling Block?', in S. Leibfried and P. Pierson (eds.), *European Social Policy between Fragmentation and Integration*. Washington, DC: Brookings Institution.

—— O'Dowd, L. and Wilson, T. W. (eds.) (2002). 'New Borders for a Changing Europe. Cross Border Cooperation and Governance', *Regional and Federal Studies*, 12(4): Special Issue.

Anderson, M. (1996), *Frontiers: Territory and State Formation in the Modern World*. London: Polity Press.

Ansell, C. and B. Di Palma (eds.) (2004). *Restructuring Territoriality: Europe and the US Compared*. Cambridge: Cambridge University Press.

—— Parsons, C., and Darden, K. (1997). 'Dual Networks in European Regional Development Policy', *Journal of Common Market Studies*, 35/3: 347–75.

Atkinson, A. (1989). *Poverty and Social Security*. Brighton: Harvester.

Bache, I. (1998). *The Politics of European Union Regional Policy: Multi-level Governance or Flexible Gatekeeping?* Sheffield: Sheffield Academic Press.

Baganha, M. (2000). 'Immigrants Social Citizenship and Labour Market Dynamics in Portugal', in M. Bommes and A. Geddes (eds.), *Immigration and Welfare: Challenging the Borders of the Welfare State.* London: Routledge.

Bailey D. and De Propris, L. (2002). 'The 1988 Reform of the European Structural Funds: Entitlement or Empowerment?', *Journal of European Public Policy*, 9: 408–28.

Baldi, B. (2002) 'Lobbying regionale e Unione europea', *Rivista Italiana di Politiche Pubbliche*, 3: 59–89.

—— (2003). *Stato e territorio. Federalismo e decentramento nelle democrazie contemporanee.* Bari: Laterza.

Baldwin Edwards, M. and Schain, M. (eds.) (1994). *The Politics of Immigration in Western Europe.* London: Frank Cass.

Baldwin, P. (1990). *The Politics of Social Solidarity: Class Bases of the European Welfare States 1875–1975.* Cambridge: Cambridge University Press.

Banting, K. (1995). 'The Welfare State as Statecraft: Territorial Politics and Canadian Social Policy', in S. Leibfried and P. Pierson (eds.), *European Social Policy between Fragmentation and Integration.* Washington, DC: Brookings Institution.

Barnard, C. (1999). 'Gender Equality in the EU: A Balance Sheet', in P. Alston (ed.), *The EU and Human Rights.* Oxford: Oxford University Press.

—— (2004). *The Substantive Law of the EU. The Four Freedoms.* Oxford: Oxford University Press.

Barr, N. (1993). *The Economics of the Welfare State.* Stanford: Stanford University Press.

Barry, B. (1974). 'Review Article: "Exit, Voice and Loyalty" ', *British Journal of Political Science*, 4: 79–107.

Bartolini, S. (1998). *Exit Options, Boundary Building, Political Structuring,* EUI Working Papers, SPN no. 98/1. Florence: EUI.

—— (2000). *Old and New Peripheries in the European Process of Territorial Expansion.* WP 2000/53. Madrid: Juan March Institute.

—— (2004). 'Old and New Peripheries in the Process of European Territorial Integration', in C. Ansell and B. Di Palma (eds.), *Restructuring Territoriality: Europe and the US Compared.* Cambridge: Cambridge University Press.

—— (2005). *Restruturing Europe. Center Formation, System Building and Political Structuring between the Nation State and the EU.* Oxford: Oxford University Press.

Baudewyns, P. and Dandoy, R. (2005). 'The Preservation of Social Security as a National Foundation in the Belgian Welfare State' in N. McEwen and L. Moreno, *The Territorial Politics of Welfare.* Oxford: Routledge

Bellamy, R., Castiglione, D., and Santoro, E. (eds.) (2004). *Lineages of European Citizenship. Rights, Belonging and Participation in Eleven Nation-States.* Palgrave Macmillan

Bendix, R. (1964). *Nation-building and Citizenship.* New York: Wiley.

Bercusson, B. (1999). 'European Labour Law in Context: A Review of the Literature', *European Law Journal*, 5/2: 87–102.

Betz, H. H. (1994). *Radical Right-Wing Populism in Western Europe*. New York: St Martin's Press.

Biersteker, T. and Weber, C. (1996). *State Sovereignty as a Social Construct*. Cambridge: Cambridge University Press.

Biorcio, R. (1997). *La Padania promessa. La storia, le idee e la logica d'azione della Lega Nord*. Milano: Il Saggiatore.

Birch, A. H. (1974). 'Economic Models in Political Science: The Case of Exit, Voice and Loyalty', *British Journal of Political Science*, 5: 69–82

Boeri, T. and Brücker, H. (2001). *The Impact of Eastern Enlargement on Employment and Wages in the EU Member States*. Brussels: DG Employment and Social Affairs.

Börzel, T. (2000). 'From Competitive Regionalism to Cooperative Federalism', *Publius: The Journal of Federalism*, 30/2: 17–42.

Bommes, M. and Geddes, A. (eds.) (2000). *Immigration and Welfare*. London: Routledge.

Bonoli, G. (2000). *The Politics of Pension Reform*. Cambridge: Cambridge University Press.

—— (2003). 'Two Worlds of Pension Reform in Western Europe', *Comparative Politics*, 35/4: 399–415.

Bosco, A. (2000). 'Are National Social Protection Systems under Threat?', *European Issues*, no. 7. Paris: Notre Europe.

Bourne, A. K. (2003). 'The Impact of European Integration on Regional Power', *Journal of Common Market Studies*, 41: 597–620.

Breuilly, J. (1998). 'Sovereignty, Citizenship and Nationality: Reflections on the Case of Germany', in M. Anderson and E. Bort (eds.), *The Frontiers of Europe*. London: Pinter.

Briggs, A. (1961). 'The Welfare State in Historical Perspective', *European Journal of Sociology*, 2: 251–8.

British Department for Work and Pensions (2002). *National Strategy Report on the Future of Pension Systems*. London.

Brubaker, R. (1992). *Citizenship and Nationhood in France and Germany*. Cambridge, MA: Harvard University Press.

Brückner, J. K. and Boeri, T. (2003). *Potential Migration from Central and Eastern Europe, an Update*. Brussels: DG Employment and Social Affairs.

Brusse, W. A. and Hemerijck, A. (2002). 'Deepening Social Europe in an Enlarged Union', in M. Dauerstädt and L. Witte (eds.), *Work and Welfare in the Enlarging Euroland*. Bonn: Friedrich Ebert Stiftung

Buchanan, J. and Wagner, R. (1977). *Democracy in Deficit*. New York: Academic.

Bukowski, J., Piattoni, S., and Smyrl, M. (eds.) (2003). *Between Europeanization and Local Societies. The Space for Territorial Governance*. Boulder, CO: Rowman and Littlefield.

Burley, A. M. and Mattly, W. (1993). 'Europe Before the Court', *International Organization*, 47/1: 41–76.

Busse, R. (2002). 'Health Care Systems in EU Pre-accession Countries and European Integration', *Arbeit & Sozialpolitik*, 56/5/6: 40–9.

Caporaso, J. (1996). 'The European Union and Forms of States: Westphalian, Regulatory or Post-Modern', *Journal of Common Market Studies*, 34: 1243–61.

—— (2001). *'Citizenship and Equality: A long and Winding Road'*. Paper presented at the International Studies Association Meeting, Chicago, 22–5 February.

—— (2003). *Rights Through Thick and Thin (or 'Polany in Luxembourg')*. *Prospects for Market Driven Rights in the EU*. Unpublished paper, Seattle: Dept. of Political Science, University of Washington.

—— and Jupille, J. (2004). 'Sovereignty and Territoriality in the European Union: Transforming the UK Institutional Order', in C. Ansell and G. Di Palma (eds.), *The Restructuring of Territoriality*. Cambridge: Cambridge University Press.

Cappelen, A., Castellacci, F., Fagerberg, J., and Verspagen, B. (2003). 'Regional Support, Growth and Convergence in the EU', *Journal of Common Market Studies*, 41: 621–44.

Castel, R. (1995). *Les métamorphoses de la question sociale*. Paris: Fayard.

Cerny, P. (1994). 'The Dynamics of Financial Globalisation: Technology, Market Structure and Policy Response', *Policy Sciences*, 27: 319–42.

Cesarani, D. (1996). 'The Changing Character of Citizenship and Nationality in Britain', in D. Cesarani and M. Fulbrook (eds.), *Citizenship, Nationality and Migration in Europe*. London: Routledge.

CGIL-SPI (2003). 'Osservatorio sulle Politiche Sociali: la spesa per il welfare dei comuni'. *Rassegna Sindacale*, 27 (suppl.).

Christiansen, T. (1999). 'Territorial Politics in the European Union', *Journal of European Public Policy*, 6/2: 349–57.

Ciampani, A. and Clari, D. (2005). *Il movimento sindacale transfrontaliero nella governance interregionale europea*. Torino: Transalp.

Clark, G. (2003). *European Pensions and Global Finance*. Oxford: Oxford University Press

—— and Whiteside, N. (eds.) (2003). *Pension Security in the 21st Century*. Oxford: Oxford University Press.

Cohen, A. P. (1986). *Symbolising Boundaries: Identity and Diversity in British Cultures*. Manchester: Manchester University Press

Coheur, A. (2001). 'Integrating Care in Border Regions: An Analysis of the Euregio projects', *Eurohealth*, 7(4): 10–12.

Conant, L. (2001). *Contested Boundaries, Citizens, States and Supranational Belonging in the European Union*, Working Paper RSC No. 2001/27. Florence: European University Institute.

—— (2004). *Justice Contained: Law and Politics in the European Union*. Ithaca, NY: Cornell University Press.

Conzelman, T. (1995). 'Networking and the Politics of EU Regional Policy: Lessons from North Rhine-Wesphalia, Nord-Pas-de-Calais and North West England', *Regional and Federal Studies*, 5/2: 134–72.

COR (Committee of the Regions) (2003). *Review of the European Employment Strategy and the Employment Guidelines for 2003 based on the Communication on Taking stock of five years of the European Employment Strategy*. Brussels: COR 15/2003 fin.

Cornelissen, V. R. (1996). 'The Principle of Territoriality and the Community Regulations on Social Security', *Common Market Law Review*, 33: 13–41.

Coron, G. (2003a). 'Pension by Capitalization and the European Union: Appraisal of the Impact of the Occupational Pension Institutions Directive', *La Revue de l'Ires*, 43(3): 11–41.

—— (2003b). *La construction d'un référentiel européen en matière de retraite à travers le droit communautaire: l'exemple français*. Report for the CNRS program 'European Identity in Question', GREE–CNRS.

Council of the European Union (2002). *Joint Report by the Commission and the Council on Employment*. Brussels: doc. Council.

—— (2004). *Joint Report by the Commission and the Council on Social Inclusion*. Brussels: doc. Council 7101/04.

Cross, G. (1983). *Immigrant Workers in Industrial France: The Making of a New Labouring Class*. Philadelphia: Temple University Press.

Crouch, C., Finegold, D., and Sako, M. (1999). *Are Skills the Answer?* Oxford: Oxford University Press.

Daalder, H. (1973). 'Building Consociational Nations', in S. Eisenstadt and S. Rokkan (eds.), *Building States and Nations*. Beverly Hills, CA: Sage.

Daly, M. (2000). *Gendering Welfare States*. Cambridge: Cambridge University Press.

—— (2004). *EU Social Policy After Lisbon—A New Approach?* Paper presented at the ESPAnet Annual Conference on 'European Social Policy: Meeting the Needs of Europe'. Oxford, September 9–11.

Davies, P. (ed.) (1996). *European Community Labour Law: Principles and Perspectives*. Oxford: Oxford University Press.

Deakin, R. (1996). 'Labour Law as Market Regulation', in P. Davies (ed.), *European Community Labour Law: Principles and Perspectives*. Oxford: Oxford University Press.

Delhey, J. (2004). *European Social Integration. From Convergence of Countries to Transnational Relations between Peoples*. Discussion Paper SP I 2004–201. Berlin: Wissenschaftszentrum.

De la Porte, C. and Pochet, P. (2005). 'Participation in the Open Method of Coordination: The Case of Employment and Social Inclusion', in J. Zeitlin and P. Pochet (eds.) with Lars Magnusson, *The Open Method of Coordination in Action: The European Employment and Social Inclusion Strategies*. Brussels: PIE-Peter Lang.

Della Porta, D. (1999). *La politica locale*. Bologna: Il Mulino.

De Matteis, A. and Giubboni, S. (1998). 'Rapporti di Lavoro con Elementi di Internazionalità e Sicurezza Sociale', in F. Carinci, R. De Luca Tamajo, P. Tosi, and T. Ten (eds.), *I Contratti di Lavoro Internazionali*. Turin: Utet.

Deschouwer, K., Keating, M., Anderson, J., O'Dowd, L., and Wilson, T. M. (2002). 'New Borders for a Changing Europe: Cross-border Cooperation and Governance', Special issue of *Regional and Federal Studies*, 12/4.

De Swaan, A. (1988). *In Care of the State*. Cambridge: Cambridge University Press.

De Winter, L. and Türsan, H. (eds.) (1988). *Regionalist Parties in Western Europe*. London: Routledge.

Diamanti, I. (1993). *La lega. Geografia, storia e sociologia di un nuovo soggetto politico*. Roma: Donzelli.

—— (1996). *Il male del nord. Lega, localismo, secessione*. Roma: Donzelli.

Diani, M. (1996). 'Regional Federalism and Minority Rights. The Italian Case', in L. De Winter, D. della Porta, and K. Deschouwer (eds.), *Partitocracies between Crisis and Reform*. Special issue of *Res Publica*, 37: 413–28.

Dowding, K., John, P., Mergoupis, T., and Van Vugt, M. (2000). 'Exit, Voice and Loyalty: Analytic and Empirical Developments', *European Journal of Political Research*, 37: 469–95.

Doyle, M. (1996). *Empires*. Ithaca, NY: Cornell University Press.

Ebbinghaus, B. (2000). *Between State and Market: Occupational Pensions, Welfare Regimes and Labor Relations in Comparison*. Paper presented at the conference on Social Protection in a New Era, ISA-RC19, Tilburg, 24–7 August.

EFRP (European Federation for Retirement Provision) (2001). *Activities Report 2001*, Brussels.

Eichenhofer, E. (2000). 'Die Sozialversicherung—Hinterlassenschaft Bismarcks', in E. Eichenhofer (ed.), *Bismarck. Die Sozialversicherung und deren Zukunft*. Berlin: Arno Spitz.

Eisenstadt, S. N. and Rokkan, S. (eds.) (1973). *Building States and Nations*. Beverly Hills, CA: Sage.

Elkins, D. J. (1995). *Beyond Sovereignty: Territory and Political Economy in the Twenty-First Century*. Toronto: University of Toronto Press.

Emmerson, C. (2003). 'Pension reform in the United Kingdom: Increasing the Role of Private Provision?', in G. Clark and N. Whiteside (eds.), *Pension Security in the 21st Century*. Oxford: Oxford University Press.

Ertman, T. (1997). *Birth of the Leviathan: Building States and Regimes in Medieval and Early Modern Europe*. New York: Cambridge University Press.

Esping-Andersen, G. (1985). *Politics against Markets*. Princeton, NJ: Princeton University Press.

—— (1990). *The Three Words of Welfare Capitalism*. New York: Polity Press.

—— and Gallie, D., Hemerijick, A and Myles, J. *Why We Need a New Welfare State*. Oxford: Oxford University Press.

European Commission (1993). *White Paper on Growth, Competitiveness and Employment: the Challenges and Ways Forward into the 21st Century*. Brussels (COM(93), 700 final).

—— (1994). *Social Europe: Supplementary Pension in the European Union*. DGV, Brussels.

—— (1997). *Supplementary Pensions in the Single Market: A Green Paper*, COM (97), 283.

—— (1999a). *Commission Communication: Towards a Single Market for Supplementary Pensions*, COM (99), 134.

—— (1999b). *Commission Communication: Implementing the Framework for Financial Markets. Action Plan*, COM (99), 0232.

—— (2000). *Acting Locally for Employment—A Local Dimension for the European Employment Strategy*, COM (2000), 196.

—— (2001a). *How European See Themselves. Looking through the Mirror with Public Opinion Surveys*. Luxembourg: Office for Official Publications of the European Communities.

—— (2001b). *Commission Communication: The Elimination of Tax Obstacles to the Cross-Border Provision of Occupational Pensions*, COM (2001), 214.

—— (2001c). *The Future of Health Care and Care for the Elderly: Guaranteeing Accessibility, Quality and Financial Viability*. Brussels, COM (2001), 723 def.

—— (2003a). *Commission Communication on Immigration, Integration and Employment*. Brussels, COM (2003), 336.

—— (2003b). *Directive of the European Parliament and of the Council on the Activities and Supervision of Institutions for Occupational Retirement Provision*. Brussels, 2003/41/EC.

—— (2004a). *Follow-up to the High Level Reflection Process on Patient Mobility and Healthcare Developments in the European Union*, Communication from the Commission. Brussels, COM (2004), 301 final.

—— (2004b). *Proposal for a Directive of the European Parliament and of the Council on Services in the Internal Market*. Brussels, COM (2004), 2 final.

—— (2004c). *Eurobarometer 62, Spring 2004*. Brussels.

—— (2005). *Green Paper on an EU Approach to Managing Economic Migration*. Brussels, COM (2005), 811 final.

—— and Council (2003). *Joint Report by the Commission and the Council on Adequate and Sustainable Pensions*. Brussels, 6527/2/03 REV 2.

—— and Eurostat (2003a). *European Social Statistics. Social Protection Expenditure and Receipt*. Brussels.

—— (2003b) *The Social Situation in the European Union 2003*. Brussels.

European Parliament (2000). *Resolution on Supplementary Health Insurance*. 2000/2009 INI OJ C 223, 8.8.2001.

Eurostat (2004) *Population Statistics*, Luxembourg: Eurostat

Ewald, F. (1986). *L'Etat Providence*. Paris: Grasset.

Fabbrini, S. (2004). 'L'Unione europea come democrazia composita?', *Rivista italiana di scienza politica*, 1: 13–42.

Fagerberg, J. and Verspagen, B. (1996). 'Heading for Divergence? Regional Growth in Europe reconsidered', *Journal of Common Market Studies*, 34: 431–48.

Faist, T. (1997). 'Migration in Contemporary Europe: European Integration, Economic Liberalization and Protection', in J. Klausen and L. Tilly (eds.), *European Integration in Social and Theoretical Perspective: From 1850 to the Present*. Lanham, MD: Rowman and Littlefield.

—— (2001). 'Social Citizenship in the European Union: Nested Membership', *Journal of Common Market Studies*, 39/1: 37–58.

Fargion, V. (2000). 'Timing and the Development of Social Care Services in Europe', in M. Ferrera and M. Rhodes (eds.), *Recasting European Welfare States*. London:. Frank Cass.

Ferrera, M. (1987). 'Italy', in P. Flora (ed.), *Growth to Limits. The Western European Welfare State since World War II*, vol. 4. Berlin/New York: De Gruyter.

—— (1993a). *Modelli di solidarietà*. Bologna: Il Mulino.

—— (1993b). *EC Citizens and Social Protection*. Brussels: European Commission, DGV Report. (http://europa.eu.int/comm/public_opinion/archives/ebs/ebs_068_en.pdf)

—— (1995). 'The Rise and Fall of Democratic Universalism. Health Care Reform in Italy, 1978–1994', *Journal of Health Politics, Policy and Law*, 20/2: 275–302.

—— (1996). 'The Southern Model of Welfare in Social Europe', *Journal of European Social Policy*, 1: 17–37.

—— (2004). 'Social Citizenship in the European Union: Towards a Spatial Reconfiguration?', in C. Ansell and G. di Palma (eds.), *The Restructuring of Territoriality*. Cambridge: Cambridge University Press.

—— (ed.) (2005). *Welfare State Reform in Southern Europe—Fighting Poverty and Social exclusion in Italy, Spain, Portugal and Greece*. London: Routledge/EUI Studies in the Political Economy of Welfare.

—— and Gualmini, E. (2004). *Rescued by Europe? Italy's Social and Labour Market Reforms from Maastricht to Berlusconi*. Amsterdam: Amsterdam University Press.

——, ——, Graziano, P., and Alti, T. (2001). *Policies for Labour Market and Social Policy Integration in Italy*. Milan: Poleis, Università Bocconi.

—— and A. Hemerijck (2003). *Recalibrating European Welfare Regimes*, in J. Zeitlin and D. M. Trubeck (eds.), *Governing Work and Welfare in a New Economy*. Oxford: Oxford University Press.

——, ——, and Rhodes, M. (2000). *The Future of Social Europe*. Lisbon: Celta editora.

—— and Rhodes, M. (2000). 'Building a Sustainable Welfare State', in M. Ferrera and M. Rhodes (eds.), *Recasting the European Welfare States*. London: Frank Cass.

—— Matsaganis, M. and Sacchi, S. (2002). 'Open Coordination Against Poverty: The New EU "Social Inclusion Process" ', *Journal of European Social Policy*, 12: 227–39.

Finer, S. (1974). 'State-building, State Boundaries and Border Control', *Social Science Information*, 13/4/5: 79–125.

Flora, P. (1986). 'Introduction', in P. Flora (ed.), *Growth to Limits: The Western European Welfare States since World War II*. Berlin and New York: De Gruyter.

—— (ed.) (1986–87). *Growth to Limits: The European Welfare States Since World War II*, vol. 1 (1986), vols. 2 and 4 (1987). Berlin and New York: De Gruyter.

—— (1993). 'The National Welfare States and European Integration', in L. Moreno (ed.), *Social Exchange and Welfare Development*. Madrid: Consejo Superior de Investigaciones Cientificas.

—— (1999). 'Introduction and Interpretation', in P. Flora, S. Kuhnle, and D. Urwin (eds.), *State Formation, Nation Building and Mass Politics in Europe: The Theory of Stein Rokkan*. New York: Oxford University Press.

—— (2000). 'Externe Grenzbildung und Interne Strukturierung: Europa und seine Nationen. Eine Rokkanische Forschungsperspektive', *Berliner Journal für Soziologie* 10: 157–66.

—— and Alber, J. (1981). 'Modernization, Democratization and the Development of Welfare States in Western Europe', in P. Flora and A. Heidenheimer (eds.), *The Development of Welfare State in Europe and America*. New Brunswick, NJ: Transaction.

—— and Heidenheimer, A. (eds.) (1981). *The Development of Welfare State in Europe and America*. New Brunswick, NJ: Transaction.

—— with Kuhnle, S. and Urwin, D. (eds.) (1999). *State Formation, Nation Building and Mass Politics in Europe: The Theory of Stein Rokkan*. Oxford: Oxford University Press.

Flora, P., Alber, J., Eichenberg, R., Kohl, J., Kraus, F., Pfenning, W., and Seebohm, K. (1983–1987). *State, Economy and Society in Western Europe, 1815–1975.* Frankfurt Campus and Chicago: St James Press, vol. 1 (1983), vol. 2 (1987).

Follesdal, A. (1999). 'Third Country Nationals as European Citizens: The Case Defended', in D. Smith and S. Wright (eds.), *Whose Europe? The Turn Towards Democracy.* London: Blackwell.

—— (2001). 'Union Citizenship: Unpacking the Beast of Burden', *Law and Philosophy*, 20/3: 313–43.

Fouchet, M. (1991). *Fronts et frontières: Un tour du monde geopolitique.* Paris: Fayard.

Franklin, M. N., Mackie, T., and Valen, H. (eds.) (1992). *Electoral Change: Responses to Evolving Social and Attitudinal Structures in Western Countries.* Cambridge: Cambridge University Press.

Freeman, R. (2000). *The Politics of Health in Europe.* Manchester: Manchester University Press.

Friedman, K. V. (1981). *Legitimation of Social Rights and the Welfare State: A Weberian Perspective.* Chapel Hill: University of North Carolina Press.

Friedman Goldstein, L. (1997). 'State Resistance to Authority in Federal Unions: The Early United States (1790–1860) and the European Community (1958–94)', *Studies in American Political Development*, 11: 149–89.

Gallego, R., Gomà, R. and Subirats, J. (2005). 'Spain from State Welfare to Regional Welfare', in N. McEwen and L. Moreno (eds.), *The Territorial Politics of Welfare.* Oxford: Routledge

Garret, G. (1995). 'The Politics of Legal Integration in the European Union', *International Organization*, 49/1: 171–81.

—— and Weingast, B. (1993). 'Ideas, Interests, and Institutions: Constructing the EC's Internal Market', in G. Judits and K. Robert (eds.), *Ideas and Foreign Policy.* Ithaca, NY: Cornell University Press.

Geddes, A. (2000). *Immigration and European Integration: Towards Fortress Europe?* Manchester: Manchester University Press

—— and Favell, A. (1999) (eds.), *The Politics of Belonging: Migrants and Minorities in Contemporary Europe.* Aldershot: Ashgate.

Gilpin, R. (1987). *The Political Economy of International Relations.* Princeton, NJ: Princeton University Press.

Giubboni, S. (2001). 'Politiche sociali e leggi dell'economia. L'integrazione sociale europea rivisitata', *Rivista del diritto della sicurezza sociale*, 1: 26–102.

—— (2003). *Diritti sociali e mercato: La dimensione sociale dell'integrazione europea.* Bologna: Il Mulino.

—— (2004). *Lavoro e diritti sociali nella 'nuova' Costituzione europea: Spunti comparatistici*, Working Paper No. 5. Turin/Moncalieri: Unità di Ricerca sulla Governance Europea (www.urge.it).

Gold, M (ed.) (1993). *The Social Dimension: Employment policies in the EC.* Basingstoke: Macmillan.

Golub, J. (1996). 'The Politics of Judicial Discretion: Rethinking the Interaction Between National Courts and the European Court of Justice', *West European Politics*, 2: 360–85.

Graziano, P. (2004). *Europeizzazione e politiche pubbliche italiane. Coesione e lavoro a confronto*. Bologna: Il Mulino.

Gualmini, E. (1998). *La politica del lavoro*. Bologna: Il Mulino.

—— and Alti, T. (2001). 'Le regioni e le politiche del lavoro', *Le istituzioni del federalismo*, 3/4: 707–50.

Guerin-Gonzales, C. and Strikwerda, C. (1993). *The Politics of Immigrant Workers: Labour Activism and Migrations in the World Economy Since 1830*. New York: Holmes and Meyer.

Guibentif, P. (1997). 'Changes in the Portuguese Social Security System', in M. Ferrera (ed.), *Comparing Social Welfare Systems in Southern Europe*, Vol. 3. Paris: Mire, 47–66.

Guillemard, A.-M. (1986). *Le déclin du social*. Paris: PUF.

Guillen, A. M. (1997). 'Welfare State Development In Spain: A Historical And Explanatory Approach', in M. Ferrera (ed.), *Comparing Social Welfare Systems in Southern Europe*, Vol. 3. Paris: Mire, 67–92.

—— (2002). 'The Politics of Universalisation: Establishing National Health Services in Souhern Europe'. *West European Politics*, 25 (4): 49–68.

—— and Palier, B. (eds.) (2004). 'EU Enlargement, Europeanisation and Social Policy', *Journal of European Social Policy*, 14/3 (special issue).

Guiraudon, Virginie (2000). *Les politiques d'immigration en Europe*. Paris: L'Harmattan.

Hagen, K. (1999). 'Towards a Europeanization of Social Policies? A Scandinavian Perspective', in MiRe (eds.), *Comparing Social Welfare Systems in Nordic Europe and France*, Vol. 4. Nantes: MiRe, 661–87.

Hall, P. (1986). *Governing the Economy: The Politics of State Intervention in Britain and France*. Cambridge: Polity Press.

Hammar, T. (1990). *Democracy and the Nation-State: Aliens, Denizens and Citizens in a World of International Migration*. Aldershot: Gower.

Hatzfeld, H. (1989). *Du paupérisme à la sécurité sociale. Essai sur les origines de la sécurité sociale* (2nd edn.). Nancy: Presses Universitaires de Nancy (1st edn., 1971, Paris: Colin).

Heater, D. (1990). *Citizenship: The Civic Ideal in World History, Politics and Education*. London: Longman.

Heclo, H. (1974). *Modern Social Politics in Britain and Sweden*. New Haven, CT: Yale University Press.

—— (1981). 'Towards a New Welfare State', in P. Flora and A. J. Heidenheimer (eds.), *The Development of Welfare States in Europe and America*. New Brunswick, NJ: Transaction.

Hine, D. and Kassim, H. (eds.) (1998). *Beyond the Market: The EU and National Social Policy*. London: Routledge.

Hinrichs, K. (2002). *Basic Security Plus Private Employment Related Pensions: Do Australia, Denmark, the Netherlands and Switzerland Show the Way for Public Pension Reform in European Social Insurance Countries?*. Paper presented at the 15th World Congress of Sociology, Brisbane, 7–13 July.

Hirschman, A. O. (1970). *Exit, Voice and Loyalty*. Cambridge, MA: Harvard University Press.

Hirschman, A. O. (1974). ' "Exit, Voice and Loyalty": Further Reflections and a Survey of Recent Contributions', *Social Science Information*, 13/1: 7–26.

—— (1978). 'Exit, Voice and the State', *World Politics*, 31: 90–107.

—— (1993). 'Exit, Voice and the Fate of the GDR', *World Politics*, 45: 173–202.

Hollifield, J. F. (ed.) (1992). *Immigrants, Markets, and States: The Political Economy of Postwar Europe*. Cambridge, MA: Harvard University Press.

Holloway, J. (1981). *Social Policy Harmonization in the European Community*. Westmead: Gower Publishing.

Hooghe, L. (1998). 'EU Cohesion Policy and Competing Models of European Capitalism', *Journal of Common Market Studies*, 36: 457–77.

—— and Keating, M. (1994). 'The Politics of European Union Regional Policy', *Journal of European Public Policy*, 1/3: 367–93.

—— and Marks, G. (2001). *Multi-level Governance and European Integration*. Boulder, CO: Rowman and Littlefield.

Huber, E. and Stephens, J. (2001). *Development and Crisis of the Welfare State: Parties and Policies in Global Markets*. Chicago: Chicago University Press.

Hunger, U. (1998). 'Arbeitskraftewänderungen im Baugewerbe der Europäische Union. Problemanzeigen, Regelungsversuche und Schlüssefolgerungen für die Zukünftige Beschäftigung von Ausländern in Deutschland', in D. Threanhardt (ed.), *Einwanderung und Einbürgerung in Deutchland, Yearbook Migration 97/98*. London, Münster: Lit.

Ignazi, P. (2003). *Extreme Right Parties in Western Europe*. Oxford: Oxford University Press.

Ikenberry, G. J. (1986). 'The State and Strategies of International Adjustment', *World Politics*, 39: 53–77.

Immergut, E. M. (1992). *Health Politics. Interests and Institutions in Western Europe*. Cambridge: Cambridge University Press.

Irish Department of Social and Family Affairs (2002). *National Strategy Report to the EU, Commission on its Pension System*. Dublin.

Jacobson, K. (2005). 'Trying to Reform the "Best Pupils in Class": The Open Method of Coordination in Sweden and Denmark', in J. Zeitlin and P. Pochet (eds.), with Lars Magnusson, *The Open Method of Coordination in Action: The European Employment and Social Inclusion Strategies*. Brussels: PIE-Peter Lang.

Jeffery, C. (ed.) (1997). *The Regional Dimension of the European Union: Towards a Third Level in Europe? London: Frank Cass*.

Jessoula, M. and Ferrera, M. (2005) 'Italy: from Policy Stalemate To Comprehensive Reforms', in G. Bonoli and T. Shinkawa, (eds), *Ageing and Pension Reform Around the World*. Cheltenham: Edward Elgar.

Jobert, B. and Muller, P. (1987). *L'État en action. Politiques publiques et corporatismes*. Paris: PUF.

Kahler, M. (2002). 'The State of the State in World Politics', in I. Katznelson and H. V. Milner (eds.), *Political Science. State of the Discipline*. New York: Norton and Company.

Kangas, O. and Palme, J. (1992a). 'Class Politics and Institutional Feedbacks: Development of occupational Pensions in Finland and Sweden', in M. Shalev (ed.),

Occupational Welfare and the Welfare State in Comparative Perspective. New York: Plenum.

—— —— (1992*b*). *Statism Eroded? Labour Market Benefits and the Challenges to the Scandinavian Welfare States.* Turku: Studies in Social Policies, University of Turku.

Keating, M. (1998). *The New Regionalism in Western Europe: Territorial Restructuring and Political Change.* Cheltenham: Edward Elgar.

Keohane, R. and Hoffman, S. (1991). *The New European Community: Decisionmaking and Institutional Change.* Boulder, CO: Westview Press.

Kildal, N. and Kuhnle, S. (2005). *Normative Foundations of the Welfare State: The Nordic Experience.* London: Routledge.

Klatt, H. (1989). 'Forty Years of German Federalism: Past Trends and New developments', *Publius: The Journal of Federalism,* 19/4: 185–202.

Klausen, J. (1995). 'Social Rights Advocacy and State Building. T. H. Marshall in the Hands of Social Reformers', *World Politics,* 47: 244–67.

—— and L. Tilly (eds.) (1997). *European Integration in Social and Theoretical Perspective. From 1850 to the Present.* Lanham, MD: Rowman and Littlefield.

Kohler-Koch, B. *European governance and system integration,* European Governance Papers, No. C-05-01

Korpi, W. (1980). 'Social Policy and Distributional Conflict in the Capitalist Democracies: A Preliminary Comparative Framework', *West European Politics,* 3: 296–316.

—— (1983). *The Democratic Class Struggle.* London: Routledge.

—— (2000). *Contentious Institutions* (Working Paper 4/2000). Stockholm: SOFI.

Krasner, S. D. (1999). *Sovereignty: Organized Hypocrisy.* Princeton, NJ: Princeton University Press.

Kristensen, P. H. and Zeitlin, J. (2005). *Local Players in Global Games: The Strategic Constitution of a Multinational Corporation.* Oxford: Oxford University Press.

Kuhnle, S. (1986). 'Norway', in P. Flora (ed.) (1986–87), *Growth to Limits. The European Welfare States Since World War II,* Vol. 1. Berlin/New York: De Gruyter.

Kvist, J. (2004). 'Does EU Enlargement Start a Race to the Bottom? Strategic Interactions among EU member States in Social Policy', *Journal of European Social Policy,* 14: 301–18.

Lamping, W. (2003). *European Integration and Health Policy: Sorting out the Issues* (Discussion Paper No. 3). Hannover: Center for Social and Public Policy, University of Hannover.

Lamy P. and J. Pisani-Ferry (2002). *L'Europe des nos volontés.* Paris: Plon.

Laponce, J. (1974). 'Hirschman's Voice and Exit model as a Spatial Archetype', *Social Science Information,* 13/3: 67–81.

La Spina, A. (2003). *La politica per il Mezzogiorno.* Bologna: Il Mulino.

Le Galès, P. (2002). *European Cities, Social Conflict and Governance.* Oxford: Oxford University Press.

—— (2003). 'The Changing European State: Pressures from Within', in J. Hayward and A. Menon (eds.), *Governing Europe.* Oxford: Oxford University Press.

—— and Lequesne, C. (eds.) (1998). *Regions in Europe.* London: Routledge.

Leibfried, S. and Pierson, P. (eds.) (1995). *European Social Policy between Fragmentation and Integration*. Washington, DC: Brookings Institution.

—— (2000). 'Social Policy', in H. Wallace and W. Wallace (eds.), *Policy-Making in the European Union*, 4th edn. Oxford: Oxford University Press.

Lemke, C. (1997). 'Crossing Borders and Building Barriers: Migration, Citizenship and State Building in Germany', in J. Klausen and L. Tilly (eds.), *European Integration in Social and Theoretical Perspective: From 1850 to the Present*. Lanham, MD: Rowman and Littlefield.

Levi, M. (2002). 'The State and the Study of the State', in I. Katznelson and H. Milner (eds.), *Political Science. State of the Discipline*. New York: W. W. Norton

Levy, J. (2000). 'France: Directing Adjustment?', in F. Scharpf and V. Schmidt (eds.), *Welfare and Work in Open Economies. Volume II. Diverse Responses to Common Challenges*. Oxford: Oxford University Press.

Lewis, J. (1992). 'Gender and the Development of Welfare Regimes', *Journal of European Social Policy*, 3: 159–73.

Liakos, A. (1997). 'Welfare Policy in Greece (1909–1940): From the Private Needs to the Social Question', in M. Ferrera (ed.), *Comparing Social Welfare Systems in Southern Europe*, Vol. 3. Paris: Mire, 93–108.

Lijphart, A. (1968). *The Politics of Accommodation: Pluralism and Democracy in the Netherlands*. Berkeley: University of California Press.

Lindert, P. H. (2004). *Growing Public. Social Spending and Economic Growth Since the Eighteenth Century*, 2 vols. Cambridge: Cambridge University Press.

Lipset, S. M. (1963). *The First New Nation*. New York: Basic Books.

—— and Rokkan, S. (1967). *Party Systems and Voter Alignments*. New York: Free Press.

Longo, M. (2003). 'European Integration: Between Micro-Regionalism and Globalism', *Journal of Common Market Studies*, 41: 475–94.

Ludlow, P. (1982). *The Making of the European Monetary System*. Oxford: Oxford University Press.

Lynch, J. F. (2005). *The Age of Welfare. Citizens, Clients and Generations in the Development of the Welfare State*. Cambridge: Cambridge University Press.

Lyon Caen, G. and Lyon Caen, A. (1993). *Droit Social International et Européen*. Paris: Dalloz.

Lyons, F. (1963). *Internationalism in Europe, 1815–1914*. Leyden: Sythoff.

Mabbet, D. (2000). 'Social Regulation and the Social Dimension in Europe: The Example of Insurance', *European Journal of Social Security*, 2: 241–57.

—— and Bolderson H. (2000). 'Non-discrimination, free movement and social citizenship in Europe: contrasting provisions for the EU nationals and asylum-seekers', in ISSA, *Social Security in the Global Village*, International Social Security Series. New Brunswick, NJ: Transaction.

McAleavy, P. (1993). 'The Politics of European regional Development Policy: Additionality in the Scottish Coalfields', *Regional Politics and Policy*, 3: 87–107.

McEwen, N. (2002). 'State Welfare Nationalism: the Territorial Impact of Welfare State Development in Scotland', *Regional and Federal Studies*, 12/1: 66–90.

—— and Parry, R. (2005). 'Devolution and the Preservation of the British Welfare State', in L. Moreno and N. McEwen (eds.), *The Territorial Politics of Welfare*. London: Routledge.

—— and Moreno, L. (eds.) (2005). *The Territorial Politics of Welfare*. London: Routledge.

McKee, M., Mossialos, E., and Belcher, P. (1996). 'The Influence of European Law on National Health Policy', *Journal of European Social Policy*, 6: 268–9

McKinnon, C. and Hampsher-Monk, I. (eds.) (2000). *The Demands of Citizenship*. London: Continuum.

Maino, F. (2001). *La politica sanitaria*. Bologna: Il Mulino.

—— (2003). 'L'europeizzazione della sanità. La politica sanitaria italiana tra patti esterni e patti interni', in S. Fabbrini (ed.), *L'europeizzazione dell'Italia. L'impatto dell'Unione Europea sulle istituzioni e le politiche italiane*. Roma/Bari: Laterza.

Mair, P. (1998). 'I conflitti politici in Europa. Persistenza e mutamento', *Rivista Italiana di Scienza Politica*, 3: 425–50.

Mancini, F. (1999). 'Principi Fondamentali di Diritto del Lavoro nell'ordinamento delle Comunità Europee', in *Atti del Convegno su 'Il lavoro nel diritto comunitario e nell'ordinamento italiano*. Padua: Cedam.

—— and Keeler, J. T. (1994). 'Democracy and the European Court of Justice', *Modern Law Review*, 57/2: 175–90.

Mann, M. (1986). *The Sources of Social Power*. Cambridge: Cambridge University Press.

Manow, P. (2005). 'Germany—Cooperative Federalism and the Overgrazing of the Fiscal Commons', in H. Obinger, S. Leibfried, and F. Castles (eds.), *Federalism and the Welfare State: New World and European Experiences*. Cambridge: Cambridge University Press.

Mantino, F. (2002). *Fondi strutturali e politiche di sviluppo*. Milan: Il Sole 24 Ore.

March, J. and Olsen, J. (1998). 'The Institutional Dynamics of International Political Orders', *International Organization*, 52: 943–69.

Marks, G., Hooghe, L., and Blank, K. (1996). 'European Integration and the State: Multi-level vs. State Centric Governance', *Journal of Common Market Studies*, 34(3): 341–78.

—— Haesly, R., and Mbaye, H. (2002). 'What do Sub National Offices Think They Are Doing in Brussels?', *Regional and Federal Studies*, 12/3: 1–23.

Marshall, T. H. (1950). *Citizenship and Social Class*. Cambridge: Cambridge University Press.

—— (1992). 'Citizenship and Social Class', in T. H. Marshall and T. Bottomore (eds.), *Citizenship and Social Class*. London: Pluto Press.

Martin, A. and Ross, G. (eds.) (2004). *Euros and Europeans. Monetary Integration and the European Model of Society*. Cambridge: Cambridge University Press

Martiniello, M. (ed.) (1995). *Migration, Citizenship and National Identities in the European Union*. Aldershot: Avebury.

Mau, S. (2005). 'European Social Policies and National Welfare Constituencies: Issues of Legitimacy and Public Support', in N. Ewans and L. Moreno (eds.), *The Territorial Politics of Welfare*. Oxford: Routledge.

Mazower, M. (1998). *Dark Continent: Europe's Twentieth Century*. London: Penguin.

Mény, Y. and Surel, Y. (2000). *Par le Peuple, pour le people*. Paris: Fayard.

Miles, R. and Thraenhardt, D. (eds.) (1995). *Migration and European Integration: The Dynamics of Inclusion and Exclusion*. London: Pinter.

Milward, A. (2000). *The European Rescue of the Nation State*, 2nd edn. London: Routledge.

——— , Sorensen, V., and Ranieri, R. (1993). *The Frontiers of National Sovereignty: History and Theory 1945–1992*. London: Routledge.

Mioset, L. (2000). 'Stein Rokkan's Thick Comparisons', *Acta Sociologica*, 4/3: 381–97.

Milgrom, P. R., North, D. C., Weingast, B. R. (1990) 'The Role of Institutions in the Revival of Trade: The Law Merchant, Private Judges and the Champagne Fairs', *Economics and Politics*, 13, 1: 31–46.

Missoc (2004). *Comparative tables on Social Protection. -Info 01/2004*. Brussels: DGV (http://europa.eu.int/comm/employment_social/social_protection/missoc_en. htm).

Moore, B. (1967). *Social Origins of Dictatorship and Democracy*. Boston: Beacon Press.

Moravcskic, A. (1998). *The Choice for Europe: Social Purpose and State Power from Messina to Maastricht*. Ithaca, NY: Cornell University Press.

Moreno, L. (2001). *The Federalization of Spain*. London: Frank Cass.

——— (2003). 'Europeanisation, Mesogovernments and "Safety Nets" '. *European Journal of Political Research*, 42/2: 185–99.

Morlino, L. (2003). *Democracy, Between Consolidation and Crisis*. Oxford: Oxford University Press.

Mossialos, E., McKee, M., Palm, W., Karl, B., and Marhold, F. (2001). *The Influence of EU Law on The Social Character of Health Care Systems in the EU*. Report submitted to the Belgian Presidency of the European Union, Brussels, 19 November.

Mouly, C. (1996). 'Securité sociale et concurrance: une reforme constitutionnellement possible', *Receuil de doctrine, de jurisprudence et de legislation*. Paris: Dalloz Sirey, 4e cahier.

Myles, J. and Pierson, P. (2001). 'The Comparative Political Economy of Pension Reform', in P. Pierson (ed.), *The New Politics of the Welfare State*. Oxford: Oxford University Press.

——— Quadagno, J. (2002). 'Political Theories of the Welfare State', *Social Service Review*, March: 34–57.

Natali, D. (2004). 'The Hybridisation of Pension Systems Within the Enlarged EU: Recent Reforms in Old and New Members', *Revue Belge de Securité Sociale*, 2: 353–78.

Noiriel, G. and Offerle', M. (1997). 'Citizenship and Nationality in Nineteenth-Century France', in J. Klausen and L. Tilly (eds.), *European Integration in Social and Theoretical Perspective: From 1850 to the Present*. Lanham, MD: Rowman and Littlefield.

North, D. (1981). *Structure and Change in Economic History*. New York: W. W. Norton.

——— (1990). *Institutions, Institutional Change and Economic Performance*. Cambridge: Cambridge University Press.

—— and Thomas, R. (1973). *The Rise of the Western World*. Cambridge: Cambridge University Press.

Obinger, H., Leibfried, S., and Castles, F. (eds.) (2005). *Federalism and the Welfare State: New World and European Experiences*. Cambridge: Cambridge University Press.

—— —— —— (2005). 'Bypass to Social Europe? Lessons from Federal Experience', *Journal of European Public Policy*, 12(3): 545–71.

—— Armingeon, K., Bonoli, G., and Bertozzi, F. (2005). 'Switzerland: The Marriage of Direct Democracy and Federalism', in H. Obinger, S. Leibfried, and F. Castles (eds.), *Federalism and the Welfare State: New World and European Experiences*. Cambridge: Cambridge University Press

O'Connor, J., Orloff, A. S., and Shaver, S. (1999). *States, Markets and Families*. Cambridge: Cambridge University Press.

OECD (Organisation for Economic Co-operation and Development) (1994). *The Reform of Health Care Systems. A Review of Seventeen OECD Countries*. Paris: OECD.

Offe, K. (1993). 'Politica sociale, solidarietà e stato sociale', in M. Ferrera (ed.), *Stato sociale e mercato mondiale*. Turin: Fondazione Agnelli.

Ogus, A. I. (1982). 'Great Britain', in P. A. Köhler and H. F. Zacher (eds.), *The Evolution of Social Insurance 1881–1981*. London: Pinter.

Olsen, J. P. (2000). *Organizing European Institutions of Governance*. ARENA Working Papers 00/2.

Olson, M. (1965). *The Logic of Collective Action*. Cambridge, MA: Harvard University Press.

Olson, S. (1986). 'Sweden', in P. Flora (ed.) (1986–87), *Growth to Limits: The European Welfare States Since World War II*, vol. 1. Berlin/New York: De Gruyter.

—— (1990). *Social Policy and Welfare State in Sweden*. Lund: Archiv.

Orloff, A. S. (1993). 'Gender and the Social Rights of Citizenship', *American Journal of Sociology*, 58: 303–28.

Osiander, A. (2001). 'Sovereignty, International Relations and the Westphalian Myth', *International Organization*, 55: 251–87.

Palier, B. (2002). *Gouverner la sécurité sociale. Les réformes du système français de protection sociale depuis 1945*. Paris: PUF.

—— (2003). *Facing the Pension Crisis in France*, in G. Clark and N. Whiteside (eds.). *Pension Security in the XXI Century*. Oxford: Oxford University Press.

Palme, J. (2003). 'Pension Reform in Sweden and the Changing Boundaries Between Public and Private', in G. Clark and N. Whiteside (eds.), *Pension Security in the 21st Century*. Oxford: Oxford University Press.

Panebianco, A. (2004). *Il potere, lo stato, la libertà*. Bologna: Il Mulino.

Parry, R. (1987). *United Kingdom*, in P. Flora (ed.) (1986–87), *Growth to Limits: The European Welfare States Since World War II*, vol. 4. Berlin/New York: De Gruyter.

Pavolini, E. (2003). *Le nuove politiche sociali*. Bologna: Il Mulino.

Pemberton, H. (2005). 'In the Long Run We Shall All Be Dead: Politics and Pensions in Post-War Britain'. Paper presented to the symposium 'Why has it all gone wrong? The present, past and future of British pensions' at the British Academy, London, 15 June.

Pennings, F. (2001). *Introduction to European Social Security Law*. The Hague: Kluwer Law International.

Perez Diaz, V. and Rodriguez, J. (1994). *Inertial Choices: Spanish Human Resources Policies and Practices*. Research Paper 2b. Madrid: Analistas Socio-Politicos.

Perrin, G. (1969). 'Reflections on Fifty Years of Social Security', *International Labour Review*, 99: 242–92.

Persson, L. O. (2003). 'The Nordic Welfare State and Territorial Politics: Changing Employment Trends in the Public Sector'. Paper for the European Consortium for Political Research (ECPR), Joint Sessions of Workshops, Edinburgh, 28 March–2 April.

Pierson, P. (1996). 'The Path to European Integration', *Comparative Political Studies*, 29(2): 123–63.

—— (2000). 'Three Worlds of Welfare State Research', *Comparative Political Studies*, 33: 791–821.

—— (ed.) (2001). *The New Politics of the Welfare State*. Oxford: Oxford University Press.

—— (2004) *Politics in Time. History, Institutions, and Social Analysis*. Princeton, NJ: Princeton University Press.

Poaires Maduro, M. (1998). *We, the Court: The European Court of Justice and the European Economic Constitution*. Oxford: Oxford University Press.

—— (1999). 'Striking the Elusive Balance Between Economic Freedom and Social Rights in the EU', in P. Alston (ed.), *The EU and Human Rights*. Oxford: Oxford University Press.

Poggi, G. (1978). *The Development of the Modern State. A Sociological Introduction*. Stanford: Stanford University Press.

—— (1990). *The State: Its Nature, Development and Prospects*. Stanford: Stanford University Press.

Polanyi, K. (1957). *The Great Transformation: The Political and Economic Origins of Our Time*. Boston: Beacon Press.

Powell, F. and Wessen, A. (eds.) (1999). *Health Care Systems in Transition: An International Perspective*. London: Sage.

Przeworsky, A. and Sprague, J. (1986). *Paper Stones. A History of Electoral Socialism*. Chicago: University of Chicago Press.

Putnam, R. (1993). *Making Democracy Work: Civic Tradition in Modern Italy*. Princeton, NJ: Princeton University Press.

Radaelli, C. M. (2003). 'The Open Method of Coordination: A new governance architecture for the European Union?', *Swedish Institute for European Policy Studies*, Report 1/2003 (available at www.sieps.su.se).

Rasmussen, H. (1986). *On Law and Policy in the European Court of Justice*. Dordrecht: Martinus Nijhoff Publishers.

Regalia, I. (2003). 'Decentralizing Employment Protection in Europe: Territorial Pacts and Beyond', in J. Zeitlin and D. M. Trubeck (eds.), *Governing Work and Welfare in a New Economy*. Oxford: Oxford University Press.

—— (ed.) (2005). *Regulating New Forms of Employment: Local Experiments and Social Innovation in Europe*. Oxford: Routledge.

Rees, R., Kessner, E., and Klemperer, P. (1999). 'Regulation and Efficiency in European Insurance Markets', *Economic Policy*, 29: 365–80.

Rhodes, M. (1995). ' "Subversive Liberalism": Market Integration, Globalization and European Integration', *Journal of European Public Policy*, 3: 384–406

—— (1998). 'Defending the Social Contract: The EU between Global Constraints and Domestic Imperatives', in D. Hine and H. Kassim (eds.) (1998), *Beyond the Market: The EU and National Social Policy*. London: Routledge.

Rimlinger, G. (1971). *Welfare Policy and Industrialisation in Europe, North America and Russia*. New York: Wiley.

Risse-Kappen, T. (1996). 'Exploring the Nature of the Beast: International Relations Theory and Comparative Political Analysis Met the European Union', *Journal of Common Market Studies*, 34/1: 53–80.

Rokkan, S. (1970). *Citizens, Elections, Parties*. New York: McKay.

—— (1971). 'Nation-building and the Structuring of Mass Politics', in S. Eisenstadt (ed.), *Political Sociology. A Reader*. New York: Basic Books.

—— (1973). 'Cities, States, Nations: a Dimensional Model for the Study of Contrasts in Development', in S. Rokkan and S. Eisenstadt (eds.), *Building States and Nations*, 2 vols. Beverly Hills, CA: Sage.

—— (1974a). 'Politics Between Economy and Culture. An International Seminar on Albert O. Hirschman's "Exit, Voice and Loyalty" ', *Social Science Information*, 13/1: 27–38.

—— (1974b). 'Entries, Voices, Exits: Towards a Possible Generalization of the Hirschman Model', *Social Sciences Information*, 13/1: 39–53.

—— (1975). 'Dimension of State Formation and Nation Building', in C. Tilly (ed.), *The Formation of National States in Western Europe*. Princeton, NJ: Princeton University Press.

—— (1977). 'Towards a Generalized Concept of Verzuiling', *Political Studies*, 25(4): 563–70.

—— and Urwin, D. (1981) (eds.). *The Politics of Territorial Identity: Studies of Developments in the European Peripheries*. London: Sage.

—— (1983). *Economy, Territory, Identity: Politics of West European Peripheries*. London: Sage.

Romero, F. (1993). 'Migration as an Issue in European Interdependence and Integration: The Case of Italy', in A. Milward et al. (eds.), *The Frontiers of National Sovereignty: History and Theory 1945–1992*. London: Routledge.

Rothstein, B. (1998). *Just Institutions Matter. The Moral and Political Logic of the Universal Welfare State*. Cambridge: Cambridge University Press.

Ruggie, J. G. (1982). 'International Regimes, Transactions and Change: Embedded Liberalism in the Post-War Era', *International Organization*, 36: 379–415.

—— (1993). 'Territoriality and Beyond: Problematizing Modernity in International Relations' , *International Organization*, 47: 139–74.

Ruiz Jiménez, A. M., Gorniak, J. J., Kosic. A., Kiss, P., and Kandulla, M. (2004). *European and National identities in EU's Old and New Member States: Ethnic, Civic, Instrumental and Symbolic Components*. European Integration Online Papers (Eiop), 8/11; http://eiop.or.at/eiop/texte/2004–011a.htm.

Ruiz Jiménez, A. M., Gorniak, J. J., Kosic. A., Kiss, P., and Kandulla, M. (1993). 'Teritoriality and Beyond: Problematizing Modernity in International Relations', *International Organization*, 47(1): 139–74

Sabel, C. and Zeitlin, J. (2003). *Active Welfare, Experimental Governance, Pragmatic Constitutionalism: the New Transformation of Europe*. Paper prepared for the International Conference of the Hellenic Presidency of the European Union on The Modernisation of the European Social Model and EU Policies and Instruments, Ioannina, Greece, 21–2 May.

Sacchi, S. and Bastagli, F. (2005). 'Italy Striving Uphill but Stopping Halway: The Troubled Journey of the Experimental Minimum Insertion Income', in M. Ferrera (ed.), *Welfare State Reform in Southern Europe*. London: Routledge.

Saelen, K. (1981). 'Stein Rokkan: A Bibliography', in P. Torsvik (ed.), *Mobilization, Center-Periphery Structures and Nation Building*. Bergen: Universitetsforlaget.

Sainsbury, D. (1996). *Gender, Equality and the Welfare State*. New York: Cambridge University Press.

Saint Jours, Y. (1982). 'France', in P. A. Koehler and H. F. Zacher (eds.), *The Evolution of Social Insurance 1881–1981*. London: Pinter.

Salminen, K. (1993). *Pension Schemes in the Making. A Comparative Study of the Scandinavian Countries*. Helsinki: Central Pension Security Institute.

Saltman, R. B. and Figueras, J. (1997). *European Health Care Reform: Analysis of Current Strategies*. Copenhagen: Regional Office for Europe, World Health Organization.

Sandholtz, W. and Zysman, J. (1989). '1982: Recasting the European Bargain', *World Politics*, 42: 95–128

Saraceno, C. (ed.) (2002) *Social Assistance Dynamics in Europe*, Bristol, Policy Press.

Sartori, G. (1976). *Parties and Party Systems*. Cambridge: Cambridge University Press.

Sbragia, A. (ed.) (1992). *Euro-politics: Institutions and Policymaking in the 'New' European Community*. Washington, DC: Brookings Institution.

—— (2004). 'La democrazia post-nazionale. Una sfida per la Scienza Politica', *Rivista italiana di scienza politica*, 1: 43–68.

Scarborough, E. (2000). 'West European Welfare States: The Old Politics of Retrenchment', *European Journal of Political Research*, 38: 225–59.

Scharpf, F. W. (1996). *Negative and Positive Integration in the Political Economy of European Welfare States*, in G. Marks et al. (eds.), *Governance in the European Union*. London: Sage.

—— (1988). 'The Joint Decision Trap: Lessons from German Federalism and European Integration', *Public Administration*, 66: 239–78.

—— (1999). *Governing in Europe*. Oxford: Oxford University Press.

—— (2000). 'Economic Changes, Vulnerabilities and Institutional Capabilities', in F. Scharpf and V. Schmidt (eds.), *Welfare and Work in Open Economies*, vol. I: *From Vulnerability to Competitiveness*. Oxford: Oxford University Press.

—— (2001). *European Governance: Common Concerns vs. the Challenge of Diversity*. Florence, Jean Monnet Working Paper, www.iue.it/RSC/Governance

—— (1996). 'Negative and Positive Integration in the Political Economy of European Welfare States', in G. Marks, F. W. Scharpf, P. C. Schmitter, and W. Streeck (eds.), *Governance in the European Union*. London: Sage.

Sciarra, S. (1999). 'From Strasbourg to Amsterdam: Prospects for the Convergence of European Social Rights Policy', in P. Alston (ed.), *The EU and Human Rights*. Oxford: Oxford University Press.

—— (2004). 'La constitutionnalisation de l'Europe Sociale entre droits sociaux fondamentaux et soft law', in O. De Schutter and P. Nihoul (eds.), *Une Constitution pour l'Europe. Reflexions sur les Transformations du Droit de l'Union Européenne*. Brussels: Larcier.

Schmähl, W. (1997). 'The Public private Mix of Pension Provision in Germany and the United Kingdom', in B. Palier (ed.), *Comparing Social Welfare Systems in Europe, Vol. I: France-United Kingdom*. Paris: Mire.

Schmitter, P. C. and Bauer, M. W. (2001). 'A (Modest) Proposal for Expanding Social Citizenship in the European Union', *Journal of European Social Policy*, 11/1: 55–66.

Sénat (1999). 'Assurons l'avenir de l'assurance', *Rapport d'Information*, 45 (1998–1999), Tome II. Paris: Sénat.

Sestito, P. (2002). *Il mercato del lavoro in Italia*. Roma/Bari: Laterza.

Shafir, G. (ed.) (1998). *The Citizenship Debates*. Minneapolis: University of Minnesota Press.

Sharpe, L. (ed.) (1993). *The Rise of Meso Government in Europe*. London: Sage.

Shoukens, P. (ed.) (1997). *Prospects of Social Security Co-ordination*. Leuven: Acco.

Sindbjerg Martinsen, D. (2004). *European Institutionalisation of Social Security Rights: A Two Layered Process of Integration*. Ph.D. Thesis, Florence, European University Institute

Smisman, S. (2004). *EU Employment Policy: Decentralisation or Centralisation through the Open method of Coordination?* (WP Law 2004/1). Florence: European University Institute.

Soysal, Y. (1996). 'Changing Citizenship in Europe', in D. Cesarani and M. Fulbrook (eds.), *Citizenship, Nationality and Migration in Europe*. London: Routledge.

Spruyt, H. (1994). *The Sovereign State and Its Competitors*. Princeton, NJ: Princeton University Press.

—— (2002). 'The Origins, Development and Possible Decline of the Modern State', *Annual Review of Political Science*, 5: 127–49.

Steinmetz, G. (1993). *Regulating the Social: the Welfare State and Local Politics in Imperial Germany*. Princeton, NJ: Princeton University Press.

Steinmo, S. (2002). 'Globalization and Taxation—Challenges to the Swedish Welfare State', *Comparative Political Studies*, vol. 3, no. 7: 839–62

Stinchcombe, A. (1997). 'On the Virtues of Old Institutionalism', *Annual Review of Sociology*, 23: 1–18.

Stone Sweet, A. and Caporaso, J. (1998). 'From Free Trade to Supranational Polity: The European Court and Integration', in W. Sandholtz and A. Stone Sweet (eds.), *European Integration and Supranational Governance*. Oxford: Oxford University Press.

——, Fligstein, N., and Sandhotz, W. (1998). *The Institutionalisation of Europe*. Oxford: Oxford University Press.

Stoppino, M. (1994). 'Cosa è la politica', *Quaderni di Scienza Politica*, I: 1–34.

Stoppino, M. (2001). *Potere e teoria politica*. Milano: Giuffré.

Straubhaar, T. (1988). *On the Economics of International Labour Migration*. Stuttgart: Verlag Paul Haupt.

Streeck, W. (1995). 'From Market Making to State Building? Reflections on the political Economy of European Social Policy', in S. Leibfried and P. Pierson (eds.), *European Social Policy between Fragmentation and Integration*. Washington, DC: Brookings Institution.

—— (2000). ' "Competitive Solidarity: Rethinking the "European Social Model" ', in Karl Hinrichs et al. (eds.), *Kontingenz und Krise: Institutionenpolitik in kapitalistischen und postsozialistischen Gesellschaften*. Frankfurt A. M.: Campus.

Strikwerda, C. (1997). 'Reinterpreting the History of European Integration: Business, Labour and Social Citizenship in Twentieth-Century Europe', in J. Klausen and L. Tilly (eds.), *European Integration in Social and Theoretical Perspective: From 1850 to the Present*. Lanham, MD: Rowman and Littlefield.

Szyszczak, E. (2001). 'The New Paradigm for Social Policy: A Virtuous Circle?', *Common Market Law Review*, 38: 1125–70.

Swiss Re-insurance Company (1998). *Financial Difficulties of Public Pension Schemes: Market Potential for Life Insurers*. Zurich: Prospect no. 8 of Sigma.

Tarello, G. (1998). *Storia della cultura giuridica moderna. Assolutismo e codificazione del diritto*. Bologna: Il Mulino.

Tarrow, S. (2004). 'Patterns of Political Contention in Late Modern Europe', in C. Ansell and B. Di Palma (eds.), *Restructuring Authority and Territoriality: Europe and the US Compared*. Cambridge: Cambridge University Press.

Taylor, P. J. (1993). *Political Geography, World Economy, Nation State and Locality*. New York: Longman.

Taylor Gooby, P. (2002). 'The Silver Age of the Welfare State. Perspectives on Resilience', *Journal of Social Policy*, 31/4: 579–96.

Te Brake, W. (1997). *Making History. Ordinary People in European Politics, 1500–1700*. Berkeley: University of California Press.

Thane, P. (2000). *Old Age in English History: Past Experiences, Present Issues*. Oxford: Oxford University Press.

Thelen, C. (1999) 'Historical Institutionalism and Comparative Politics', *Annual Review of Political Science*, 2: 369–404.

—— (2000) 'Timing and Temporality in the Analysis of Institutional Evolution and Change', *Studies in American Political Development*, vol. 14: 103–35.

—— (2004) *How Institutions Evolve: the Political Economy of Skills in Germany, Britain, Japan and the US*. New York: Cambridge University Press.

Therborn, G. (1989). 'Pillarization and Popular Movements. Two Variants of Welfare State Capitalism: the Netherlands and Sweden', in F. G. Castles (ed.), *The Comparative History of Public Policy*. New York: Oxford University Press.

Tilly, C. (ed.) (1975a). *The Formation of National States in Western Europe*. Princeton, NJ: Princeton University Press.

—— (1975b). 'Reflections on the History of European State-Making', in C. Tilly (ed.), *The Formation of National States in Western Europe*. Princeton, NJ: Princeton University Press.

—— (1975c). 'Western State-Making and Theories of Political Transformation', in C. Tilly (ed.), *The Formation of National States in Western Europe*. Princeton, NJ: Princeton University Press.

—— (1984). *Big Structures, Large Processes, Huge Comparisons*. New York: Russel Sage.

—— (1990). *Coercion, Capital and European States*. Cambridge, MA: Blackwell.

—— (1996). 'Citizenship, Identity and Social History', in C. Tilly (ed.), *Citizenship, Identity and Social History*. Cambridge: Cambridge University Press.

Tinbergen, J. (1965). *International Economic Integration*. Amsterdam: Elsevier

Trubek, D. M. and Mosher, J. S. (2003). 'New Governance, Employment Policy and the European Social Model', in J. Zeitlin and D. M. Trubek (eds.), *Governing Work and Welfare in a New Economy*. Oxford: Oxford University Press.

Van der Mei, P. A. (2003). *Free Movement of Persons Within the European Community*. Oxford/Portland: Hart.

Van Kersbergen, K. (2000). 'Political Allegiance and European Integration', *European Journal of Political Research*, 37:1–17.

Van Riehl, B., Hemerijck, A., and Visser, J. (2003). 'Is There a Dutch Way to Pension Reform?', in G. Clark and N. Whiteside (eds.), *Pension Security in the 21st Century*. Oxford: Oxford University Press.

Vaughan-Whitehead, D. (2003). *EU Enlargement versus Social Europe?* Cheltenham: Edward Elgar.

Venturini, A. (2004). *Post-War Migration in Southern Europe*. Cambridge: Cambridge University Press.

Viesti, G. and Prota, F. (2004). *Le politiche regionali dell'Unione Europea*. Bologna: Il Mulino.

Wallerstein, I. (1974). *The Modern World System*. New York: Academic Press.

Weber, M. (1972). *Wirtschaft und Gesellschaft: Grundrisse der Verstehenden Soziologie*. Tübingen: Mahr.

Weil, P. (1996). 'Nationalities and Citizenships. Lesson from the French Experience for Germany and Europe', in D. Cesarani and M. Fulbrook (eds.), *Citizenship, Nationality and Migration in Europe*. London: Routledge.

Weiler, J. (1981). 'The Community System: The Dual Character of Supranationalism', *Yearbook of European Law*, 1: 257–306.

—— (1991). 'The Transformation of Europe', *Yale Law Journal*, 100: 243–283.

—— (1994). 'A Quiet Revolution—The European Court of Justice and Its Interlocutors', *Comparative Political Studies*, 26: 510–34.

White S. (2003). *The Civic Minimum. On the Rights and Obligations of Economic Citizenship*. Oxford: Oxford University Press.

Whiteside, N. (2003). 'Historical Perspective and the Politics of Pension Reform', in G. Clark and N. Whiteside (eds.), *Pension Security in the 21st Century*. Oxford: Oxford University Press.

Wiener, A. (1999). 'From Special to Specialized Rights. The Politics of Citizenship and Identity in the European Union', in M. Hanagan and C. Tilly (eds.), *Extending Citizenship: Reconfiguring States*. Lanham, MD: Rowman and Littlefield.

Winterstein, A. (1999). 'Nailing the Jellyfish: Social Security and Competition Law', *European Competition Law Review*, 20/6: 324–33.

World Bank (1994). *Averting the Old Age Crisis: Policies to Protect the Old and to Promote Growth*. Oxford: Oxford University Press.

Zeitlin, J. (2005*a*). 'Conclusion. The Open Method of Coordination in Action: Theoretical Promise, Empirical Realities, Reform Proposals', in J. Zeitlin and P. Pochet (eds.), with Lars Magnusson, *The Open Method of Coordination in Action: The European Employment and Social Inclusion Strategies*. Brussels: PIE-Peter Lang.

—— (2005*b*). 'Introduction: The Open Method of Coordination in Question', in J. Zeitlin and P. Pochet (eds.), with Lars Magnusson, *The Open Method of Coordination in Action: The European Employment and Social Inclusion Strategies*. Brussels: PIE-Peter Lang.

—— Pochet, P. (eds.) with Lars Magnusson (2005). *The Open Method of Coordination in Action: The European Employment and Social Inclusion Strategies*. Brussels: PIE-Peter Lang.

Zielonka, J. (2001). 'How New Enlarged Borders will Reshape the European Union', *Journal of Common Market Studies*, 39: 507–36.

Ziller, J. (2003). *La nuova Costituzione europea*. Bologna: Il Mulino.

Zincone, G. (1992). *Da sudditi a cittadini*. Bologna: Il Mulino.

Zimmermann, B., Didry, C., and Wagner, P. (eds.) (1999). *Le travail et la nation: histoire croisée de la France et de l'Allemagne*. Paris: Editions de la Maison des Sciences de l'Homme.

Index

Index of European Court of Justice cases